Machiavelli in Brussels

Machiavelli in Brussels

The Art of Lobbying the EU

Rinus van Schendelen

Amsterdam University Press

Cover illustrations
– The Berlaymont building behind curtains (for restoration), Brussels,
  photo European Commission
– Niccolò Machiavelli, Santi di Tito

Cover design: Sabine Mannel/NAP, Amsterdam
Lay-out: Het Steen Typografie, Maarssen

ISBN 90 5356 573 6 (paperback)
ISBN 90 5356 579 5 (hardback)
NUGI 654

SUMMARY CONTENTS

DETAILED CONTENTS

3. Pushing the Buttons of 'Brussels'

4. Managing the EU Arena

PREFACE

Is it possible to influence the European Union (EU) and to achieve a desired outcome? Thousands of lobby groups based in Brussels or operating from their home country, do at least believe so, as they sniff around hoping to acquire some of the EU honey and money. They range from companies and trade associations through non-governmental organisations like trade unions and environmental groups, to so-called public interest groups like national ministries, local governments and public agencies. They come not only from all levels within the member countries, but also from others such as the USA, Japan and those in the Third World. Even people and units of the European Commission, Parliament and Council frequently act as lobby groups themselves. Like birds and bees, smelling the scents of the flowers of 'Brussels', they try to get closer in order to achieve a desired legislative, financial or other outcome.

This book is not just about the EU, but it regards this political system primarily as a most relevant machinery of decision-making within which to examine the art of lobbying. The EU produces its outputs largely under the competitive pressures from all sorts of lobby groups. Our focus is on the questions of how these groups try to score and how they can improve their scores. The answers come from two scientific disciplines. Firstly, *political science*, the mother of the study of influence, with lobbying as the special case of exerting influence in unorthodox ways. We examine the use of such influence within the EU. Its machinery is described and analysed in 'flesh and blood' terms. Lobby groups want to know how it really works and not how it is supposed to work. They want to win, or at least not to lose. The second discipline is *management science*, which regards the study of 'how to get things done as desired' or how to achieve success in management. Lobby groups want to score and to improve their scores. They want to know the best practices. Niccolò Machiavelli is a model for both sciences. He was the early modern scientist in this field, and was focused on the two questions of how influence is really exerted and how it can be made more effective. His answer to the second question is, in short: by intelligent and prudent behaviour. This is also our answer for the EU playing field.

The two streams of knowledge come together in this book as *EU Public Affairs Management* (EU PAM). Every private or public interest group has its external agenda of so-called 'public affairs' or, back to an old language, *res publica*, and it wants to manage this agenda successfully. The old practice of lobbying has been renamed and broadened to the new one of public affairs management. Its application within the EU machinery is far from easy, looking as it does like a complex labyrinth constructed on a dynamic trampoline. The many amateurish lobby groups can easily lose their way or fall off. They could learn from the best practices of the professional groups, who prudently anticipate their fieldwork through carefully prepared homework. The professionals understand the basic mechanisms of the EU arenas better and can manipulate their complexities and dynamics more successfully than the amateurs.

The *professionalisation* of EU public affairs management or, in short, EU lobbying is the main theme of this book. Its core activity is all kinds of preparatory work, which is a matter of applied methodology regarding the EU arenas. More than any other factor of influence, brains make the major difference between losing and winning an EU game. Of course, it is not always possible to win everything. Limits remain, but for the amateurish group more than for the professional one. All this finally raises the popular question regarding the democracy of EU lobbying. Our basic view on this is two-fold. Firstly, using one's brains cannot really undermine democracy, as long as people have more or less the same amount and the free choice to use them. Secondly, the more competition between lobby groups, the better for EU democracy, as long as the competition remains open to newcomers. Open competition ensures that a few cannot dominate the arena and take all. In addition, all the lobbying by groups from governments and civic societies contributes to the peaceful integration of Europe.

To put the focus of this book in academic language: the EU machinery of common decision-making is presented as a relevant variable dependent on the efforts to influence coming from all kinds of lobby groups. The machinery can be manipulated from the outside and it is really possible to get a more or less desired outcome. Many examples from case studies and research are given hereafter. Much also comes from the direct observations we have been allowed to make inside lobby groups at the EU level. Of course, we are very grateful to those who offered this opportunity and, as well, to the many who critically commented on drafts of the text. We dedicate the book to the thoughtful practitioners on the EU playing field. Every day they have to update their knowledge from practice and to apply it prudently.

Rotterdam, Easter 2002

LIST OF FIGURES

LIST OF ABBREVIATIONS

ACEA	European Automobile Manufacturers Association
ACP	African, Caribbean, Pacific
AEA	Association of European Airlines
AMCHAM	American Chamber of Commerce
BEUC	European Consumers Organisation
BINGO	Business Interested NGO
BONGO	Business Organised NGO
CASTER	Conference and Association of Steel Territories
CATS	Committee Article Thirty Six
CCMC	Committee of Common Market Automobile Constructors
CEA	European Committee of Insurers
CEFIC	European Chemical Industry Council
CFI	Court of First Instance
CIAA	Confederation of EU Food and Drink Industries
CoA	Court of Auditors
COM	European Commission
COR	Committee of the Regions
COREPER	Committee of Permanent Representatives (-tions)
DG	Directorate-General
EACEM	European Ass. of Consumer Electronics Manufacturers
EACF	European Airlines Consumer Forum
ECB	European Central Bank
ECJ	European Court of Justice
ECOBP	European Campaign on Biotechnology Patents
ECOFIN	Economic and Financial Council
ECSC	European Coal and Steel Community
EESC	European Economic and Social Committee
EFPIA	EuroFed of Pharmaceutical Industry Associations
EFSA	European Food Safety Authority
EIB	European Investment Bank
ELTAC	European Largest Textile and Apparel Companies

EMF/FEM	European Metal Workers
EP	European Parliament
EPHA	European Public Health Alliance
ERT	European Round Table of Industrialists
ETUC	European Trade Union Confederation
EU	European Union
EuroFed	European federation
FIM	International Motorcyclist Federation
GINGO	Government interested NGO
GONGO	Government Organised NGO
GMO	Genetically Modified Organism
HDTV	High-Definition Television
ICT	Information and Computer Technology
IGC	Intergovernmental Conference
MNC	Multinational Company
MEP	Member of the European Parliament
NATO	North Atlantic Treaty Organisation
NGO	Non-governmental Organisation
OECD	Organisation of European Co-operation and Development
PAM	Public Affairs Management
PGEU	Pharmaceutical Group of the EU
PR	Permanent Representative (Representation)
PSC	Political and Security Committee (Pillar II)
QMV	Qualified Majority Voting
SEM	Single European Market
SG	Secretariat-General
SGCI	SG of the Interdepartmental Committee (France)
SME	Small and Medium-sized Enterprise
UEAPME	European Association of SMEs
UNICE	Union of Industrial and Employers' Organisations
WEAG	Western European Armament Group (NATO)
WTO	World Trade Organisation

CHAPTER 1

THE EUROPEANISATION OF PUBLIC AFFAIRS

Living Together in Europe

'Europe' is almost a synonym for *variety*. In the year 2000 about 370 million people were living in the European Union (EU), more than in the USA and Japan put together. The future admission of other member states will increase the EU population by 160 million people. They all are organised by the way of a national state, frequently subdivided into more-or-less autonomous domestic (regional, provincial, local) governments, reflecting territorial idiosyncrasies and power ambitions. Their political histories usually have a long record of wars with neighbours and, many of them, with former colonies. Their political ideologies range from the extreme left to the extreme right. In their daily life the Europeans, living in free and pluralist societies, encounter a kaleidoscope of civil organisations such as companies, corporations, trade unions, political parties, churches and other interest groups. Their economies range from free-market systems in the North to more state-directed ones in the South. The EU people communicate with each other by eleven different national languages and hundreds of regional ones. In France alone one-third of the population makes daily use of one of its eight dialects.

In terms of *social statistics*, variety in Europe is even more impressive [COM, Europe in figures]. The population size of the member state of Luxembourg is less than one-half a percent of that of Germany, but has the highest GDP per capita, being two-and-half times that of Portugal. In general, a wealth contrast exists between the relatively rich North and poor South of Europe (Ireland included in the latter). Rates of labour activity and unemployment vary widely across member states and regions. Sectoral employment rates show a mountainous landscape, with Greece peaking in agriculture (about 20% of the labour force), Germany in industry (about 40%) and the Netherlands in services (about 70%). Social security in Europe is a volatile variable, mainly due to the differences of domestic government programmes for income maintenance, health, housing and education. This description of social variety could be extended for a range of variables, ranging from urbanisation rates to leisure patterns and from consumption behaviour to environmental interests.

Perhaps the most important, but certainly the least documented is *cultural variety* [Hofstede, 1984 and 1994]. In France, Belgium and Spain the dominant norms and values of social behaviour are relatively hierarchical or top-down, even inside small and decentralised units. In Scandinavian countries and the Netherlands the national culture is more bottom-up, based on self-reliant networks. Portugal, southern Italy and Greece have a culture mainly based on family values, with elderly leadership and clearly defined loyalties. In the United Kingdom it is more centred on the value of market competition, limited by the rule of law. In Germany and Austria orderly and predictable behaviour is a dominant value. These short generalisations of national cultures deserve, of course, a more detailed examination, but for the moment they suffice to underline the cultural variety. The cultural differences help to explain as well why the peoples of Europe have so little trust in each other. Except for the Italians and the Belgians, they put most trust firstly in their own countrymen, then in the northern peoples and the least of all in the southern ones [COM, Eurobarometer, 1996, 46].

All this variety is, of course, not unique to Europe. One can also find it in large geographical areas such as China, Brazil or the United States. These are already established states. Their management problem is *to keep* all the variety together. But Europe is still in a process of political integration. Its fundamental management problem is *to bring* the different parts together into a larger whole. Keeping it together comes next. Especially the irritating differences pose the problem of integration. Examples are the different domestic taxation rules, subsidy practices or technical standards. Of course, in many cases the variety is not considered irritating at all. Most Europeans tend to appreciate the varieties of music, cuisine or architecture as a non-irritating enrichment. The integration problem lies in the differences that do cause irritation. These can be anything, and may even include the way music is produced, the healthiness of the cuisine or the safety of the architecture. The management problem here is: *how to solve the irritating differences?*

Solving the Irritating Differences: the EU Method

Take the *gas hose.* By far the best, according to the French, is the 'Dormant' one: it has stainless steel helical tubing, moulded from a continuous spiral, with flare-type seals at the end and no covering. But the British believe they have a better than best gas hose: with galvanised metal annular tubing, formed into concentric circles, and with a rubber covering. The real best one is the Italian gas hose, at least according to the Italians: stainless steel annular tubing, extendable and free from covering. In fact, the German, Swedish, Spanish and any other gas hose, made in Europe, is the best as well, according to its country of manufacture. The gas hose is just one example of variety in Europe and numerous others exist, ranging from products and services to values and ideas.

So far the gas hose case does not cause any irritation. It only represents a difference and this might continue to be the case for another fifty years. Some producers may appreciate the difference, because it provides effective protection against imports from abroad. But other interest groups in the private or the public sector may feel irritated and start to politicise the difference. A few producers may want to export their gas hose, to create economies of scale and to become the market leader in Europe. Consumer groups may demand a cheaper and standardised gas hose. Governments may want to save on inefficiencies. An irritation is born and may grow into a conflict. What are the potential solutions? There are five traditional methods that have been adopted in Europe.

The first one can be called *patience*. Indeed, one might live with any difference for another time period, even if it is irritating. The costs of patience may be considered less than those of another solution. One might even count the blessings of a difference and accept the irritation as a minor element of the balance sheet. This solution may work for some time, as is the case in the field of educational diplomas, which have different attributes and values in different countries. But an enduring irritation may one day become an obsession for which patience is no longer a solution.

Leniency is a second standard solution. At least the irritation resulting from a difference may be dealt with by leniency, as a variant of tolerance. For example, the small country of Luxembourg irritates its neighbours by its flexible practices in banking, which is its major economic sector. But for a long time, the neighbouring countries have simply accepted these practices as a fact of life. France and the Netherlands have become lenient regarding each other's different (and irritating) drugs policy practices. A next step may be to equalise the differences as well. Concessions and the time involved are the costs of leniency.

An old approach to dealing with irritating differences is, thirdly, the *battlefield*, the opposite of leniency. The histories of European countries are, indeed, full of wars with neighbouring states over all sorts of irritating differences. A victory solves the irritation and equalises the difference. The method is, however, costly in terms of resources committed to it. It is only rational if the victor maintains the upper hand and can write off its war investments for a long period. This seldom happens. The hindsight wisdom in Europe since 1945 shows that the method is largely considered both inefficient and ineffective.

Imitation represents a fourth standard solution for equalising differences. Governments and companies, reconsidering the irritating caused by a difference with others abroad, may decide to follow the so-called best practice. They adapt their position to that of the other(s), thus removing the difference and consequently the irritation as well. Many a national welfare scheme in Europe is based on such imitation, being called the 'Beveridge' or the 'Bismarck' model [Flora, 1988]. In the industrial sector many companies easily adopt newly developed technology. Often they have to, due to the circumstantial pressures coming from an open and competitive environment. The costs of an almost permanent need to change are real, but accepted.

Finally there is the *negotiation* method. A government or a company may enter into negotiations with those who are responsible for an irritating difference. Through public treaties or private agreements a solution may be reached. There are thousands of good examples, ranging from the 'Rhine Treaty' to the standardisation of automotive parts. The method is based on an 'ad hoc' approach, taking each issue separately. This may be inefficient if there are many old or emerging issues at stake at the same time and ineffective if there is no sanctioning mechanism.

All these five solutions have the potential to make differences less irritating or even to settle them. Together they form the old menu of integration practices. But they have their limitations and disadvantages as sketched. The construction of what is now called the *European Union (EU)* aims to provide a better sixth method to solve irritating differences. According to many, this machinery of common public decision-making is the very essence of European integration [Lindberg, 1970]. The application of European law, always having priority over domestic law, can safeguard the settlement of an irritating difference. This approach is only obligatory for issue areas prescribed in the treaties on which the EU is based.

The sixth method is not exclusive. Most of the older solutions can also be offered as part of an attractive package. The EU provides an open forum inviting to patience and leniency. It is peaceful in the sense that fighting takes place only by word and on paper. It provides many different examples to follow as best practice and it always allows opportunity for negotiations.

The EU method of dealing with an irritating difference is also flexible in its outcomes. Settling the difference and thus erasing its irritation as well is, of course, the most effective solution, as exemplified by the many cases of EU standardisation and harmonisation. But an officially recorded irritating difference may also remain a fact of life, left to those involved. Sometimes the irritation may be reduced only temporarily, for example by an agreement to establish a task force aiming to propose a solution before a deadline. Frequently EU subsidies help to deal with an irritating difference. In short, the EU can try many different ways of bringing the various parts of Europe together into a larger whole and keeping them together peacefully.

Not Member States, but Member Countries

From the legal perspective, the national governments of the so-called 'EU member states' negotiate every new treaty, which binds their country after its ratification by the electorates (through a referendum) or the elected members of the national parliament. It would, however, be a misperception to see the EU as involving only national state governments. The EU is composed of member states indeed, but what are these?

Take the case of France [Schmidt, 1996; Safran, 1997; Guyomarch and others, 1998; Elgie and Griggs, 2000]. It has the reputation of being the most 'statist' and most centralised member state of the Union, as illustrated by the saying *Paris gouverne*. The state intervenes strongly in French society, usually in the form of specific and hard regulations. For almost any sector, trade or activity there is a detailed book of rigid codes. Through a *plan indicative* long-term policies are developed and set. State banking and subsidies give the central government financial power over society. But what is the state? It is largely the bureaucracy that issues the regulations and controls public finance. The leaders of this technocratic apparatus are not a closed group, but act in closed networks especially with the captains of industry, with whom they have enjoyed a common education in the *grandes écoles* and with whom they sometimes change positions through *pantouflage*. Major companies and business organisations are also present or represented inside the ministries by their membership of administrative *groupes d'études* or *comités*. Who influences whom in such a system? The legal perspective is only one side of it. In practice the voice of business can direct the state from within.

Or take Germany [Roberts, 2000; Helms, 2000]. This member state is, even in legal terms, a federalised collection of 16 *Länder* or regional states, each having its own government, parliament, bureaucracy and court. The umbrella-state is well over one century young and encompasses all kinds of variation. Brandenburg is not the same as Bavaria. Like Europe at large, the German states have their more or less irritating differences with each other. At both the regional and the federal level the governmental culture is only mildly interventionist, with a preference more for general than specific policies and more for encouraging than rigid interventions. The regional governments can play such a mildly interventionist role through, for example, their *Landesbanken*. They also like to make enduring agreements with the influential interest groups from organised business, labour, consumers and environmentalists, the so-called *Konkordanzpolitik*. In trade organisations, companies or neighbourhoods comparable forms of *Mitbestimmung* (co-determination) exist. Social order is valued highly, hence the extensive provision of social security. Again: who is influencing whom? There is no major government policy without at least the basic consent of the leading private interest groups.

Or take, finally, the case of Britain [Berrington, 1998; Kavanagh, 2000]. Here, the central government exerts moderate rule. Regional and functional authorities enjoy much governmental power. The interventions in society have usually a more general scope (like in Germany) and a rigid form (like in France). But all governments together have only limited domain. Much is left to the *private domain* of so-called market forces and competition. Developments of privatisation and deregulation during the Conservative years (1979-1997) enlarged and vitalised this private domain. It differs from standard practices on the European continent, particularly insofar as the central government aims to keep organised business and labour at arm's length. The Cabinet, acting as the *first committee* of the Lower House, likes to make its policies itself, free from compromising social consultations or co-determinations. It prefers the rule of law above the rule of compromise. These basics of governance have not changed very much since new Labour took over (1997). For the third time, again: who is influencing whom? The UK comes close to being an open park with many public and private playing fields.

The three country snap-shots make clear that the so-called member states, widely seen as the crucial parts of the EU construction, are not identical to the national governments. All countries have, in fact, a government, which is both more or less *fragmented* by different layers and *limited* by the private domain. The fragmentation and the limitation are, of course, variables with different loadings for the different countries. The fragmentation is relatively low in France, Denmark and the Netherlands, but high in countries like Germany, Belgium and Spain [Marks and others, 1996-B]. The limitation takes many forms. In the UK the public domain is largely restricted to the government officials, while in France, Italy and Portugal it is open to established interest groups from business as well. In Germany, Austria and Sweden the governments have their institutionalised negotiations with the major private interest groups and these groups are also characterised by their own fragmentation and limitation. This organised pluralism gives all groups only limited domain and scope for influence at home.

The member states can best be said to be so-called mixed economies [Nugent and O'Donnell, 1994; Edye and Lintner, 1996, 118-154] or, to put it more precisely, *mixed public-private* systems. The governance of a country consists of a mixture of public and private organisations, like government ministries and companies together. In between stand many hybrids or so-called non-governmental organisations (NGOs), like trade unions and consumer groups, which by function and/or status may overlap with either the public or the private organisations [Hudock, 1999]. Between the public and the private organisations two-way intervention exists. On the one way government organisations intervene in the private ones acting for profit or not. On the other way private organisations intervene in what the public organisations of government do or leave. For this reason it would be better to rename the concept of member state into that of *member country*. The former is only a part of the latter. Before we examine the consequences of this for both the understanding and the management of the process of European integration, we need to look more closely at the various patterns of relationship between the public and the private organisations at home.

Domestic Patterns of Public-Private Relationship

For the sake of clarity we keep society split into two parts: the public and the private, thus bypassing for the moment the many hybrids in between. Regarding their relationships there are three important questions. Firstly, do they each have their separate domain or are they interdependent? Secondly, is the public sector dominating the private one or is the opposite the case? Thirdly, is the quality of their relationship antagonistic or friendly? The central variables behind the three questions are, in short, respectively: *domain, direction* and *affection*. If we limit ourselves, again for the sake of clarity, to dichotomous answers (the extremes of the three kinds of relationship), then we get six logical patterns. But one is practically redundant: on the question of domain, the answer of 'interdependency' covers all the following patterns. Eliminating that one, we end up with five logical and potentially relevant patterns of relationship, typified as follows [Van Schendelen, 1990].

The first one may be called the *two worlds* pattern. Privatisation, deregulation and retrenchment of both budget and personnel are in many countries popular catchwords for implying the real or desired curtailment of government. They suggest or advocate a wide distance between the public and the private sectors. The crucial question here, however, is whether the two sectors have their own domains. If the answer is no, then all the following four patterns of relationship become irrelevant. If the other patterns have some validity, then the pure 'two worlds' pattern does not exist. Because it is always more reliable to measure the presence rather than the absence of something, in this case interdependency, we can anticipate here the second variable of direction: is the public sector intervening in the private and/or the reverse?

An absolutely separated public or private domain exists nowhere in Europe. Public organisations intervene in the private domain, as private organisations do in the public domain. This interdependency is, of course, not a constant but a variable, both across countries and in time. For example, the central government of France usually intervenes more frequently and more detailed in private organisations than its Irish counterpart. In Germany and the Netherlands the public authorities usually undergo more interventions from private organisations than their equivalents in Portugal or Britain. The conclusion is that the first pattern is practically empty and that the following ones have validity by consequence.

The second pattern is one extreme of the core variable of direction and may be called *public interventionism*. In this pattern the government establishes many of its interventions through public legislation, ultimately maintained by police and court systems. But it makes use of soft interventions as well, such as subsidies, procurements, white papers, promises, privileges and more, either in the positive variant of granting or in the negative one of refusing a desired item. Interventionism is, of course, a variable correlating with such factors as the target for the intervention, the composition of government, the sort of agenda and the estimated effectiveness [Rose, 1984]. Many governments, for example, like to target their interventions at areas of the private sector having a low mobility (big plants, farms) and/or a high concentration (chemicals, the car industry).

The reasons behind public interventionism are manifold. The core mission of the public sector can be said to be interventionist: for the provision of infrastructure, security, education, social welfare, crisis management and more. But, in practice, the extent of this mission is always contested and not self-evident. Within governments different ideologies and policy cultures compete with each other. Political parties extend their electoral competition to the realms of public decision-making [Downs, 1957]. Bureaucrats like to increase their public budget, which encourages them to intervene even more [Niskanen, 1971]. And much public intervention comes, paradoxically, from pressures exerted by private interest groups.

The third pattern mirrors the former and represents *private interventionism*. Companies and/or citizen groups, together forming civil society, intervene in the government system, in order to protect or to promote their interests. A formal indicator as regulation in the former pattern is not available for the measurement of these interventions. Only in a few so-called corporatist countries (especially Austria, to a lesser degree Sweden and the Netherlands) the major social organisations of employers and employees have some formal say about the government's socio-economic agenda. The standard indicators of private interventionism are usually less formal and two-fold. One is the transformation of the private interest group into a pressure group. The other is private pressure group behaviour, as shown, in simple terms, by the expressions of 'exit, voice and loyalty' [Hirschman, 1970] or, in popular language, the triple F: 'flee, fight, flirt'. By acting in such ways a pressure group tries to obtain from the public authorities a desired outcome.

Private interventionism through pressure group behaviour is, of course, a variable and dependent on many factors. In traditional views one category of factors is emphasised: resources, such as size, composition, budget and personnel [Dahl, 1991]. In modern views these are part of only one broader category of *capacities* to act, including coalitions and skills [Schlozman and Tierney, 1986]. Three other categories of factors are: *desires* to deal with threats and opportunities coming from government, *compulsions* due to a lack of alternatives for public action, and *invitations* to behave as a pressure group [Milbrath and Goel, 1977]. Paradoxically, in many cases a government organisation is itself a sort of 'meta-factor' behind these capacities, desires, compulsions and/or invitations. As part of its own competition with other public organisations, it tries to stimulate supportive actions from friendly private pressure groups.

The fourth pattern represents one extreme of the last core variable, affection. Its catchphrase is *public-private antagonism*. Indicators are distrust, evasion, insult and conflict. In the continental countries of Europe much antagonism is more latent than manifest, due to a national culture of preferred harmony. Nevertheless, antagonism is a very normal phenomenon everywhere. At some times it is caused by misperceptions and misunderstandings, but real in its consequences. At other times it is more objectively based on conflict of interests, on damage caused or on misconduct. It can even be part of a negotiation game, in which conflict is just a bargaining chip [Coser, 1956]. Public and private organisations can exist on both sides of antagonism, which increases the pluralism of the country. For example, on the issue of new railway infrastructure a coalition of the Ministry of Transport, the regional authorities and the green movement can act antagonistically versus a counter-coalition of the Ministry of Trade, the truckers' organisations and the local citizens groups.

The fifth and final pattern mirrors the former one and may be called *public-private partnership*. Mutual trust, co-operation, respect and harmony are its indicators. Public and private organisations feel happy with each other. The feeling may, of course, be the result of misperceptions and misunderstandings. More commonly it is based on shared preferences, mutual dependencies and, in general, common interests. A partnership can also be a negotiations chip, even if it is only played through courtesy. This happens especially in the continental countries, where a partnership garners social approval almost by definition. Partnerships frequently remain, however, quite limited by time and place. For example, a local authority with land but without money can have a temporary partnership with an investment company for land development. More far-reaching cases are both the previously mentioned corporatism and the state protection for companies seen as 'national flags'. By its creation of outsiders and losers, a partnership too can fragment both the public and the private sector. The result is once again an increased pluralism in the country.

The Europeanisation of the Member Countries

The implicit assumption so far is that national public and private organisations remain inside their national borders. Of course, they do not and especially not in the European area with its mainly medium-sized and highly interdependent countries. One indicator of this is the export ratio, which for Belgium is around 60% of its GDP and even that for Germany is around 20%. A ministry, company or whatever interest group can be more dependent on a foreign country than on its own one. Then it has to cope with foreign public and private organisations and not least with the EU.

All above-mentioned patterns of relationship, characterising the mixed public-private member countries, can thus become relevant at this *European level*. Of course, a small company or an ordinary citizen may consider that level as 'far away' and as belonging to another world. In objective terms, however, nobody can escape the interventions from the other countries and the EU. From their side, ministries like Trade & Industry, big companies like Unilever and an NGO like Greenpeace are regularly active pressure groups in other countries and at the EU level. With some parts of the EU they may have a relationship of antagonism and with other parts one of close partnership. The same holds true for the EU units themselves. A Directorate-General (DG) of the Commission intervening in a member country can develop both antagonistic and friendly relationships there. At the European level there exists an even wider international context. Issues of, for example, agriculture, steel and financial services can be dealt with at the World Trade Organisation (WTO) level. All patterns of relationship can recur even here.

We have already observed that, at the European level, the EU is relevant as a *sixth approach* to the settlement of irritating differences among the member states. We also observed that a member state is not a homogeneous entity, let alone a monolith. In practice it stands for a fragmented and dynamic collection of public and private organisations, better described as a *member country*. These two observations can be linked now. An irritating difference between two countries is never a difference between two nationally cohesive coalitions of public and private organisations. It is almost always an issue inside each country as well, both between and among its public and private organisations. Take, for example, the EU issue of state monopolies for post delivery. Member countries tend to be divided on this. On one side may be the Post Ministry, the protected state-company and the labour union, all in opposition to the liberalisation. On the other side may stand the Ministry of Economic Affairs, the couriers and the consumers, all strongly in favour. All these parties can air their preferences and disagreements over the issue at the European level and specifically within the framework of the EU. In this way they contribute to the europeanisation of public and private issues existing at the domestic level. By raising them at the EU level they also give this system a mixed public-private character [Edye and Lintner, 1996].

This term *europeanisation* is increasingly popular in both public discussion and in literature, but seldom defined [Meny and others, 1996; Goetz and Hix, 2000]. Some take it as a special case of globalisation [Wallace and Wallace, 1996, 16-19]. We define it, in general terms, as the *increase of cross-border public and private issue-formation in Europe*. The core element is the movement across borders of an irritation or an issue. The increase can take place not only by volume (more new issues), but also by contents (more intensely contested issues). The definition leaves open for research, deliberately, three related questions: the source of europeanisation, its direction and its outcome. The *source* can be one or more of the following four: a

European or a domestic pressure group, either public or private. The source is, for example, the EU itself, a European federation, a national ministry or a regional trade association. On the same issue all types of source can be active at the same time, thus reflecting the plural divisions of Europe. Europeanisation can occur in two opposite *directions*. Firstly, it can go from the European level to the domestic one. The issue is, then, created inside another country or within the EU framework and it is received at home, where one may have to adapt oneself to the external events for the time being. Secondly, the issue can start at home and be exported to another country or to the EU. In this case a domestic group influences the process of issue-formation in Europe. The *outcome* of issue-formation is left open as well. It can be a binding decision or a policy proposal made by the EU or a private agreement among companies from various countries. But the issue may also remain as it stands, like the perennial plug socket issue, or simply disappear, like the HD-television issue of the early nineties. The EU is not necessarily but increasingly a prominent source of europeanisation, an established part of the two directions and a major processor of outcomes. Many irritating differences of Europe come together here.

Vectors of Europeanisation

Elaborating our general concept of europeanisation, we will maintain the two *central dichotomies*: the national versus the European level and the public versus the private sector. Of course, every dichotomy has some grey area. Is, for example, an issue of the multinational company Siemens, headquartered in Germany, a case that belongs to the national or to the European level? The realistic answer is probably: formally national, but practically European. If Siemens, besides, creates an issue in close partnership with the German Ministry of Environment, does the case then belong to the private or the public sector? Although reality is always more shaded than any of the two dichotomies, we can fruitfully use them for analytical purposes. They help to clarify the process of europeanisation. At least eight different vectors can be distinguished: the four analytical sources multiplied by the two directions. They are presented below. The first four cover the domestic (public or private) *adaptations* to European causes and the other four the domestic *influences* at the European level. For the EU, the first four operate at its output-side and the second four at its input-side.

First of all there is the vector *from the European public sector to the national public sector*. This is, for example, the popular idea of 'Brussels governs'. It has given rise to a body of literature on adaptation. For example, an EU directive on food production or safe transport outlaws any conflicting domestic regulation. It binds the governments to its full and loyal implementation at home. Other examples of this vector are the soft EU interventions like so-called 'guidelines' and 'memoranda' and the treaties made by governments outside the EU framework, like the 1985 Schengen agreement on open borders.

A second vector goes *from the European public sector to the national private sector*. Many decisions of European governments directly bind private sector organisations, whether profit-oriented or not. General examples are the many EU decisions regarding an open and competitive market. Specific examples are the EU regulations regarding safety and health on the workplace and those regarding emissions harmful to the environment. The Rhine Treaty, signed by national governments along the river Rhine, binds both those transporting goods and the companies on the banks.

Europeanisation may, thirdly, also go *from the European private sector to the national private sector*. Many private sectors have their European federations and institutions. For the food and drink industries there is the CIAA, for the trade unions the ETUC and for motorcyclists the FIM. Their manifest function is usually to influence the EU. This falls, however, outside our definition of europeanisation, because no border is crossed here. Their most important latent function is frequently the formation of an internal agreement. To this the members are expected to be bound and to adapt. Without any public involvement the agreement can europeanise the members back home. A lot of industrial norms and standards have been produced this way.

The fourth vector runs *from the European private sector to the national public sector*. The federations and institutions referred to above may seek to influence national public organisations. This may happen through an open statement or a campaign. The European Round Table of Industrialists (ERT), for example, addressed its well-known 1984 campaign for an open EU common market directly to the national governments, which decided accordingly in their 1986 Single European Act (SEA). For the 1992 Slots Dossier, regarding the distribution of landing rights for air transport, the national carriers, united in the Association of European Airlines (AEA), orchestrated informal influences on their national ministries at home [Van den Polder, 1994].

From here we leave the vectors running from the European to the national level and provoking a national adaptation to the European level. The next four represent, reversely, national influences at the European level. First of all there is the vector *from the national public sector to the European public sec-*

tor. The most institutionalised target here is the EU Council of Ministers. National ministers meet together in order to suggest, approve or reject proposals for new legislation coming from the Commission and maybe amended by the European Parliament. But they can also meet informally or outside the EU framework, with the same or a different composition, in order to develop a common line. A semi-formal example is provided by the thousands of national civil servants meeting in expert committees of the Commission.

A second influence vector goes *from the national public sector to the European private sector.* Not very often, but sometimes national public authorities seek to influence directly a European private sector group. In 1998 the French government wanted to have its air-defence industry Aerospatiale included in an eventual European consortium with the British Aerospace and the German Dasa. To tempt these companies into an agreement it even partially privatised Aerospatiale. Local governments can appeal to European companies to make a common cause, like local authorities in steel regions suffering from declining employment managed to do in 1995. Together with the major European steel companies and the trade unions they established Caster, a public-private umbrella for steel interests.

A third influence vector runs *from the national private sector to the European private sector.* Every membership of a private European federation involves this vector. As members of the EU Pharma Group (PGEU), all national professional groups of pharmacists discuss some of their issues within this federation. They try, first of all, to monitor and to influence each other. The same sectoral approach is followed by thousands of other national private organisations, profit-oriented or not, from telephone companies to consumer groups. By making a cross-sectoral deal at home, they can even orchestrate their influence on more than one European sector.

Finally there is the influence vector *from the national private sector to the European public sector.* This vector covers the many popular cases of EU lobbying by private companies and citizen groups [Pedler and Van Schendelen, 1994]. Another example is provided by the thousands of private sector representatives sitting in expert committees of the Commission. Most complaints regarding unfair market behaviour are brought to the Commission by private groups feeling aggrieved. Multinational companies frequently approach foreign governments under the flag of their subsidiaries there, in order to orchestrate a pan-European symphony of lobby sound directed at the EU, as Philips managed to do in 1986 in order to get EU protection for its compact disc 'infant industry'.

The Fuller Story of Europeanisation

The eight different vectors are useful for the better understanding of the reality of europeanisation. They represent eight hypotheses or stories of europeanisation, thus stimulating the mental mapping for both research (description and explanation) and practice (evaluation and optimisation). But they also remain a schematic model, which can never tell the full story of any case of europeanisation. Four more complex and dynamic elements should be added: the public-private transactions not crossing borders; the volatility of the two dichotomies; the connection of vectors; and the wider global level.

In our definition of europeanisation, all issue-formation by public and private organisations at only the national or the European level falls outside any vector. These events *not crossing borders* can, however, be relevant for the cross-border issue-formation. A company or NGO, observing a rising political threat or opportunity coming from elsewhere in Europe, frequently asks selected public officials at home to support its position at the European level. Likewise, a national ministry can ask private groups at home for information and support. At the EU level, the Commission and the many European federations (EuroFeds) have their regular direct communications and interventions. Even events happening only among the public or the private organisations can be relevant for some European issue-formation. Domestic companies and NGOs frequently support or fight each other over action at the European level. In July 2001 the European Employers Association UNICE intensified its dialogue with European consumer groups. Such events at only one level can be seen as side stories of europeanisation: relevant, but not the main story.

Secondly, the two dichotomies are in real life not as clear as suggested. The previously mentioned grey areas in fact amount to a *volatile* variable being an issue of europeanisation in itself. Many an organisation operates at both *the national and the European* level. The clearest example is the multinational company (MNC) acting in various countries and inside both European federations and EU expert committees. But national ministries, local governments and NGOs can occupy positions at both levels as well. They themselves function across borders and their issues go with them. The dichotomy has even become an issue itself. In 1987 UK Prime Minister Margaret Thatcher pleaded for a more clear separation between the two levels and, re-launching the old notion of subsidiarity, for the supremacy of the national level. The same also applies to the second dichotomy between *the public and the private* organisations. There is more and more grey area in-between. Many governments organise their own NGOs, to be called GONGO or Quangos in the past [Van Thiel, 2000], functioning as mixed public-private types of agency. The antipode is the BONGO, the business-organised NGO, like any trade organisation and also many citizens' groups, for example in the fields of health, transport, consumption and the environment. NGOs can make themselves hydra-headed as well. As a lobby group they act as a government-interested NGO, thus as a GINGO. By selling special products and services, as the simoniacal clericals did in the past and Greenpeace and Oxfam do today, they become business-interested or a BINGO. This distinction between the public and the private domain has also become an issue itself. The competitive notions are privatisation and nationalisation.

Thirdly, the cross-border formation of an issue is seldom carried by only one vector. Most cases of europeanisation are caused by a number of vectors *connected* in parallel or series. An example is the Decker/Kohll case. In the mid-1990s these two citizens, one from Luxembourg and the other from Germany, had to buy medical services (from an optician and a dentist) during their holidays in another EU country. Back home they wanted to get the costs reimbursed by their public health insurance companies, which refused to do so. Then they appealed to the European Court of Justice. In 1998 the Court came to the decision that medical services are not exempted from the open market, thus breaking open the formerly closed national public health insurance systems. Most public insurance companies were not amused and, as a side story of europeanisation, many approached their national ministry. They also raised the Court decision with their European federations, such as the CEA. Various national ministries discussed the issue in the EU Health Council of April 1998. Encouraged by the 1999 Amsterdam Treaty chapter on public health, the Commission began to prepare specific proposals for the liberalisation of the public health insurance market. The insurance companies soon started to lobby. In this single case, in short, the first two adaptation vectors and three of the four influence vectors have clearly been operative in series or even in parallel. All together they form only one episode of this case.

Finally, there are the complexities and the dynamics coming from the wider international or *global level*. For example, with regard to bananas, beef and biotechnology many issues have already been created at the EU level, but the three 'B's have subsequently become a global issue as well. In 1999 the USA chief negotiator Charlene Barshefsky placed them on the WTO agenda. She also looked for support from national governments and private companies in Europe, thus exploiting divided positions and useful vectors there. In fact, some governments and private interest groups from the EU supported the USA against the EU, in order to change the EU policies disadvantaging their interest. The reverse frequently happens as well. Then, USA state-governments and/or private interest groups, having lost in Washington, support the more benign EU side around the WTO table.

The EU is clearly not the only chapter in the full story of the europeanisation of its member countries. But for the domestic public and private sector organisations and for the European private ones as well, it has become the single most important *focus and source* of europeanisation. The EU deals with all sorts of irritating differences between domestic public and private organisations from different member countries. It has political, legal and other capacities to channel many issues and to bring at least some of them to accepted outcomes. In academic terms, the EU is both a dependent and an independent variable of europeanisation. It is a focus of national public and private pressure group behaviour and also a source of European interventionism.

Influence Challenges from Europeanisation

It is old wisdom that, in the pluralist countries of Europe, every organisation usually has some capacity for influence, but this is always limited and fragile in both scope and domain. An organisation always remains more or less dependent, for good or bad, on the *challenging environment* [Thompson, 1967]. This outside world is perceived as having two faces. One looks promising and full of opportunities, the other threatening and reluctant. The permanently changing complexities of the environment make adaptive and/or influencing behaviour continuously necessary. More specific challenges come from other organisations and groups acting as either friends or opponents, in short as *stakeholders*. They too require adaptive and/or influencing responses. Given this existential dependency on a challenging environment, every organisation has two main interests. Firstly, at its input side it has to acquire the means of operation it needs from the outside, for example budget, support, information and other resources. Secondly, at its output side it has to deliver what is demanded from the outside, for example special products and services, support and other contributions. In this functional sense, every organisation is an interest group. This is not less true for a ministry or the EU itself than for a company or a group of citizens. To survive they have to take the opportunities and to tackle the threats as assessed, at both their input side and their output side.

Only with regard to its internal operations can an organisation act more or less independently, but this *autonomy* is not sufficient for survival. There are usually strong variations depending on, among other things, the organisational size (big or small), type (public or private), resources (affluent or poor) and reputation (good or bad). An important factor is the awareness of the challenging environment. The more an organisation is conscious about the external challenges, the better it can exert its autonomy and do more than merely adapt itself to the good or the bad luck coming in from outside. If it is alert, it can decide to influence the environment by pushing the opportunities and by blocking the threats. Paradoxically, an unfriendly environment frequently sharpens this awareness better than a friendly one. Particularly serious and specific threats coming from public interventions and market competitions contribute to it. A calm and friendly environment tends to make one sleepy and lazy, with the risk of being caught by surprise. As soon as Shell or a public agency is insufficiently aware of its environment, it runs a high risk of losing leadership, income or function. No organisation is secure in this respect.

To this old wisdom the vectors of *europeanisation* have added a new experience. Since the rise of the EU, the environment of every organisation in Europe has acquired a stronger cross-border dimension. The wider environment presents new and more dynamic complexities, related to both the other member countries and to the EU. The vectors from the European to the domestic level create challenges of adaptation. They can bring good fortune in terms of new opportunities, for example for the export of products or for some policy change at home. But they can also bring new threats and increased costs incurred through adaptation. They can not, as in the past, be easily filtered or blocked by the national state [Hall, 1993; Frieden and Rogowski, 1996; Kohler-Koch and Eising, 1999]. The influence vectors, going from the domestic to the European level, have two different faces as well. They can create new opportunities, for example a more level playing field or a specific EU decision as desired. But they can also create new threats, for example because they provide a comparative advantage for a competitor at home or abroad. The fight for survival, in short, is shifting from the domestic to the European level. The challenging European environment, encompassing the domestic one, has to be met more internationally and, as far as the EU is concerned, transnationally.

Inevitably, the challenging European environment affects, positively or negatively, the autonomy of every public or private organisation. By being aware and acting alert, the management of an organisation can diminish the chances of being caught by surprise. Due to the europeanisation this alertness needs to have a cross-border dimension as well. It must be *focussed* on the sources of europeanisation, particularly on the EU and the other member countries. This is, in short, a matter of three forms of preparation or homework, to which we return at length in the chapters to follow. First of all, new facts and trends occurring in the European environment have to be monitored. The observations have, secondly, to be assessed in terms of threats and opportunities, which assessments are always value judgements, derived from the organisational values and objectives. They result, thirdly, in so-called interests, which are chosen positions regarding facts and trends occurring in the environment and being labelled as either threats or opportunities. These interests are usually contested by other stakeholders and, as such, are taken as *issues*. The contested nature of interests applies to both public and private organisations. A public interest is not an interest of a higher or lower order than a private interest, but merely an interest of a public organisation like a ministry, agency or party, whereas a private interest is one held by a private organisation.

The more alert or conscious an organisation is in defining its interests, the more it is capable of preserving and strengthening its *autonomy* amidst the challenging European environment. Alertness to the challenges from europeanisation does not imply, however, that a public or a private organisation always has to decide to influence that environment. As will be shown later, there are many situations in which adaptive behaviour is more rational than an effort to influence a growing threat or opportunity. This rationality can only be based, again, on conscious homework. In the daily life in Europe, however, adaptive behaviour is frequently not the consequence of conscious homework regarding the challenging environment, but of precisely the opposite, namely the neglect of it. In this case, the organisation can only adapt itself to the europeanisation of its environment. Sometimes it may enjoy some good luck from a free opportunity, but usually it suffers more from the bad luck of a neglected threat.

If a public or a private organisation comes to the decision that on an issue some action to influence would be rational, it changes from an interest group into a so-called pressure group. In the European area it can choose, then, from two sets of basic alternatives. One option is to move the issue at either *the national or the European* level. The choice will be dependent on the value attached to the estimated outcome. For example, Europe-wide operating companies and NGOs, wanting to get rid of a domestic filter or veto, frequently push an issue at home up to the European level. But small-sized enterprises and homebound ministries are frequently inclined to move their issue down from the European to the domestic level. Another example regards issues of safety and health on the workplace. The trade unions from northern Europe frequently prefer EU regulations above national ones, but those from the south usually have mixed feelings, while the employers' organisations tend to want only a level playing field [Daemen and Van Schendelen, 1998].

The second option is to go *public or private*. Many a pressure group is inclined to influence an issue only in that part of its environment in which it sees its cause or origin. Wanting to save the opportunity or to solve the threat, it goes to the source. It therefore tries to tackle a challenge coming from either the public sector in that sector and one from the private sector there. It behaves like Pavlov's dog. A more sophisticated pressure group, informed about the many vectors, can decide to change the type of vector. In response to the 1992 EU policy programme on the Single European Market (SEM), with all its threats and opportunities for competition, many multinational companies (MNCs) reacted not by lobbying the EU, but by the early exploitation of the private sector [Calori and Lawrence, 1991; Mayes, 1992; Urban and Vendemini, 1992]. In the early 1990s, however, the European Federation of Largest Textile and Apparel Companies (ELTAC), suffering from cheap imports from non-EU low-wage countries, raised this market issue at the EU level. It presented itself as a sort of NGO against child labour and it lobbied for (high) price protection. Many a public or private pressure group creates a GONGO or a BONGO only in order to change its face of government or, respectively, business so that it can exploit another group of vectors more easily.

From Old to New Influence Techniques: Public Affairs Management

A pressure group, wanting to influence its challenging European environment, can choose from a menu of at least four traditional techniques.
The first is the use of *coercion*. A national ministry can coerce its home environment by issuing legislation that is ultimately maintained by police, court and jail systems. It can also try to do so through the EU Council of Ministers. Private pressure groups have to play a less formal game. NGOs may set up a blockade or a hate campaign, as Greenpeace did against Shell in the 1995 Brent Spar affair. A company can threaten to move production to another country. The EU itself is ultimately based on coercive legislation.
A second old technique is *encapsulation*. Major stakeholders are made more dependent by nominating their leadership and/or by granting them a budget. A subtler variant is the establishment of procedures of decision-making, which keep them subordinate. Ministries in particular keep many a so-called independent agency or private organisation under sufficient control in this way. Many a group of citizens is financially dependent on a

government and has to apply for a new budget every year. The EU relies heavily on subsidy allocations to get things done the way that it wants. A company or an NGO may use part of its budget to make others dependent on them.

Advocacy is a well-established third technique. In its informal variant it comes down to propaganda, for example through an advertisement or a mass media campaign. NGOs and trade organisations, smelling an opportunity or fearing a threat, frequently rely on this technique. A semi-formal variant is the lodging of a complaint. Competition authorities at both national and EU level receive most complaints about unfair market practices from companies feeling hurt. The formal variant of advocacy is litigation in court, where self-interest is advocated with reference to the laws. In relatively formal societies like Germany and France, litigation is more often used than elsewhere, a national characteristic which is also visible at EU Court level [Stone Sweet and Caporaso, 1998].

The final traditional technique is *argumentation*. Here, self-interest is hidden behind seemingly intellectual reasoning, based on logically sound inferences and empirically credible references. Its impact is, of course, dependent on its credibility. In the Brent Spar case, neither Shell nor Greenpeace had a credible position, Shell because it neglected the logical alternative of dismantling the platform and Greenpeace because it provided incorrect data about the degree of pollution. Argumentation is frequently used in four situations: when important stakeholders are still wavering (they might be won over); when an issue is in an early phase (many have not yet adopted a position); when an issue gets publicity (the audience wants argumentation); and when it needs an upgrade (to present it as a more general interest). In all these cases the argumentation comes close to salesman's talk.

These traditional techniques of influencing a challenging environment are still used in practice, but they have a limited and frequently even decreasing effectiveness and efficiency. This is especially the case on the EU playing field. Competition here is usually among the fiercest in Europe. Many players are relatively experienced public or private pressure groups. Parts of EU institutions, pressuring for their own interests, belong to this league as well. Representing the irritating sides of European variety, they fight intensely in order to get the EU outcomes, as they desire. They increasingly realise that they can not rely solely on the traditional techniques. These are, essentially, based on an *arrogant* belief of superiority. It holds that the opponents can be coerced, encapsulated, overruled and/or converted to do what is desired. In contemporary Europe most established pressure groups, however, possess sufficient capacity to oppose such arrogance effectively. Many find it even easier to block what they dislike than to push what they prefer. They are, in short, neither easily influenced nor influential.

In the search for better techniques of influence *public affairs management* (PAM) has become the new catchword. The public affairs (or, in Latin, the *res publica*) of an interest group refer to its external agenda. This is simply the group of interests to be protected and promoted by influencing the challenging environment. The decision to do so is seen as an essential part of general management. So far, the new catchword might be considered a new container for an old wine. It contains, indeed, some fine old wine. Under the label of management the objective remains to influence the challenging environment by solving problems and/or enjoying opportunities, as they are perceived. The task is to internalise the environment and to externalise the actions to influence it. In the field of public affairs management, the term 'influence' is frequently replaced by 'management', derived from the Latin *manu agere*, which means something like 'directing by hand', 'taking in hand' or 'having a hand in the game'. It has almost the same meaning as manipulation, coming from the same language (*manu pulare*). Although the former word sounds much better than the latter, both refer, ironically, to the same effort to obtain a desired outcome from the environment, in short to influence the environment.

Yet, there are two sorts of new wine in the container as well. Firstly, public affairs management implies specific *internal homework* for the external influence process. The awareness of this, namely that one has to prepare and to organise oneself for a game or fight outside, is in itself far from new in the field of pressure group behaviour. Niccolò Machiavelli recommended it to Lorenzo dei Medici, the ruler of Firenze, as Ignatius Loyola did to the Roman Catholic Church. But in contemporary times that insight has got the specific notions of both analytical and organisational homework. New catchwords, among others, are short-list, arena analysis, ad-hoc team and Public Affairs official, to which we will return in the chapters that follow. They refer to a more systematic and methodical or, in short, a more professional way of transforming an interest group into a potentially more successful pressure group. By doing its homework carefully, the pressure group hopes to sharpen its alertness and to strengthen its autonomy with regard to the environment.

Secondly, public affairs management contains techniques of influence, which are subtler than the four traditional ones. They are not one-sidedly directed at the environment, but highly interactively intertwined with it.

The pressure group opens its windows. It goes *window-out*, in order to monitor the environment, to do field research and/or to lobby for information. It also brings crucial stakeholders *window-in*, in order to form a coalition, to negotiate a deal and/or to lobby for support [PARG, 1981]. The pressure group uses these interactions as a major source of inspiration for the definition of its interests, the formulation of its targets and the selection of its activities. In this way it searches for an optimal match between its preferences and what it may achieve. The pressure group does not hold the arrogant belief that it can simply coerce, encapsulate, overrule and/or convert an opponent. The new techniques are, in contrast, based on the belief that the domain and the scope of influence are always limited. The domain has to be scanned by going window-out and the scope has to be enlarged by acting window-in. The popular catchword for both is lobbying. A lobby group, thus, is a pressure group acting window-out and window-in. This general definition we shall make more specific in chapter 6.

Public affairs management or PAM, in short, is more than a new container for an old wine. The traditional techniques are, in essence, only the arrogant form of window-in activities. Under PAM they have the more politic reform of interactive coalition formation and negotiations. They are also extended through preceding window-out activities and a lot of homework. All this can be performed, of course, with different levels of quality, ranging from amateurish to professional. It indicates that the modern playing field is regarded as more level than before and as not permitting a mainly arrogant style of influence behaviour. The new insights might even be labelled as a case of *public marketing*, as they have many parallels in the influencing of the consumers' market [O'Shaughnessy, 1990; Andrews, 1996; Harris and Lock, 1996; Harris and others, 2000]. Here too, the desired outcomes, as sales and profit, can not any longer, as frequently in the past, just be imposed, tied-in, advertised or talked-up. They may need a great deal of homework beforehand in the form of research and development (R&D). The consumers, capable of resisting, have to be won by window-out and window-in techniques as well. Both on the commercial market and on the EU playing field the old techniques may, however, remain a part of the influence package. In many an EU case a little bit of coercion, encapsulation, advocacy and/or argumentation can support the formation of a coalition, a deal and, finally, a desired outcome. But this supplementary use requires a prudent fine-tuning of influence behaviour. Otherwise its implied arrogance can boomerang back onto the user.

Extra: the Extending Family of EU Public Affairs Management

The basics of EU Public Affairs Management come from two main sources. The first is *academic* and has two origins: business management and political science. This should not be surprising, because the relationships between business and politics or, taking it broader, the private and the public sector form the crux of any modern society characterised by a mixed public-private governance system. Since World War II, many US scholars have contributed to this field of study [Dean and Schwindt, 1981]. Those in business management adopted the view of business and particularly big companies and trade organisations. They regarded them in their dual roles of both a receiver and a sender of influence efforts, as business is both influenced by and influences its environment. Their basic question of research was, how these organisations (can and/or should) cope with the threats and opportunities coming from that environment. The scholars in business management gave birth to both the core idea and the concepts of public affairs management. Their colleagues in political science adopted the view of government and they focused mainly on its receiver's role. Reflecting the traditional democratic belief that a government should not act as a pressure group against civil society, they implicitly denied the government's role as an influential pressure group. With regard to the receiver's role they were able to draw on a large amount of studies about private interest groups, pressure groups and lobby groups [Laurencell, 1979]. They questioned particularly how government officials, elected or not, (can and/or should) cope with the pressures and lobbies from the private sector. Their initial focus on the profit-oriented organisations was extended to the NGOs later on. The two US academic origins had their spillover into Europe via the United Kingdom.

The second main source is *practice*, again especially in the USA after World War II. Due to a lack of formal training, many people in both the private and the public sectors simply had, and still have, to find out how best to cope with threats and opportunities coming from their challenging environment. On the basis of daily experiences, they have collected empirical insights and wisdom, frequently resulting in so-called 'do's and don'ts'. In the private sector, many have joined peer group organisations, such as the *Public Affairs Council* (1954), thus making their personal experiences more collective. In the public sector, both at the state and the federal level, many officials have in particular politicised the supposed threats from business lobbying. In an effort to cope with these, they most often used the traditional technique of coercion and issued regulations, registration forms and codes of conduct [US/Congress, 1977; US/GAO, 1999]. Again, it was the United Kingdom that became the first country in Europe to follow the US example in examining the management of public affairs. The first stimulus here came from the Labour government in the 1970s, with its proposals for specific interventions in the world of business, including the nationalisation of private companies. The second stimulus came, paradoxically, from the Conservative government of Margaret Thatcher. She wanted to create a sort of 'two worlds pattern' between the public and the private sector and particularly to abolish the organisations representing labour and management [Willis and Grant, 1987; Grant, 1989]. Large UK companies followed the American example of public affairs management.

Since the mid-1980s the small family of people interested in public affairs management in Europe has been rapidly expanding as a result of both internal and external developments. On the internal side, first of all, the separate worlds of academia and business became linked. In the UK the *European Centre for Public Affairs* (ECPA), founded in 1986 and originally based at the University of Oxford, became a meeting place for both groups. From its inception it launched conferences, workshops and studies in its field. Another major British initiative has been the launch of the *Journal of Public Affairs* (JPA) in 2001. The second internal development has been the dissemination of experiences with public affairs management in Northwest Europe, among both academics and practitioners. For example, in the Netherlands four different peer groups of people practising public affairs management in, respectively, big companies, public interest groups, trade associations or at junior level have been formed since the mid-1980s.

On the external side, the *changing methods of government* in many countries in Northwest Europe have become a major factor of growing awareness of public affairs management. Although happening a little later, the pattern of change has come close to the British one. Many companies in Scandinavia and the Netherlands were unhappy with the government's politicisation of the economy in the 1970s and were subsequently surprised by a swing towards liberalisation, deregulation, privatisation and budget retrenchment in the 1980s [Van Schendelen and Jackson, 1987]. Both changes they could hardly control. They perceived the national governments as acting arrogantly, unpredictably and unfriendly towards the intermediate organisations of management. This created antagonisms. The large companies and the leading NGOs subsequently wanted to find new ways of managing their public affairs. Another change came with the Single European Market (SEM) in the early 1990s. Thanks to the previous changes at home, the private organisations in the northwestern countries could easily shift their focus from the domestic to the European level. They could act more independently of national governments than their counterparts in the south and east of Europe. The experience of public affairs management at home was applied resolutely to the even more unfamiliar system of the EU.

Public Affairs Management at EU Level

The EU is a most appropriate place for the application of practices of public affairs management. At the EU level exist thousands of organisations, which functionally act as interest groups. They come from the public and the private sides of both the member countries and many foreign ones. Brussels, the EU capital, is the main location of their activity. Most interest groups make only *irregular* visits to this meeting place, for example when something of relevance to them is at stake in a Commission expert committee, a Parliament hearing or a European Federation (EuroFed). The rest of the time they try to monitor and to influence what happens at distance by remote control, for example via a trade organisation, through their domestic government or a consultant. Like their domestically based equivalents, most of these EU-based interest groups have a private sector background, either profit-making or nonprofit-making and their numbers continue to increase. Less numerous but running up are both the interest groups of the public sectors of Europe, like the independent agencies and the decentralised governments (regional, urban), and those of the private worlds of small and medium-sized enterprises (SME) and NGOs. Foreign interest groups are increasingly active as well, ranging from the American Chamber 'AmCham' to the Turkish employers Tusiad and from the Mauritius Sugar Syndicate to the Thailand government.

At the beginning of the year 2000, about 2,600 interest groups even had a *permanent office* downtown Brussels [Landmarks, 2000]. Their distribution is roughly as follows: European trade federations (32%), commercial consultants (20%), companies (13%), European NGOs in such fields as environment, health care and human rights (11%), national business and labour associations (10%), regional representations (6%), international organisations (5%) and think tanks (1%). In addition there are the permanent representations of the member-state governments and around 150 delegations from foreign governments. Quoting Eartha Kitt, 'they all do it'. The interest groups are particularly focused on the EU policy fields of the internal market, the environment and health, the agriculture, the social affairs, the research and development, and the transport [Fligstein and McNichol,

1998]. Even the EU institutions, offices, agencies, committees and other parts of the official machinery may be seen as interest groups with a permanent office on the spot.

All these public or private pressure groups, with or without a permanent office in Brussels, import their own interests into the EU system of decision-making. They see this as a most challenging environment. Present or represented they want to monitor it at an early stage and to create a desired outcome. Many transform themselves into lobby groups. They clearly dislike being only part of the adaptation vectors of europeanisation. They want to join the influence vectors. Due to the variety of Europe, their interests inevitably clash with those of others. New issues are continuously rising by consequence. These lobby groups are the most manifest *carriers of europeanisation*. The fact that they channel their issues into the EU indicates that they consider the five old European methods of conflict resolution as either outdated or insufficient. Apparently they see the EU method as more promising in terms of effectiveness and efficiency. Being unfamiliar with both each other and the EU officials, most groups are aware that the traditional techniques for coping with a challenging environment will also be insufficient. At EU level no group can influence another stakeholder, such as a Commission official, a national government or a European federation, by coercion, encapsulation, advocacy and/or argumentation alone.

The main *reasons why* are the following. Coercion, if based on established EU law and taking the form of litigation, usually has only short-term effectiveness. The risk of receiving a retaliating boomerang from the coerced opponents always remains high. Encapsulation requires both a strong position of power and an affluent financial footing, which preconditions rarely exist. Advocacy leads to little more than counter-advocacy, as every barrister gets an opponent, and thus easily to stalemate. Litigation, in its Court variant as well, frequently incurs high costs, unpredictable outcomes and probably a vengeful opponent. Argumentation is seldom sufficient, as most pressure groups in Europe can produce a position paper with logical inferences and credible references. The real issues, of course, lie in the hidden values and interests. Like in an ancient Greek drama, all characters may then be right in their argumentative acting but, if unwilling to compromise, dead in the final act. Argumentation is even more useless, insofar as strong allies are already convinced and difficult opponents are unwilling to be convinced. At EU level, in short, one has to play a more prudent and politic game. The conflicting issues have to be managed by negotiating a deal and a compromise, by researching the stakeholders and the issues in advance and by doing a lot of homework, in short by practising public affairs management.

Private lobby groups from Northwest Europe have largely been responsible for increasing confidence in practices of public affairs management at EU level. Thanks to their antagonisms with their national governments since the 1970s, they had become experienced in those practices much earlier than their counterparts elsewhere. They became leading players within the Brussels-based peer groups in the field of public affairs management, such as in the *Society of European Affairs Practitioners* (SEAP), the *Public Affairs Practitioners* (PAP) and the *European Federation of Lobbying and Public Affairs* (FELPA). There are even Brussels-based national EU groups in public affairs management, such as the Dutch *European Public Affairs Platform* (EPAP). Most 'Brussels' consultancies also have a northwestern and particularly British background. The same holds true for newsletters like the *Public Affairs Newsletter* and the weekly newspaper *European Voice*. The previously mentioned British ECPA established a Brussels facility (ECPAB) in 1995. From the other countries of Europe, especially the French-language groups are following Britain's lead by establishing in Brussels their own consultancies, peer groups and training centres. They are in the lead with information services, such as *Agence Europe, European Information Services* and the *European Public Affairs Directory*. Major companies and a few NGOs from Italy, Germany and applicant member states in Central Europe show an increasingly active interest in EU public affairs management. The family is extending and growing all the time.

There seems to be in development even a sort of *premier league* of EU lobby groups trying to manage their public affairs professionally. Usually they have learnt their EU lessons through games lost in the past. They did not give up, but braced their nerves and body. Many had already tasted the honey: fewer threats and more opportunities. Now they keep open their organisational windows for going out and getting in. These professionals are, however, not necessarily the same as those having either a permanent office in Brussels or a full-time profession as an EU lobbyist, commercial or otherwise. The latter may also neglect the essentials of EU public affairs management, just as much as the amateur interest group. It is also true that some pressure groups without a facility in Brussels and operating from their headquarters elsewhere are excellent players. The same may be true for the many part-timers on the EU playing field. Quality is the only indicator of professionalism, not permanency or job profile. Nobody is excellent just by definition. Nevertheless, the reputation of professionalism particularly belongs to those having a facility in Brussels [Green Cowles, 1998]. Their abilities are sharpened through learning from each other.

EU public affairs management is, of course, not a panacea. If applied professionally, by careful homework and fieldwork, it provides only better chances to win or, at least, not to lose an EU game. The professional public affairs manager clearly operates by a set of norms or prescripts regarding, in our case, better playing in the EU. Its contents will be revealed in the chapters to follow. Our approach, however, is not normative, but *advisory*. Every interest group remains free, of course, to manage its public affairs amateurishly, to use only the traditional techniques of influence, to solve its challenges by non-EU activities, to feel satisfied with mere adaptation to EU outcomes, or to rely on the old non-EU methods of integration in Europe. But, *if* an interest group wants to improve its chances to create a desired EU outcome, *then* it should practice the insights from public affairs management professionally. In this sense our approach is advisory.

CHAPTER 2

THE PLAYING FIELD:
EU COMMON DECISION-MAKING

Deus Ex Machina

In the previous chapter, integration was defined as bringing parts together into a larger whole and, specifically, as managing or settling irritating differences. This accommodation may take place, of course, through the five old practices referred to, such as leniency, fighting and negotiation. But through a permanent machinery of common decision-making the many irritating differences might be settled more effectively and efficiently. The EU is this kind of *machinery*. At its input side it takes on board the many issues from the public and the private interest groups. Through its procedures and practices it can settle many an issue, at least provisionally. This peaceful accommodation of irritating differences can be seen as its ultimate product. Many stakeholders intervene in the production process, especially at the most concrete *dossier* level. Of course, whether they apply the new practices of public affairs management or not, they may also still apply some of the old practices, except that fighting is now only a matter of spirit. The common machinery is, however, more than a new container for the old practices. It has its own mechanisms, which are appreciated for their assumed higher effectiveness and efficiency. Integration is like a goddess, in our case *Europa*, which emerges from the machinery.

The organisation of this machinery for integration is not static, but highly dynamic. Its current functioning is quite different from, for example, its oldest forerunner, the European Coal and Steel Community (ECSC, 1952), and each subsequent variant has taken a different approach. The machinery is, in fact, permanently *in development*. This should not be surprising, given the fact that the EU is quite a young political system, being almost of the same age as the average mid-African developing state. The two and frequently interdependent sources of its development are the well-intended reconstructions of its architecture and the modes of life of its inhabitants.

At irregular times the member-state governments agree upon a new blueprint, called Treaty [Edwards and Pijpers, 1997; McDonagh, 1998]. They re-engineer or reconstruct the machinery. For example, they allocate more formal powers to the European Parliament (EP) or they open up new policy areas for common decision-making. The latter was done under the 1993 Maastricht Treaty for the areas of foreign and security policies (Pillar II) and justice and home affairs (Pillar III), in addition to the established policy fields of the Economic Community (Pillar I). But in many cases such a formal modification of the machinery is, in fact, merely a codification of incipient or even fully existing new practices. The EP, for example, has frequently exerted more influence on the EU decision-making process than its (in the past: weak) formal powers suggested, a positive difference which was codified in a follow-up Treaty [Van Schendelen, 1984]. Such a dynamic difference between the *formalité* and the *réalité* is a normal fact of life. The use of any machinery is in practice always somewhat different from how it was planned. A house gets its living signature from both the architect and its inhabitant.

Our focus here is not on the broad concept and practice of European integration. It is limited to the machinery of EU common decision-making, especially as it operates in practice. This is the playing field for all management of EU public affairs, the theme of this book. Anatomising the machinery, we shall pay less attention to its formal structure or *skeleton* than to its working practices or *flesh and blood*. The skeleton may help to understand, of course, some of the characteristics of the flesh and blood in real life. But the other characteristics, the main ones, are determined by the behaviour of the participating actors. On every issue the stakeholders tend to shape and to reshape the playing field, insofar as not forbidden by the skeleton.

In this chapter we shall summarise the most *basic characteristics* of the EU playing field. We shall do so in particular for its most established and active Pillar I. It is clearly not our objective to present a fully updated and comprehensive description of EU decision-making, which covers all its aspects, issue areas, changes and implications. One may question whether anybody can arrive at such a description of the transitional and prismatic EU system in any case [Bellier, 1997]. In the EU approach of public affairs management it is seldom important to know all the ins and outs of, for example, the voting points at Council level. It is, however, crucial to know whether the Council takes a decision, by which method of voting and what this means in daily practice, wherein a vote is taken rarely. Regarding the basics of the EU machinery we shall present briefly the skeleton and more extensively the flesh and blood.

The Skeleton of the EU Machinery

Its basic design for common decision-making goes back to three dominant political beliefs among the original six member-state governments (France, Germany, Italy, the Netherlands, Belgium, and Luxembourg) in the early 1950s. Firstly, any common decision made under the Treaty (so-called *primary law*) is first and foremost a case of foreign policy and thus falls under the responsibility of the ministers of Foreign Affairs. Secondly, both the main political parties and the major interest groups should be consulted in formulating a common decision. Thirdly, the new decisions should be maintained by law, which is binding either directly (regulations, decrees) or, via national implementation, indirectly (directives), together forming the so-called *secondary law*.

The first belief resulted in the rule that every new common decision has to be approved by the national ministers of (originally) Foreign Affairs, meeting in their General Council on behalf of their governments. Permanent Representatives (PRs), located in Brussels and meeting in their joint committee Coreper, assist the ministers in their approval of a common decision. The drafting of a common decision has been given exclusively to a new body, supposed to stand above parties: the Commission, with a College of Commissioners (two from each of the larger countries and one from each of the smaller ones) plus a bureaucracy of so-called statutory civil servants. The second belief resulted in the establishment of both the European Parliament (EP), representing the national parliaments and their main political parties, and the European Economic and Social Committee (EESC), standing for the main national socio-economic interest groups (particularly from management and labour). These two bodies have to be consulted on major proposals for a common decision. The third belief resulted both in the prescript that European law, as published in the Official Journal, always has priority over domestic law and in the establishment of the European Court of Justice (ECJ).

The plan of the architecture was laid down in the 1957 Treaty of Rome, in particular, as agreed upon by the member-state governments. Acting as both the principals and the shareholders of this architecture, the member-state governments have changed it whenever they agreed a new Treaty, and this has happened more than ten times already [Bainbridge, 1995, 451]. They made the changes not radically but incrementally or step by step. The old skeleton has got a different appearance now, as the following shows (*figure 2.1 left side*).

Main EU decision-making flows and member countries

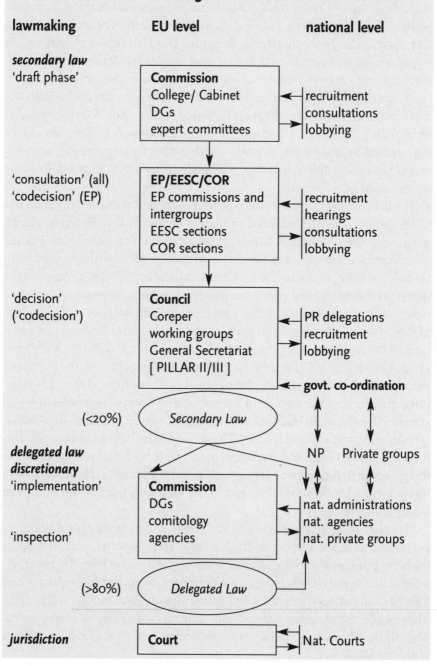

lawmaking	EU level	national level
secondary law 'draft phase'	**Commission** College/ Cabinet DGs expert committees	recruitment consultations lobbying
'consultation' (all) 'codecision' (EP)	**EP/EESC/COR** EP commissions and intergroups EESC sections COR sections	recruitment hearings consultations lobbying
'decision' ('codecision')	**Council** Coreper working groups General Secretariat [PILLAR II/III]	PR delegations recruitment lobbying
		govt. co-ordination
(<20%)	*Secondary Law*	NP Private groups
delegated law discretionary 'implementation' 'inspection'	**Commission** DGs comitology agencies	nat. administrations nat. agencies nat. private groups
(>80%)	*Delegated Law*	
jurisdiction	**Court**	Nat. Courts

Figure 2.1

The Skeleton in Development

The *Council* in Pillar I [Hayes-Renshaw and Wallace, 1997; Westlake, 1995] has become a collection of about 15 specialised Councils, such as the Transport Council and the Health Council. The Council in Pillar II consists of the ministers of Foreign Affairs and, since their first informal meeting in the year 2001, the ministers of Defence. In Pillar III the Council is run by the ministers of Home Affairs and Justice. Most Councils meet only a few times a year, but the Agricultural Council has almost monthly meetings. All the ministers are entitled to act on behalf of their governments. If they fail to come to a common decision, the General Council, formed by the ministers of Foreign Affairs, can at present take over the issue in order to reach a decision. This General Council now has another layer above it, the European Council, consisting of the heads of government (presidents and/or prime ministers). A General Secretariat of almost 2500 people assists all Councils administratively. The preparatory layer of Coreper has acquired a formal position, two chambers (Coreper I and II) and about 300 working groups for the specialised preparation of a common decision. These working groups are officially composed of mainly specialised national civil servants, plus people from the much-enlarged offices of the PRs (amounting to about 800 people in all in the year 2000).

On most proposals for a common decision the Council in Pillar I no longer decides by unanimity (the intergovernmental way), but by a qualified or simple majority (the supranational way). This means that every member-state government can be overruled; in Pillars II and III the intergovernmental way prevails [Maurer, 1999, 14]. Treaty texts prescribe which *voting regime* applies to a proposal. In the case of qualified majority voting (QMV), the majority consists of about two-thirds of the voting points, of which every member state has been assigned a proportion. In most cases of secondary legislation the Council is still the sole formal decision-maker. But since the 1987 Single European Act (SEA) the EP, until then having only been consulted, has increasingly acquired in Pillar I the position of a *codecision-maker*, being equal to the Council. In 2000 the Council concluded 255 secondary laws introduced in the years before, of which 80% were still subject to consultation and the remainder subject to codecision. But up to 50% of the new proposals introduced that year were subject to codecision [General Report 2000, X]. The Treaty texts, again, prescribe the appropriate procedure.

Most EU legislation falls, however, under so-called *delegated legislation.* By its secondary acts the Council can transfer formal powers of legislation to the Commission and particularly to the around 450 special committees, which is called *comitology* [Christiansen and Kirchner, 2000; Andenas and Türk, 2000; Vos, 1999; Joerges and Vos, 1999]. These special committees are established by a Council decision and officially composed of people representing the member states. On the basis of a proposal from the Commission they contribute to the implementation of secondary laws. There are three categories of special committee. *Advisory* committees, comprising roughly half the total number, can only advise on implementation proposals from the Commission. This has to give the utmost attention to the advice, but remains free to do what it proposes. *Management* committees, which manage a policy field (mainly agriculture), and *regulatory* committees, which act as regulators, have a formally stronger position. By QMV they can express their disagreement with the Commission. In such a situation the Council may decide, by QMV as well and before a short deadline, that the Commission must reconsider its proposal; otherwise the Commission proposal is executed. Since 1994 by an informal *modus vivendi* and since 1999 by a Council decision, the EP has been able to interfere if it believes that a decision goes beyond the limits set in the basic act of secondary law, if this act was subject to codecision. In the year 2000, the volume of delegated legislation has been more than 82% (1,201 acts) of the total EU legislative output, the remaining 18% being the previously mentioned 255 secondary laws. In fact, under delegated legislation 38 directives, 606 regulations and 557 decrees have been produced [General Report 2000, chapter X].

By the year 2000 the *Commission* had become an apparatus of about 22,000 civil servants [Edwards and Spence, 1994; Cini, 1996; Page, 1997; COM Designing, 1999; Nugent, 2001]. About 80% of them hold a statutory position. Two-thirds of the others are temporarily contracted persons and one-third national civil servants working on secondment. The main organisational units are the around 20 specialised Directorates-General (DGs) and the around 10 general Departments (such as the General Secretariat and the Translation Service). In addition, more than 10 formally established Agencies, which are linked to the Commission, have the combined tasks of implementation and inspection [Kreher 1996 and 1998]. The Commissioners, meeting as a College almost once a week, are in overall charge of the operation. They are nominated by their governments (and its chairman also by the European Council) and the College is approved by the EP. They all have a small Cabinet with personally selected people to serve them politically. The Commission has remained the body that exclusively drafts proposals for binding decision-making by either the Council or the comitology.

In addition it has, directly through the Treaties, some formal powers of legislation of its own, particularly in the policy fields of competition and external trade.

The *Parliament* [Corbett, Jacobs and Shackleton, 2000; Westlake, 1994-A] has undergone perhaps the biggest changes. The number of Members of Parliament (MEPs) increased more than eightfold from its beginnings in the ECSC to 626 people in 1994. Since 1979 the EP has been directly elected. The large majority of MEPs have held a seat only in the EP and no longer, with a dual mandate, in their national parliaments as well. In cross-national perspective, the budgetary powers of the EP have always been strong. It has the final say over both the total EU budget and the so-called non-obligatory (mainly non-agricultural) expenditures, which now form the largest part of the total budget. In the process of EU legislation the EP has acquired a gradually stronger position: from mere advisory (consultation) to also amendment powers (co-operation) under the 1987 SEA and to veto powers (codecision) under the 1993 Maastricht Treaty; and through the 1999 Amsterdam Treaty co-operation became part of codecision. In special cases such as international agreements and enlargement the EP also has an advisory position (assent). Since 1999 the EP can intervene in the delegated legislation, if this is based on a Council decision under the codecision rules. The new power of codecision particularly covers the expanding policy fields of Pillar I, except agriculture, and needs an absolute majority of all MEPs. Assisted by a staff of about 4.000, the MEPs arrive at a common position in plenum after preparatory work by a rapporteur from one of the about 15 specialised EP commissions.

The most important other parts of the skeleton of the EU machinery are the following. The *EESC* can be said to be the body that has undergone the least change. Due to the subsequent enlargements of the EU, it has acquired more members (222 in the year 2000), but in its policy domain it has still only advisory (consultation) power. As a result of the Maastricht Treaty it was given a companion in the form of the new *Committee of the Regions* (COR). This is also an advisory body, again composed of 222 representatives (mainly elected politicians) from subnational governments. The EESC and COR have a mainly joint staff (and building) of about 700 people. The *Court*, having one judge per member state, has undergone much change due particularly to its workload [Dehousse, 1998]. The number of cases has increased more than eightfold. In order to manage the workload better, the Court established in 1989 a special Court of First Instance (CFI) with five chambers for the fast-track processing of individual (not government-involved) cases. The Court staff counts about 800 people, of which about one-third work as translators. The unchanging authority of the Court is quite remarkable. Without an effective sanction (police and jail) system of its own, it manages to get its judgements largely accepted by individuals, governments and EU bodies. Finally, a few other bodies exist, such as the *European Central Bank* (ECB), the *Court of Auditors* (CoA) and the *European Investment Bank* (EIB). Because they act at a formal distance from the EU common decision-making machinery, they do not need a further description here.

Formal Policies and Powers

The changing skeleton of EU decision-making is certainly an ongoing process. There is always a next intergovernmental conference, for the making of a new Treaty. Those who want to influence the EU machinery should have a basic understanding of its skeleton, both as it is at any moment and as it develops by formal re-engineering. Knowing its causes and consequences, irrespective of their desirability, helps in anticipating particular changes more effectively. Two specific developments deserve more attention here.

Firstly, there are the formal changes of *policy regime*. This always has two main components: the fields in which it operates and the instruments of their cultivation. The EU policy fields formally expanded from just coal and steel to almost the same broad policy landscape controlled before exclusively by the member-state governments *(figure 2.2)*. The 1993 Maastricht Treaty can be seen as the watershed between the mainly market sector-orientated EU and the one also covering policy areas that belong pre-eminently to the government sector, such as defence, public health and migration. In the new millennium only a few policy areas, such as housing and recreation, which are characterised by marginal cross-border impacts, still fall virtually outside any EU involvement and are still almost purely run by domestic public and private organisations. All the others have undergone a more or less intense europeanisation, resulting in a shifting division of labour from the national capital to 'Brussels' [Schmitter, 1996-B, 125-6]. Policies in such fields as competition, transport and trade largely emanate from the EU capital now [Fligstein and McNichol, 1998; Nugent, 1999, 347].

The wider and more intense policy-making does not imply that the various policy fields are cultivated in the same way, or that a sort of hotchpotch Union is in the making. The Treaties offer a *menu* of policy instruments. One choice is between soft interventions (like subsidies, benchmarks

Official key-dates of main EU policy formation

	1952-1957	1958-1972	1973-1985	1986-1993	1994-
Coal & Steel	+	+	+	+	+
Open Market	–	+	+	+ ('1992')	+
Competition	–	+	+	+	+
Euratom	–	+	+	+	+
Agriculture	–	+ (1962 EAGGF)	+	+	+ (MacSharry)
Transport	–	+	+	+	+
Regional Policy	–	+ (1957 EIB)	+ (1974 ERDF)	+	+ (Cohesion Fund)
Social Affairs	–	+ (1957 ESF)	+	+	+ (Social Protocol)
Developmental Aid	–	+ (1963 Yaounde)	+ (1975 Lomé)	+	+
Environmental Policy	–	–	+ (1973 Action)	+	+
Consumers Policy	–	–	+ (1975)	+	+
Monetary Affairs	–	–	+ (1979 EMS-ERM)	+ (1990 EBRD)	+ (ECB)
SM-Enterprises	–	–	– (1983)	+	+
Fishing	–	–	– (1983)	+	+
Industrial Policy	–	–	–	+ (1986 R&D)	+
Energy	–	–	–	+	+
Education	–	–	–	+	+
Social Health	–	–	–	+	+
Security/Foreign Policy	–	–	–	–	+ (pillar 2)
Justice/Home Affairs	–	–	–	–	+ (pillar 3)
Member States	1952: 'Six'		1973: +UK, DK, Ire 1981: +Gr	1986: +Sp, Por	1994: EEA 1995: +Au, Fi, Swe
Institutional Reform	1952: ECSC	1957: 'Rome' 1967: 'merger'		1987: SEA 1993: 'Maastricht'	1999: 'Amsterdam'

Figure 2.2

and guidelines) and hard ones (like legislation and levies). Another one is between specific measures (for a single sector, trade or even item, like for agriculture, meat or the compact disc) and general ones (applying to many sectors, trades and items, like the policies on competition and social affairs). A third choice is between the delineation of common policies (so-called positive integration, such as on agriculture, environment and working conditions) and the removal of barriers to free interaction (so-called negative integration, as applies to competition and education). The EU decision-makers tend to have their quarrels over these options when trying to agree a common line. Going *à la carte* is not a formal option. Since the 1990s, the trends of the common choices made have moved from soft to hard intervention, from specific to general measures, and from positive to negative integration.

The second formal development deserving special attention here regards the *power balance* inside the EU. For a long time intergovernmental decision-making was the leading power principle, resulting in unanimity voting in the Council and little or no role-playing by the EP, the Commission and/or the Court. The 1987 SEA strengthened, especially for the Single European Market (SEM) policy area, the principle of supranationalism, implying both QMV in the Council and stronger powers for the three previously mentioned other bodies. The 1993 *Maastricht Treaty* introduced at least four new power principles. Firstly that of subsidiarity, which holds that there should not be an EU decision unless it appears to be a better option to find a common solution to a problem [EIPA, 1991]. Parliament, secondly, must have the formal power to reject draft legislation in specific policy areas (the codecision position). Regional governments, thirdly, must acquire at least an advisory position via their newly established COR. And, finally, under the Social Policy Agreement (a protocol to the Treaty, with the United Kingdom abstaining) the representatives from organised management and labour were given the joint right to make specific proposals for the EU agenda and to implement the eventual decisions subsequently. The 1999 *Amsterdam Treaty* adopted this Agreement as part of its Social Chapter (UK now joining). It also re-emphasised the principle of co-ordination, which recommends soft guidelines rather than hard legislation for sensitive policy areas like public health and taxation.

A single answer to the question of the formal EU power balance is not easy to find. There is much *variation* according to policy field and, indeed, no hotchpotch at all [Nugent, 1999, 347]. Any principle is always applied somehow and somewhere. For example, around the year 2000 market issues fall mainly under supranational decision-making, defence issues under intergovernmental one, social insurance under mild co-ordination and domestic crime under subsidiarity. However, in diachronic perspective, there is a clear trend towards supranational decision-making. The indicators are the following. Until the 1987 SEA, market issues fell under intergovernmentalism, but since that date have been dealt with mainly under supranational procedures. Issues in Pillar II and III came from subsidiarity or soft co-ordination and already show the first signs of supranational decision-making. For issues still treated nationally, like civil liberties and income taxation, co-ordination is the way to bring them under the aegis of the EU. Examples refuting the observed trend of *creeping supranationalism* hardly exist. By consequence, if the member-state governments have ever possessed sovereignty at all [Christianen, 1994; Krasner, 1999], they are increasingly losing much of it. At the Council level their independence, equality and veto power, being the three main indicators of sovereignty [Morgenthau and Thompson, 1985, 331-2], are declining. Under the supranational regime they need support from other governments for getting through a desired decision, they are treated unequal by weighted voting points and they can be overruled by QMV. At most, they are pooling their sovereignties within the EU [Keohane and Hoffmann, 1991]. Through their common power in the Council they may have control over the other bodies, but this control is being scaled down and weakened. The Commission, EP, EESC, COR, Court and other bodies have acquired their own powers, and they also add to the skeleton their flesh and blood.

The Flesh and Blood of the EU Machinery

The work floor of the EU decision process is our chief concern from now on. The metaphor of 'work floor' stands for the places where the work of decision-making is really done. *Figure 2.1* shows the main parts of the whole machinery containing this work floor. Although the decision-making is, strictly, only one early phase of the full decision process, it is often used as *pars pro toto*. The skeleton may be a determinant of this EU work floor, but the *flesh and blood* make it real. More or less the same players are presented as in the skeleton approach, but now they are regarded for their behaviour in daily practice. Many different observations will be the outcome. Two differences of approach deserve attention first.

In the previous section our key concept was formal power, as distilled from the Treaties. From now on, the central concept is *influence*. We define it in terms of a relationship between two or more actors: A influences B, if B's behaviour changes (either in accordance with the wishes of A or in any other direction) due to the behaviour of A [Dahl, 1991]. Like any relationship, influence is not a constant but a variable factor, dependent on time, arena, intelligence, supply and many other circumstances. By consequence, only repeated and controlled observations may permit some generalisations in terms of patterns. Like any causal relationship, influence cannot be proven perfectly, but only in terms of plausibility [Van Schendelen, 1998, I]. Formal powers can, of course, be a determinant of the work floor or, in our terminology, a resource of potential influence. In such a case, for example, a hierarchically superior person or body actually determines the behaviour of a lower-placed one. But the reality is frequently different, because a lower-placed person can have stronger resources of influence, such as time, information and support. Private lobbyists are the best-known example of persons usually having minimal formal powers and sometimes exerting maximal influence. For measuring influence, formal powers have scant value.

A second difference from the previous section is the reversal of our starting point. In the formal approach, the Treaty and, subsequently, the Council form the basis of EU decision-making. The other bodies, like the Commission and the Parliament, have formally a more or less subsidiary position. In the work floor approach we focus on the reality of EU decision-making, as it evolves from start to finish in the main Pillar I. The best metaphor for it is the initially *blank A4-format* piece of paper. At the end of the process this may be published, full of text, as a common decision in the Official Journal. The filling of the paper usually starts somewhere in or around the Commission. Insofar as the Council has the ultimate say over a proposed decision, it usually gives this only as a last say at the end, when the paper is already full of text. In the many cases of delegated legislation, it rarely even has the option of a last say. The difference between the skeleton and the flesh and blood and thus the relevance of our metaphor can be exemplified by the practitioners' saying that 'it is not those who sign the decision, but those who draft it, who are the most important people'.

The Commission's Work Floor

Except in two respects, the Commission is a very normal bureaucracy, like one can find at more or less any level in any member country. The first exception is its *multicultural* composition. The Commission reflects the variety of Europe. At all levels, from Commissioner to technical assistant, the people have very different languages, customs, values and norms. This variety far exceeds that of the national bureaucracy of a federal country like

Germany or Spain. The apparatus is also an example of multicultural integration, stimulated by such factors as a common location, the pragmatic use of only a few working languages (English, French) and shared expectations. It has a developing *esprit de corps*, although many cultural differences continue to play a role. The second exception regards the *underresourced* nature of the Commission. Its total EU budget is almost equal to that of only the Belgian federal government. To make another comparison: in June 2001 US president George Bush ordered a federal tax relief of almost twice the size of the whole EU annual budget. Its own (statutory) administrative staff is much smaller than that of the local government of the city of Rotterdam and has only 2% of the size of the US federal government. The staff are about 30% secretarial (so-called C level), 10% linguistic (LA level) and 5% technical (D level), leaving about 55% of the staff (about 10,500 persons) for policy work (A and B level) [Nugent, 2001, VII]. The Commission has, because of this, a strong appetite for information and support from outside, to which we shall return below.

The Commission behaves, in daily practice, *multifunctionally* [Cini, 1996, I; Page, 1997, VII]. The Commission is the main gatherer of issues from the member countries' public and private interest groups that add to the EU agenda. It is also the main collector of information and expertise for the drafting of proposals to deal with the issues. It also acts as the leading broker for negotiating the required consensus among the stakeholders. The Commission has economic functions as well. Within the limits of the financial funds and the policy programmes, it allocates both financial means and public procurements to interest groups, particularly in the fields of agriculture, regional development and enlargement. Its managerial functions regard the good conduct of its apparatus and the scrutinising, by itself or its Agencies, of other EU bodies and stakeholders, like member-state governments. The Commission also acts as a plaintiff and an adjudicator in certain policy fields, particularly on competition issues. When its legislative function described below is included, the Commission practically holds *trias politica*, not exclusively but shared with others, such as with the Council and the EP on legislation, with the member states on implementation (the directives) and with the Court on adjudication.

For four reasons, legislation can be considered as the main function of the Commission. Firstly, regarding *secondary* legislation (the aforementioned 18% of total EU laws in 2000) it holds the monopoly on drafting proposals for new Council decision-making. Without such a proposal the Council cannot decide. In most cases the final Council decision is largely identical to the proposed text [Bellier, 1997, 110]. In other words: the Commission, representing formally the drafting phase of EU decision-making, is practically involved in the decision phase. The blank A4-format piece of paper receives its contents here. Secondly, regarding *delegated* legislation (82% of the laws in 2000) the Commission sits practically in the driver's seat. In the field of competition policy it has its own powers. Between 1991 and 2001 it blocked, *inter alia*, 15 cross-border take-overs, including some from outside the EU. It also runs the comitology. For every committee it assigns the *chef de dossier*, decides the agenda, presents the proposals and allocates the budget. In most cases the Commission gathers support from a committee and can forward the decision to the Official Journal. Thirdly, the Commission makes so-called *discretionary* legislation: specific binding decisions considered justified and not forbidden by EU law, for example regarding the awarding of a subsidy or a procurement. The current laws always provide some room for discretionary interpretation and manoeuvre, useful for the making of a binding decision. Finally, the Commission produces a great deal of so-called soft or *supplementary* legislation, which is not binding legally but is taken as authoritative in practice. Examples are its green papers (for defining problems), white papers (for suggesting solutions) and other papers framing an issue.

The Commission, in short, is the *major EU legislator* [Majone, 1996-B]. Some suggest, however, that much of its legislation is, not by quantity but by quality, of minor relevance as it regards the mainly non-political, routine-like, so-called technical details agreed upon by nominated officials, and is far from the so-called high politics of elected politicians [Nugent 1999, 257; Greenwood, 1997, 13]. However, an objective criterion to assess the relevance of the content of legislation does not exist. It is EU practice to regard issues of disagreement among politicians as belonging to the realms of high politics, and those for settlement by officials as a 'low politics' matter. The level of the issues has, however, little to do with relevance. For example, the 1989 Framework Directive in the field of Safety, Health and Hygiene on the Workplace was widely regarded as a case of high politics finally concluded by the Council. It empowered the Commission to regulate this field in detail, and soon the Commission produced almost 40 directives through its Advisory Committee, part of comitology [Daemen and Van Schendelen, 1998]. It is not the Framework directive, but these 40 follow-ups, that have been considered most relevant by the lobby groups from management and labour. For them and for most other lobby groups the devil (or the saint) is usually in the detail.

The Commission: how it Works

As the Commission is multifunctional in its behaviour, it is polycentric in its organisation [Cini, 1996; Page, 1997, II]. Viewed *vertically*, it has different layers. The Commissioners have to run a policy area (portfolio), which seldom coincides with a Directorate-General (DG): most Commissioners have their feet in more than one DG and most DGs have more than one Commissioner. In practice, the Director-General himself has to maintain order inside the DG. Every DG consists of several Directorates and these have their specialised bureaux or units. As in any normal bureaucracy, the substance of policy work is done at the mid-level. Most important are the *chef de dossier* (usually lower-A level), the Head of Unit above this person and his/her associates (upper-B). They produce the draft paper for the higher official, who normally only makes comments in the margin (and therefore might be called marginal) but, of course, he or she can have issued an instruction beforehand. They co-ordinate their expert groups and their comitology. In practice, the mass of policy papers moves like an iceberg through the Commission: only its small top is in the hands of the upper-A civil servants and the Commissioners. Their range of control tends to be limited to the dossiers that need approval by the College, such as proposals for secondary legislation, and to the most politicised issues of the month.

Viewed *horizontally*, every DG has its own set of policy tasks and its aforementioned structures to realise them. But this administrative segmentation or sectorisation does not fall in line with that of the policy fields. For example, the europeanisation of the working times for the cross-bordering truckers falls under DG Transport, but is, as well, an issue for DG Social Affairs, DG Internal Market, DG Enterprise and, regarding enlargement, DG External Relations. The result is bureau-political behaviour: the bureau that is formally in charge tries to keep the lead and to win the game, while the other offices try to intervene at the earliest phase. At the proposal of the Commission's General Secretariat a dossier is assigned to one or another DG, whose decision may make all the difference for the outcome. For example, regarding the 1998 draft Directive on Biotechnology, the DG Environment took the lead over DG Enterprise, DG Agriculture and DG Research, much to their regret afterwards. Inconsistent policy-making always lies in wait.

One can, thirdly, take a *diagonal* view of the Commission: the structures and cultures, which crosscut the layers and the policy tasks. Examples of crosscutting structures are the College, the General Secretariat, the inter-service consultation (interdepartmental meetings), the joint task forces, the Cabinets (observing each other) and the mixed task set of a Commissioner. The most important cultural crosscut is the so-called *double loyalty*, which may even quadruple. Firstly, there is nationality [Page, 1997, III], and here the Commissioners set an example. Nominated by their national governments, they frequently act as national watchdogs for all policy fields [Donnelly and Ritchie, 1994]. National (party-political) figures can be appointed (parachuted) at the highest A level [Page, 1997, 82]. The positions at the A and B levels are still largely distributed according to an unofficial *fourchette*, largely based on the size of the member states, although the Belgians are overrepresented and the new member states underrepresented [General Report, 1998]. The 1999 Prodi Commission has opted for a move from spoils (nationality) to merit (diploma) appointments [COM, Reforming, 2000]. The second variant of double loyalty is regional affiliation. The regional governments, getting more importance in most countries, want to have their region represented inside the Commission. Many civil servants, especially those from federal countries, hold a special sympathy for their own region and behave accordingly. Thirdly, there are the sectoral loyalties, for example those of the hi-tech freaks at DG Research, the environment worshippers at DG Environment and the farmers' clan at DG Agriculture. Sectoral interest groups often try to install their experts at the (most important) lower-A level. Finally, there are the many crosscutting informal groups, based on personal characteristics such as language, education, age, friendship, years in Brussels, family networks and character.

The Commission and its Assistant Bureaucracy

As said before, the Commission is an exceptionally small bureaucracy. The average size of a policy unit is less than 20 persons [COM, Designing, 1999, annexe 7]. The Commission totters almost permanently on the brink of both volume and content overload. In order to manage this, it has to rely on various techniques. On the one hand it tries to reduce the overload, for example by selecting priorities, combining issues and phasing policies [Deutsch, 1963; Easton, 1965]. On the other hand it tries to expand its capacities by two ways. Firstly, by the outsourcing of work particularly to national governments (as for implementation and inspection) and private consultancies (mainly for research and management). Secondly, by bringing in people from outside ('insourcing'), particularly those belonging to the following categories: temporary personnel, employed for all sorts of expert work; national civil servants, on secondment; and representatives from lobby groups, who get an open door for their provision of sectoral information and who are particularly invited to take place in committees. It this *committee method*, in particular, that has given the Commission a large assistant bureaucracy [Pedler and Schaefer, 1996; Van Schendelen, 1998].

Most committees are so-called *expert groups*, also bearing various names like task force, scientific committee, interface and platform. They are composed of so-called experts believed to be representative of a public or a private interest group. The number of expert groups, as officially registered for the reimbursement of their variable costs, is at least 1,000. But there may be twice as many, because they are often unregistered [Landmarks, 1999, 240]. All these expert groups, lacking any formal power at all, have only semi-formal advisory status. About 50,000 experts meet in the groups that are registered, and these are drawn from (in roughly equal numbers) the public and private interest groups in the member countries. They contribute on only a part-time basis, dependent on the workload, for example once a week or a month. If they meet, on average, only ten days a year, then these experts represent an additional workforce equivalent to roughly 2,000 people. The second category of committees comprises the around 450 falling under the aforementioned *comitology*, practically run by the Commission. They do have formal powers, ranging from advisory and management to regulatory. The numbers of the two categories are increasing [Dogan, 2000], as new issue areas get their own committees and more specialised new committees are established to deal with existing issues. For example in the field of waste management, once covered by only the 1976 Waste Management Committee, about 20 committees are involved now [Van Kippersluis, 1998].

All these committees are semi-formal meetings of experts connected in parallel. There are, however, functional equivalents. Firstly, there are the *virtual committees* of experts being consulted on the same issue one after the other, thus connected in series instead of parallel. Secondly, there is *engrenage*, by which domestic bodies are brought together into an EU network [Leonard, 1999]. Recent examples can be found in the fields of competition control, central banking, food safety and diploma inspection. Starting with a benchmark or an expert group, the Commission is spinning its web here. In due time the network may develop into an EU Agency with national and even regional branches, functionally comparable to a highly institutionalised and deconcentrated committee composed of representative experts from all over.

This committee-based assistant bureaucracy reflects an old European government practice and is maintained by many *positive functions* [Van Schendelen, 1998]. The first parliaments in Europe have, essentially, been budget committees ('no taxation without representation'), composed of expert representatives from the citizenry [Bisson, 1973]. Since the beginnings of the EU in the form of the ECSC there have always been committees. For the (understaffed) Commission the representative experts provide excellent and cheap labour, which is highly valued for its provision of field information, its articulation of support and its aggregation of interests. The Commission receives all of this almost for free. For example, the average costs of a committee under comitology are about 40,000 Euro a year, which is about half the price of one B-level civil servant [Vos, 1999, 118]. In return for this investment the Commission can monitor the represented lobby groups and influence the experts. The committee method helps the Commission to depoliticise the issues, by dissolving them in a Cartesian (rational, scientific and technical) way. It also helps to legitimise its own decision-making, because 'organised Europe' has participated. The experts and their home organisations appreciate the committees as well, as these provide a low-cost and semi-formal channel to influence each other, the Commission and, ultimately, the Official Journal.

Case studies show that both the expert groups and the comitology committees can, indeed, be highly influential [Van Schendelen, 1998]. By defining 'problems' and suggesting 'solutions', they at least influence the policy climate in an area, thus creating chances for desired outcomes in the future. In many cases they have a more immediate impact on the agenda and the proposals of the Commission in their field. Sometimes they are even so influential that, in fact, they make the text for the Official Journal. The formal distinction between expert groups and comitology is hardly relevant in practice. An expert group can be involved in the preparation of delegated legislation and a committee under comitology can be consulted for a proposal of secondary legislation. Such role changes happen regularly. Many committee members are ignorant and even indifferent about the formal status of their committee. Their interest is to exert influence. The precondition of this is having at least the image of both expertise and representativeness, which they cultivate carefully. Many committee members behave, however, rather as experts with a free mandate than as instructed representatives [Egeberg, 1999; Schaefer, 2000].

The main direct factor of influence is the formation of an internal consensus. The *chef de dossier* is usually most prepared to accept a consensus reached. Many a proposal from the Commission for either secondary or delegated legislation is, in fact, not exclusively the product of a mid-level civil servant, but the outcome of political manoeuvring with the relevant committee (or its Very Important Persons) beforehand. The possession of formal powers (the status of comitology or not) is not a systematic factor of influence at all. A formally powerful committee may be without influence and a powerless expert group may be highly influential. Additional factors affecting committee influence are a monopolistic position and a simple procedure. Due to the proliferation of committees, these factors are becoming rarer. Among the committees there is increasing policy competition and procedural complexity, as shown in the case of waste management.

Taken as a whole, the committees function for the Commission as an inexpensive shopping centre full of representative expertise, articulated interests and discursive deliberation [Joerges, 1999]. Paradoxically, the single committee is tending to lose influence, while the system of committees is becoming, more than ever, the basic work floor of the Commission. By the creation of this assistant bureaucracy the small-sized Commission has shown itself to be smarter than the member states [Lord, 1998, 29].

The Parliament's Influence Role

The approximately ten political *parties* of the EP are not its basic working units. They are more or less loose networks of so-called sister parties from different member countries [Gaffney, 1996; Hix and Lord, 1997]. The two largest parties together, the socialist PES and the christian EPP, hold an absolute majority in theory and might dominate the EP in practice. In the 1994-1999 EP they managed to do so in slightly more than half the cases of roll-call voting; in three-quarters of the cases, at least, most of their members were in agreement [Hix, 2000]. Perfect bloc voting remains an exception [Raunio, 1997], and has been even more unusual in the new 1999-2004 EP, after its high turnover of members in 1999. A substantial number of MEPs hold more sympathy for a special (national, regional, sectoral or personal) interest than for the not-so-common ideology of their party. Most MEPs clearly act under competing pressures from both the EU and the domestic level [Deschouwer, 2000]. In fact they can behave as trustees with a free mandate [Katz, 1999-B]. The parties have more problems in voting as a bloc on policy issues than on issues of the EP's housekeeping, particularly the adoption of budget, positions and privileges for their own.

About 15 EP *commissions* provide the main work floor, each being a kind of a micro-parliament for a specific policy field. The number of seats the various parties have in the commissions roughly depends on their size in the plenum. However, the size of the EP commissions, between 50 and 80 MEPs, is too large for effective action. To deal with this corpulence, every major item on a commission's agenda, such as a Commission proposal or an initiative of its own, is given to a *rapporteur*. This MEP has the task of drafting a resolution acceptable to the majority of the commission and, finally, the plenum. It is a prestigious role, frequently given to senior MEPs from the larger parties. The rapporteur, usually working highly informally and proactively, is closely watched by the so-called shadow rapporteurs from the other parties and is intensively approached by people from lobby groups, including those from the Commission and the Permanent Representatives (PRs). In order to produce an acceptable draft resolution, the rapporteur has to anticipate many of their demands and to communicate intensively.

Also forming part of the work floor are the around 80 (in the year 2000) *intergroups*, which do not have any formal status at all. They are merely meetings of MEPs having a similar interest or concern, such as on disarmament, mining regions or Jewish affairs. People from outside, representing an interest group, can be members of an intergroup. The common objective is to create an issue and to push it onto the EU agenda, through a recommendation or a resolution, accepted by the plenary EP. Although this cannot formally bind the Commission or the Council, it frequently influences them. The Commission often feels very sympathetic towards any new issue-creation by an intergroup. With normally a time lag of about four years, the issue then frequently appears on its official agenda. A fine example of success is the intergroup on animal welfare [Jacobs and Corbett, 1990, 151-4]. A recent example is the 2000 Intergroup on Safety at Sea, formed after the Erika oil-tanker disaster.

The case of intergroups illustrates that the influence of the EP can be far larger than its formal powers of decision-making suggest [Van Schendelen, 1984]. The EP is a major creator of EU issues and agendas, particularly in such policy fields as social affairs, the environment and consumer affairs. Civil interest groups in these fields keep close contact with MEPs. In EU decision-making as well, the EP's *influence* often far exceeds its formal position, which anyhow has been strengthened under all Treaties since 1979. Even through consultation, being the main procedure until at least 1999, the EP can exert real influence by making use of other resources. It can link the dossiers under consultation with those under codecision, or mobilise lobby and media support from outside. It can also profit from divisions inside the Council. Frequently it wrestles a gentleman's agreement from the Commission (like the 1999 Prodi promise to fire a Commissioner at the EP's request) or from the Council (like the 1994 *modus vivendi* on comitology).

Formal resources can strengthen a position of influence too, particularly the *codecision* procedure (and the co-operation variant from the 1987 SEA until 1999). Between 1993 and 1999 the EP held these formal powers in 31% of the 1608 proposals for secondary legislation in Pillar I (apart from budget and assent), the rest falling under consultation [Maurer, 1999, 18]. In 2000 as many as 50% of the new proposals were codecision cases, particularly relating to transport, the environment, social affairs and development [General Report 2000, VII]. From 1993 to 1999 165 codecision cases were concluded [EP, Activity, 1999, 11]. In 63 of these, the EP and the Council reached an agreement without any amendment, in 36 cases the Council adopted all the EP's amendments and in the other 66 cases the conciliation committee had to discuss a total of 913 remaining amendments. The Council finally accepted 27% of these as they stood and 51% in some compromise form. On 22% of the amendments no agreement was reached. Three of the 165 codecision cases finally failed through EP blocking (the 1994 Voice Telephone, the 1995 Biotechnology and the 1998 Transferable Securities). The EP's formal impact on secondary legislation looks impressive in both quantitative [Maurer, 1999, VI] and, insofar as data are available, comparative terms [Blondel and others, 1970; Kurian, 1998]. Behind the scenes the reality of conciliation is, however, highly informal and more determined by influence practices than formal powers [Shackleton, 2000; Wurzel, 1999; Garman and Hilditch, 1999; Westlake, 1994-B]. In small-sized *trialogue* meetings people from the EP (the commission chairman and the rapporteur), the Council and the Commission try to reach a compromise.

Like the Commission, the Parliament, in short, behaves in a *polycentric* and *multifunctional* way. Its openness provides a supportive group of MEPs for almost every issue or interest. The mere choice of a specific commission or even rapporteur may determine the policy outcome, as happened in 1999 when the commission on the Environment successfully achieved a moratorium on the trade and the production of genetically modified organisms (GMOs), to the displeasure of some other commissions. In comparison to many a more centrally controlled national parliament, the EP runs the higher risk of inconsistent decision-making and enjoys the greater opportunity of discursive deliberation reflecting the variety of Europe. This is particularly due to its independence from any government at EU or national level. It is the only parliament in Europe which cannot be dissolved and which is free from the Trojan horse of a government-controlled majority. Together with the Commission it usually acts as a lobby group in favour of further europeanisation [Franklin and Scarrow, 1999; Corbett, 1998]. Enjoying their freedom of action, the MEPs themselves lobby for all sorts of interest groups. They also launch new issues, contribute to the EU agenda formation, negotiate with the Commission and the Council, scrutinise their activities and act as barristers 'in first instance' on proposals from the Commission. All together, they belong to the influential players of the EU decision-making machinery.

EESC and COR: More Influence than Power

Expert representatives from national socio-economic interest groups, meeting in the *EESC*, have to be consulted on major proposals from the Commission in their field. They can also advise on their own initiative. As a Grand Committee, the EESC comes close to an advisory committee under comitology: its advice has to be given the utmost attention, but not necessarily any response. Its logic of influence is similar: as long as its expertise and representativeness are acknowledged, it may exert influence far exceeding its weak formal powers. The main influence factor is the formation of a sufficient consensus. The EESC is certainly an active committee. In the late 1990s it produced each year on average about 100 reports by request and another 100 on its own initiative [General Report 1998]. They comprise varied issues, such as on the environment, agriculture, social affairs and transport. The real work floor is at the level of sections and subcommittees, led by a chairman, assisted by the bureau and, for every dossier, a rapporteur.

Although its own reports praise its *influence* on EU decision-making, outside observers are more reserved [Van der Voort, 1997 and 1998]. They see the EESC as having only rarely an observable direct impact on Commission proposals. Its influence is more indirect and mid-term: by changing the policy climate, an issue or an agenda inside the Commission. The major explanation for this is that the EESC has great difficulty in coming to a common position on a concrete and specific issue. It produces a lot of output, but its contents either sum up the diverse views on the concrete issue or suggest a consensus at the most abstract level. The main reasons for this are its internal divisions, challenges to its expertise and representativeness, strong competition from other committees and bodies, and the openness of its policy area. The employers' and workers' groups have their strong divisions both between each other and internally, especially between the Northern and the Southern members. EESC membership, then, is particularly used for the monitoring of another group and to block its preferences. Thus the influence is more negative than positive. Many members consider this quite useful and do their positive lobbying elsewhere in the system.

Similar divisions can be observed over the former *Social Dialogue*, then the Social Policy Agreement and now the Social Chapter. This procedure is formally distinct from the EESC, as it has its own place in the Treaties of Maastricht (as a protocol) and Amsterdam. But the main players are the same: the organisations of management and labour [Treu, 1992]. Between 1993 and 1999, the two groupings, together possessing the formal powers of corporatist-like self-regulation [Gorges, 1996; Falkner, 1998], have produced three directives (1996 Parental Leave, 1997 Part-time Work and 1999 Fixed-term Contracts). Since 1987 they have also arrived at 23 joint positions, phrased in general terms (such as on disabled people, vocational training, and employment). Their dialogue, even if one of the deaf, at least contributes to the EU policy climate. In addition, it triggers dialogue at the sectoral level (like on insurance, construction, road transport). About 20 formal committees and informal groups do the real work here.

The other Grand Committee *COR* is in many respects comparable to the EESC. It also has only advisory position, the same size, similar internal operations and a high level of activity. It covers a variety of issues as well, ranging from structural funds to employment and public procurement, but all related to regional affairs. Four differences are its young age (formed in 1994), its regional focus and background, its composition of mainly elected regional politicians, and its internal organisation by political groupings operating like those in the EP. A fifth difference is its *reputation for influence*, as recently underlined by its impact on the text of the Treaty of Amsterdam [Bindi, 1998]. That the COR is rather successful in reaching an internal consensus, is not self-evident. The members score high on representativeness, but low on (sectoral) expertise. They also operate in highly competitive and open policy fields. Those four differences can be regarded as resources that have been beneficial from its inception. As a young body the COR is full of ambition and without a history of old scores and sores. Its regional focus is strongly supported by the rise of regionalism in Europe [Sharpe, 1993; Jones and Keating, 1995; Leonardi, 1995; Telò, 2001; Loughlin, 2001]. Its elected politicians usually have close links with their national politicians in the Council and their party colleagues in the EP. Its party political organisation gives it the image of being the second parliament of the EU, as a kind of *Bundesrat* next to a *Bundestag*. Of course, these influence resources may not last. In the near future, for example, the high ambition may create frustration, the internal consensus may stagnate and the EP may openly challenge the COR. For the time being, however, the COR has a reputation of influence.

The Council: More Power than Influence

Viewed vertically, the Council in Pillar I moves like a layered iceberg [Hayes-Renshaw and Wallace, 1997; Westlake, 1995]. The Council ministers at the top meet only a few times a year (ranging from roughly one to, for the Agricultural Council, 15 times), and many ministers attend meetings like migrating birds. Due to national political dynamics, the turnover of Council ministers is high. For example, in the second part of 1998 eight of the fifteen ministers of the Agricultural Council were replaced. The real Council work is done at the lower levels of Coreper and the working groups [De Zwaan, 1995]. If Coreper believes that the ministers, given the required procedure for decisions in the Council (unanimity, QMV or other), can accept a Commission proposal subject to a Council decision, then it puts an *A-mark* on that dossier. Such a dossier, either single or brought together as a package, is rubberstamped at the next meeting of the Council ministers. Case-study research into the Agricultural Council reveals that 65% of all (about 500 in the years 1992 and 1993) items for Council decision-making are rubberstamped in a second. Most of these items (60%) deal with EU legislation. Of the remaining 35% of the cases (so-called B-dossiers), most (61%) remain undecided and return, with the minutes of the Council discussion, to Coreper and the Commission, with the request to present a proposal that can be accepted more easily. Only the remaining few (13% of all cases) are somehow (*de facto* or *de jure*) decided by the ministers themselves [Van Schendelen, 1996].

Due to the extension of the QMV since the 1987 SEA, most cases of Council decision-making have come to be subject to this *voting* system, but the ministers rarely apply it in reality. The first time was for the December 1992 Banana Trade Regime in the Agricultural Council [Pedler, 1994]. The ministers dislike the QMV for its revelation of their position on an issue and prefer to come to a silent and preferably rubberstamped agreement. During 1996-1998 a member state voted against a legislative proposal about 60 times a year. Top scorers have been Germany (37), Italy (28) and the Netherlands (22, mainly in 1998, to press for its 'money back'). Abstentions during those years vary between 14 (1996) and 34 (1998), with Germany again at the top (14 in total). On average 22% of the proposals were subject to negative votes and/or abstentions [EP Question E-0917/00]. Only in the few cases of unanimity was the proposal blocked, usually for only one session. In most QMV cases the country voting against or abstaining was only registered as such and could not block the proposal, which thus went through.

But the real work floor is not Coreper but the system of about 300 *working groups*. Functionally, they can be compared with the committees at the Commission level: representative experts do the real work. They explore the acceptability of a proposal for Council decision-making. If they conclude positively, they mark the dossier with a *roman I* and send it to Coreper, which makes the final check. The large majority of A-dossiers for the Council's rubberstamping are I-dossiers from the working groups. Compared with the Commission committees, the Council working groups are, however, different in two respects. Firstly, they are less specialised. A working group deals with related policy dossiers, thus covering a broader policy area than a committee does and being able to combine issues to some extent. Secondly, they are expected to consist of only nationally appointed administrative people. Most working group members have, indeed, an officially national government status, either as visitors from their ministry (the majority) or as part of the national PR in Brussels. But the growing practice is for people from both private interest groups (sectorisation) and subnational governments (regionalisation) to appear as their national government representatives. Austria exemplifies the former and Germany the latter.

There is even more verticality at Council level. Among the specialised Councils exists, firstly, a sort of a caste system. The Economic and Financial Council (Ecofin), in particular, including its (high-level) working groups, is a *primus inter pares*. The Youth Council has always been an example of low prestige. Secondly, above the specialised Councils there still stands the General Council, being originally the mother of all Councils and since the 1993 Treaty of Maastricht in charge of Pillar II. In the main Pillar I it is supposed to act as a brokerage platform for issues at stalemate in the specialised Councils. In practice, however, these specialised Councils more often review their unsettled B-points themselves than hand them over to the General Council, which has the reputation of being more interested in overall agreement rather than in the contents. On top of the Council pyramid there is, thirdly, the European Council [Werts, 1992]. Consisting of 'the heads of state', it increasingly acts as the real broker for the most fiercely contended stalemate issues and usually solves them by package-dealing. In issuing manifold declarations and memorandums, it has also become a major EU agenda-builder giving the green light to the Commission, which usually acts quite responsively. Finally, at all Council levels, there is the special position of the Presidency: the role that passes to another member-state government every six months and that regards chairing any meeting, overseeing the Council General Secretariat and representing the Council to the outside [Hayes-Renshaw and Wallace, 1997, V; Kirchner, 1992]. Thanks to these role privileges, the Presidency can subtly steer the whole process.

Viewed horizontally, the Council is also a fragmented arena. Firstly, in addition to the main Pillar I, there are *Pillars II and III* with the Council acting as both the beginning and the end of EU decision-making. The Commission, Parliament, Court and other bodies play at most an informal role here. Most of the real work is done by special committees, parallel to Coreper, such as the Political and Security Committee (PSC) in Pillar II and the Committee Article 36, in short CATS (named after that article in the Amsterdam Treaty) in Pillar III. Under these leading committees, lower-ranking working groups again do the real work. In practice, however, in Pillars II and III the Council begins only a little decision-making and finishes even less. The Pillar II Council has its contests with the Commission DGs of External Relations, Enlargement, External Trade, and Development. Its output is still mainly declaratory [SG Council, November 21, 2000]. The Pillar III Council competes with Commission DGs as well. By the 1999 Treaty of Amsterdam much of its agenda has been transferred to Pillar I, thus in fact to the Commission, which is highly motivated to give it a push.

Secondly, there is often strong competition among the various *Pillar I Councils* and working groups [Westlake 1995, VIII and IX]. As at Commission level, the task areas of these Councils do not perfectly coincide with the EU policy areas, let alone with the policy issues of a specific dossier. For example, the previously mentioned dossier on GMO trade and production encompasses issues of agriculture, research, industry, health, development, employment, environment, external relations and more. It could be handled by tens of different working groups and half the number of Councils. In practice, the choice for a particular Council is an important determinant of the decision on the matter. The General Secretariat Cabinet and the Presidency normally make the choice and act under different pressures from rival Councils. This *General Secretariat*, thirdly, is a somewhat segmented bureaucracy as well, but less so than the Commission [Westlake, 1995, XIII; Hayes-Renshaw and Wallace, 1997, IV]. Its ten DGs run more aggregate policy areas; half of these could have handled that GMO case too.

Taking a *diagonal view* of the Council makes its polycentric character even more clear. The ministers in the Council and the civil servants in the working groups tend to have, first of all, loyalty to the perceived interests of their own ministry at home. Policy competition between ministries at the national or, as in Germany, the subnational level is often continued or begun at Council level. The competition may even extend to other Councils when the ministers experience a lack of congruence between their policy tasks at home and those at Council level. For example, a national Ministry of

Transport may find to its chagrin that the dossier on Working Hours for Truckers is handled by the Social Council, that is by the minister and the civil servants from a competing ministry at home. For a country with many governments, such as Germany, this partially explains why frequently more than one domestic minister shows up in the same Council meeting, and why the country so often prefers to abstain from voting, if a vote is taken at all [Hosli 1999-A and 1999-B]. Such a vote could reveal embarrassing internal divisions.

The Council: the Shareholder as a Stakeholder

The member-state governments, having established the Union by Treaty, can be seen as its shareholders and their Council as the shareholders' meeting. According to the Treaty, they remain the chief decision-makers. In practice, the ministers do not really take decisions. They mainly formalise the smallest part of the EU legislative proposals (17.5% in the year 2000) that needs Council approval. The delegated and discretionary legislation by or on behalf of the Commission falls, in daily practice, beyond their scope. Most of what the Council formally decides is in any case made by Coreper and the working groups. New Treaty formation, being the major case of primary legislation, is still in the hands of the member-state governments, but under a different umbrella: not the Council, but the (highly informal) Intergovernmental Conference (IGC). The mainly *formalising* role of the Council in secondary legislation is, of course, not unimportant. Without this, there is no new formal decision at all. In this formalising role the Council of Ministers, in short, develops into a sort of Upper House or Senate, having the last, but mostly not the really decisive, word on only secondary legislation. In 2001 German Chancellor Gerhard Schröder proposed to codify this development and to redefine the Council as a sort of EU *Bundesrat*.

The Council meetings have at least three other important functions, which come close to variants of lobbying. First of all, the leftovers from Coreper (the B points) are brought into the discussion. Usually this does not result in an immediate solution, but indicates a possible compromise. The Council meeting, then, is a mild version of a *dealing room* for negotiations [Lewis, 2000]. Secondly, at the end of any Council meeting there is always time for 'various other points'. The ministers, then, can raise new issues, brought up either on the national agenda or as a result of irritation caused by imperfections of previous EU decisions. In this way, they contribute also to *agenda building*. Their products here are declarations, recommendations and memoranda, in short (soft) supplementary legislation giving a green light to Coreper and/or the Commission. Thirdly, the Council meetings are used for *playing home politics*, for example to satisfy the national parliament or to bypass another ministry at home. The Environmental Council in particular, in taking decisions without them being discussed by nationally based ministries, has acquired a reputation for this. The three additional Council functions are, however, not exclusive, but shared with other bodies and platforms and particularly with those belonging to the Commission and the EP.

The Council's polycentric character and its limited functions make it, in daily practice, more a meeting of competitive *stakeholders* than that of dominant shareholders. Some centripetal forces keep the competition under control. Coreper and the General Secretariat take care of both the production and the cohesion of the decisions. The General Council and the European Council can overcome stalemates among and inside specialised Councils. By co-ordinating ministries at home, a national government can limit competition with them at Council level. By instructing his/her people in the working groups and in the PR, a minister can at least speak with one voice. A minister can also arrange informal 'bilaterals' with other national or foreign ministers, in order to come to an earlier agreement. All this may be possible, and it happens sometimes and to some degree, but the centripetal forces at home are usually particularly weak. For example, the civil servant in a working group may act as a self-instructed trustee for the minister or the national co-ordination may simply be too late.

Some Other Decision-Makers

The *European Court of Justice* is frequently a major EU decision-maker [Dehousse, 1998]. Its decisions on cases brought to trial are formally binding on the parties involved. By the setting of a precedent, such decisions become fully part of EU law. As division of the Court, the Court of First Instance (CFI) heard in 1997 more than 600 cases, mainly of two types: disputes involving EU personnel and appeals from private parties against Commission decisions, particularly regarding subsidies and competition [Nugent, 1999, 276-7; Harding, 1992]. Closely following these were complaints in the new policy fields of health, insurance and taxation. The European Court itself heard more than 400 cases, about 10% appeals against the CFI decisions and the rest directly coming from private parties (individuals, companies, organisations), national governments (including national courts) and EU institutions. Examples of individual cases are the previously mentioned two brought by Mr Decker and Mr Kohll regarding their public health insurance abroad. National courts, requesting an authoritative interpretation of EU law, bring about one half of all cases [Sweet and Caporaso, 1998]. For the Commission the Court procedure is the main touchstone for the maintenance of competition law, over which it has its own authority. The Parliament and the Council may go to the Court if they believe that their formal powers and/or position, as laid down in Treaty, are not sufficiently respected.

The Court, including the CFI, frequently acts as an engine of europeanisation, usually started by both public and private actors from either the domestic or the European level and oiled by its referendaries [Wincott, 1996]. The direction of its decisions, which ultimately have to be based on Treaty text, tends to be in favour of further European integration. Frequently the Court functions as the alternative route for secondary legislation. For example, its famous 1978 *Cassis de Dijon* decision ordered the free circulation of goods, a decision that could also have been decided by the Council at the proposal of the Commission and after EP consultation. The Court is usually highly effective in getting its decisions accepted by the contesting parties. They comply voluntarily or under legal pressure exerted by the national legal system, which functions as an annexe to the Court. Even member-state governments, being in the past often the most reluctant parties to comply with Court decisions, can be brought to compliance, as (following the 1993 Maastricht Treaty) the Court has the authority to impose financial penalties. In July 2000 it did so for the first time against the government of Greece, which repeatedly neglected EU environmental legislation and received a fine of 20,000 euros for every day it continued to do so.

The *Court of Auditors* (CoA) can act as a decision-maker as well. In fact, it is another fine example of the paradox that weak formal powers, in this case in the field of financial inspection, do not necessarily exclude real influence, especially in the longer run. Its usually critical reports on EU revenue and expenditure can formally be neglected by the Commission and the Council or be taken as read by the Parliament, which is entitled to give sanction to the Commission for its financial behaviour. In practice the CoA's criticisms and recommendations often fuel the EP's agenda with regard to the operations of the Commission and contribute to decisions made at a later stage. The 1999 fall of the Santer Commission was set in motion after the critical CoA report on the 1997 budget, for which the Parliament refused to give discharge in December 1998.

Finally, there are the special *Bodies and Agencies* for specific policy sectors. Having a formally autonomous position, most deal with the so-called implementation, monitoring and inspection of EU policies at the domestic level [Everson and others, 1999]. The European Central Bank provides the most institutionalised example, with its own operations on common monetary policy-making. The Bilbao Agency for Safety and Health at Work is an example of a monitoring agency connected to the DG Social Affairs. The EU Ombudsman can inspect policy decisions in the case of a citizen's complaint. Whatever their formal status is, they can all contribute practically to EU decision-making, either by influencing the other EU bodies and institutions or by making use of their delegated and discretionary powers. The distinction between, on the one hand, decision-making and, on the other, implementation and inspection is, in practice, highly artificial. The so-called implementation is simply the continued decision-making at a more detailed level; and the results of inspection, almost always exposing a difference between the legal norms and the social reality, tend to feed back into new EU issue and agenda formation. New decisions can be taken either by the responsible Agency itself (discretionary decisions) or by the Commission (by delegated legislation), the Council in codecision with the Parliament or not (by secondary legisation) or the Court (by jurisprudence).

The Playing Field in Two Catchwords

As said before, the focus of this book is on the influencing of the EU decision-making system. Therefore, we are more interested in the flesh and blood of the system than in its skeleton, although the latter can be a factor influencing the former (and, for the codification of new practices, the reverse may be the case). In the coming chapters we shall see how this system relates both to the independent variable of EU public affairs management and the dependent one of the desired outcome, whatever its contents and form. The desire may encompass any opportunity or threat from the EU, including no decision at all. But first we will characterise the playing field by the means of two academic catchwords: complexity and dynamics.

EU complexity
By its atypical design and workings, the EU machinery can be perceived as extremely complex [Previdi, 1997]. Its skeleton is made up of different pillars, institutions, procedures, positions, powers, authorities, competencies and more, and its flesh and blood looks no less complex. In spite of its formal construction, the machinery moves polycentrically and multifunctionally. The many semi-formal and informal practices on the work floor may seem *labyrinthine*: those involved in the making of a decision have their interdependencies and try to anticipate the multiple reactions. The members

of, for example, an expert group have to watch each other, their home organisation, the attentive outsiders, the Commission unit and many more
stakeholders. The variety of Europe is all around and is reflected by, among
other things, different policy values, regime practices, personal backgrounds and interest positions. Such divisions are crosscut by both formal
arrangements, as part of the skeleton, and informal networks based on, for
example, regionality, character and common interest. By no means the least
complex are the multi-level linkages between the EU and the member
countries, resulting in, for example, many problems of implementing EU
directives at the national level [Azzi, 2000]. On its input side the EU
absorbs experts, interests and lobby groups from the member countries.
On its output side it implements and inspects the common decisions at
member country level. Maybe the greatest complexity, not to say *miracle*, is
behind the birth of a decision on whatever issue. It is almost always the outcome of wheeling and dealing or negotiations among the stakeholders, taking place behind the scenes and giving rise to intricate trade-offs.

Every complexity has, of course, its *unique configuration* of specific causes. For example, the QMV mechanism in the Council is the outcome of such
specific factors as the rivalries between France and Germany, the demands
from smaller countries, the desires to get rid of the old veto, the compromises with positions taken by both the Commission and the Parliament and, especially, the search for a sword of Damocles rather than a real one. The
many semi-formal committees, to give another example, each have their
own life histories, related to factors like the old European traditions of governance by committee, the need to reduce the irritating differences regarding so-called technical questions, and the demands for influence of both
Commission officials and pressure groups. The two examples make clear
that at least two general causes are in operation.

One is the construction of the skeleton. Its many complexities are the direct result of the well-intended *engineering* by people entitled to do so, such
as those sitting in an IGC, the Council, the Commission College or the EP
Presidency [Keohane and Hoffmann, 1991]. They once decided to establish
a Commission with few more formal powers than its monopoly of drafting
laws and with only limited resources of budget and manpower. They have
also formulated the various procedures regarding, for example, the role of
the Parliament, the making of legislation and the implementation of common decisions. The establishment of the Pillars, the Agencies and the
comitology is their product as well. On policy matters they developed the
various principles, ranging from supranationality to subsidiarity, and the
different instruments like negative integration and exemptions from the

law. But the construction of the skeleton is not a satisfying explanation for the many complexities. Firstly, it assumes that the skeleton is all that the daily functioning of the machinery amounts to, but given the different flesh and blood practices this is clearly not the case. Secondly, insofar as the skeleton determines that functioning in reality, why has it been made seemingly so complex?

The second and major cause of the complexity, of both the skeleton and the flesh and blood, is the *pluralist variety* of the European countries. On every single issue they are internally divided along the lines of, for example, policy values, market positions, regional competitions and social differences caused by language, religion, age, class and more. All this pluralism, represented and presented by public and private lobby groups, easily permeates the EU at its open and receptive input side [Wessels, 1997]. Without much boundary control, the understaffed Commission in particular invites the many different stakeholders not only to deliver their demands, but also to participate in various informal and semi-formal roles. All together they give the machinery its flesh and blood. Its complexity is anything but based on a grand design. It is the outcome of a continuous and incremental engineering, which reflects the wide variety of governance traditions, practices and styles in Europe. The variety of both the input and the throughput makes its imprint on the EU output side as well. The EU decisions are, essentially, the result of many compromises among the different stakeholders.

The complexity of the machinery gets very different *evaluations*. In fact, the term 'complexity' is already a value judgement made by those lacking in understanding. Any machinery is only complex for the layman, not for the mechanic. In particular, ordinary citizens, mass-media journalists and national politicians lacking sufficient knowledge often feel themselves lost in a labyrinth. Experienced stakeholders frequently make only an opportunistic judgement: the complexity is welcome if it favours one's interests but irritating if it hinders. Thanks to the complexity, the same desired outcome can be acquired in different ways (multicausality) and the same way can lead to various acceptable outcomes (multifinality). All one has to do is understand how the machinery works. The academics are, as usual, divided. Some see much of the complexity as a source of 'garbage-can' legislation, inadequate implementation, insufficient communication and other so-called shortcomings [Curtin, 1997; Kohler-Koch, 1997, 51; Richardson, 1996-B and 1996-C; Hayward, 1995]. Others see positive functions, particularly the flexibility provided for decision-making [Wallace and Wallace, 1996, I; Caporaso, 1974]. Their view comes close to that of the stakeholding practitioners: in complex machinery, contrary to a simple one, there is always a way of finding a solution. For example, by combining a stalemate issue with other ones a consensus can always be found.

Some scholars take a more *philosophical* view and assess the complexity as an integrating force. Thanks to, for example, the polycentrism of the machinery, the different interests and the many competitive stakeholders can place their multifaceted imprint on every common decision, thus integrating the pluralism of Europe within a compromise [Cini, 1996, 150; Page, 1997, VII]. Thanks to its lack of resources, the Commission has to take many interest groups on board and to expand its *engrenage*, thus integrating the variety of Europe within a machinery at the grass roots. But whatever the evaluations, one may wonder whether there exists an alternative to the so-called complexity of the EU playing field. In modern society, the management of a local area requires complex machinery, and so the EU area will require much more.

EU dynamics

A popular *party game* among EU watchers is to name the five most important recent EU changes. Unable to choose, they may end up with a long list containing, among others, the transfer of Pillar III functions to I, the increase in delegated legislation, the stronger roles of the EP and the Court, the further enlargements, the trend towards negative integration, the increasing role of lobby groups from civil society, the regionalisation of governments, the Council's transformation from decision-maker to agenda-builder, the decline of national co-ordination, and the globalisation of the playing field. In comparison to the domestic dynamics, the EU machinery looks like a *trampoline*, as the following examples indicate. The contents and domains of policies are frequently redefined, expanded and intensified, and stakeholders change their positions continually. Regime values and policy practices may come and go as a pendulum swings [Wallace and Young, 1997-B; Wallace and Wallace, 1996, I]. The Commission, Parliament, Council and Court now function in ways very different from ten years ago and they do so at a pace of change without parallel at many a domestic level. The assistant bureaucracy of expert groups around the Commission has expanded by many hundreds following the 1987 Single Open Market programme. Member countries have replaced the member states as the basic units of the EU. Private lobby groups have found their nests inside the machinery. Perhaps the best indicator of the dynamics is that every handbook on the EU is outdated after a few years.

One general and direct cause of the high level of dynamics is the *reforms* of the skeleton of EU decision-making [Keohane and Hoffmann, 1991; Neunreither and Wiener, 2000]. The most formal ones come from the newly established Treaties. For example, the 1999 Amsterdam Treaty defined many new policy targets, regime values and institutional settings. Administrative reforms can add even more dynamics. The Santer Commission adopted in 1994 the project for 'less but better legislation', based on criteria such as proportionality and subsidiarity, and it resulted in both the thinning out of old laws and the more selective launch of new ones. At its inception the 1999 Prodi Commission launched major reforms of the organisation, formation and operation of its institution. They dealt with, among other things, the rules of procedure, the organisation of the DGs, internal co-ordination, the personnel policies and the code of conduct. All such reforms can contribute to a modification of the flesh and blood of the EU machinery. Past examples are the overruling of national governments in the Council, the role of the regional governments and the growth of delegated legislation. But the planned reforms can also just remain on paper or be merely codifications of already existing practices. Anyhow, the question remains why those reforms have been decided.

The answer to this question has to be found in the second general cause of the dynamics: in short, it is the *pluralistic variety* of Europe again. The functioning of the machinery itself is a continuing case of issues, tensions or controversies. One category of these comes from outside the EU system (exogenous), and examples are the development of new technologies, changes of national governments, the rise of regional pressure groups, protests from civil society and economic globalisation. They usually create new irritating differences among the interest groups in Europe and subsequently new impacts on at least the EU input side. The second category comes from the machinery itself (endogenous), and examples here are the spill-over effects of established policies, the enlargement negotiations, the agenda overload, the distribution of scarce resources like positions of power and the budget, the outcomes of policy inspection, the transparency of the machinery and, not least, the contents of specific policy dossiers. Some stakeholders want to keep the machinery unchanged, as it protects their interests, but many others want to change it continually. One way is to make formal pleas for reform. Another way is simply to make use of the existing opportunities for re-interpreting the formal procedures, positions and powers and to do what is not clearly forbidden, thus developing new flesh-and-blood practices. Examples here are the proliferation of expert groups, the inception of public health policies, the centralisation of inspections and the EP scrutiny of agricultural expenditure. These occurred in the absence of an official reform plan, let alone a common decision in favour of them.

As with the complexity of the decision mechanism, the dynamics are subject to mixed *evaluations*. Of course, the term 'dynamics' may be a value judgement held by those finding the pace of change exceptional. Ordinary citizens, mass-media journalists and national politicians often find EU developments unpredictable and feel themselves taken by unwelcome surprise. They lack the understanding of the EU practices, such as the trends of policy expansion and supranationalism or the chain reactions from national deviant behaviour and stagnating common policies to growing irritations and finally accelerated integration [Corbey, 1995; Haverland, 1999]. The trained stakeholders understand the basic dynamics as patterned changes, and at least they take them as new opportunities. A trivial example is the 1999 decision of the Prodi Commission to relocate the Commissioners from one common building to their respective DG buildings. For the experienced lobby groups this was an opportunity to divide the College. They cope proactively with the dynamics, and if a change proves to be unfriendly, they take early measures to deal with it. Thanks to the dynamics, they always see a better moment. On a trampoline they can make a big jump forwards, as long as they have the expertise for doing this. Scholars make different evaluations, according to their appraisal of the effects of the dynamics on their chosen dependent variable. Some consider the dynamics of, for example, the enlargement and the budget allocations as 'imbalances' endangering the integration achieved so far [Andriessen, 1999]. Others see the rise of Council QMV, EP codecision or Commission inspections as auspicious for further integration. Others, taking national sovereignty as the yardstick, assess the same trends negatively [Majone, 1996-C]. Others again take a philosophical approach, and see the dynamics, patterned or not, as normal for an adolescent system of about five decades.

Extra: the Wandering Scholars

Many academics studying the EU still walk in the footsteps of the EU founding fathers like Jean Monnet, Walter Hallstein and Henri Spaak, who were driven by the desire to integrate the frequently bellicose European states peacefully by the means of a machinery of common decision-making. The scholars take, explicitly or implicitly, the integration process as either the main dependent variable of their empirical study or the crucial criterion of their normative one. They tend to see, as well, the EU as a unique machinery, as a system *sui generis*. But they also have their differences, like the wandering scholars in the Middle Ages [Waddell, 1952].

First of all, there is the difference between the *disciplines* that, so far, have made the largest contribution to the study of the EU. The two oldest are international law and international relations. The lawyers describe, explain and assess the EU mainly as ruled by primary law (the Treaties). They keep their focus on the formal institutions, procedures and powers, in short on the EU skeleton. Scholars in international relations describe the EU as a regional case of synchronic multilateral foreign policy-making by state governments [Pollack, 2000-A; Howell, 2000]. They ascribe its integrating performance to the negotiations among these governments and regard the EU as being led by the Council. In the mid-1970s political science appeared as the third major discipline, at first borrowing much from the international relations approach and later on applying or developing its own concepts and theories [Rosamund, 2000]. In particular, the dependent variable was changed from integration to decision-making, broadly taken as the process of converting the inputs from the environment (like from public and private interest groups, public opinion, citizens) into more or less binding outputs (like laws and policies) [Hix, 1999, XIII].

Secondly, the academics follow many different *approaches*. Neil Nugent [1999, part IV] breaks the literature down into three categories: conceptualising, grand theorising, and mid-level approaches. To the first category belong old *concepts* considered relevant in the field of European integration, such as sovereignty and (con-)federation, which depart from the concept of domestic politics. New ones, among others, are multilevel governance [Scharpf, 1994; Hix, 1999; Massey, 1999; Kohler-Koch and Eising, 1999] and consociation [Taylor, 1996]. In the second category figure old *grand theories* such as (neo)functionalism, institutionalism and supranationalism and new ones like interdependency theory [Keohane and Nye, 1977; Keohane and Hoffmann, 1991; McCormick, 1999; Rosamund, 2000] and constructivism [Christiansen, 1999; Wind, 1996]. The third category of *mid-level* approaches may overlap with the previous two, but its claim is less general or comprehensive and more modest. It frequently contains a shift of the dependent variable, from integration to some intermediate variable. Established examples are the three-fold reinterpretations of decisions [Rosenthal, 1975] and the five modes of decision-making [Wallace and Wallace, 1996, II]. Recent mid-level concepts are, for example, bargained administration [Molle, 1993], policy convergence [Schmitter, 1996-A] and policy networks [Fligstein and McNichol, 1998]. New mid-level theories cover, among other things, transactional exchange [Stone Sweet and Sandholtz, 1997 and 1998], principal-agent relationships [Pollack, 1998] and garbage-can incrementalism [Richardson, 1996-B; Mazey and Richardson, 1996].

A third difference involves the appreciation of the various academic products. Among many academics the *dissatisfaction* with the 'state of concepts and theories as religions' [Young, 1968, 103-6] is so widespread that it comes close to a consensus in disguise. To quote a few EU scholars: 'the imprecision of theory' [Schmitter, 1996-B, 137], 'we, the prisoners of our concepts' [Wallace, 1990-B, 19], 'the crisis of legal studies' [Shaw, 1995], 'the either...or approaches' [Wallace, 1997] or 'the tribalism of specialisms' [Jørgensen, 1997]. Some react with efforts to synthesise or to amend the current concepts and/or theories [Moravcsik, 2000; Corbey, 1995]. Others develop even more new ideas, aiming to replace the old ones [Schmitter, 1996-B; Stone Sweet and Sandholtz, 1998]. But most scholars acquiesce in the fragmented state of EU studies, silently accepting it as normal and maybe as a richness [Rosamund, 2000, VIII; Peterson, 2001].

We belong to the latter, taking that fragmented state as *normal* for a field of study focused on a fairly young and unique phenomenon. We can even share much of the dissatisfaction regarding the current concepts, theories and observations applied to the EU. In research, there is almost nothing better than a good (well-developed, useful) concept and theory, as there is almost nothing worse than bad ones. They determine both the validity and the reliability of the observations, which may lead to sound empirical knowledge. We consider the large room for improvement an opportunity rather than a problem, because it would be worse if there were no room left. Many of the aforementioned differences we see as quite *acceptable*. It is reasonable that lawyers come to different observations from, for example, political scientists. They have different academic approaches and interests. It is also reasonable that the shift of the dependent variable, from integration to something like decisions and/or policies, produces different concepts, theories and, again, observations. Because the EU is, essentially, a transitional and prismatic system [Bellier, 1997, 115], it is equally reasonable that scholars at different times and with different questions come to different conclusions.

Many differences are more apparent than really existing at the epistemic level. *Older* European academics in particular have, in spite of their various differences, many beliefs in common regarding the EU. They believe in EU uniqueness rather than comparability, in deductive over inductive reasoning, in integration rather than decision-making, in the skeleton over flesh and blood, in factors of national government rather than those of civil society, in theory construction above empirical research, in general rather than specific statements, and in evaluation above explanation. The *younger academics* increasingly adopt the opposite beliefs. Almost inevitably they take the mid-level approaches, and in fact follow the example of older American scholars, such as Ernst Haas [1958], Leon Lindberg [1963], James Caporaso [1974], Glenda Rosenthal [1975] and Leon Hurwitz [1980]. Long before the birth of the EU, the Americans had already gathered much empirical knowledge about their own 'multi-country' US system and considered more specific variables than merely integration. Many of them applied their advanced expertise to the empirical study of EU common decision-making. Our approach comes close to theirs. The EU decision process, how it works and can be explained, is our main concern here. The knowledge can, at this moment, best be gathered by specific and inductive empirical research into the machinery as it functions in reality. In this chapter that concern with knowledge has been only intellectual. In the next chapters it will also be applied to the question: how can EU public affairs management influence the outcomes produced by the machinery?

EU Governance and EU Public Affairs Management

The two academic catchwords describing the EU playing field can be augmented with a third one: *relevance*. This is, of course, a subjective matter, defined by every lobby group differently. Most groups make their definitions sooner or later. They consider the EU outcomes as relevant opportunities or threats. They believe that many interesting prizes can be won or lost by EU decision-making, and of these legislation is normally seen as the big prize. In its hard forms in particular (primary, secondary and delegated legislation plus Court jurisdiction), it outlaws conflicting domestic legislation and practices. By encouraging EU legislation, the public and private lobby groups can overcome irritating domestic situations and they can come to comfort for the whole EU area. By blocking it, they can save domestic situations pampering their interests. Legislation is thus usually the major way of getting things done in the EU. The businessman's saying on Open Market legislation: 'he who has the standard, gets the market' illustrates this. Legislation, finally, is often also the carrier for winning or losing small prizes, such as by financial decisions (levies, subsidies), procurements (goods, services) and privileges (powers, procedures, positions).

This EU *supply side* attracts many public and private interest groups from both the domestic and the European level. By wanting to come nearby and to win, or at least not to lose, a prize, they function as influence vectors of europeanisation. This is, in a free world, not different from the birds and bees which, according to Jewell Akens' song, are attracted by the flowers and the trees in the garden. But on the EU playing field, more so than in nature, there is too little bread and honey for the many birds and bees. The logical result is strong competition among the stakeholders. Due to the proliferation of lobby groups from the member countries, which has increased further through the enlargements, the competitions become even stronger. Many an issue, indeed, is for some time a drama of fights and stalemates. However, the Official Journal, continually publishing new agreements, proves that the stakeholders can frequently reach a common decision regarding the distribution of a scarce value. This result is almost a political *miracle*. It is seldom explained by the dominance of one or a few stakeholders, as if one big bird can take most from the garden. On the EU playing field, the many stakeholders usually reach an agreement only by wheeling and dealing: on either a single issue or a package of issues they negotiate and make a compromise [Elgström and Smith, 2000]. This provides the basis for the consensus as required and as formalised, for example, by unanimity, (qualified) majority or silent acceptance in the Council.

The metaphor of *political market* is useful for the understanding of this decision mechanism. On one side there is a rich supply of desired values. To some degree it comes close to being a staple market, a concept of harbour economics, where every desired value can be delivered, either immediately from stock or soon after arrival. On the other side there is a strong and varied demand. Only if there is a match or a balance between supply and demand can a transaction take place. The parallel of price formation in the commercial market is the formation of consensus in this EU political market. One may, of course, criticise the consensus as being a compromise falling short of rational (effective, efficient) decision-making. Selfish lobby groups wanting to take all frequently do so, and British groups do so almost by national character. The criticism has had its parallel in the old economics debate on the *pretium justum*. Adam Smith brought this debate to a close by pointing out that, under the precondition of open competition, the correspondence between demand and supply results in the most rational (effective, efficient) price. Similarly, the formation of political consensus through compromise can be considered the best possible decision method. Whether the EU meets the precondition of open competition as well is a question to which we will return in the last chapter. If it does so, then the EU practice of deciding by compromise is a case of political rationality, which makes the aforementioned sixth method of solving irritating differences in Europe effective.

Provided that the playing field is open and competitive, its complexity and dynamics are not at all disadvantageous or negative for decision-making by compromise; in fact, they are most helpful and functional for it.

Thanks to the complexity, there is always a way through the labyrinth to a desired destination, and thanks to the dynamics, there is always a movement on the trampoline to a better moment. The EU machinery allows one to be optimistic that, one way or another, and sooner or later, demands and supplies can balance and result in a compromise decision. The stakeholders only have to know how and when. The extent of *knowledge* and *understanding* of the EU machinery frequently makes the big difference between the winners and the losers of the game. Amateurs from either inside or outside the EU machinery, who hardly understand or know how to handle it, may abhor its complexity and its dynamics, regarding them as hindrances to getting a desired outcome. Professionals do not make such complaints. They can cope with the various labyrinths constructed on different trampolines. Their first reward is that the amateurs get lost and fall off, so making it easier for the professionals to develop a compromise among themselves. Proactive professionals may try to make the machinery even more complex and dynamic, thus setting the semi-amateurs at distance as well. The fewer the stakeholders, the less the competition over an issue. During the 1992 EP hearings on the proposals to subject lobby groups to a code of conduct and registration, some companies and consultancies provided a fine example of such proactive engineering. They were much in favour of the proposals, which they knew would hinder the amateurs more than themselves.

Such *EU political expertise*, reflecting both the knowledge and the understanding of the EU machinery, is not the only factor differentiating between winners and losers. But it indicates a potential influence of exceptional strength. In the political science of EU decision-making, with the desired outcome as the dependent variable, the expertise of the stakeholders can be taken as the most important independent one. In applied political science the latter can also be improved, as will be shown in the following chapters. But even the best expertise meets its limits and, therefore, demands prudent and politic application. How this can be done and whether the EU variant of Darwin's Law, under which it is the most expert and prudent lobby groups that survive, still meets the criterion of democracy, are the questions for the last two chapters.

CHAPTER 3

PUSHING THE BUTTONS OF 'BRUSSELS'

Managing the Crucial Variables

The ultimate goal of public affairs management (PAM) is to achieve a complete victory in a supposedly interesting game. The victory is complete if one has gained the desired outcome from the EU, received substantial support from the other stakeholders, and succeeded in overcoming opposition at home comfortably. The chance of such a full score is, however, low. In real-life, competition in the EU is usually extremely strong and hard. EU officials act under many cross-pressures, competitors quietly hold the belief that it is in their common interest to prevent one player gaining all, and other interest groups at home may feel threatened if one achieves a full score at EU level. Every player, therefore, has reason to be already satisfied if it has won the game only partially and/or has maintained its position in the fighting arena and/or has kept its home organisation on its side. *Compromise, respect* and *backing* might be seen as second-class prizes to win, but are in reality frequently valued as the highest attainable and thus as satisfying ones. They give a prolonged licence to operate.

Of course, one may completely lose as well. In this case, one is not party to the compromise and/or one gets less respect from others and/or one loses backing at home. But as long as a pressure group continues to play actively and prudently, it seldom runs this risk. By participating actively it usually becomes part of the compromise and by acting prudently it can both retain respect for its position and maintain its backing at home. In short, the full score is normally only a *daydream* and the complete defeat only a *nightmare*. Both rarely occur, but, paradoxically, both have their useful functions. Without the daydream of becoming the complete winner and without the nightmare of ending up as the complete loser, no sportsman can ever hope to become a competitive player.

The *desired outcome* can be anything coming from the EU. The main field of desires is usually legislation, because this is expected to be binding on those whom it concerns and to supersede domestic laws. An interest group may desire, for example, a change to the Treaty, a piece of either secondary or delegated legislation (a directive, regulation or decree), a Court decision, or the granting of an exemption to a rule. Equally desired may be a derived act of legislation, such as the allocation of a subsidy or a levy, the granting or the withholding of a procurement, and the launch or the postponement of an inspection. It may even be apparently a mere detail: a deadline, a sanction, a form, a word, a definition, a number, a comma or whatever else that is regarded as relevant by a player. Whether the other players consider such a desire irrelevant or silly does not matter. Because of the lack of an objective criterion to distinguish between relevance and irrelevance, every value is always a relative and subjective affair. A desire that seems silly to others even has the great advantage that it may attract less competition from those others.

Legislation may be the main field of desires, but it is not the only one. One reason is that its assumed effects of both binding others and superseding subordinate laws are not perfectly realised in practice. If one cannot be guaranteed to win through the law, one cannot really lose either. Even if one has lost a game of legislation, it is possible to find an escape. Another reason is that *other outcomes* rather than legislation may also be desired. EU officials can provide many different values on a discretionary basis, such as their support for one's cause, the building of a preferred agenda, a seat in a committee, crucial information, a financial favour, and priority under a tender. The other stakeholders can provide such desired items as respect, information, support, a network, burden-sharing and even favours unrelated to the EU, for example a commercial contract or co-operation on policy. The interest groups at home can also make available everything ranging from backing to opposition. An exhaustive catalogue of all these outcomes other than legislation cannot be made. Everything, even if it does not yet exist, can be desired.

Furthermore, the desired outcome, may not necessarily be a positive outcome from the EU decision process, eagerly longed for as a daydream. It may also be a negative one, feared as a nightmare but not produced. Such a so-called *non-outcome* could be the rejection of a legislative proposal, the delay of a decision, the fading away of an issue, the jamming of the decision machinery and anything else desired to produce a non-event. For example, at the spring 2001 Stockholm Summit, France successfully delayed the Energy Liberalisation Dossier, thanks to which its major utility EdF was able to get control over the Italian Montedison. In fact, the more competitive an arena is, the more the influence behaviour is directed at preventing the undesired outcomes rather than promoting the desired ones. On a competitive playing field, being complex and dynamic as well, it is always easier to block than to push a development and it is more prudent to play defensively than offensively. Every single player simply has more nuisance value than pushing power. But no pressure group can only play the negative game; if it did, it would become an outcast. It also has to push for some positive outcome. This may, of course, amount to a nuisance in a pleasing disguise, for example the desire to review a policy area substantially. Most pressure groups have, indeed, not just one desire, but a mixed package of both positive and negative outcomes to be obtained from EU officials, the other stakeholders and groups at home.

The positive or the negative achievement of a desired outcome is, in other words, the *dependent variable* of EU public affairs management. This ambition is held by all sorts of pressure groups. Profit-oriented private ones and especially the multinational companies (MNCs) may have the strongest reputation for it. But non-profit-making NGOs, sub-national governments and national ministries or even parts of them may have the same ambition. So have those with an established position inside the EU machinery, such as parts of the Commission (a Directorate-General, Directorate, Commissioner, Agency, committee, group or person), the Parliament (a commission, an intergroup, a party, a national delegation, an MEP) and the Council (a special Council, a working group, a group of ministers, a DG of the Secretariat-General) or of other bodies like the COR, the EESC and the Court. Frequently they act as public lobby groups from within, wanting to create a desired outcome. As being both subjects and targets of EU public affairs management, they can play dual roles.

The traditional techniques of influence, outlined in the first chapter, are still used in the EU arena. However, coercion, encapsulation, advocacy and argumentation appear to have insufficient effectiveness and efficiency. More and more, the players also have to go both *window-out* for monitoring and researching the other players and *window-in* for building coalitions and deals with them. In short, they have to lobby. The characteristics of the EU decision machinery, defined by the catchwords of complexity and dynamics, can be exploited as lobby opportunities: there is always an open door and a suitable moment. The crucial *independent variable* here is knowledge, to which we return in the following chapters. The influence process is, however, seldom a straight line between the knowledgeable player and the final decision-maker. If one wants to influence 'Brussels', one has to push many buttons. They may connect the desire to the decision.

The Manageable Machinery: General Approaches

Thanks to the characteristics of the EU machinery, there is really no shortage of buttons to push; in fact, there is an oversupply. This creates, however, its own puzzles. Every player has to make, each time, a careful selection of buttons to push. Otherwise they may push the wrong button, lose momentum, awake competitors, enter a dead lane, make a short circuit, irritate the official or cause whatever damage to their interests. All this is, again, a matter of knowledge. But before they can make the choice, they need to be familiar with the menu of existing or potential buttons. In the following menu we distinguish between three general categories of decision buttons: *the actors to approach, the factors to use* and *the vectors to create*. The actors are the people who contribute to the making of a decision, the factors are the determinants of their decision behaviour and the vectors are the newly created factors, which may influence that behaviour.

As with every menu, ours is selective and not exhaustive for all potential items under the three categories. It is always possible to identify more actors and factors and to develop more vectors, which are useful for pushing the desired outcome or for blocking the undesired one. All together, they form the *intervening variables* of the EU lobbying process. The logic behind this is that one makes use of the multicausality and the multifinality of the EU decision machinery. This is a matter of political management or, as explained before, political manipulation. The creation of a desired outcome by the use of intervening variables is more than a profession; it is highly creative work or even an art.

Actors to approach

Which actors play a crucial role in the making of an EU decision? The answer depends, of course, on the dossier, the arena, the procedure, the setting, the time and many other circumstances. But in the flesh and blood process of EU decision-making some patterns and configurations are discernible. The metaphor of the *A4-format* piece of paper, that starts blank and may end up full of text in the Official Journal, remains helpful here. Much paper, of course, may never get the final and authoritative signature and, as such, may be the subject of successful blocking actions. But every authoritative decision has begun life as a first draft on paper and has been subject to successful pressure. As said in the preceding chapter, those who draft the decision are frequently more important than those who finally sign it. Our question therefore is: which actors are, not formally but practically, the major and the regular contributors to the paper that may carry the final decision and which of these can best be approached?

Actors inside and around the *Commission* play a more or less crucial role in almost every process of decision-making. They are normally dominant in the production of both delegated and discretionary decisions, take the lead in secondary legislation, make the bulk of supplementary decisions, and contribute to both primary legislation and Court jurisdiction. The key people inside the Commission are usually ranked at the levels of lower-A and upper-B. As *chefs de dossier* they make the first draft of a final decision or receive this from the outside, particularly from the experts involved in a committee or as individuals. Their assistants (lower-B) and secretaries (C level) tend to act as desk managers and gatekeepers. The upper-A civil servants, like the Head of Unit, usually set only the objectives, check the draft texts and, if required, push for approval at political level of the Commission, such as by the Commissioner, his Cabinet or the College. The top levels can, of course, influence the bureaucrats at the mid-level, but they usually do so only in the early phases of agenda-making, when the paper on the desks here is still blank. Otherwise they distract the mid-level people.

The relevant people inside the Commission have to meet two more criteria. The first relates to their involvement in the decision-making process. One has to keep an eye on both the actors in the formally responsible unit and those holding positions in potentially conflicting policy areas. The latter can act as intervening stakeholders via the *inter-service* procedure or otherwise. For example, on an issue of food production one should not only deal with the relevant people in the policy sector of Agriculture, but also those in the adjacent sectors of, for example, R&D, Consumer Affairs or External Trade. The second criterion regards their policy preferences. One has to identify both policy *friends and enemies*. They stimulate the daydream or, respectively, the nightmare. Their preference may be based on sectoral values, but also on crosscutting domestic or even personal values. One can often find a number of policy friends inside the most closely related Directorate, expert committees and agencies and particularly among one's national or regional countrymen in these bodies. The policy enemies usually belong to units with different sectoral interests, especially if they come from other nations or regions. The majority of both friends and enemies are frequently the experts representing their private or public organisations established elsewhere, and they can be approached already there.

The key people of the *EP, COR* and *EESC* are, first of all, the rapporteurs and, secondly, the chairmen of the commissions (or the intergroups and sections) and the co-ordinators of the political parties (in EP and COR) or the interest groups (in EESC). Among them and their opponents one can find one's own friends and enemies. The third relevant category is the ordinary staff members of the aforementioned role-players, who may play a major part in the process. In each of the three bodies the total number of key people involved with a dossier is usually under ten. They practically make the plenary resolution, which has potential influence on the wider decision-making process. Their impact may be limited to the framing of the issue or the agenda, but this can be decisive for the final result. Insofar as the MEPs hold a codecision position, they can also formally intervene in the secondary legislation being formulated and, to some degree, in the delegated one. All members of the three bodies have their feet in domestic public or private organisations. Again, they can be approached within these organisations as well.

At *Council level* the most relevant actors are, first of all, those who in fact determine the Council position: the mainly national civil servants sitting in the working groups under Coreper and in the special committees of each Pillar. They make the bulk of the decisions, which are rubberstamped by the ministers. They are all appointed nationally and they can be influenced in their member countries. The second relevant category of actors is the civil servants of the Council's Secretariat-General. They handle the dossiers 'administratively', which is an euphemism for all sorts of political manoeuvring. We can illustrate this for the third relevant category: the hundreds of people who belong to the Presidency for half a year. Formally they do nothing more than just technically chairing the numerous sessions at all levels (working groups, Coreper, Councils, Summits). In addition they have to control the SG and to represent the Council before the other bodies, the mass media and the rest of the world. Under Pillars II and III, they are also responsible for the introduction of proposals and the implementation of decisions. In practice, however, by playing the Presidency's role, they can set times for the meetings and thus the arenas, push the issues up or down the agenda, make the difference between A and B points, arrange both the order and the debate, settle the conclusions and the minutes, mediate between divided members, suggest compromises, determine that a proposal has met the voting majority required, intervene in the division of labour and the recruitment for vacancies inside the SG, fine-tune the messages to the outside world, and effectively frame the decisions under Pillars II and III.

Thanks to the polycentric and fragmented character of the EU, *many more officials* can usefully be approached. The advocates-general and the referendaries of the Court of Justice usually have a strong impact on the Court's decisions, as do the researchers at the Court of Auditors on theirs. The intendants of the inspection agencies can almost always identify some difference between the norms and the practice of policy-making. Thanks to the imperfect rule of law, these intendants can be used for getting an issue back on the agenda. The jurists of the legal service, belonging to every institution and many a DG, are important as consultants to the high officials. Changing their minds will mean they give different advice. The many translators convert the legally binding decisions into all the official languages, but no two languages have fully identical semantics and a small change to the wording can make a big difference. High-ranking people frequently play important 'meta-roles' in decision-making, for example by dividing the work, assigning the positions and allocating the resources. By approaching them, one may change the arena and get, for example, another DG, expert group, commission, rapporteur or special Council to be in charge. Even a small change can make a big difference for the outcome, as a gradual change of course can take a ship miles away from its original destination.

Other important actors to approach are the stakeholders not formally belonging to the EU system, such as the *other pressure groups* at both EU and domestic level. For example, the Brussels-based PRs, MNCs and NGOs have their established links and networks with parts of the EU machinery. Regional governments, units of national ministries, trade organisations and citizens' groups frequently have such linkages between home and the EU as well. These all can be used as channels of access to the EU. In addition, many hold positions at the cross-points of various networks. They can be approached from different sides and be used as transporters of interests. Because every country is normally divided over every dossier, one can always mobilise domestic pressure groups to push the government's position in the Council in the desired direction. Most useful is the expert sitting in an expert group for drafting a decision, in a working group for assessing it and in a comitology committee for implementing it. People with the same (sub-)national identity often meet informally, as the Irish do in their Brussels pub *Kitty O'Shea*, thus linking their different functions. Many actors also play roles outside the EU, for example in relationships with non-EU countries or at the level of the OECD or the WTO, and so again they can be approached from the outside. For example, the WTO is frequently used to effect a U-turn from EU decision-makers, as happened in the 1990s on bananas, steel, the environment and many forms of standardisation.

Approaching crucial actors is a strategy practised not only by all sorts of public and private lobby groups, but also by the *EU officials as lobbyists* themselves. They also want to create desired outcomes. Every Commissioner initiates meetings with leading figures of, among others, the EP, the relevant

EuroFeds and his/her national government. A *chef de dossier* frequently consults directly with the crucial experts of a relevant committee and, sometimes, the private or the public organisation represented by them. Officials of the PRs, who in the past focused their attentions on the Council alone, now increasingly go to the Commission and the EP in order to get more desired outcomes. Politicians of the EP and the COR may arrange a get-together with their party-political friends at home, in order to promote some common interest. Members of the EESC create their concerted actions with the private interest groups of the employers, the trade unions and the consumers. Officials of the Court of Justice and the Court of Auditors are the main exceptions to this EU practice of lobbying each other. In fact, most officials play dual roles, with other players approaching them as relevant actors and they in turn doing so to others. If the two roles coincide, a relevant deal can arise.

There is, in short, indeed no shortage of actors who can be approached and thus be influenced. The puzzle for EU public affairs management is to find the optimal selection, the best connection, the right timing and the correct approach. All this and more is a matter of homework, to be discussed in the following chapters. The main point here is that there are many actors available as co-producers of outcomes, whether desired positively or negatively.

Factors to use
The number of relevant EU actors may be numerous, but it is modest in comparison to the total sum of factors affecting their behaviour. Any interest group can make use of these factors, as a green farmer exploits the natural conditions for growing and flowering or as a shopkeeper uses the market opportunities of supply and demand to make his family wealthy. Manipulating the different factors of behaviour is certainly more sophisticated than approaching the actors. The increasing policy competition among EU stakeholders has resulted in this sophistication becoming a current trend. From the long list of numerous factors useful for the promotion of a desired outcome we select the following ones and gather them under four categories: cultural, formal, operational and decisional.

Policy concepts, policy values and regime values are cases of *cultural factors*, which may be highly instrumental in determining decision-making. Their formation is usually prompted by an issue or irritating difference among the stakeholders. In 1999 there appeared to be no common concept or definition of, for example, 'chocolate' or, taking the wider issue of genetically modified organisms (GMO), 'risk'. This situation could be taken as either an opportunity or a threat. In the end, the Belgian chocolate industry finally took it as a chance to reposition itself as the sole producer of a pure product in Europe. Environmental groups could block the approval of new GMO products by openly pleading for zero risk, thus creating a cultural constraint for both DG Industry and the food industry. New policy values come and go like the wind: if it is friendly, one can hoist the sail, and if not, one can at least steer a middle course. Green and white books and memoranda are often carriers of new values. In the 1990s they covered such topics as the environment, security, competition, growth, employment, human rights and sustainability. Through the old technique of argumentation many lobby groups try to pour their old wine into such a new container. New regime values, such as subsidiarity, transparency, proportionality, coordination and reciprocity, all launched in the 1990s, can be used likewise by lobby groups for pushing or blocking a policy development and, like squirrels do in the wood, for dragging their interests to a better arena. For example, subsidiarity has often been used for challenging EU environmental or social policies, transparency for hindering efficient negotiations, and reciprocity for retarding an open gas or railway market.

The use of *formal factors* is widespread and indicates that the skeleton of the EU decision-making machinery can work as a determinant of its flesh and blood. Especially useful in this are procedures allocating formal powers to selected actors. It may make a big difference for the outcome whether, for example: a decision-making process follows the secondary or the delegated procedure; the EP decides under consultation or codecision; the Council concludes by unanimity or majority; a dossier is dealt with by the one or the other Commission DG, EP commission or Council working group; the implementation or the inspection is done by EU civil servants, national bureaucrats, regional authorities or private organisations; or a decision gets the formal status of a non-binding guideline or a binding directive, regulation or decree. Seldom have such dilemmas been settled in detail by existing formal decisions, which in specific cases thus provide some room for interpretation and lobbying. If formal factors are linked, they even provide repeated opportunities for blocking or pushing. When a lobby group feels itself damaged by a Commission proposal for secondary legislation, it can use firstly the EP to appeal against the Commission, secondly the Council against the EP, and thirdly the Court against each of them. This is what the German government did in the 1993 Banana Case [Pedler, 1994]. In 2001, the Commissioner on Taxation, Frits Bolkestein, announced the lodging of a complaint at the Court against governments putting up fiscal barriers against the open market.

A change of the Treaty, which is the mother of all procedures, may provide many new opportunities. Thanks to the 1993 Maastricht Treaty, the Commission, with the support of the trade unions federation ETUC, managed to get adopted in 1994, after nearly 20 years of stalemate, its first directive on the workers council for multinational companies [Van Rens, 1994]. By making use of the 1993 Social Protocol, the Commission tried in 1997 to push more co-determination in such companies and it managed to get the directives on parental leave and part-time work passed. For many policy areas the 1999 Amsterdam Treaty changed, at the date of its coming into force (1 May 1999), a number of procedures, particularly the one on codecision. For example, on the specified issues of both food and transport policy, the EP was given codecision powers and the COR advisory ones, while some specific issues of Pillar III were moved to Pillar I, thus providing new arenas. In 1998 the EP decided to delay its proceedings on the Water Framework Directive until after the coming into force of the Amsterdam Treaty.

For their daily operations the EU stakeholders are much dependent on material resources such as staff and budget and less tangible ones like information and support. Such *operational factors* can make a large difference for the desired outcome. The underresourced Commission has no alternative to opening its doors and calling in a great number of inexpensive experts. This is an opportunity for all interest groups. They can provide the Commission with what in lacks in specific information and support. Some Commission units may have, of course, more or less resources than others. In 1995, the DG Social Affairs, unit V, had to call off a meeting of its Advisory Committee on Safety, Health and Hygiene, owing to a lack of means at the end of the year. The representatives from organised management took the delay as an opportunity [Daemen and Van Schendelen, 1998, 135]. Similar imbalances between workload and resources may arise in the EP, the Council and the Court. The EP's Friday session in Strasbourg, having a low turnout of MEPs and therefore abolished in 2000, was an example of underload, which made it easy to get any resolution adopted by a simple majority. The imbalance may be caused not only by sheer volume, but also by conflicting contents. In such cases, the EU official will prefer to deal with combined interests, and sophisticated groups can take advantage of this by aggregating a broader coalition.

There are more operational factors, three of which deserve special attention. The first one is *friendship*. In the multicultural EU this is often quite an important factor. Actors tend to like (or dislike) each other, for whatever reason. By using friendship as a tool, one may further a desired outcome. Then, for example, a DG civil servant may be prepared to raise an issue with his/her friend in another DG, an EP commission or a Council working group; or a MEP may mediate with a fellow party member in the Commission, the COR or the Council. The second is the personal *ambition* of an actor. Normally he/she wants to score with a dossier and to make a career. As a result of paying a person and his/her principal a compliment on what is done, a favour may be received in return, as courtesy repays in a comity of politics. The third is *language*. Normally, a decision is made by the use of a working language (usually English or French), but published in every official language. Many a key word goes into translation without a common definition. No two languages have, besides, fully identical semantics. A pressure group can use the differences for pushing its interests and a clever group always checks various language editions. In the 1999 dioxin case (on polluted animal food) the French farmers could claim that the sludge they used (in itself forbidden, but undefined at European level) was not sludge, but really fertiliser.

Finally, there are the *decisional factors* that can be used. On every issue some lobby groups are in favour of a common decision and others are against. Each category tends to have, in addition, its internal divisions regarding the best policy outcome. There is, in short, always some room for pushing or blocking a decision or a policy as desired. In the absence of a dominant side, every outcome is a matter of giving and taking or decision-making by compromise. For successful negotiations, two factors are most important. Firstly, one's position or demand regarding the issue at stake has to be raised in the EU dealing rooms, because otherwise one cannot be taken into account. Secondly, one has to offer something of interest or advantage to other important stakeholders, because otherwise one will be neglected or opposed. By using its 'green papers' and 'white papers' as a sort of marketing tool, the Commission has developed a sophisticated method of producing a more attractive supply side. The two factors of demand and supply, necessary for every desired outcome, are always variables. The former comes from one's own desires and the latter encompasses items advantageous to the stakeholders in the arena. Both the identification and the management of the two are, substantially, a matter of homework, to which we will return in the following chapters.

Vectors to create
The number of potential vectors is as unlimited as human creativity. A vector is a newly constructed factor, comparable with the use of chemicals or GMO technology by a farmer or with the manipulation of supply and demand by a shopkeeper. The conditions under which EU officials and other

stakeholders behave are not simply used for the promotion of the desired outcome, as in the above-mentioned factor approach. The threats and opportunities are now changed and reconstructed, in order to maximise the chances of the desired result. In the vector approach the lobby group is manipulating a relevant arena proactively, thus hoping to achieve the anticipated influence as desired. The method of doing this is essentially the result of homework and full of *feedforward* thinking regarding actors, issues, time and other conditions. The lobby group needs to focus on the desired outcome in order to engineer the most favourable conditions right from the start. Of all three approaches the vector one is the most sophisticated. Because of the increasing competition among EU stakeholders, it is also the trend-setting example provided by the smartest players. They try their utmost to manage or to manipulate *the various labyrinths constructed on different trampolines*, as the EU machinery was described in the previous chapter. Major examples of cultural, formal, operational and decisional vectors are the following.

Policy concepts, policy values and regime values provide excellent *cultural vectors*. A sectoral or a regional interest group can collect more EU subsidies if it creates a more acceptable concept of, for example, poverty. Even a different indicator may help: in 1994 the wealthy Dutch province of Flevoland managed to receive more than 150 million *ecu* (now *euro*) from the regional fund ERDF by excluding from its poverty indicators its most wealthy commuters. Policy values are frequently used as a vector. In the early 1990s, European textile manufacturers, organised in the ELTAC, promoted the value of human rights particularly for children in order to prevent cheap textile imports from the Third World, which uses child labour. Also in the early 1990s, the German beer industry, disliking an open beer market, promoted at first the value of public health, referring to its *Reinheitsgebot* of the Middle Ages. After the failure of this, it seized on the value of the environment, by demanding that every empty bottle or tin should be repatriated to the country of origin, which would mean increased transport costs for their foreign competitors. A central value is thus not simply used, as in the factor approach, but is now amplified or newly constructed in a proactive way. The issue is reframed to reach a culturally higher level. For example, the financial support from DG Agriculture for the destruction of livestock plagued by diseases is demanded as a matter of ethics rather than economy. The self-interest is transformed into a so-called general interest, for which many people tend to have sympathy spontaneously. As a technique of argumentation it is typical salesman's talk.

Regime values are equally fit for this sort of *issue manipulation*. Those who are against the europeanisation of a policy item often preach subsidiarity, proportionality or reciprocity. Southern countries sometimes enthusiastically press for the setting of minimum EU standards in the fields of the environment and social affairs. They restrict themselves to the minimum level and chuckle about the northern countries, whose NGOs covering these fields push their own governments to go far above the minimum level, to the advantage of the southern economies. In the 1990s, the UK government acquired the reputation of promoting the enlargement ('widening') of the EU merely as a means of hampering the trend towards a more supranational Union (its 'deepening'). The regime value of co-ordination, also sounding reasonable, is frequently used to catch reluctant interest groups in the EU net. Those wanting to delay EU decision-making smartly push the regime value of transparency, thus trying to involve critical stakeholders and the mass media. In all these cases the key is to find a higher value, which can be exploited as a catapult for the creation of a desired outcome. The real art is to bring into being the next spectacular value, as fresh and attractive as the young lady Lorelei of German legend. To this we will return in chapter 6.

The reinterpretation of formal procedures and powers, as laid down in Treaty texts and other formal agreements, ranks top among the *formal vectors*. Such documents refer almost only to general issue areas, such as agriculture or health, and seldom to specific issues, such as a new margarine which lowers cholesterol. Every fight over EU decision-making is, however, not general but specific. It may be won by bringing the specific issue under a different general label, for example health instead of market competition. The issue may then be entrusted to a more benign Commission DG, EP commission or special Council, with different procedures and powers. The arenas of agriculture, the environment or consumer affairs may indeed result in very different outcomes for Unilever, the food producer that wanted market admission for that new margarine in 1999. At the same time the European federation of biotechnology firms Europabio pressed for redefining GMO products as consumer concerns rather than environmental ones, in fact for moving them to a more benign DG. Other popular procedural vectors involve the legislative procedure (secondary or delegated), the position of the EP (consultation or co-decision), the voting in the Council (unanimity or majority) and the ways of implementation and inspection (European or national). In 1997, Germany claimed that the Commission's draft Tobacco Advertising Ban Directive was wrongly based on article 100a of the EU Treaty and should have been based on article 129, which does not permit a ban at all, and this was agreed by the Court. Inspection vectors can be found under the notification procedure, which obliges the governments to notify the Commission about their new laws. It enables lobby groups to hinder a competitor. All this is lawyers' work and they can always find some room for new manoeuvring. The Commission itself is frequently an expert on this.

The formal vectors can be made even more ingenious. For the better risk assessment of GMO products, Unilever pleaded in 1999 for the establishment of an European Food Authority, which would act professionally like its US counterpart and would liberate the company from the existing procedures, which it considered messy. The linking together of formal vectors may create more new opportunities. For example, when a regulatory committee (comitology type III) cannot come to a valid decision regarding a Commission proposal, it must take the case to the Council, which has to decide within a limited time; otherwise the Commission proposal goes through as the regulation. Thus, a national pressure group can win its case by first getting a Commission proposal which supports its line and by subsequently blocking valid decisions by both the committee and the Council. On the free trade of transgenic maize, France managed to get this desired result in 1996 [Bradley, 1998; Töller and Hofmann, 2000]. The formation of a new Treaty always attracts proactive efforts to create new vectors, such as a changed procedure, a new regime value or a redistribution of powers.

The *operational vectors* are frequently activated. Many a lobby group tries to influence the desire of an official for the help of special experts, better facilities, information and support. The dream is to get a sustainable monopolistic position and to become the sole supplier of scarce items, thus largely encapsulating the official. All governments try to parachute some of their experts into Commission DGs, as in 2001 the Dutch Ministry of Transport managed to achieve the nomination of one of its experts as a staff member of the EP. Consumer electronics firms, farmers' organisations and environmental groups all have a reputation for such parachuting. A smart lobby group also tries to stimulate the demand for supporting its own case and for refuting that of its opponents. Not only by volume, but also by contents can the workload and subsequent behaviour of a player be predetermined. Pressure groups can invest varying amounts of energy in bringing together their conflicting issues. Through the high officials responsible for internal management they can also play 'meta-games', such as the shift of tasks and resources to another unit or the outsourcing to a consultancy firm under their reach. In their committees the experts from ministries or companies can make great play of their own expertise and play down that of their opponents.

Special operational vectors again encompass friendship, ambition and language. *Friendship* in political settings is a diplomat's game. One has to be(come) understanding and charming, and most people appreciate an empathetic word. Background information about the hobbies and the life styles of the high officials is for sale in Brussels. Even to opponents and enemies a lobby group can profess friendship and community. The personal *ambition* of an EU actor can be satisfied proactively by the creation of career opportunities, for example through lobbying in his/her favour for getting a better position inside a DG, a national ministry or an European federation. In the Babylonian EU, *language* is a crucial vector. To work in one's own language gives an advantage, as does preventing the opponent's language being used. A lobby group can try to get a loose translation of some decision in an official language; this gives more room for manoeuvring afterwards and may destabilise a competitor. In 1991 the Dutch Frisia Dairy was enraged by an EU decree prescribing metal instead of carton packaging for milk products. It appeared to be a mistranslation of the French word *boîte*, which means any packaging. According to the official excuse, the error was made by a Belgian translator from the French-speaking Wallonia, where the contested word was said to have the specific meaning of metal packaging. Frisia Dairy, however, believed it was a trick of mistranslation caused by the French, their main competitors in the dairy business.

Decisional vectors cover all the variables of negotiation. One possibility is the creation of a strong and preferably cross-sectoral coalition. In 1995 the steel regions managed to do this by bringing together local authorities, trade unions and steel companies under the umbrella of Caster. Another game is the politicisation (or depoliticisation) of an issue by raising (or lowering) its profile, and thereby creating a different playing field and outcome. In order to achieve a better compromise one can majorate one's own demand, pay concessions on instalment, push or block an exemption, combine with another dossier and, in short, manipulate every element of one's demand and supply side. UK lobby groups have some reputation for creating fancy cleavages, cleverly enabling them to ask for something in return for their support for a compromise, even if they do not have an interest in the issue at all. The engineering of such decisional vectors requires, of course, a lot of proactive homework.

The Meta-Game of Triple P

Well-known is the pious wish for a level playing field in Europe to achieve the integration or accommodation of irritating differences. This piety is comparable with the call for a free and open competition on the commercial market, in which every merchant still strives to become the single monopolist. As long as all merchants have this same ambition, they all end up as competitors indeed. But some, thanks to their smarter buying and selling techniques, may be successful in gaining market advantage. On the EU political market the behaviour of the players is not very different. Many pressure groups say they love a level playing field, but privately they almost all prefer to have a most unlevel playing field, of course with themselves at the top and their opponents at the bottom. The level playing field is only their next-best preference.

The game of *Triple P* is intended to make the playing field more unlevel. In this smart game one tries to place, like pickets in the field, the friendliest *persons* in the best *positions* in the most beneficial *procedures*. The lobby group tries to achieve its aims by setting the principles before the match starts. Triple P is thus a proactive and coherent meta-game, which prearranges or rearranges the playing field. Those who have arranged the field to their comfort, enjoy the greatest chance of scoring with the ball subsequently. Every IGC for a new Treaty is substantially a Triple P game, placing the pickets on a policy field for the next few years. In the daily life of 'Brussels' both the Commission officials and the French lobby groups often play the game excellently. When others start to argue over the contents of the issue, they have already prearranged the playing field and limited the other players' movements by their early settling of the procedures, positions and people favourable to their cause. The meta-game of Triple P requires a systematic selection of vectors to create, factors to use and actors to approach. Its rich menu is regularly further enriched with new discoveries *(figure 3.1)*.

The First P of *procedures* is no different from our category of formal factors and vectors, as far as they prearrange or rearrange the field. By getting a benign procedure applied to one's issue, one automatically gets a distribution of formal powers that are fairly likely to protect one's interests. That benign procedure may be the Parliament having codecision or not, Council voting by unanimity or majority, legislation by secondary or delegated procedure, or whatever other procedure is considered to be beneficial for the desired outcome. The issue may even be rephrased in advance, so that it makes the benign procedure more suitable. For example, under the Social Protocol of the Maastricht Treaty, any proposal in favour of co-determining workers' councils in multinational companies had to be subject to unanimous decision-making by the Council. But after its rephrasing in terms of consultation, the first proposal became subject to QMV and was accepted in

The meta-game of triple P

First P: Procedures, such as

- EP: consultation, codecision
- Council: unanimity or (Q)MV/subsidiarity
- implementation: EU (comitology) or national
- Court involvement

Second P: Positions, such as

- membership committees, working groups
- Special DG, EP Commission, Council
- inside PR, SG Council/Council Chair
- Inspection Agency/policy consultancy

Third P: People, such as

- Commission: 'Chef de Dossier', cabinets
- EP, EESC, COREG: friends as rapporteur
- parachuted friends in Commission, SG Council
- Court members and staff

Figure 3.1

1994 [Van Rens, 1994]. In the 1990 EU tender for food supply to Russia, French interest groups in the meat trade managed to get included in the tender conditions sizes of cans for potted meat that were normal in France but strange to their Dutch competitors. They won the tender. Under the First P there is, of course, much room for full issue manipulation as well. National market protection, in itself forbidden, might be preserved through the different procedures resulting from its reframing in terms of health or environmental interests. Commission proposals for common taxation are subject to unanimous voting in the Council, unless they are re-framed as, for example, open market measures.

The Second P of *positions* is, in our terminology above, a mixture particularly of formal and operational factors and vectors. The lobby group now tries to acquire crucial positions in the flesh-and-blood process of decision-making, like the position of chairman or rapporteur of a relevant committee, commission or working group, or at least to prevent opponents getting such positions. The position is not necessarily formally the top of the hierarchy, but it must confer control over the issue in practice. French pressure groups often claim and take the positions of chairman, and in doing so are often more formalistic than pragmatic [Legendre, 1993]. Their northern competitors frequently feel happier with the low-key position of the *apparatchik* who does the work. It has been recently found that holding a position close to a consultancy firm contracted by the Commission may provide control over the advice given. Issue manipulation can, of course, be part of the Second P game. In 1999 the lobby groups on the environment managed to get various issues of agriculture, transport and trade reframed in the white books of the Commission as issues of sustainability. In doing so, they brought themselves and their friends in DG Environment closer to being in the drivers' seat when considering later proposals.

The Third P of *persons* is in our terminology a mixture of mainly cultural and operational factors and vectors regarding crucial people. A friend or an associate in a relevant position to take advantage of a beneficial procedure can apply the finishing touch to the ball in the real match. Highly valued is the old friend who already shares common values and perhaps interests and thus hardly needs a cultural massage. New friends can be won by stressing a common value and creating a common interest, based on either the dossier or the person in question, including, for example, common background and career expectations. A good friend in a relevant position can distribute material resources such as staff and budget and less tangible ones as information and support as desired. When the real match starts, the other stakeholders hardly have an alternative to coming along and offering a deal. Friends might be made, recruited or parachuted in to all institutions and units and at all levels considered to be relevant. These friends may be lower-A civil servants of the Commission, referendaries of the Court, translators of the Council, inspectors of an agency or experts of a management committee. Their recruitment and promotion, officially called personnel policy, frequently develop into a fight with others over the selection of friends. By manipulating such issues as representative versus merit recruitment one can arrive at totally different personnel outcomes.

The Triple P meta-game usually has a bad reputation among the players who find themselves at the far end of the playing field. They find it aggressive, Kafka-like and sneaky. They only want to play the real match when it comes to, for example, a standardisation or a food regulation, and not, far before this, the sort of devious manoeuvrings over such abstractions as procedures, positions and people in charge. Many pressure groups, however, quickly learn in practice. As soon as they understand this meta-gaming, they start to apply it themselves and to appreciate its sophisticated efficiency and effectiveness. The aggression is then reassessed as a professional skill, the Kafka style as an interesting composition and the snake as a part of the Paradise worth to enjoy. In fact, there is hardly anything new about the Triple P game: it is classical political behaviour [Loewenstein, 1973; Machiavelli, 1513]. At EU level it has merely acquired new applications. The paradox, encouraging for less smart players, is that the higher the number of lobby groups playing this meta-game, the smaller the chance that a single one can prearrange the playing field solely for its own benefit. If the playing field is unlevel, it indicates that many lobby groups have neglected both their competitive fieldwork and their preparation for new conditions.

Specific Trends in the Management of EU Affairs

On the EU playing field the thousands of public and private lobby groups have one thing in common: the ambition to win, or at least not lose, a game relevant to their interests. They try to achieve this by one or more of the three aforementioned general methods: approaching actors, using factors and creating vectors. One trend is to use the first method more often combined in some way with the others, for example in the sophisticated meta-game of Triple P. Of course, in their daily lobbying the many EU stakeholders exhibit striking and variable differences as well. They all have their idiosyncratic preferences, resource lines, forms of management, lobby styles and more. These differences, however, are often patterned in three particular ways: by origin, by type of organisation and by time. Lobby groups coming from the same country, region or sector or having organisational similarities of size, desire or experience frequently show more or less similar patterns of EU behaviour, as will be demonstrated in the following sections and chapters. The third pattern, by time, is under discussion here. In their efforts to push the 'buttons of Brussels' the lobby groups reveal some specific trends and developments.

These trends seem to have at least one common cause: the *increased competition* on the playing field. For the understanding of this we refer to the previous chapter or, in short, to the logic of EU lobby-group action: the more relevant 'flowers and trees' that are seen in the EU policy gardens (supply side), the more 'birds and bees' will try to gather nectar (demand side), which is scarce like in nature (competition). In addition to this deepening of the lobby competition, there is, because of the further enlargements of the

EU and the growth of non-EU stakeholders, also a widening of it. At the end of the first chapter we could, indeed, observe a burgeoning number of interest groups registered in Brussels. Their increasingly active presence on the EU playing field indicates, in general, the strength of the factors behind their participation: strong desires, sufficient resources, irresistible compulsions and seductive invitations [Milbrath and Goel, 1977]. This growth of competitive players causes a lot of *overcrowding* on the playing field or, more precisely, in crucial parts of the machinery of EU decision-making, particularly near the Commission, the Parliament and the Council. This overcrowding eventually causes problems of influence efficiency and effectiveness. The following three specific trends can be seen as, at least partially, common responses to these problems. The trends are, as always in life, set by a few players and more or less followed by the many others. The few are apparently the quickest to learn and the most innovative in the game.

From national co-ordination to self-reliance

In the past the individual interest groups wanting to influence EU decision-making preferred to take, as a matter of course, some national route to Brussels. At their micro-level they contacted their national associations (meso-level), such as trade and professional organisations. These associations stood at the crossing of the routes to their EuroFeds and the national government (macro-level). The latter felt happy to bring together all sorts of interests, to co-ordinate them both by a procedure and through having a desk at central government level, and to defend the selected interests at its Brussels Council level. On the national playing field every government ministry thus had a triple position: as a public interest group (micro), as a sort of public association for the interest groups in its policy domain (meso) and as a participant in the national co-ordination procedure (macro). In the past the national government has clearly functioned as a centre of gravity for many interest groups at home. To a large extent, that *government co-ordination*, exaggeratedly labelled as national co-ordination, made sense as well. For a long time most EU decision-making was still secondary legislation with, until the 1987 SEA, a veto position for the national minister in the Council. Thus, with the help of central government, a domestic lobby group could at least prevent or block an undesired EU decision. With a few exceptions, like the MNCs and the agricultural associations, most interest groups lacked, in addition, any experience of cross-border lobby activities. They felt uncertain and looked for help from their national governments.

Although all national governments still hold, at the highest level (Cabinet, Prime Minister or President), such a procedure for national co-ordination [Kassim and others, 2000], they have found that it has become a *quag-mire* [Wright, 1996]. In practice, national governments hardly co-ordinate anymore [Van Schendelen, 1993]. They try to co-ordinate usually in only four cases: (a) if for the next Council meeting the national voting position has to be formalised, (b) if the national parliament pressures for a national position on some issue, (c) if there are heavy interdepartmental conflicts over an issue, and (d) if the government holds veto power in the Council, for example regarding Treaty reform or Pillars II and III. But even in these cases the attempt at national co-ordination often remains symbolic and/or ineffective. The specialised ministry and/or the other lobby groups at home usually decide the voting position for the Council long before and from the bottom up. Most national parliaments receive mainly symbols of coherence rather than co-ordination, such as solemn statements, promises and registers listing standpoints. Conflicting ministries soon discover that their common interest is at least not to be co-ordinated centrally. Only in the case of the Council veto can national co-ordination, if attempted, be really effective for the blocking of an undesired outcome, but not for pushing for a desired one. In any case, because of the power of the veto, the blocking could even be achieved without using co-ordination.

The growing new practice can be summarised by the catchword *self-reliance* [Van Schendelen, 1993]. Pressure groups may like to co-ordinate others actively, but they abhor being co-ordinated by others passively. Those feeling they have a specific interest increasingly prefer to act on their own. This is the case with all sorts of interest groups, even those that otherwise preach co-ordination. Many a trade association, wanting to co-ordinate its members, prefers to bypass its national umbrella, and ministry units often find their way to Brussels long before informing the co-ordinating office about it. Ministries of Foreign Affairs, which in most countries are charged with the dual task of both national government co-ordination and foreign policy-making, frequently act self-reliantly on their second concern in Pillar II. In the early 1990s even in France, officially the most centralised country of the EU, more than 100 interest groups, including units of central government, escaped the national co-ordinating office SGCI (the General Secretariat of the Interministerial Committee) by setting up their own lobby offices in Brussels [Legendre, 1993]. So-called national co-ordination is now almost only requested by the national parliament wanting to bind the government structurally and by the ministry concerned wanting to control other ministries according to circumstances. The trend of self-reliance, found among all sorts of interest groups, justifies the view that the EU is not a collection of member states, but of member countries.

Self-reliance has a *threefold rationality*. Firstly, on every EU issue every member country is, normally, internally divided. The country or society always contains more varied interests than the state and the latter more than the central government. From the perspective of democratic pluralism the central government ought to split its voting position in the Council partially in favour and partially against any Commission proposal, but this does not happen. In denying pluralism at home, the central government stimulates willy-nilly the many stakeholders who are worried about losing the game in the national capital to look after their interests themselves in Brussels. By excluding the decentralised governments and the private interest groups from its so-called national co-ordination procedure, the central government stimulates these stakeholders in particular to work on their own. Secondly, the advantages of national co-ordination can only exist if the Council plays a role and if the national position can make a difference here. But, as shown in the previous chapter, the Council usually plays an only formally decisive role on less than 20% of EU legislation. Under the QMV voting practice a single member state rarely makes a difference in any case. Thirdly, the disadvantages or costs of national co-ordination can be serious: an interest group still relying on it runs all the risks of losing its case, diluting its interests at home with heterogeneous other ones, being too late in the early phases of EU decision-making and/or failing to be part of an European coalition in development.

The threefold logic of self-reliance, based on considerations of efficiency and effectiveness, applies not only to the macro-level of national co-ordination. It also applies to the co-ordination at the meso-level of a national association or a ministry and to that at the micro-level inside a heterogeneous organisation like a big ministry or an MNC. In the open and free European countries almost every specific interest group has the option of self-reliance. This is rarely effectively prohibited by the parent organisation. As shown in *figure 3.2*, it can choose to take a national, an international and/or a transnational route to the EU and make use of the many lanes, junctions and roundabouts. By such self-reliance a specific interest group can make itself faster and better adapted to the EU playing field and thus just escape the overcrowding by lobby groups there. Instead of being part of standing co-ordination procedures at home, it co-operates with others selectively. If considered helpful, it may ask government officials at home for additional information and support, in return for some compensation. Such shopping behaviour is a matter of lobbying at home.

From individual to collective EU action
Every lobby group would love to be the single player on the EU playing field, but this is only a daydream. Even in the old Community of only six member states there was always competition among lobby groups, even in a niche of a policy sector. But the number of competitors was clearly smaller then than at the turn of the millennium. Even until the 1987 SEA, with its application of QMV, individual EU action could be effective only for blocking EU decision-making at Council level. Then one only had to ask the national government to veto a proposal in the Council. This possibility has almost disappeared, except for a minority of dossiers under Pillar I and for the majority under Pillars II and III. But pushing for a decision has always required collective action, although in the past the group involved could be quite small. For example, on EU issues of air transport, only six national carriers, closely associated with their national ministries and thus practically running their

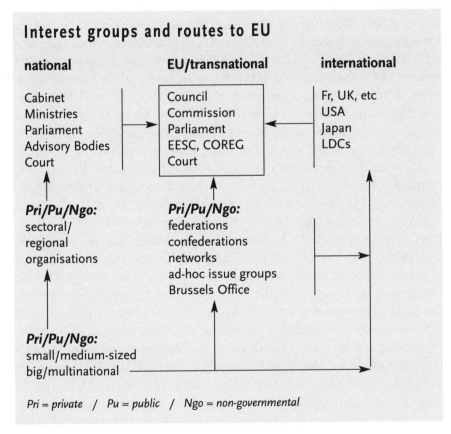

Interest groups and routes to EU

national	EU/transnational	international
Cabinet	Council	Fr, UK, etc
Ministries	Commission	USA
Parliament	Parliament	Japan
Advisory Bodies	EESC, COREG	LDCs
Court	Court	

Pri/Pu/Ngo:
sectoral/
regional
organisations

Pri/Pu/Ngo:
federations
confederations
networks
ad-hoc issue groups
Brussels Office

Pri/Pu/Ngo:
small/medium-sized
big/multinational

Pri = private / Pu = public / Ngo = non-governmental

Figure 3.2

own Transport Council, could settle the outcomes. In each niche of a policy sector the number of competitive interest groups is nowadays so high that more than ever collective action is necessary. The pressure group may fly alone from home, but, when it arrives near the EU playing field, it usually has to become part of a *flock of birds*. It may still contact people in the Commission, Parliament or Council individually [Kohler-Koch, 1998], but such action is done for the window-out monitoring rather than the window-in negotiations. The latter in particular need a collective approach.

The factor providing the impetus for interest groups is the so-called *logic of influence* [Schmitter and Streeck, 1999], which to some extent is related to the size of a political system. At local level even a medium-sized interest group may have sufficient mass and weight to present its interest to officials. But at the regional, the national and, most of all, the European level it needs to create more mass and weight in order to attract attention for its interest. It does so by acting collectively: the single bird joins a flock of similar birds. In addition to this factor pushing for collective action, there are pull factors as well. Other interest groups in the same position will be looking for associates with similar interests, and seek to bring them into a group to act collectively. EU officials, wanting to interact with interest groups, prefer to do so not at the individual, but at the aggregate level, and are even prepared to subsidise such aggregation [Greenwood, 1998, 106]. They then suffer less from volume and content overload. DG Social Affairs, for example, has always promoted the idea of management and labour organising themselves in a better way and meeting together on a sort of platform, which once developed into the Social Protocol procedure. In 1997 DG Small and Medium Sized Enterprises initiated measures to promote the formation of EU-wide associations and foundations in its field.

For every lobby group, the puzzle is to find the optimal form of a European collectivity or flock; this optimum is a combination of *homogeneity* and *control*. With similar birds (homogeneity) the issues are shared, but the interests may be extremely competitive. It is as easy to list the items for the common agenda as it is difficult to come to a common position. With different birds (heterogeneity) one usually has little community of issues and interests, so that the formation of a common agenda results in endless waffle, making it even more difficult to come to a common position. Most interest groups prefer homogeneity, mostly on a sectoral basis, and they want to exert control over the collectivity. Large-sized interest groups, like multinationals and trade organisations, may possess the capacity for direct control [Coen, 1998; Bennett, 1999], but the large majority of small- and medium-sized interest groups remain much dependent on remote control, starting with some domestic umbrella and extending it to the EU level.

The model for collective action is the so-called European Federation or *EuroFed*. Groups with a common specific interest area meet together in a common transnational organisation close to the EU machinery, as shown in *figure 3.2*. Variants of it are the more heterogeneous confederation, the informal network and the most specific ad-hoc coalition. In addition, many groups also establish their own offices here too. The collective group usually hopes to achieve the four functions of providing a platform for watching each other, aggregating specific interests, saving on the costs of lobbying and, ultimately, influencing the EU successfully. These groups are also the largest category of Brussels-based lobby groups, and they exist particularly for private interest groups and decentralised governments. The national ministries do not have a form of EuroFed; they mix the four functions with their Council function of finally formalising secondary legislation. This hardly works in practice, and the formation of EuroFeds consisting of national ministries may be expected as an inevitability in the future. Only the Ministries of Defence, insofar as belonging to NATO located in the north of Brussels, have a Europe-wide collective platform useful for the EU action here.

The EuroFeds and their variants are a *well-established* phenomenon. Pharmaceutical companies and associations meet in EFPIA, chemical ones in CEFIC, small- and medium-sized enterprises (SMEs) in UEAPME and food-producers in CIAA. The NGOs and their variants ranging from GONGOs to BONGOs meet in different groups: the consumer groups in BEUC, the employers' organisations in UNICE and the trade unions in ETUC. Regional and professional groups also come together, for example the steel regions in CASTER, the big cities in EUROCITIES, the architects in ACE and the journalists in AJE. But an EuroFed is seldom representative of the whole of the sector. There exist, for example, about 15 Euro-Feds dealing with construction, 20 with packaging and 75 with chemicals [Landmarks, 2000]. Many of them are not broadly European for their sector, but regional (for example, only Southern or Teutonic) and trade-specific (such as for only a certain group of chemicals). In spite of all differences, most EuroFeds have a basically similar organisational form [Greenwood, 1997]. There is a General Assembly having as members the national associations and sometimes also the major individual organisations. Stakeholders from outside but operating inside the EU, like US companies or Turkish associations, can usually become members as well. The Assembly appoints an Executive Board and President, supported by a Secretariat or Bureau and having its own budget. Through preparatory commissions and standing procedures the Board and the Secretariat achieve a common position.

The model of the EuroFed is widely seen as *efficient*: at low cost a community of interests with a European face is formed. But its *effectiveness* is frequently criticised by members, as case studies show [Greenwood and others, 1992; Mazey and Richardson, 1993; Pedler and Van Schendelen, 1994; Greenwood, 1995; Wallace and Young, 1997-A; Greenwood and Aspinwall, 1998; Greenwood, 1998]. The external influence of an Eurofed is considered as quite limited, and it is usually highly dependent on such contributive but scarce factors as homogeneity, past experience, leadership, multinationality, sectoral status, and focus [Greenwood, 1995, 44-7]. Ironically, the same factors may previously have hampered one's own internal influence. For example, inside EACEM, the homogeneous EuroFed of the manufacturers of consumer electronics, the few large-sized multinational and prestigious companies (including Thomson, Philips, Nokia and Siemens) had to learn painfully how to arrive at internal compromises [Knill and Lehmkuhl, 1997]. In spite of all their criticisms of EuroFeds most interest groups are direct or indirect members of a transnational lobby platform. Apparently, they consider the costs of non-membership as higher than those of membership, even if the external effectiveness is low. As a member they can at least more easily monitor, control and approach the other members and the EU stakeholders, including the EU officials. If a common position is achieved, then they can really enjoy the taste of influence [Greenwood, 1997].

For many interest groups the membership of a standing platform like an EuroFed is merely one route or means of influencing the EU. If one has lost inside an Eurofed, there remain other opportunities of influencing the other EU stakeholders in the desired direction, and many interest groups continue to search for more optimal platforms that will provide more homogeneity and control [Pollack, 1997]. Four *additional trends* of collective action can be observed. Firstly, flexible ad-hoc coalitions are increasingly being established for a specific dossier of interest [Pijnenburg, 1998]. The costs of development may be high, but are limited in time, while the return on the investment is seen as better. In the mid-1990s all members of EACEM created such coalitions with, for example, the trade unions (on labour conditions), the publishers (on intellectual property) and the customers (on standardisations). Secondly, the business EuroFeds present themselves more and more as forms of NGO, in fact as BONGOs, as they believe this appearance provides additional influence [Warleigh, 2000]. Thirdly, the EuroFeds become more and more connected to the EU machinery, particularly its work floor of expert groups and comitology. They ask and get invitations to parachute in their members. Finally, on a particular dossier the members constituting an EuroFed, and especially the MNCs, increasingly make use of multiple collective routes to influence the EU. In addition to their direct actions from their Brussels' office, they act simultaneously through, for example, a national association, a national ministry, an EuroFed, an ad-hoc coalition and an expert committee and frequently they do so through more than one of these. Whether they intend to or not they contribute much to the integration process [Greenwood and others, 1999].

From ready-made to tailor-made action
In the past, a lobby group tended to show little variation of behaviour regarding EU decision-making. It acted as relatively *ready-made*. It took the traditional routes to its national association and/or ministry and followed the officially co-ordinated link to the relevant EuroFed and/or EU institution. It hardly differentiated its approach regarding the various issues or dossiers. At the EU (and its forerunners), there was equally little variation in the response to lobby groups. For example, the bulk of legislation was secondary and based on unanimity; the concept of comitology had not even yet been given the name. The number of players was as small as a village. Among the old Six existed a fair amount of common understanding. In short, the EU complexity and dynamics were low-scoring variables. Inevitably, the interest groups acting through their national governments reflected in their behaviour their governments' characteristics, for example type of regime (presidential or parliamentary), structure (central or federal) and size (large or small).

To some degree the government-related differences of behaviour still exist. They have been augmented with even more, such as rich versus poor member states, 'Catholic' versus 'Protestant' administrative cultures, and old versus new member states. But the differences are becoming less clear-cut, making each of the them less dominant and the lobby behaviour *more varied*. In addition, pressure groups have become more and more self-reliant. Their behaviour reflects less than before the imprints of their national governments and much more those of themselves and their social environment. They behave, for example, typically as a big trading company or like an association of notaries based in Finland or France. They reflect, first of all, their organisational traits, such as size (large versus small), sector (industry versus services), focus (profit-oriented or not) and status (private versus public). Secondly, they reflect societal positions on, for example, transparency (the northern versus the southern countries), governance (market versus government-oriented) or pluralism (competitive versus corporatist). All these idiosyncrasies have scattered the formerly government-related differences even more, but even they have not become the main, let alone the sole, determinants of EU lobby behaviour. Two multinational food producers or two public health insurers from the same country may behave quite differently on the EU playing field. The same applies to, for example, two food-policy units from the same national government, one belonging to the Ministry of Health and the other to that of Industry. In spite of their similarities of public accountability, control by politicians, bureaucratic procedures and food domain, they behave differently at the EU level.

As far as there exists one single initial determinant of lobby behaviour, it is, increasingly, the issue at stake, as perceived by the interest group itself. *Issue perception* drives behaviour initially, and is encompassed by other organisational and societal factors, including governmental ones. The perception may be a Pavlovian reaction, but is seldom so among the self-reliant lobby groups. They themselves assess a growing EU issue as either a threat or an opportunity, and develop a plan of action. If they want to interfere on the EU playing field, they construct their most efficient route to Brussels and develop their optimal coalition there. From the EU side they choose from the rich menus of actors, factors and vectors, including the metagame of Triple P. They make, in short, their prudent selection from the multiple issues, routes, stakeholders and access points available. They set the trend from ready-made towards *tailor-made* behaviour. As such they behave like the self-reliant chess players. Kasparov does not play in a standardised and thus predictable way, but always varyingly and thus surprisingly. Even more than the chessboard, the EU playing field requires a tailor-made approach, simply because it contains a higher number of options. Here there is neither a limit of time, players or strict rules, not even only one ball or one referee. An EU match is potentially infinite.

Even the lobby styles are tailored, so producing much more *campaign variety*. For example, the formal request to the Commission or the Parliament is increasingly shaped by semi-formal activities through expert groups or intergroups and even more by informal lobbying. As with a girl-friend, the desired support is usually substantially gathered informally, subsequently safeguarded by a semi-formal engagement, and formalised only at the successful end. Reversing this order will bring a bad result. The request itself, giving expression to one's demand side, is increasingly balanced by supplying behaviour. This demand side is, of course, not a negotiation chip and can best be kept in one's mind or on one's position paper, as it is only relevant for home consumption. One makes friends with one's supply side, even if this is only a show-case of charming flattery. The prudent lobby group even tailors its profile, usually beginning not with a high profile, but low-key and quietly. This style is less upsetting to the desired partner and causes less alarm for competitors. The high profile is kept in reserve for an emergency situation. An actor is not simply approached directly, but also frequently indirectly, such as through a trusty contact, a friendly coalition, an authoritative person or another effective U-turn. All this (and more) tailoring serves the ambition of escaping the overcrowded arena of competition and pushing the buttons of Brussels more efficiently and effectively, in short to achieve greater success. Self-reliance, prudent choice and tailor-made action are, in fact, three connected catchwords. They clearly require a lot of professional preparation or homework. We will return in the chapters to follow to this professionalisation of EU lobbying, which may be seen as a fourth specific new trend.

Extra: Country Profiles of EU Lobbying

Comprehensive and diachronic research into the styles of EU lobbying by pressure groups from the member countries does not exist, but a few studies at least give some insight. In the mid-1960s the styles were summarised [Spinelli, 1966] as 'the easy and smoothly operating Belgians, not making too much trouble'; 'the most difficult and obstinate Dutch, distrusting their southern neighbours and niggling about the most minute details'; 'the opportunistic Italians, with their fine sayings and lazy doings, and more obsessed with Rome than Brussels'; 'the dedicated Germans, wanting to reacquire esteem and acting with great sense of primordial duty'; and 'the ambivalent French, being both antagonistic and constructive, sending their best officers, and holding them to co-ordinated instructions'. The modest Luxembourgers were even then overlooked. A more recent study [Van Schendelen, 1993] provided evidence from different countries of the three aforementioned trends towards self-reliance, new collective platforms and tailored actions. More incidental observations are provided by the recent case studies referred to of EU interest group behaviour and by some country comparisons [Rometsch and Wessels, 1996; Meny and others, 1996; Hanf and Soetendorp, 1998; Siedentop, 1999; George and Bache, 2001; Kassim and others, 2001]. In addition there are the few studies using interviews with MEPs, consultants and trade organisations [Kohler-Koch, 1998], the many single-country studies and the views of practitioners in the field, as recorded in interviews and memoirs like Spinelli's above. Because of the lack of systematic research, the following summary of country profiles can only be a tentative sketch, to the best of our knowledge. It is limited to the member countries and thus neglects the lobbying of the EU from abroad, for example from applicant states and US companies [Andersen and Eliassen, 1993; Henning, 1993; Winand, 1998]. The summary is focused on the three trends above and on the major alleged differences in behaviour.

The larger countries

French interest groups have an old reputation of acting under co-ordination from the central government SGCI office. Much of this reputation is dubious. The large-sized SGCI (in 1999 about 50 co-ordinators plus 130 support staff) has become little more than an internship programme for young graduates from the *hautes écoles*, before they move to the specialised ministries or elsewhere. The main SGCI product is not the co-ordination of behaviour but the *cohérence* of policy standpoints. As the *plan indicative* (political planning) it is put on paper and believed to mean effectiveness. Many ministries, such as the one of Finance, have an even bigger and certainly more experienced office dealing with EU affairs. The conflicts between the *Matignon* (Prime Minister) and the *Elysée* (President) weaken central co-ordination, especially in times of *cohabitation*. Among and inside the many ministries, agencies, state companies, regional authorities, professional groups, private companies and other interest groups the issues tend to be perceived differently. This stimulates self-reliant behaviour to move in different directions at the EU level. The main exception to this rather pluralist pattern encompasses the issue areas of security (Pillar II) and IGCs (Treaty reform). But the unified approach here, with its regular emphasis on French autonomy, is the outcome more of dominance by the *Elysée* than of any co-ordination.

The main French areas of interests are agriculture and industry, which both have their own strong organisations. Strong trade and umbrella associations run agriculture, mainly based on small farming. Industry, from car manufacturing to consumer products and from chemicals to utilities, is highly concentrated and run by multinationals. Through a *pantouflage* of leaders the profit-oriented interest groups are closely connected to the specialised ministries in Paris and may even have a special desk there. The NGOs and particularly the trade unions lack such a connection. At the EU level most French interest groups prefer positive above negative integration and specific rather than general regulation. Their preference frequently exhibits a bias towards *mercantilism*. Political planning, with a strong input from experts and led by a hierarchy, is still popular, but now done by the pressure groups themselves. Inside the EU machinery, originally of French design, they usually turn the Triple P game into an art form, especially regarding formal actors, factors and vectors. They like to get their people nominated as the high officials of the bodies already positioned in the procedure that they have engineered as they desired. Their special appetite is for comitology. But often they mistake this meta-game for the end game, thus attaching more value to the formal setting than to the practical result. This partially explains their frequent problems with implementing EU decisions and the high incidence of infringement and Court procedures. Having decided on their plan of action, they tend to stick to it rigidly and to neglect the tailoring of their approaches. Their resulting behaviour is frequently formal, demanding, visible and direct, and as such not very surprising. In short, they are more inclined to apply the traditional influence techniques than the modern ones of public affairs management, although the latter become a close second.

British interest groups are marked by self-reliance. There is a Cabinet Office for EU Affairs, which has fewer than ten people, circulating between the specialist ministries. In addition to its standard preparation of the UK voting position for a Council meeting, it works mainly for the settlement of interdepartmental conflicts and for the special interests of the Prime Minister. The number of such conflicts is usually small, because the least that the different ministries want is the involvement of the full Cabinet. Under the John Major Cabinets, the special interests of Downing Street became more and more closely related to the survival of the Conservative Party. The practice of self-reliance was encouraged under the Thatcher Cabinets, as a side-effect of the general ideology of privatisation. The management of EU affairs was seen as a part of general management, for which not the central government but each regional or sectoral interest group itself is primarily responsible.

This *privatisation* of EU management has prompted many UK interest groups to develop their own EU routes, alliances, agendas and access points. While the UK government did not participate in the EU Social Protocol or the EMU, the British trade unions and financial organisations (the City) belonged to the most supportive EU lobby groups in Brussels. Many UK companies, regional authorities (particularly, but not only, from Scotland) and NGOs have given birth to new EuroFeds and particularly to ad-hoc groupings. They also tend to prefer negative above positive integration, general above specific regulation, and hard above soft law. Their approach is often at least partially tailor-made: informal and indirect in the promotion of an EU issue and agenda, but visible and demanding during the negotiations. The British largely developed the new styles of informal lobbying in the EU corridors, also partly as a result of their feelings of discomfort regarding both the formal institutions and the semi-formal work floors. Mainly UK interest groups stimulated the birth of EU agencies, officially for controlling the allegedly wrong practices of implementation and practically for using them as new access points for the relaunch of issues.

The *German* interest groups reveal in the EU the stamp of their federal or decentralised state, their sectoralism, and the economic weight of many of their organisations. The country has not one government, but sixteen (the regional *Länder* governments) plus one (the Federal one in Berlin), all fully equipped with their own ministries, parliament and court. Unlike other countries, the German regional governments are frequently less EU-minded than the national government. They already have a strong position inside their federation and feel less reason to substitute 'Berlin' for 'Brussels'. They all have a Brussels office, which they use particularly for watching both each other and the official federal Permanent Representation. Through their *Bundesrat*, the *Länder*-controlled federal 'Upper House', they even distribute the seats for the Council working groups. All ministries at the two levels tend to cherish the *Ressortprinzip* of rigid sectoralism, deepened by their *Expertenkultur* and making them reluctant to compromise with the other ministries at home on the policy positions they have developed and see as the best. Because of its internal disagreements, Germany is represented in many Council meetings by more than one minister and/or has to abstain from voting or to reject the proposal. National co-ordination is, in short, more a German daydream or nightmare than a reality. The implementation of EU decisions at home is another common problem, resulting in a lot of infringement procedures.

The many established German pressure groups usually prepare their EU position papers self-reliantly and thoroughly, drafted by many experts and signed by a hierarchy of chefs. This applies not only to the ministries and the agencies, but also to the private groups, from the Siemens company to the trade unions. Many have their own facility in Brussels, where for example the *Rue d'Arlon* is almost a *Deutsche Strasse*. However, most prefer to further their interests, first of all, as part of a German collective action on a sectoral and/or regional basis and frequently including a public-private partnership or *Konkordanz*. Subsequently they bring this to a European platform. Thanks to domestic practices they are accustomed to act through a multi-layered collectivity. In consequence, many German lobby groups find it difficult to tailor their approach, especially at the level of the Commission. Due to their multiple internal deliberations, they frequently arrive too late on the playing field and thus become dependent on the more formal and direct approaches. Their lobbyists in the field tend to have only a limited mandate. While the game is going on outside, they still wait for new instructions from their headquarters. Demanding and vociferous behaviour is, however, seldom a characteristic of German interest groups. In many cases, however, this is less a result of their tailor-made approach than of their fortunate position between the French and the British regarding issues of positive or negative integration, general or specific regulation and hard versus soft intervention.

For *Italian* interest groups self-reliance is hardly a choice. It is a necessity, because the country is fragmented by the *partitocrazia* of party politics, the regional antagonisms and the strong competition between big companies in particular. The country is more or less kept together by the formalistic bureaucracies of 'Rome'. Ministries, regional governments and private organisations are expected to allow their EU interests to be dealt with by the national government. Here the President's Council, the Ministry of Foreign Affairs and the Ministry of European Affairs cover EU affairs. Most other ministries have their own EU office as well, as do the regional governments, the major associations and the multinationals. The government of Rome they see as taking too much time, with formalities and other hindrances, and hardly encouraging expectations, let alone achieving great success in Brussels. The private interest groups usually operate through their domestic umbrellas, like *Confindustria* for business, which have their established or ad-hoc platforms at the European level. The larger ones and the regional governments have an office in Brussels as well, although they prefer to remain here within their *apartenenza*, their Italian network.

On the input side of the EU machinery the Italian interest groups and particularly the ministries have the reputation of more words than deeds, except for the collecting of subsidies. They hardly participate in the important policy debates, are frequently absent or simply applaud whatever the EU decides. Their record of implementing EU directives is usually one of the poorest in the EU. They even find it difficult to spend collected subsidies according to the rules. But, since the end of the 1990s, change is in the air. The new inspection practices on the EU output side were feeding back into Italian behaviour on the input side. The regional and sectoral interest groups from the north of Italy increasingly set the example of tailor-made actions. Playing the game with charm, informality and secrecy fits closely with the traditional virtues of their national politics. Additional U-turns are provided by sophisticated alliances, such as the fusion between the region of Piemonte and its main company Fiat or the cross-bordering axis from the

Lyon region in France to the state of Slovenia with the region of Lombardia in the middle.

The *Spanish* pressure groups in Brussels reveal their own mixture of features. They come from a German-like federal state, with 17 autonomous regions, almost all having a facility in Brussels. Both party politics and formalistic bureaucracies like those in Italy determine their central government in Madrid. As in France, the public and private interest groups want to have their EU actions prepared by many experts and approved by the high officials, with *coherencia* on paper as the ultimate criterion of success. Owing to the lack of large interest groups, like multinationals, there are hardly any trend-setting players at home. The main exception is the *Junta de Catalunya*, one of the first regions in Europe with an office in central Brussels. The many small-sized interest groups start their collective action at home through numerous domestic umbrellas, which usually travel the long route to Brussels self-reliantly.

On the playing field in Brussels, Spanish interest groups are notorious for arriving late, particularly at the Commission level. Like the Germans they spend too much of their time at home. Unlike the Italians, they remain committed players, keeping their words more in line with their deeds, which are usually poor as indicated by their low levels of implementation. Often discovering new proposals for legislation at a fairly late stage, after the draft has been published, they tend to resort to the next-best game of the so-called *exemption* lobby, which is more or less a Spanish innovation in the field of EU lobbying. Not being able to block the proposal, they try to get attached an additional article giving Spain an exemption to the rule for a number of years, as happened with the 1997 Telecom Liberalisation Directive. Thus, like the Italians, they do not comply with the ruling, but, unlike them, they manage to make it legal. Another Spanish speciality, also a next-best game and an exception to their slow behaviour, is the *subsidy* lobby. The regional and sectoral interest groups in particular tailor their actions in this area. Low-key, indirect, charming and informal, they try to influence, inside the Commission, the objectives and conditions of the coming subsidy programmes, so increasing their chances of gaining a greater share of the euros. But the Spanish negotiators at the Council level, mainly from the central government, frequently exhibit the exact opposite styles, making them unpopular here.

The smaller countries

The major *Dutch* public and private interest groups usually have a utilitarian preference for more supranational and negative integration. They believe in having more room to manoeuvre inside the Commission and the Parliament than inside the Council, where country size can be at their disadvantage. The high export ratio of the country (about 55% of GDP) makes many of the groups highly dependent on the open market, especially in such sectors as food, chemicals, electronics and transport. The traditionally autonomous interest groups have at their disposal numerous domestic umbrellas, public-private networks and European memberships. In the EuroFeds the Dutch frequently control the secretariat, which gives them some power over the agendas, meetings and budget. They feel, in short, at ease in EU collective groups and like to act self-reliantly. Trendsetters have been the Dutch multinational companies, some NGOs (like environmental groups and trade unions) and a few units of the central government, all having sufficient autonomy and size for an EU lobby. For example, the Ministry of Transport has almost as much policy personnel as the Commission. The Dutch pressure groups reveal a loose bureaucratic approach, and their lobbyists behave as *apparatchiks* with a free mandate. Most groups, however, have difficulties with tailor-made approaches. They like to make themselves widely heard and often see their demands as a generous offer to Europe. Their living at a short distance from Brussels is frequently turned into a disadvantage, because many tend to commute to the city by arriving in the morning and leaving in the evening, thus neglecting the informal networking. Even their Permanent Representative is eccentrically located on a road leading homewards out of the city. All this undermines the effectiveness of their favourite semi-formal behaviour.

The *Belgian* and *Luxembourger* interest groups belong to young states with a low sense of nationalism. Owing to their high export ratio (about 65% of GDP), they usually have strong utilitarian support for EU market integration, except for the (protected) banking sector. Their behaviour may be best characterised by the catchword of 'pragmatism', being the academic name for the absence of a clear pattern of behaviour. They can afford to behave like that, because, living at an extremely short distance, they can hardly escape the informal networking, and they enjoy the overrepresentation of their countrymen at almost all levels of the Commission, totalling roughly one-quarter of all personnel. Due to the language issue at home, most Belgian interest groups, however, are organised at only the regional level and subsequently linked to the EuroFeds. The three Belgian regional governments (Flandres, Wallonia, Brussels) have their own people inside the Belgian PR. The public interest groups, in particular, from both countries are French-styled bureaucracies: driven by experts and bound by formalistic chefs. Their mutual distrust is a major source of self-reliance. The behaviour of most lobby groups looks tailor-made: informal, silent, indirect and charming. They are well known for linking up with a stronger foreign lobby group to achieve their ends, but this free-riding behaviour is mainly the result not of their homework but of their 'Catholic' feeling for opportunities.

The *Nordic* countries (Denmark, Sweden, Finland) have a strong sense of nationalism, a practice of decentralisation and an open market orientation. Their interest groups have many conditions in common: Brussels is far away, which is a hindrance for intense informal networking. The Swedish and Finnish groups are, as late members (1995), neither widely nor deeply nestled inside the EU machinery. Free collective action at EU level is seen as normal and practised especially by the few multinational firms. The majority of small-sized interest groups tend to approach Brussels via a national public-private partnership. Their main method of entry is via the PR at the Council level, which is late in the process and detached from most dossiers. Their limited governments hardly intervene in the lobby behaviour of the interest groups, except when their national parliaments make use of their power to instruct a minister on the voting position in the Council. The value of national democracy is, then, often at odds with that of EU success, because an instructed minister can hardly negotiate. To solve the problem, the new trend is for the government to draft the parliament's instruction. Coming from wealthy countries with a strong tradition of welfare, the Nordic groups inside the EU are usually in favour of careful spending and social and environmental policies in particular. Their 'Protestant' home culture makes them supporters of EU regime values such as transparency and accountability. By keeping their words in line with their deeds, they have the reputation of predictability, which frequently reduces their lobby effectiveness. Tailor-made behaviour mainly comes from the few multinational companies and the national umbrellas. The lobby groups from the government, however, often excel in direct, formal, vociferous and demanding behaviour, especially at the Council level.

The *Irish, Portuguese* and *Greek* interest groups have, of course, many differences between themselves. For example, the Irish groups have relatively strong interests in the issue areas of industry, trade and the open market, while those from Portugal and Greece have their bias towards protected agriculture and small enterprises. The Irish groups act highly informally and via self-determined national alliances, often in a public-private partnership and led by their few MNCs. They meet in, for example, the Irish pub *Kitty O'Shea* in central Brussels, which functions as a sort of informal PR for all Irishmen. Portuguese and Greek groups come from a much more formalistic society. Their government likes to control its ministries and to intervene in the private sector. The two countries lack MNCs to counter the government. Due to their lack of sufficient size and other resources, the private groups can hardly act self-reliantly. For the remote control of the EU, they remain dependent on their government and their national umbrellas, which are frequently linked to the government. But their government puts more effort into the production of coherent position papers at home than in the active lobbying of Brussels. The three countries have, however, much in common too: they are at a far and geographically isolated distance from Brussels; both clientelistic party politics and rising regionalism fragment all three; their people usually play a marginal role on the input side of the EU machinery; like the Spanish they keep their focus on both the exemption and the subsidy lobbies; they have achieved a great reputation for milking the structural funds; and their records on implementing EU legislation and the subsidy allocations effectively are weak. In tailoring their actions, the Irish are more politic than the Portuguese and the Greek, especially by acting informally and low-key.

Finally, the *Austrian* interest groups are stigmatised by their national corporatism, the academic euphemism for being held together by distrust. Formalistic as they are, they see the Council level as decisive and many have managed to get representation in the Austrian PR's office, primarily for watching each other. Found here are representatives from the federal government and all nine *Länder* governments, the organisations of employers and employees, and major business groups like the Chamber of Commerce and banks. This large and mixed public-private PR, entitling the major private groups to be present in the Council working groups, is the recent (1995) Austrian contribution to EU influence practices. Other interest groups are found in the Austrian House, central Brussels. Only a few have their own separate office as well. Various government units at both the federal and the *Länder* level try to co-ordinate the Austrian public and private interest groups. These units, in their turn, are often instructed by the formally powerful parliaments at the two levels. This creates the same dilemma between national democracy and EU effectiveness as in the Nordic countries. Big organisations, which might act as trendsetters of EU lobbying, are absent. National group formation is seen as a necessity, but takes much time and energy and means that Austrian interest groups arrive late within the EU processes. Since some have their own links with both the EU work floors and the EuroFeds, there is a rising trend of self-reliance, particularly among the regions. Tailor-made actions remain an exception, but on many an EU dossier the Austrian interest groups form part of the winning coalition. The explanation for this is that, like for the Germans, they hold centre positions, which lie close to the final compromise. An example is the 1999 EU policy programme on Sustainable Agriculture, which comes close to the Austrian practice of farming.

Professional EU Public Affairs Management

Of the three previously mentioned trends in lobbying practices, the first two are most visible. Self-reliance and collective action are becoming the rule rather than the exception. The third trend of tailored lobbying is still new, but increasingly visible among MNCs, large NGOs, regional governments and parts of a few central governments. Other pressure groups see it as an example to follow. The growing belief is that in any EU arena tailored behaviour is necessary and should be much improved. The catchword for this is *professionalisation*, which stands in contrast to amateurism. The professional should, of course, not be confused with the full-time lobbyist or consultant, who may also behave like an amateur.

The professional is somebody who is capable of identifying more options for behaviour and can optimise choices that score better on effectiveness (goal realisation) and efficiency (cost-benefit ratio). The professional in EU Public Affairs Management (EU PAM) fine-tunes the approach of actors, the use of factors and the creation of vectors. The meta-game of Triple P is typically the work of the professional. Of all this 'pushing the buttons of Brussels' the objective (dependent variable) remains the winning of the game or, as secondary pay-offs, an encouraging compromise, respect or backing. By professionalisation, the factor (independent variable) of political expertise can be brought to a higher level. As the precondition for all this tailor-made fieldwork is seen as *intelligent and prudent homework*, it is useful to compare it with the thinking of Kasparov before he moves a chess piece. The motives behind each are comparable: the game is difficult, because the playing field is complex and dynamic; the outcome is seen as highly relevant, since the prizes are so interesting; and the increasingly strong competition gives birth to a 'premier league' of smart players. Darwin could have rephrased his law in terms of the survival of the political fittest here. The difference is made particularly by political expertise.

Regarding the fieldwork, intelligent interest groups frequently puzzle over the question *'what is better to do?'*: for example, to strive for supranational or intergovernmental EU decision-making, to have co-ordinated or self-reliant units, to politicise or depoliticise an issue, to enter a standing or a flexible alliance, or to behave actively or passively? The amateur player hardly considers such dilemmas or solves them dogmatically. For the professional the answer always is: '*it depends*'. The next question, then, is: '*on what?*'. This is a matter of consideration or homework regarding the crucial variables, many of which can be manipulated for the creation of the desired outcome. These variables are countless, as they include all sorts of actors, factors and vectors. The amateur may see this infinite menu of options as a confusing problem and may prefer to play at random. The professional, however, sees it as an opportunity for greater effectiveness and efficiency, because it provides many ways and means to the desired outcome and enables optimisation of the fieldwork. Tailoring the fieldwork also is full of questions that need consideration, regarding both oneself and other players, such as '*who acts, why, for what, to whom, where, on what, when, how, and with what result?*'. They apply to all lobby groups, including the EU officials.

These questions of professional EU public affairs management are summarised in *figure 3.3*, with a breakdown for key activities respectively of homework and fieldwork. The figure can be seen as composed of modules for learning. The player at *Kindergarten* level has only an emotional approach to some perceived event (or non-event) and only one question: how to promote or to prevent that event? Without further thoughts, the player immediately tries to lobby others on the field and to open some door, a revolving door. Then the learning process starts. At *primary school* level the

Professional public affairs management

Question	Homework: analysing	Fieldwork: organising
1. who acts?	the internal organisation	improving the organisation
2. why?	threats and opportunities	choosing the strategy
3. for what?	options	determining the targets
4. to whom?	crucial actors	making relations, networks
5. where?	arenas	forming coalitions
6. on what?	dossiers and issues	bargaining
7. when?	time and agenda phase	timing, agenda-building
8. how?	methods, techniques, routes	lobbying
9. & result?	process evaluation	learning

Figure 3.3

player begins to wonder about reality and to pose a range of questions (the first column in the figure). Advancing to the *secondary school*, the player believes he or she understands the world and even knows how to improve it. Quick answers are provided (third column). If a clear strategy is needed, it is arrived at within three months. If a network has to be built up, a start is made on networking; with whom hardly matters, but there will be a network soon. The player becomes a doer, full of energy, spending many resources, but hardly scoring. A few players go on to the *university* level. They learn to think about all options for playing and about the best choices to make (middle column). They think about ways of doing better. They are more and more taken as an example to follow by others.

The various questions in the figure have been placed in a seemingly logical order. They start with oneself (Q 1-3), are followed by those regarding the arena, with issues and stakeholders involved (Q 4-6), continue with questions related to precise timing and tailored lobbying (Q 7-8), and end with the question of whether the desired result has been achieved at all (Q 9). In practice this order is rarely the real order. Usually all the questions are on the table at the same time, and remain so. Neither is the presented order necessarily logical or politico-logical. Players may start to approach the world from their own standpoint and preferences, but they may be wiser if they reverse this direction and first try to understand the world around them before taking a position. This is our approach from now on. In the next chapter we shall focus on the questions regarding the EU arena with its issues and stakeholders (Q 4-6). Chapter 5 is focused on the EU public affairs agenda inside the home organisation (Q 1-3 plus 9). Chapter 6 is devoted to the external fieldwork, including timing and lobbying (Q 7-8).

CHAPTER 4

MANAGING THE EU ARENA

How to Lobby Better?

The simple-minded or amateurish lobby group will regard this question as superfluous. It knows what it wants to get from the EU officials and it finds their names and addresses in some EU directory. Then it approaches them as directly as possible and it tries to convince them that their best response is to comply with the demand soon. If it gets a refusal, it will probably make a lot of noise, on both the national and the EU scene, and launch a second strike, now joined by a number of 'friends' that it has found in the meantime. It may also get some advice from a semi-amateurish or semi-professional group already with some experience on the EU playing field. Then it may follow some rules of thumb. For example, that the best actors to approach are one's national PR officials, one's countrymen in the Parliament and one's regional officials in the Commission DG, and that the best way of approaching them is a free lunch together with some friends. The conscious or professional lobby group watching the meeting critically considers this charming, informal, quiet and indirect approach as usually better than the opposite, confrontational style, but not necessarily the best.

The professional group knows that, in the competitive EU arena, the best way to lobby always depends on the specific situation. Sometimes even a formal, demanding, noisy and/or direct style may be the best. The professional group considers, first of all, the broad concept of 'the situation'. Nowadays it is taken as a synonym for arena and broken down into at least the four elements of stakeholders, issues, time and arena boundaries. The second thing to think about is how to collect useful information on these important elements. By making such an *arena analysis* the professional group can identify its friends and enemies, the issues at stake, the time aspects and the differences between the insiders and the outsiders. All this is a matter of window-out preparatory work at home. Then it may know how to lobby, whom to lobby, where and on what issues most effectively and efficiently. Through window-in activities it can subsequently apply the best practices of managing an EU arena and its four constituent parts. All this puzzling regarding an EU chessboard may nowadays be seen as sensible and logical, not to say self-evident. However, in daily practice the majority of lobby groups still behave more amateurishly than professionally. The quest for useful knowledge is apparently not so obvious a requirement as is assumed. Anyhow, it has taken three waves of intellectual thinking before it has become established, in at least the theory. The driving force behind it has come from mainly scholars in the USA.

The Predecessors of Arena Analysis

The first wave may be called the *ruler analysis*. It is the oldest and most classical one. A group or, at the lowest level, a citizen may feel to have a strong interest in the outcome of some political decision-making and may want to influence the authority formally entrusted with making the decision. For this purpose it tries to collect useful information about the highest official in charge, in order to increase the chance of success. In modern language, this approach is a form of actor analysis, but limited to the top official. In the old days the King or the Prince was the highest ruler to be approached. In his *Il Principe*, Machiavelli gives both free advice to his ruler, Lorenzo dei Medici, on how to survive politically and, more implicitly, a code of conduct to his fellow citizens on how to approach Lorenzo successfully. More recently, until the mid-1970s, the US scholars studied interest group behaviour particularly for its impact on the formally ruling institutions such as the Congress and the President [Key, 1964] and on the elected officials such as the Congressmen [Milbrath, 1963; Scott & Hunt, 1965]. Examining the safety of private investments in foreign countries, US scholars also developed the study of political risks coming from changes of rulers there [Coplin and O'Leary, 1976 and 1983]. An American scholar applied the ruler analysis to the EU [Gardner, 1991] by equating 'effective lobbying' with an understanding of the EU institutions. This type of knowledge is certainly still necessary, but it is also insufficient. Its drawback is the assumption of political hierarchy or central rule, neglecting the presence of both negotiable issues and stakeholders intervening from outside the formal leadership of the organisation.

The second wave is described as *issue analysis*. It started in the late 1960s, as a chapter of ruler analysis, under the flag of policy studies. Authoritative institutions and officials came to be placed in a dynamic perspective, namely as producers of public policies. They make their choice, called policy, from a surplus of more or less contested specific facts, values and instruments, in short from a menu of issues [Heath, 1997, 44 and 84]. American scholars have linked the study of policy-making to that of interest groups from business in particular[Bauer and Pool, 1960; Bauer and others, 1963]. Others, subsequently, broke the concept of policy down into issues and presented their issue analysis as a tool, called issue management, to interest group managers [Brown, 1979; Kingdon, 1984; Buchholz and others, 1985; Heath and Nelson, 1986; Buchholz, 1990; Frederick and others, 1996; Heath 1997]. They also made a key distinction between opportunities and threats, which are assessed as issues having respectively a positive and a negative effect on a specific interest group. US-educated people within the EU [Andersen, 1992; EC Committee, 1994] were soon promoting this approach. In many cases the issue analysis remained closely linked to the ruler analysis, resulting in the study of issues inside, for example, the US Congress [Hojnack and Kimball, 1998] and the EU Commission [Emerson and others, 1988].

One chapter of issue analysis has become most popular among interest groups: *the life cycle of an issue*. The contestation or dispute over a specific fact, value or instrument may start life silently. At this stage, it is, for example, widely considered to be futile or it remains unnoticed. At some point it may emerge into the public arena, usually lasting at the most ten years, and attract public attention in the form of a bell curve: rising boisterously, achieving some settlement and sinking to slumber or death [Tombari, 1984]. A similar biography may apply to a set of connected issues, called a policy dossier. The *dossier life cycle (figure 4.1)* begins with the rise of a so-called 'social problem' (phase 1), which may attract mass public attention and thus get the status of a political problem (phase 2), whereupon it may be placed on the official agenda (phase 3) and become subject to decision-making (phase 4), after which the decision may be implemented (phase 5) and then inspected for its effectiveness (phase 6). This life cycle has a stylised order here, but, anticipating chapter six, its real life may be like that of a human being and, for example, suffer an early death, never get wide recognition or remain indeterminate. Viewed in retrospect, however, any established policy has more or less followed the life history of the cycle, like an *éminence grise*. All this knowledge, derived from issue analysis, is still useful and necessary. It may help, for example, to cosset a growing opportunity or to kill a new threat in its early phase. But it is also insufficient, with its main default being that it is based on a closed system of communication and interaction between the interest group as sender and the group of officials as receiver. It neglects the open and dynamic competition from intervening stakeholders.

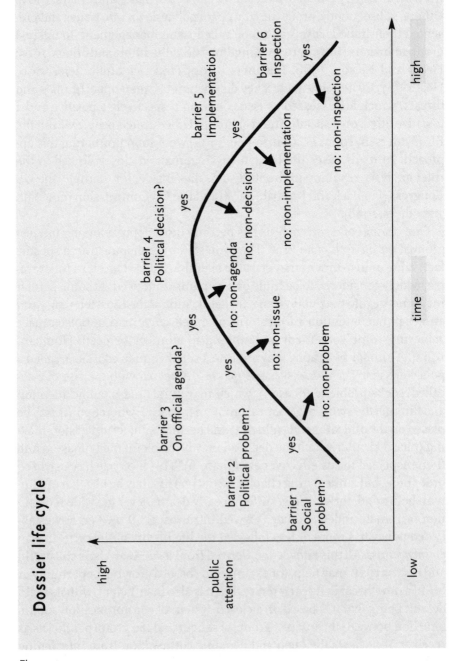

Figure 4.1

The third wave of research is *stakeholder analysis,* which took hold in the USA during the mid-1980s [Freeman, 1984; Carroll, 1989; Alkhafaji, 1989; Huxham, 1996; Freeman, 1999]. A stakeholder is broadly defined as another player affecting the performance of an interest group or, in turn, being affected by the group [Mitchell and others, 1997]. The other player may be a competitive private or public lobby group, or possibly the ruling authority itself, for example the Commission official or the Parliament commission sitting in the driver's seat on an issue. A stakeholder, in short, is an interest group as well. It holds a stake or a position in an issue area. In a pluralist society an interest group has always to cope with a variety of stakeholders having an interest in the same issue or the same dossier. The study of their behaviour is, technically, a multiple actors analysis. The stakeholders want to push their own interest and to block any opposing interest. They intervene in both the policy process and in the relationships between competitors and officials. Usually adopting a position during the life of the dossier at stake, they may become either a supportive friend or a determined enemy and join some coalition. Others remain ambivalent or indifferent, as a result either of really mixed feelings or of calculated negotiation behaviour [Savage and others, 1991]. There may even be capricious stakeholders, who give the impression of having an interest in the matter, but who in fact only want to build up nuisance value to be used regarding a different matter. At EU level, the stakeholder analysis is applied both by practitioners and in a few case studies of EU lobby behaviour [Pedler and Van Schendelen, 1994; Greenwood, 1995; Wallace and Young, 1997-A]. All this knowledge is still quite useful and necessary, but its strength is also its drawback. Its focus on the stakeholders suggests that the political outcome is essentially produced only by their interplay.

Arena Analysis: Going Window-Out

Whereas all three aforementioned types of analysis are considered both necessary and insufficient, they deserve to be synthesised into one more comprehensive approach. This fourth wave is called *arena analysis.* An arena here is not a physical place, but the virtual collection of all the stakeholders, including the officials, together with their issues regarding a specific dossier at a specific moment. Taken as a whole, it means 'the situation' on which the answer to the question 'what is the best thing to do?' depends. Neither issues nor stakeholders are the sole impetus towards the best action, although both are relevant, and include the lobbying group itself. In addition to these two elements of every arena, time has also to be taken into account as a third relevant one. Time provides both opportunities and constraints, so here the concept of the dossier life cycle is again appropriate. The fourth and last relevant element is the composition of all stakeholders and issues at any moment. This is never limited or fixed, but always variable and dynamic. Old stakeholders and issues can leave and new ones enter and so the boundaries of an arena have to be researched carefully. In order to optimise its actions, the professional lobby group is, in short, *situation-driven*. However, most EU lobbying is still merely issue-driven and/or stakeholder-driven, as it neglects time and boundaries. Therefore, most lobby groups can still improve the quality of their actions.

Arena analysis is aimed at neither more nor less than the acquisition of *realistic insights* regarding a particular dossier at a specific moment, to enable a more successful lobby action. In the best case it is not performed once, like taking a still photograph, but repetitiously, like filming the battle-field. It is as useful for a company or an NGO as for a national ministry or an EU Directorate. The analysis of the arena precedes the action, as the description of the arena precedes the analysis. In fact, it is all a matter of risk assessment [Fischoff and others, 1981; Douglas, 1985; Gigerenzer and others, 1989]. The homework of description and analysis takes time and other resources, but usually much less so and with better results than random action. Going window-out before the action starts is almost always cost-saving and highly rewarding. As such it is clearly not a goal in itself, but a major instrument with which to make the window-in lobby more effective and efficient. As in the complex and dynamic games of chess or war, proactive investigation and critical reflection are the best investments. Frequently they make the major difference between the winners and the losers.

The volume of preparatory work varies, of course, with each game. Complexity and dynamics are always variables, and really simple games seldom exist. Even a game under Pillar II or III is complex. True enough, the Commission, the Parliament and the Court play hardly any or no formal role here at all, but in informal ways or via side-dossiers they might participate, like other interest groups do. The unanimity rule, which prevails in these Pillars, looks easy, but is only so if one wants to prevent an undesired decision. If one tries to push for a decision, the unanimity game becomes extremely intense. It requires a lot of homework regarding the issues and the positions of the national ministers, even on different dossiers that can be linked together. On the other hand, not all games in Pillar I are necessarily difficult, as the 1992 Slots Case may show [Van den Polder, 1994]. National air carriers, like Lufthansa and Air France, were easily able to keep their private distribution of landing rights (slots) safe from EU intervention, which was demanded by new carriers like Virgin and Lauda Air, by jointly mobilising their ministers in the Transport Council. As a compromise, to please the Commission, they ceded ten percent of the slots to the new carriers. In this case all four arena elements were relatively easy to handle.

Describing the Arena

What is the best thing to do, depends on the situation. Believing this, the studious lobby group wants to know in what sort of an arena it is before it starts any action. For each selected dossier, it wants to identify again and again the relevant stakeholders, the issues at stake, the aspects of time and the boundaries of the arena. It goes window-out.

Stakeholders
The serious lobby group starts with drawing up an *inventory* of the stakeholders, including the officials and itself. They are all players or actors, who can affect or are affected by its performance and, because of this, may intervene. A few officials even play a dual role, as they are both a stakeholder and, in a (co)decision capacity, a (co)'ruler'. In this chapter we assume that the lobby group itself is cohesive and that its objectives are stable; in the next chapter we will challenge this assumption. The inventory is not biased towards only friends or enemies or towards only formal entities. One can best compare it with military scouting: all warriors, whatever their preference, are respected for their weapons and thus taken seriously. On a specific dossier a Greek group of farmers may be as relevant as the French President or a Commission expert. Even non-EU players may have to be taken into account, such as the Thai exporters on the tapioca dossier, the mid-American countries on bananas and the World Trade Organisation (WTO) on external trade liberalisation.

All this may sound trivial, but in practice most interest groups fail to perform satisfactorily at this first step of arena monitoring, and many are in fact *biased* in their approach to scouting. National ministries tend to neglect both local governments and private interest groups and to see the EU arena as a sort of intergovernmental field of battle. Many a business group neglects the intervening role of some national ministry, frequently because it does not want to see this. On the other hand, NGOs are often comparatively good at unbiased scouting in the arena. A second regular mistake made by many interest groups is to *deify* the stakeholders, putting them in, for example, 'the British position', as if such a stakeholder ever exists. However, every country is pluralistic and thus always divided regarding every dossier. At best, there may be a statement from the British Cabinet or Prime Minister, which is only perfunctorily supported by the national ministries. In reality they may go their own way, as do many other UK stakeholders. The same holds true for the position of, for example, Greenpeace, Siemens or the Commission. Accurate scouting requires that stakeholders be inventoried at the lowest relevant level. This level may be just a person or a unit of a larger organisation. An unbiased and specific inventory usually results in a long list of stakeholders, especially in the early phase of a game. In later phases its length is usually reduced to only a few coalitions. Anyhow, no information potentially relevant for a later phase should be lost at the start.

The identified stakeholders must be assessed in terms of relevance. A relevant stakeholder is one who is expected both to intervene actively and to possess sufficient influence capabilities to become effective. The stakeholders are, as it were, placed along two continua: one ranging from active to passive and the other from strong to weak. Regarding the first continuum, falling under the study of political *participation*, it is not enough to include only the stakeholders who are obviously participating. Many others may be active in an indirect or hidden way, for example via a caretaker, or they may become active soon. Key variables, discussed in the first chapter, are their desires, capabilities, invitations and compulsions to participate. The second continuum covers particularly those capabilities, maybe better known as the study of political *resources*, such as financial means, expertise, skills, affiliations, personnel, reputation, networks and other assets [Schlozman and Tierney, 1986]. They indicate the stakeholder's potential to become an influential player. Potential influence should, however, never be equated with real influence, as an army with many capabilities is not necessarily victorious. Most relevant are the so-called primary stakeholders, identified as both prone to action and potentially highly influential. Those who are assessed as remaining passive and/or as falling short of sufficient potential influence can be treated as stakeholders of secondary importance. They should not be deleted, but be placed on a memory list. In another phase in life of the dossier they may become primary, and the reverse may happen as well. The drawing up of the inventory of relevant stakeholders clearly requires a lot of intelligent monitoring. The smartest stakeholders will try to play both passivity and impotence, like a cat apparently sleeping on the roof but really watching the birds. The most assertive stakeholders, suggesting they can hardly refrain from strong action, may be like barking, but seldom biting, dogs. The outcome of all this preparatory homework is nothing more than a reasoned estimate, but this is much better than nothing. It enables prudent measures to be taken with regard to every major stakeholder [Hunger and Wheelen, 1998, 112].

Issues

Every stakeholder is driven by its own interests, which are chosen positions regarding what happens in its environment. They represent the daydreams and nightmares regarding, in the case we are considering, the EU playing field. The stakeholder likes to promote and to preserve the daydreams and prevent or resolve the nightmares. Together they determine its lobby agenda. The chosen positions are always a balance between the values it cherishes and the facts it perceives. How a stakeholder comes to a chosen position or to the definition of its interest and how it can come to a better choice or definition, will be discussed in the next chapter. The focus now is on the *identification* of interests covering the cherished values and the perceived facts, as held by the stakeholders in an arena. Many of them will dispute the values and facts, and the same holds true for the policy instruments put forward to preserve a daydream or resolve a nightmare. Issues are, in short, disputed facts, values and instruments. A professional lobby group wants to know about these issues precisely. Because of the EU practice of decision-making by compromise, it has to know what the issues are and for which conflicting interests they stand. If it possesses this information, it can make itself more interesting to the other stakeholders and thus become part of the final compromise. That relevant information is, of course, necessary but never sufficient for getting the desired or satisfying outcome. However, without it a lobby group cannot influence the outcome and remains dependent on sheer luck.

Again this may sound trivial and self-evident, but this makes it even more surprising that most lobby groups fail to acquire this type of knowledge. They live in their own world and see the EU officials as the formal and only rulers. On their chosen values and perceived facts, they feel that their interest position is perfectly right. Subsequently, they can make two big mistakes. The first is one of *arrogance*: believing that their own position is perfect, they may expect that many other stakeholders, maybe after some enlightenment, will finally share their excellent position. The second is one of *naivety*: still believing they are right, they may come to the conclusion that those not sharing that position must be wrong. They are like the theatre-goer who considers that the other members of the audience that evening must either share his opinion about the play or be stupid. All theatre-goers, however, see the same play from a different position, interpret it differently and go home with a different intention for tomorrow [Cherry, 1966]. Likewise, the other stakeholders may be perfectly right about their different lobby agenda, simply because they cherish different values and perceive different facts. For example the 1998 Laying Hen Dossier, aimed at allocating more space and comfort for laying hens, was considered by the industrial egg producers as an additional cost, by the traditional farmers as a comparative advantage, by the suppliers of cages as new business, by the animal welfare groups as free publicity and by some northern ministries as a subsidy expenditure, and that is just to mention five of the stakeholders. All this pluralism of interests reflects the relativism of values and facts in practice. The amateurish groups may finally learn to accept the different positions of the other players as a matter of fact. But being late and frequently still lacking respect for them, they can hardly develop an early and interesting supply side, necessary for the acceptance of their own demand side.

The identification of current issues is, indeed, not easy at all. It is especially difficult to identify the *real agenda* of the primary stakeholders in particular. Their official statements can never be taken at face value. On a single issue or a specific dossier the other professional players can disguise their internal divisions, remain silent or cover their real interests. The many amateurish stakeholders may hardly have a real agenda at all. Behind their so-called interests, then, lie only badly reasoned values and poorly perceived facts, which may need reassessment soon. The discovery of the real agendas clearly requires a lot of knowledge and understanding of the stakeholders. As in diplomacy one has to monitor their internal arenas at home, their dominant values and their perceptions of reality. From this information one may deduce their real interests or real agendas. On every dossier almost every stakeholder appears to have various real interests, which are taken as friendly, hostile or indifferent by the other stakeholders. On the friendly ones one can build a coalition, over the hostile ones one may have to fight and for the indifferent ones one can give support cheaply. One can even mix it up and make a trade-off between friendly and hostile interests. Such preparatory homework to examine a reluctant stakeholder can be used on another dossier. The five stakeholders mentioned on the Laying Hen Dossier are all involved in other EU dossiers as well. By bringing together different dossiers one can settle almost any current issue. It is all a matter of knowledge first.

Time

An EU arena continuously changes with time. The professional lobby group is conscious of the relevance of *time analysis*. From general experience it knows that in the early phase of a dossier's life normally many stakeholders and issues are at stake; that during the dossier's life most stake-holders become part of larger coalitions and most issues part of a package; and that in the end-phase of an EU decision process usually only two groups still exist, namely the proponents and the opponents of the proposal, and only a few issues are left, such as 'the envelope' (who pays the bill), the date of taking effect and any exemptions demanded. The professional group also knows that the dossier's life is only partially regulated by procedures setting deadlines, for example of formal consultation or codecision. In most cases, it just develops naturally. Then, somewhere in Europe a difference is seen as irritating, is raised to the EU playing field, adopted on an official agenda, challenged by other stakeholders, mixed up with different issues, processed into the EU machinery and, finally, decided, implemented and inspected, or not, as the case may be. Some stakeholders act under pressure of time, others have all the time in the world. Those in a losing mood like to delay, those in a winning one to speed up. Time, therefore, distributes both constraints and opportunities. All this is general wisdom that the professional organisation possesses, but in every real situation it has again to define it precisely, or else the group cannot fine-time its activities.

Most lobby groups are *nonchalant* about time. Usually they enter an arena after the dossier has received public attention, which is frequently halfway through its life. Most dossiers falling under delegated decision-making will never get that attention and be missed altogether. The nonchalant groups are often too late to join a growing opportunity or to stop a growing threat. In a later phase, they may yet become aware of the many different players and issues. If they take a still photograph of the arena at all, they can easily mistake it for the film. They are hardly aware of the developments of coalition building and package-dealing. They believe that they can meet the few formal deadlines at 'five to twelve', or even later, thus neglecting the unfixed nature of the dossier's life. They easily underestimate or overestimate the urgency of any state of affairs. They are also not aware of the winning or losing moods of the other stakeholders. In short, they can hardly act effectively, let alone proactively. Delaying or speeding up the process is beyond their capacity. Their lobbying is like extinguishing one fire after another and is directed only at preventing the growing threats, not at promoting opportunities. They may consider fire-fighting as efficient but it is much less effective than setting up a fire-prevention programme.

The *calculation of time* is clearly not easy. The dossier's life cycle remains an abstraction of reality, to be updated at any time. For example the early phase of problem definition may be full of implicit decision-making that is binding subsequently. The early framing of the Laying Hen Dossier as a problem of animal welfare strongly determined its outcomes. The so-called inspection phase may be full of additional decisions, now at the more detailed level, which is for many stakeholders the most relevant one. The best thing, of course, is to remain alert. The professional lobby group regularly updates its inventories of stakeholders and issues, links these with the formal deadlines, if existing, reassesses the newly found situation in terms of time constraints and opportunities, and tries, if necessary, to delay or to speed up the process. It can, of course, be misled by other professional stakeholders, who suggest that there is either all the time in the world or no time left. By verifying this it may avoid being ultimately misled by itself. Even if all this time knowledge is based on an estimate, it is still better than nothing. It enables intervention to be more carefully timed and less haphazard.

Boundaries

Just as an arena is permanently changing over time, it is also always changing in composition, and so the studious interest group explores the *arena boundaries*. They are never fixed. Every stakeholder can introduce new issues and every issue can attract new stakeholders. Formal procedures can also partially determine the composition of an arena. When a dossier attracts wider public attention, many more stakeholders and issues may become part of the arena. This frequently happens in the formal decision phase, especially at the Council level. The Laying Hen Dossier started as a mini-arena on animal welfare, but subsequently it attracted the attention of the egg producers, thus raising the issue of cost. But costs are a relative affair on a market being partially a global market, and so the importers of non-EU eggs, used in the food-processing industry, saw a great opportunity for themselves. The trade unions, however, assessed this shift from production to trade as a threat to employment and raised the issue of health conditions for labour under the new cage system. Stakeholders can also leave the arena, for example because they see another arena as more promising, and thus they take their issues with them. Such volatility of the arena boundaries is normal for every open society and no different from the case of the garden where animals searching for food come and go.

Most lobby groups neglect the arena boundaries. They consider the composition of an arena to be static, like a photograph. They hardly pay attention to the stakeholders and the issues that disappear from the arena, nor do they notice those that enter. By consequence, they seldom care about the causes and the consequences of this *boundary traffic*, which may be highly relevant for their own position as well. Through this lack of understanding they can hardly anticipate future events, and they are taken by surprise. Proactive action, aimed at attracting new stakeholders and new issues or at removing old ones, is almost beyond their mental scope. In the Laying Hen case the animal welfare groups should have tried to keep the boundaries closed. At least they should have anticipated the entrance of the farmers, the producers and the trade unions, all raising new issues. Their entrance changed the arena and the outcome for the animal welfare groups radically.

The professional lobby group explores the *volatility* of the arena boundaries. It monitors those who enter or leave and their agendas. From these traffic statistics it tries to deduce the next developments for the coalition-building, the package-dealing and the time schedule. Thus it gives itself the opportunity to anticipate events. Proactively, it can try to get new supportive stakeholders and issues on board and maybe to get rid of annoying ones. It also broadens its homework to neighbouring dossiers or arenas. Their partial overlap can be used for either stimulating cross-traffic or for erecting roadblocks, in short for pushing or blocking the combination of issues. It also knows that the public's attention to a dossier is the single most important determinant of the entrance of new stakeholders and issues. It is therefore prudent in making a noise itself. Only in a real emergency case full of threats may noise help to prevent at least an immediate loss, as it may attract new stakeholders and issues and thus delay the decision-making process. This fine-tuning is dependent on the quality of the boundary analysis. Even if this is only based on estimates, it is much better than nothing. It can make the difference between winning and losing.

The Satisfactory Description

A lobby group may consider the description of the four arena characteristics to be costly and troublesome homework. There are, of course, always problems attached to getting valid and relevant insights into the state of the arena at a specific moment. The perfectly complete and reliable summary of an arena is beyond human reach. This is partially due to practical circumstances, such as the volatility of an arena, particularly in its early phases, or the lack of time for arriving at the ultimate description. And partially it is caused by the extremity of the two norms of completeness and reliability confronting the desire for the greatest realism. As often, the best is the enemy of the better here. By critically reviewing the two norms one can come to satisfying next-best solutions.

The norm of *completeness* should be considered an utopia. Because of the absence of fixed arena boundaries, there is by definition no stable criterion of completeness. New stakeholders and issues may arise and old ones may disappear continually. By internal divisions a stakeholder may break down into many different ones and by successful negotiations these many may form a new coalition. A current issue may have a similarly turbulent life. Completeness, as every historian knows, exists at the most for only a moment, and even then it is almost a daydream. This is still more so for the diachronic description over a longer time period. The second norm of *reliability* can be considered equally impossible to realise perfectly in practice. Among the stakeholders there are always some who give the impression of having an interest, who remain silent as the cat on the roof, or who bark like only apparently vicious dogs, in short who mislead the observer. Some relevant stakeholders who would normally take a position may even be absent, owing to, for example, internal problems. The perceived relevance of stakeholders is, by definition, only potential and not yet proven by their impact. Every stakeholder can, in addition, always reassess a threat as an opportunity or the reverse and thus redefine its stake in the dossier. Because of the practical and the fundamental obstacles of arriving at the perfect description of the arena, it is better to accept satisfying next-best outcomes through reasoned estimate and repetition.

The *reasoned estimate* is an educated guess regarding the composition of an arena, in addition to direct monitoring. It can be based on at least five techniques of making arena observations more complete and reliable. The first is memory retrieval. Although every arena is unique in its composition, no arena is totally new, because some stakeholders and issues are regularly involved. The corporate memory or experience is thus a source of information, which only has to be opened and kept available. The comparative study of homologous dossiers is a second technique. An interest group of road haulage companies or transport ministries can, for a dossier on working hours, learn from the parallel dossier in the industrial sector. Theoretical knowledge of EU decision-making, on for example the role of expert groups, is, thirdly, an inspiring source of conjecture, which may lead to more complete and reliable observations. These three techniques are typically the work of specialist staff in EU public affairs management. A fourth one makes use of other staff and particularly line people having their own experiences, comparisons and conjectures. A company like Siemens consults its leading staff and line people in both product divisions and country units regularly, by sending them a questionnaire in which they are asked to identify, among other things, the major stakeholders and the issues relating to a selected dossier. The fifth technique is similar to the fourth, but not limited to one's own organisation. Outsiders, such as consultants or friendly stakeholders, are asked to identify the arena. The five techniques can be used in combination.

The second method producing satisfying outcomes is the *repetition* of the homework by a second researcher for either the same moment in time (duplica research) and/or for a later moment (replica research). The duplica variant almost always creates, thanks to the intellectual competition, better insights. Two (or more) researchers, using the same five aforementioned techniques, may come to different observations regarding the same arena, because no technique is watertight. They all have their good reasons for coming to their own description of the arena. In order to get a better synthesis, a dialectic exchange of arguments should be organised. The replica variant needs to be practised as well, because the arena is continually changing. If one observes at a given moment the presence of a new stakeholder or a new issue (or the disappearance of an old one), one must question whether this has happened because of the arena's dynamics or because of shortcomings in one's earlier reasoned estimate. If the latter, one must improve monitoring and/or applied techniques.

For those still considering all this homework regarding the description of the arena to be a troublesome affair, there is a *quadruple consolation*. The first is the aforementioned reward of getting onto the table valid and relevant insights into a specific arena, which are as complete and reliable as possible. They enable more efficient and effective lobbying. Secondly, the more complexity and dynamics one unveils, the easier one can come to the desired outcomes. The most difficult fight is with only one's spouse on only one issue. If many different people, issues, moments and environments are involved, the easier one can come to outcomes satisfying all or many. Thirdly, action without homework usually creates even greater troubles. This gives a great risk of wrongly identifying some relevant stakeholders, crucial issues, best moments and/or boundary traffic. The comparative costs of losing the game are most probably much higher in such a case than those of the preparatory work. The fourth consolation is that, as time goes on, the homework becomes easier. At the end of a decision-making process there are usually only two major stakeholders, namely the coalition in favour and the one against, and only a few hot issues, particularly 'the envelope' (who pays the bill), the commencing date and a possible exemption. After some time one can also determine which stakeholder is merely a comedian, or really a passive cat on the roof or a dog whose bark is worse than its bite. In the meantime the lobby group can have achieved more complete and reliable insights by the additional techniques of reasoned estimates and repetitions. The competitors also enjoy these facilities at the same time, of course. So, one receives the greatest return on homework in the troublesome early phases, just as one gets the commercial profit better in a difficult rather than in a simple market.

The 1992 *High Definition Television* (HDTV) case provides a fine example of the comparative costs of poor preparation. In the late 1980s the major European consumer electronics manufacturers, such as the French Thomson, the Dutch Philips and the German Bosch companies, demanded from the EU both a legal standard and a fat subsidy for the development of HDTV [Verwey, 1994; Cawson, 1995]. They soon received privately from the DG R&D Commissioner Filippo Pandolfi, once a board member of Olivetti, the strongest support, including a promise of 850 million ecu (now euro). But in 1992 it appeared that they had neglected relevant opposing stakeholders with their own issues, such as the broadcasters (fearing the costs of rebuilding their studios), the satellite companies (offering a competitive alternative) and the consumer groups (who were against compulsory purchase of new television sets). The mass media, smelling a rat, finally helped to bury the dossier. Neither the standard nor the subsidy ever materialised. With a good description of the arena in advance, the companies could have known the relevant stakeholders and the crucial issues better and could have done their timing and boundary control more successfully. Now they were collecting their wisdom about the arena not by foresight, but by hindsight.

The Quick Arena Scan

The preparatory homework on the description of the arena clearly includes a synthesis of the older issue and stakeholder (including ruler) approaches. They are connected both to each other and to the variables of the dossier life cycle and boundary traffic. Frequently, however, there is no time or need for such thorough homework for a dossier. If this is the case, the *quick arena scan* may suffice. This is a simple two-dimensional matrix, with the left-side vertical axis representing the stakeholders and the upper-side horizontal axis the issues *(figure 4.2)*. It is, in fact, no different from what most people do in their mind when they are thinking about an arena. Then they consider only the major players and the key issues. The mind has however a limited capacity to consider many stakeholders and issues at the same time and also to store the collected insights. It is already much better to collect them on the reverse side of a cigar-box, but this may be lost when it is empty. The best thing is to make the quick scan on a piece of paper or on a computer spreadsheet.

On the vertical *stakeholders axis* there is endless room for listing all sorts

Dossier Homework

Dossier 1 : .... (2 and ff = agenda analysis)
Moment t : .... (t−x .... t+x = time analysis)
Analyst A : .... (B and others for control)

Stakeholders	Issues involved		
	1 2 3 4 5 6 7 8 n...		
own organisation			
national - public and private - sectoral - cross-sectoral - regional - others: media etc			
foreign - governments - sectoral - cross-sectoral - regional - others: media etc			select items for trade-offs
transnational - COM (DG's, agencies) - committees - EP, ESC, COREG - COREPER, council - Court - EuroFeds, NGOs - others: media etc			Identify coalitions for or against

assess their actions
+ influence =
relevance
	assess relevance of issues and make
	
	adverse columns: loss scenario
	favourable columns:
	   win-win/free ride scenario
	unsettled columns:
	   negotiations scenario
			other
			dossiers
			and
			players

Figure 4.2

of stakeholders, even with breakdowns made at the lowest relevant level, for example a government unit or a person. The criterion is whether they can become single warriors in the arena. They can be grouped into three categories. Firstly, the domestic stakeholders, including oneself, insofar as they have some interest in the same dossier. For example, national ministries, private companies, NGOs, trade associations, regional interest groups or whatever others. As interested players they may try to intervene on the dossier, in order to enjoy its opportunities and/or to eliminate its threats. Secondly, there are the foreign stakeholders. Their composition may be similar to those at home, multiplied by the number of their countries. They may come from both EU and non-EU countries. The interest groups from Eastern Europe, Asia or the Americas, including the global platforms like the WTO, can be as active and effective as those from inside the EU. They may have their informal activities, semi-formal positions and even formal linkages with the EU. Thirdly, there are the many stakeholders inside the EU machinery, ranging from Commission officials and experts to Parliament rapporteurs and Court referendaries.

On the horizontal *issues axis* there is endless room for registering all contested facts, values and instruments, in short all the specific issues of the various stakeholders. They are grouped in homogeneous categories by column. If necessary, every issue can be split into more, which results in still more columns, and every issue on top of a column should be defined in precise terms indicating what is in dispute. On the HDTV dossier, for example, the issues on top might have been labelled as 'an EU standard', 'subsidies to the producers', '850 million ecu', 'studios' compensation' and so on. In the cells, being the crossings of the two axes, one can put the estimated position or preference of every stakeholder regarding any issue. It can be done in a simple way, for example by putting a plus sign (+) in the cell if a stakeholder is assumed to support the issue as defined at the top; by placing a minus sign (-) if one observes that the issue is perceived as a threat; or by putting a zero (0) in the cell if one believes that a stakeholder is wavering or ambivalent on the issue and thus can become either in favour or against. If one observes no position at all, one leaves the cell empty. Of course, one can use shaded scores, ranging from for example +5 to -5, expressing the intensity of a stakeholder's preference as well.

This simple arena description for one dossier at a specific moment, made by one observer, is indeed not substantially different from what every person can do in his mind or on the reverse side of a cigar-box. But by putting it down on paper or using a computer one saves the data for a longer time and adjustments can easily be made. By applying the aforementioned five additional techniques of monitoring, one can give the estimates a more reasoned basis. Adding to the description both a duplica (by another observer) and a replica (at a later moment), one can greatly improve their quality. The grid provides even more facilities. To the inventory of the stakeholders on the vertical axis one can easily add a measure of their relevance, as defined by their probable action and their potential influence. Then one can continue with the short list of primary stakeholders. On the horizontal axis of issues, one can also easily make a distinction between those being probably real and those being maybe false or fake. Using the data in this way, one in fact shortens the axes without losing potentially relevant information.

The greatest facilities, however, one can never get through using either the mind or the cigar-box, but only through the grid. Firstly, the manifold *empty cells* (without any sign), representing many interesting question marks, one would otherwise miss. Stakeholders with empty cells are probably unconscious or unconcerned about the related issues, seeing them at best as issues only of interest to others. But sooner or later they also might (want to) take a position on these, in order to use them as free bargaining chips, like the cigars from another man's box. Secondly, the grid allows replicas to be made regularly and thus to give the description a *diachronic perspective*. One replaces the still photograph with a moving picture, giving a view in an early phase of the centrifugal or centripetal developments involving both the stakeholders and the issues. This is valuable information for the action to come. Finally, to the two axes one can easily add findings from the exploration of the *arena boundaries*. This is, as it were, a matter of rotating the two axes. In the course of research into the stakeholders, one finds more dossiers and issues of interest to them, and when researching the issues, one finds more interest groups. The new dossiers, in which primary stakeholders are involved as well, can be recorded on the rows at the right side and can be brought together at a later moment. The new interest groups that might become involved on some issue can be recorded in the columns at the bottom. They can be mobilised at a later moment. All this additional information may help to push or block either a single issue or the full dossier when the moment for action comes. But preferably before this moment one will have analysed the descriptive materials.

Analysis for the Action

The simple form of *figure 4.2* is also most helpful for the analysis of the described arena. The serious lobby group may start with the columns, which give information about the state of affairs on an issue. By the *vertical analysis* of the stakeholders involved in an issue it can rationally discover its room for action on every issue. Starting from the top with its own position, it can always arrive at one of the following three conclusions regarding the situation. Firstly, its own position, being either plus or minus, may be widely shared by the majority of primary stakeholders. The wind, in short, is friendly, blowing strongly from behind. It is most likely that one's own preference will come through and finally be approved by the EU officials. The lobby group may, secondly, also observe that its position is hardly or not at all shared by the other major stakeholders. Now it meets an unfriendly and cold headwind. The chances of its preference prevailing are almost zero. Thirdly, the lobby group may observe that in a column most primary stakeholders hold positions that are indifferent, ambivalent or still blank on the issue. Thus, mainly side winds are blowing now, or there are no winds at all. The column is indeterminate, the game open and the outcome unpredictable.

The *horizontal analysis* of the rows reveals the great surprise that every stakeholder is always, without any exception, open to negotiation. On its row it has pluses, which it wants to score with, and minuses, which it wants to eliminate. If a lobby group complains, as happens frequently, that it cannot negotiate effectively with some other stakeholder, then almost certainly it has carried out badly or neglected its homework. For example, when in 1998 the Parliament gave the first reading to the Biotech Dossier regarding the research, production and trade of genetically modified organisms (GMOs), the European food-producing companies on one side and the lobby groups on environment and health on the other were not on speaking terms. Good homework could have revealed two openings for negotiations. First of all, both coalitions were internally divided. Even at organisational level a company like Unilever or an NGO like the European Public Health Alliance had mixed feelings. Secondly, both coalitions also had some overlapping interests. Unilever had to be extremely prudent regarding for example consumers' trust, while the Alliance acknowledged the biotech benefits for patient groups. The costs of good homework are clearly much lower than those of unplanned conflict.

One can also make a *diagonal analysis*, which is the helicopter view. The order of both the horizontal and the vertical axis is nominal and, because of this, may be changed. By reordering one can bring the pluses and the minuses together into aggregates, which in fact are potential coalitions in favour or against a single issue or the full dossier. Sooner or later most stakeholders will discover these coalitions as well, but the studious interest group can see the potential coalitions far in advance and anticipate them by smart actions. These potential coalitions are, in addition, of a high quality, clearly based on common interests and providing more solidity than that of, for example, common language, tradition or location. The diagonal analysis provides two further pieces of interesting information. Firstly, no potential coalition is perfectly unified. Thus there is always some room for undermining an opposing coalition, as there is always a need for strengthening one's own. Secondly, every coalition is always a uniquely mixed collection of interest groups, which includes some national and local governments, NGOs, business groups, non-EU stakeholders and Brussels officials. Thus one has many entrances into the EU decision-making system, and with well-prepared homework one can know them and use them.

Finally, one can make a *diachronic analysis,* which is an assessment of developments over time or, in short, the film instead of the still photograph of the arena. Its first benefit is that one can check one's previous analyses and expectations, for example regarding the boundary traffic, the coalition formation and the package dealing. The more one is surprised, the more one should improve the description of the arena. The second benefit from the diachronic analysis is insight into the next development of the dossier's life cycle within the arena. Gradually most stakeholders will take a clear position, filling in their previously empty cells. Many stakeholders will come together, settle their mutual issues and combine their interests in some way. Others may fail to do so and become vulnerable to isolation. As time goes on, the two axes become much shorter, but the friction between the remaining stakeholders and issues tends to become more intense as well. This happens especially when the dossier enters another phase, for example on the eve of the Commission's proposal, the Parliament's rapportage, the Coreper's determination of A-points or the launch of an inspection procedure. The lobby group with diachronic insight can, if necessary, reposition itself in plenty of time. It acts not merely reactively, but preferably proactively.

Pro-Active EU Arena Management: Window-In

The integrated and research-based analysis of issues and stakeholders involved with an EU dossier is not a goal in itself, of course, but a means to more successful action on the playing field. Due to the complexities and the dynamics of the arena, the action has to be reasoned and precise or, in short, be based on good preparation. Thanks to the complexities and the dynamics, the investment in homework can bring great rewards. It gives a major comparative advantage over the competitors who have neglected to carry out preparatory work and act as amateurs seeking gold without checking the ground beforehand. Thanks to their homework, the studious lobby group can see, each and every morning, reasonable options for both trading off issues and forming other coalitions. Of course, every afternoon it might have to update this work, based on new information and reflection, thus getting ready those new options for the next morning. The professional group is frequently chastened by the luxurious paradox of *embarras du choix:* because it sees so many attractive options, it may have difficulty in deciding what to choose. But the pressure of time will finally bring the embarrassment to an end. Something like the intuition or the craft of an artist like Kasparov will help to make the better choice in such circumstances. The proactive, research-based management of the EU arena can be described for both the short and the long term. The only difference is the room for manoeuvre, which increases if there is more time.

Short-term EU arena management

The basic principles are based on the four key characteristics of an arena, each containing a major dilemma. Firstly, there is *issue management*. Here the main dilemma is whether to push both one's own opportunities and the threats to the opponents or to block one's own threats and the opportunities for the opponents. In the EU arena the blocking strategy is usually both easier and less risky than the pushing one, just as one controls a car on a slippery road surface better with the brake than with the accelerator. The more risk one takes, the bigger the chance of either winning or crashing. The second principle regards *stakeholder management*. This contains the dilemma of whether to exploit both one's own strengths and the opponents' weaknesses or to reduce one's own weaknesses and the strengths of the opponents. In the EU arena, once again, the defensive strategy is usually both easier and less risky than the offensive one, in the same way as one survives an ambush on a battlefield better by improving one's shelter than by launching an attack. But by remaining under shelter nobody wins the battle. Thirdly, there is the *dossier life cycle or time management*. This brings the dilemma of whether to speed up or to delay the EU decision-making process. The delaying strategy is usually easier and less risky than the accelerating one, just as it is easier to keep one's balance on a slow- rather than on a fast-moving treadmill. But if it is slow, more competitors can leap on as well. Finally, there is *arena boundaries management*. This involves the dilemma of whether to widen or to narrow the arena boundaries or, referring to figure 4.2, adjust the two axes. Here, the narrowing strategy is usually easier and less risky than the widening one, just as one negotiates more effectively in a small group than in a mass meeting. However, the stakeholders and issues left outside may become disruptive at a later stage.

Easiness and low risk are, however, not necessarily the best criteria for the decision about what to do on the playing field 'to whom, where and on what'. A bias towards *easiness and low risk* usually results in poor rewards as well. The lobby group accepting greater problems and risks may become the winner almost taking all, or it may fall victim to its ambition and lose successively the desired outcome, respect from the other players and backing at home. Nevertheless, most EU lobby groups seem to prefer low risks. They see a good chance of winning a little as more attractive than the bad chance of losing almost all, even if the latter may include the small chance of winning the big prize. The rationality behind this risk avoidance is usually their interest in many more dossiers than just one. The sum of many small but easily and safely obtainable prizes is seen as more attractive than the big prize with greater troubles and with high risks of severe losses.

The question, however, remains of whether such risk avoidance is really rational. In fact, the standard practices of blocking, defensive, delaying and restrictive behaviour are nothing more than *rules of thumb*. Once a dossier or issue area has been selected as highly relevant, to which we will return in the next chapter, the rational choice of acceptable troubles and risks should not depend on such popular and unscientific rules, but on the situation in the arena. Three major types of situation can be distinguished: *friendly, unfriendly or indeterminate*. These labels should not be taken as absolute but, as with any value judgement, only as relative. Every arena, like every human being, has varying degrees of difficulty and risk. For example, a friendly arena is one perceived as having more friends than enemies, containing benign rather than difficult issues, promising better rather than worse moments and being less unpleasant than the outside world, in short as having a relatively favourable wind blowing. It may still be no heaven, but it could be much worse. Instead of the full arena only a part of it may be friendly, for example a category of issues and stakeholders. Every arena type requires specific management of the stakeholders, the issues, the moments in time and the boundaries. The *best practices* can be summarised as follows *(figure 4.3)*.

In a mainly *friendly* (section of the) arena the wind is nicely turning into a following wind or already strongly blowing from behind. The general strategy here is to keep the situation as it is and to harvest the fruits. The interest group can confine itself to a few securing actions. The identified friendly stakeholders should be brought together and, regarding the common interests, be bound to a common action [Knoke, 1990; Knoke, 1996]. From

Best practices of arena management

if the arena is:	favourable	unfavourable	indeterminate
then, best for			
general management	keep status quo	change situation	influence components
stakeholders management	secure support take free ride	divide opponents approach waverers	maybe argumentation negotiate
issues management	keep issues high block others	compensate loss manipulate issues	manipulate the issues
dossier time management	speed up	delay	wait and see
boundaries management	keep restricted	widen the arena	wait and see

Figure 4.3

among the many supporters, a strongly influential one should be selected for both taking the lead and giving a free ride. The potentially opposing coalition(s), which are weak according to the analysis, can be undermined by highlighting their internal issues. Maybe one of their influential groups can be induced to defect. To keep the following wind up to strength, new evidence supporting the benign issues must be distributed regularly and precisely. But this should not be overdone; the few counter-issues can be blocked by counter-evidence. Since the wind is blowing favourably, time management should be directed at speeding up the decision-making process. There is no need to widen the arena boundaries; it is better to keep them restricted to, as far as possible, only the friendly stakeholders and issues already at hand.

In a mainly *unfriendly* (section of the) arena the wind is unpleasantly turning into a headwind or already coldly blowing against. Here the general strategy is to stimulate a change in the situation. The strong coalition(s) of opponents should be divided by highlighting their internal issues as revealed through the homework. This also shows which opponents are waverers and may be open to persuasion or negotiation. They might leave their coalition and thus help to turn the wind around. Regarding the unbenign issues, the best practice is to find compensation for those assessed as probably lost. Even a dead horse may have a market value, especially among the amateurs who believe it is still alive. Alternatively, one can start to lobby for an exemption, to avoid the loss. A more advanced approach is the search for issue manipulation, as explained in the previous chapter. By reframing a difficult issue it may get a better meaning and attract more support. Time management must be directed at delaying the decision-making process, for example by urging the need for additional research and consultation. A delay will, most probably, temper and warm the wind. The widening of the arena boundaries can also make the tide more friendly. New issues and new stakeholders at least delay the decision-making process, provide more options for combining issues and create new coalitions.

A mainly *indeterminate* (section of the) arena has increasingly or primarily either sidewinds (mixed positions) or no winds at all (empty cells). In the case of sidewinds the general strategy is to turn them into friendly ones. Most important here is the management of the stakeholders and the issues. In the indeterminate situation many stakeholders are looking for information and support and appear to be open to negotiation. They may accept traditional arguments regarding the disputed facts, values and instruments, and pleasant behaviour and compromises may bring them onto one's side. A little bit of issue manipulation may be enough, in which case one tries to push better-sounding and more comfortable interpretations of the facts, values and instruments at issue and to block those from the opposing side. There is no good reason to speed up or to delay the decision-making process. That depends on the turn of the tide, which is still to come. The same holds true for either the widening or the narrowing of the arena boundaries. There is sufficient room for playing inside the existing arena, and no need to change it, unless one is sure, thanks to the homework, that widening it will bring in mainly benign issues and stakeholders, or narrowing will repel mainly the difficult ones.

The other indeterminate variant, in which the winds are absent, is usually only to be expected in the early phase of a dossier's life, when the issues are still in formation and the stakeholders nonexistent or just arriving. The general strategy here is to mobilise support for one's own issue preferences. This, too, is mainly a matter of managing stakeholders and issues. Most stakeholders with empty cells, hardly believing they have a real interest, tend to be more open to direct deals than to traditional argumentation. The same applies to one's own empty cells. On these issues one is indifferent, and they can be used as free gifts, like another man's cigars. Issue manipulation may help to convince others that their interest lies on one's side. Of course, everybody can also play the comedian, suggesting indifference and thus trying to get free cigars. In this indeterminate situation it is hardly logical to speed up or to delay the process, or to change the arena boundaries. It is better to follow a wait-and-see approach.

The *best practices* are clearly different from the rules of thumb mentioned above, which advocate blocking, defensive, delaying and restrictive behaviour. In a friendly situation, the action should be directed towards pushing one's coalition and issues offensively, speeding up the process and keeping the arena restricted. The first three rules of thumb are better not applied here, but only in an unfriendly situation. The fourth rule on boundary management should be applied in reverse. In an indeterminate situation it is frequently best to wait and see. The popularity of the aforementioned rules of thumb suggests that many EU lobby groups consider their arenas to be unfriendly. An alternative interpretation is that they have neglected their homework and, without reflection, are simply relying on popular but unjustified rules of thumb. If so, they are behaving not professionally, but amateurishly. The two interpretations are not mutually exclusive. In fact, the more amateurishly a lobby group behaves the more unforced errors it makes and, as a result, the more it feels that it is in an unfriendly arena. Paradoxically, the aforementioned criteria of easiness and low risk may yield the greatest difficulties and highest risks. Rational risk avoidance should be based on a risk assessment study alone. The cautious behaviour based on the rules of thumb should be replaced by the *prudent* behaviour based on the best practices derived from the ongoing preparatory homework. Notwithstanding all this, every lobby group can make mistakes and errors, not necessarily unforced ones. Some come from the imperfections of the preparation, discussed above, and some from both the organisation at home and lobby interactions, which will be discussed in the next two chapters.

Long-term EU arena management
The long-term management of an EU arena has both an *early start and a late finish*. So has the preparatory work. The earlier one starts it, the sooner one can possess in-depth insights regarding the arena, allowing one to play proactively. This sounds self-evident, but is often hard to realise in practice. There is usually an imbalance between (scarce) available resources and (manifold) pressures from games in progress. Early preparation will contribute to a rebalancing and reduce the chance of unforced errors. This not only saves resources during the action, but also reduces the number of pressures caused by one's own errors. The higher efficiency and effectiveness of the fieldwork clearly remain the sole objectives and the only justifi-

cations for the early preparatory work. It is important to keep monitoring the situation in the arena because a political game is never completely over: the losers may take revenge; a win may turn out to be a disaster in disguise; unforeseen side effects may open new arenas; mistakes may return as boomerangs. For all these reasons one should continue with homework for a longer time and certainly not stop when the EU officials have taken their formal decision. More dossier life phases are still to come.

The long-term approach to EU arena management yields three more advantages other than those contained in the short-term approach alone. First of all, one can *fine-tune the dossier phases*. In every phase there is usually a different demand for action. When, for example, an issue is becoming irritating to many more interest groups, then the EU officials in particular have a special need for information relevant for the definition of the underlying problem. Through early preparation a lobby group can supply that information which, firstly, may bring the official problem definition closer to its interests and, secondly, may make the proposed solutions friendlier. In the decision-making phase, however, both the officials and the other stakeholders have less appetite for information than for support. Again through early preparation, a lobby group can choose to supply the most efficient and effective type of support. In the long-term perspective the interest group can even consider an integrated process-oriented approach instead of a phase approach. The homework in such a case anticipates the future and the action is organised backwards into the present. An example is the aforementioned Slots Case, with the backward action by the national air carriers against the proposals from the Commission.

Secondly, the long-term approach permits more than the proactive management of the impending stakeholders, issues, dossier phases and boundaries. One can also apply the *general influence approaches*, as outlined in the preceding chapter and there applied only to the EU officials. The actors' approach, focused on those who really make a decision, can be extended to all sorts of stakeholders, for example the key member of a EuroFed. More sophisticated are the approaches based on the manipulation of factors and vectors. Their cultural, formal, operational and decisional variables can be equally relevant for whatever stakeholder, issue, phase or boundary. For example, the vector of issue manipulation can change an opponent into a friend, shorten a phase and move a boundary as desired. The game of Triple P, with its prefabricated procedures, positions and people, can promise a most friendly arena situation. All these approaches require proactive management and thus an early preparation, which has to be continued for a long time.

The third advantage of the long-term perspective is the possibility of *scenario management*. This is, first of all, also a matter of homework. Its basic formula is the question: 'What will happen, if x-y-z occurs?' [Van der Heijden, 1996; Ringland, 1998]. The answers must be based on logical and/or empirical relationships between the independent variables x, y, z on one side and the expected outcomes or dependent variables on the other. The alleged relationships should meet the tests of relevance, consistency and plausibility, but not of probability. In the field of EU arena management the most relevant independent variables are the stakeholders (including the officials and oneself), the issues, the time developments and the arena boundaries. But one can also take as independent such intervening variables as the factors and the vectors regarding a particular stakeholder or the components of the Triple P meta-game. Possible questions arising when preparing for a scenario are: *what will happen,* if this or that stakeholder disappears or changes its position?...if a particular issue is traded off or rephrased?...if a potential coalition achieves cohesion or becomes divided?...if the arena becomes widened or narrowed?...if the process is speeded up or delayed?...if, regarding a stakeholder, a particular (cultural, formal, operational or decisional) factor is influenced or vector is created?...if a Triple P game is played differently?

The answers to such analytical questions provide different windows onto possible futures. An example are the five possible futures for Europe, respectively called 'Triumphant Markets', 'Hundred Flowers', 'Shared Responsibilities', 'Creative Societies' and 'Turbulent Neighbourhoods' [Bertrand and others, 1999]. They are not assumed to be probable. The least advantage they offer is that one can better prepare oneself for the future. Some day a possibility may become a probability and then the lobby group will be less surprised than it would have been otherwise and it will be able to use the analysis of the scenario for arena planning. This advantage is no different from the analysis of a scenario by the chess player, who wonders what will happen if the opponent moves one or another piece. The greatest advantage, however, is that one can base an action in the arena on one or more of the possible futures. The scenario analysis, then, turns into *scenario management*. A very attractive possible future, at present still considered a daydream, might be promoted or managed in such a way that it becomes self-fulfilling, whereas a horrible possible future, at present only a nightmare, might be turned into a self-denying possibility. The precondition for such scenario management is, of course, the early and ongoing study of possible arenas.

Extra: the GMO Food Arena

On 23 February 1998 the Commission published its *document 598PC0085*, prepared by its DG Environment, Nuclear Safety and Civil Protection. The code stands for the proposal for secondary legislation to the Parliament and to the Council to revise the old Directive 90/220/EEC on the deliberate release into the environment of genetically modified organisms (GMOs). Its objective was a stricter regulation, but not a full prohibition, of the research, the production and the (both external and internal) trade regarding GMOs produced through biotechnology. On 24 June 1999 the ministers of the Environment Council reached an informal agreement of a mainly procedural character: any acceptance of GMOs for experimental or market releases should be based on both a risk assessment and a decision of a competent authority (mainly by Regulatory Committee procedure) and must meet special standards of risk management, monitoring and public information (such as labelling). France, wanting to protect its traditional farming, also pushed for a *moratorium* on further permission for products containing GMOs (so far there had been 18 permitted). With UK, Ireland and Portugal abstaining, this proposal was adopted under the formula 'no further permission, unless no risk'. Formally these agreements were only non-binding declarations, but they expressed the controversial nature of GMOs among and inside the member countries, and they indicated to the Commission and to the Parliament what might be acceptable.

On 18 October 1999, the Parliament, under the codecision empowering it to make amendments and to veto, discussed the first report of its commission on the Environment, Public Health and Consumer Protection. It adopted 39 amendments to the Commission proposal. They were all directed towards stricter regulation and almost all adopted by the Commission. On 13 December 1999 the Council rubberstamped its common position (at the first reading), almost fully in line with the Parliament, but with France, Ireland and Italy abstaining. Some new principles were also supported: the *precaution* (if risk, no permission), the *traceability* (regarding the origin of GMO products on the market), the *authorisation* period (a maximum of ten years) and the need for *global* agreements on exports ('Biosafety Protocol'). Of course, it was up to the Commission to make proposals based on these principles. Soon the DG Environment (headed by Margot Wallström) presented its white papers regarding both those principles and the new policy idea of environmental *liability* (not limited to GMOs only). DG Consumer Affairs (led by David Byrne) became more involved, especially on the idea of *labelling*, which would enable the consumers to decide for themselves. In exchange for all this, the Commission offered the ending of the moratorium, which was not binding legally but merely discretionary.

In the meantime the revision of the Directive 90/220 continued in the Parliament and the Council. The two bodies kept their disagreements at the second reading, after which a conciliation procedure came into operation. Finally a compromise was reached, which allowed the principles of traceability and labelling and the lifting of the moratorium. At the plenary session of 14 February 2001, the European Parliament approved it and *concluded the dossier*. As usual, the Revised Directive contained many provisions for further delegated legislation by the Commission, *inter alia* regarding further permissions, traceability and labelling. Again as usual, the devil (or the saint) is more in the detail than in the general text of the secondary legislation, although even the latter can be full of drama. Indeed, the next conflict became apparent as early as May 2001. Regarding the measures of traceability, Wallström wanted to set minimum levels of permitted GMOs immediately, while Byrne proposed that special committees set maximum levels in due time.

Between 1998 and 2001 the whole dossier, in short, has been a clear example of many *cleavages* inside and between the Commission, the EP and the Council. During this period, the three bodies have functioned primarily as forums for conflict between different stakeholders from inside and outside, and hardly as bodies to promote cohesion. The Commission was particularly divided between the DGs. Sitting in the driver's seat was DG Environment, but DG External Trade (for settling GMO issues with the USA), DG Industry (for economic growth) and DG R&D (for new technology) wanted to hit the brake pedal. DG Agriculture was internally divided between traditional and modern farming, as DG Consumer Affairs was between consumer benefits (price, quality) and safety (health). In the EP, the environment freaks, meeting in the commission on Environment, were firmly in the driver's seat, with strongest support coming from the Green Party, while all the other groups were divided to some extent. The ministers of the Environment Council disagreed among themselves. Instead of making decisions, they quarrelled about principles and procedures, thus failing to inform the Commission and the EP about what might be acceptable. Many ministers had to cope with domestic cleavages as well, particularly between ministries, industrial groups and NGOs. Not surprisingly, many issues had to be left unsettled in the end and, as part of the compromise of conciliation, to be delegated to the Commission. Since the dossier had become so politicised, it also collected a gathering of lobby groups from outside, closely connected to the different stakeholders inside the three institutions. To cut a long story short, those groups can be reduced to two main coalitions: the anti-GMO and the pro-GMO one.

The *anti-GMO movement* was led by Greenpeace and included lobby groups from health, religion, ethics, animal welfare and development aid. It also received some support from traditional farming (averse to new technology) and retailers (fearing consumer protests). Now nestled within DG Environment and the EP's commission, the anti-GMO movement had realised the wind was blowing their way even before the 1998 revision of the old directive. The adoption of that old directive in 1990 had turned out not to be an easy pill to swallow for those from industry. It became an Ancient Greek drama, full of ideological conflicts and power play between different Commission DGs, EP commissions and Councils and, gradually, with the officials on environment getting into the driver's seat [Gottweis, 1999; Patterson, 2000]. In 1996 the acceptance of transgenic maize proved to be a Pyrrhic victory for the traders [Bradley, 1998], with Italy, Austria and Luxembourg refusing to implement the decision. In 1997 the Biotechnology Patent Directive narrowly came through, after fierce opposition from inside the Commission (DG Environment), the EP (across parties), and the Council (from Denmark, Austria and the Netherlands). To fight this directive Greenpeace had constructed the European Campaign on Biotechnology Patents (ECOBP) and it was soon able to use this platform as the take-off for the campaign against the release of GMOs. To strengthen the growing following wind it mobilised public opinion and thus the national and European politicians who were sensitive to this. The mass media smelled and fanned the fire of public concern about 'Frankenstein food'. The anti-GMO coalition got its great impetus when the dossier came under the control of their friends in the DG Environment and subsequently those in the EP and the Council. It enjoyed the Triple P game. Observing that the arena was turning friendly now, it tried to speed up the process and to keep the arena restricted to its own issues and allies alone. It applied the best practices of arena management rather professionally.

The *pro-GMO coalition* was led mainly by Europabio, a EuroFed of companies active in the research, the production and/or the trade of pharmaceuticals (like Glaxo-Smith-Kline) and food products (like Unilever). It was not against regulation of GMOs, but wanted one based on sound risk assessment, allowing research, enabling consumers to choose, and keeping the trade competitive. Inside Europabio the GMO-dossier became more a challenge for the companies involved in food production than for those in pharmaceuticals; in health cure the patients tend to consider any risk an opportunity rather than a threat. Soon the food companies came to be almost isolated. They received some support from a few DGs (Industry, R&D and increasingly Consumer Affairs) and some MEPs (Socialists and Christian Democrats), but this support was initially hardly effective. Most national governments took shelter from the issue area. The noisy and aggressive support from US producers like Monsanto and Cargill soon proved to be more embarrassing than helpful. The mass media constantly fanned the flames. Only in 2000 did the arena become a little bit less unfriendly for the food producers. In this year, the EP plenum rejected the most adverse amendments, the Commission presented its package deal including the lifting of the moratorium and the Council accepted this with a delegation of powers to the Commission. For Unilever this came too late: in May 2000, the company decided to end, for the time being, the production and trade in Europe of products containing GMOs. Three months later the Swiss giant Novartis followed this example. The food companies were clearly weary of feeling that they were on the lower side of an unlevel playing field, with the wind blowing coldly and fiercely against them. They should not have been surprised. The previous decisions on the old 1990 Directive, the transgenic maize and the Patent Directive had shown a rising headwind. In 1997 the Commission, preparing the revision of the 1990 Directive, was already an open forum for conflict. All this was publicly known, and it should have stimulated the food companies to prepare themselves for the headwind. Instead of the exit option, a company like Unilever could have applied the best practices of surviving in an unfriendly arena.

A good *stakeholders analysis* would have shown that the opposing coalition was far from unified. For example, the environment movement was divided into a polemic European faction and a moderate Third World faction. The latter considered the GMOs as less disastrous for the environment than the current use of chemicals and, in fact, as the poor man's fertiliser. The health movement, partly organised in the European Public Health Alliance (EPHA), was divided into a 'caring' and a 'curing' faction, the latter acknowledging the benefits of GMOs for specific patient groups. The consumer organisations like BEUC were not against GMOs, but concerned about consumer safety and price/quality ratio. Only some of the traditional farmers were orthodox green peasants, averse to any new technology, the rest being small farmers fearing stronger competition. The food retailers, composed of multinationals like Carrefour (France), Sainsbury (UK) and Delhaize (Belgium), were divided by the market competition both among themselves and with the alternative retailers like the health food stores. Last, but not least, the Commission, the Parliament and the Council were notoriously divided over the whole dossier. In short, the advocates of GMOs could have weakened the unstable coalition of opponents. They could have won over at least the many moderate and partly wavering opponents by a mixture of argumentation and negotiation.

Proactive *issue analysis* could have provided the clues to all this, and at an early stage the food companies could have promoted the issues controversial among their opponents, such as development aid, medical benefits, price/quality advantages for consumers, crop benefits for small farmers, and market opportunities for alternative retail channels. Then they would have deprived their opponents of the political room to build up a broad coalition around the single issues of environment and safety, with wide mass-media support shackling the politicians. By early issue manipulation they could have reframed those issues in terms of higher social values, such as global nutrition, agricultural development, public health, consumer welfare, economic growth, quality employment, and environmental savings. They also could have found better compensation for early losses than the lifting of a moratorium that had no legal basis in the first place. Examples might have been the granting of EU subsidies to R&D free from GMOs, the transfer of GMO-related dossiers from DG Environment to DG Consumer Affairs and the setting-up of more efficient permission procedures. Unilever has indeed pushed the latter, and in 2001 this resulted in the European Food Authority. However, it did so not for its GMO interests but for its GMO-free new margarine that lowers cholesterol.

In an arena becoming hostile or already unfriendly, one should try to delay the process. As long as one is not hanged, one is still alive. The companies should have made a thorough *time analysis* as the preparatory basis for delaying practices. For example, regarding the disputed GMO benefits for Third World countries the companies could have facilitated a round of consultations with developing countries. Through the befriended pharmaceutical companies inside Europabio, patient groups could have been mobilised to lobby for exemptions complicating the process. For every specific issue there is a whole menu of delaying techniques. Some involve an actors approach, which ranges from a special hearing in the Parliament to a series of expert meetings or a media campaign for national politicians. There is a choice of factors to delay the decision-making process as well. For example, the companies could have elicited new research to confuse some opponents, challenged the Treaty basis of the Revised Directive, or evoked an early complaint from the WTO. Alternatively, they could have engineered delaying vectors, for example by lobbying for more subsidiarity, for a moratorium only on GMO imports from abroad (thus evoking WTO complaints) and for reconsidering the dossier in the perspective of EU enlargement. The objective of all these possibilities would have been simply to win time.

By *boundary analysis* the companies could have created their last safe resort. In such an unfriendly situation they should have striven for a widening of the arena. By provoking new issues and stakeholders they might have won at least more time and at most many benign issues and stakeholders. They could have reactivated, for example, the issues of stagnating employment and global competitiveness, which are dependent on innovative technology. That would have motivated the trade unions and the socialist parties fearing a loss of employment to US producers. Even DG Social Affairs and DG Industry might have joined the arena actively. The companies could also have demanded that the precautionary principle (if risk, no permission), if adopted, should be applied, as a matter of legal fairness, to totally different policy areas as well, such as to transport, chemicals, regional development and, not least, traditional agriculture. This would have encouraged many new stakeholders into the arena to fight against that same principle. The companies could even have linked their interests to the Agenda 2000, being decided in March 1999, for which the issues of employment and growth were central, as a means to further the Open Market, to finance the Union and to enlarge it.

Arena Analysis: Necessary, but not Sufficient

The short exercise looking at the GMO food arena is no magic show, but a specimen of thoughtful arena management. It also provides a few illustrations of the many reasoned options obtainable through systematic descriptive and analytical homework. The professional lobby group considers this preparatory work necessary in order to find sound answers to the questions *'to whom, where and regarding what'* it should direct its arena actions. After the identification of the crucial stakeholders and issues, together making up the arena, and after the consideration of the time and the boundaries, the professional group can see the best options for networking, coalition formation and bargaining. The semi-professional group limits the homework to dealing with only a few stakeholders and issues and perhaps points in time, and accepts the arena boundaries as they are. It will not be able to match the performance of the professional. The amateur group is even weaker, taking into account little more than a few EU officials, its own issue perspective and usually a moment for decision at a late stage in the game. It hardly has a chance of winning. As with the performance of a sportsman, the preparation is, however, a necessary but not a sufficient condition for success. At least four factors may contribute to losing a game regularly, a set sometimes, and a match perhaps.

Firstly, there is always a degree of *uncertainty*. This is inherent to any complex information process. Completeness and reliability remain fundamental problems, although there are next-best solutions. The sheer volume of both the described data and the analysed options makes their all-round processing a cry for the moon. This has already been proven for the game of chess [Simon, 1960], which is clearly simpler than the game of EU arena politics. Every player decides to the best of his knowledge, but the level of knowledge may vary significantly. Intuition or an artist's feeling, based on experience, may do the rest, even in the case of Kasparov. Every player, secondly, can have some *bad luck*, even if this is only the good luck of a competitor. The luck may be some special information or support. In the 1992 HDTV case the Commissioner Filippo Pandolfi, personally in favour of this new technology, was the embodiment of luck himself: good for the producing companies and bad for the opponents [Verwey, 1994], and when he left in 1994 the situation became reversed. But luck is not always a message from heaven or hell. In many a case it can be (or could have been) foreseen by developing scenarios and possibly managing one of them. Thirdly, the *chance of winning* is a factor. The excellent player at the lower side of a most unlevel playing field may have less chance of winning than the amateur player on the higher ground. In the 1998 GMO case the food companies found themselves in such a disadvantageous position on an unlevel playing field. Chance, however, is not a metaphysical category. By studious homework the companies could have noticed the wind changing beforehand and have taken appropriate measures subsequently.

Finally, an otherwise professional lobby group can lose a game, and more, if its *internal organisation* has become disorderly or in bad shape. It may have carried out its preparatory homework on the arena excellently, but if this is not used as input for the strategy or the tactics of the organisation, then it cannot result in a winning performance. And, the other way around, if the organisation has insufficient capacity for arena management, lacks a clear strategy, leaves its targets undefined, or does not learn from its errors, whether forced or unforced, then it will bring even its best professional to despair instead of high performance. This is the theme of the next chapter.

CHAPTER 5

MANAGING THE HOME FRONT

Who Is Acting, Why, for What Reason, and With What Result?

The simple-minded lobby group gives the answer before the question is posed. It takes its self-image as self-knowledge, its motivation for the action as self-evident and its objectives as clear enough. It divides the results into two categories: the losses are to be blamed on the others and the gains are, of course, due to its own performance. In daily practice, such an interest group will continually blame the others and whitewash itself. The conscious interest group, in contrast, knows that its internal affairs are always an incomplete puzzle, its motivations characterised by uncertainties and its objectives full of dilemmas. It divides the results into at least four categories: both the losses and the gains can have been caused by either its own behaviour or by outside (f)actors. Its aim, however, is to strengthen the *causal* relationship between its behaviour and the results, in short to get the desired results and to prevent the undesired ones. Therefore, it has to define its desires clearly, to consider its motivations thoughtfully, and to review its organisation critically. The person responsible for doing this usually faces much internal dissent. Many a Public Affairs official has the experience that organising public affairs at home takes at least 60% of his/her energy. The remainder is spent on the EU officials and the other stakeholders. The own organisation is usually a difficult arena.

Our approach is, once again, not normative but *advisory*. There is no good reason why a lobby group or even a citizen should not be allowed to act in a simple-minded or amateurish manner. It may hold values that sufficiently justify such behaviour. But *if* an interest group (or a citizen) wants to create real chances to influence its challenging EU environment, *then* it should take the EU arenas as sources of inspiration for the development of its own organisation, strategies and agendas. For this reason chapter 4 came before this one. Every lobby group with the ambition to create a desired outcome from EU decision-making should not be introvertively focused primarily on its own inner world. Otherwise it cannot go window-in and -out. It has to adapt its organisation, strategies and agendas to EU constraints and possibilities. Without the required variability and flexibility in its internal affairs, it cannot act in a potentially effective and efficient way. The ambitious lobby group is also eager to learn all the time from both its own experiences and those of others [Kobrin, 1982, I and II]. This difference between amateurish and professional behaviour remains our focus.

In this chapter, the unit for analysis is not necessarily the *formally established* interest group. Of course, it may be the Siemens company, the NGO of Animal Welfare, the EuroFed CIAA (food industry), the London local government, the Regional Affairs Ministry of Italy, AmCham in Brussels, the Commission or any other established organisation of either a public or a private nature, and based either inside or outside the EU area. Every organisation has two further relevant layers, which are more semi-formal or informal than established. Firstly, *part* of an organisation can act as a lobby group itself. For example the subsidiary of a company, the bureau of a ministry, a Commission DG, a unit of a Commission DG, an intergroup of the Parliament, graduates from the same year or the junior staff of MEPs. Secondly, every established interest group participates in external *networks*, platforms or groups, which can develop into lobby groups as well. They may be an ad-hoc coalition, a cross-sectoral platform, an interface between industrialists and Commission officials, an Irishmen's club, a meeting of French and German officials, or a joint dinner of ministers from applicant-member states. The formally established interest group remains, however, our frame of reference.

The Acting Interest Group

From the various aforementioned case studies of EU interest group behaviour it is possible to distil a number of variables, which differentiate between amateurish and professional behaviour. We condense them here into four closely linked but distinguishable indicators of a professional lobby organisation: sufficient cohesion, useful knowledge, an optimal mix of resources and skills, and a good image.

Sufficient cohesion
In the previous chapter we made the assumption, for the simplicity of the discussion, that an interest group acting on the divided EU playing field is internally cohesive. Cohesion we define here as the end-situation of both a *coherence* of preferences and a *co-ordination* of actions. The assumption of cohesion is usually false. Under normal circumstances every group is inter-

nally divided, with its members arguing for their chosen facts, values and instruments. They have, in short, their internal issues, which become manifest as different preferences and divergent actions at all levels of the organisation.

At the informal level, there exists the *pluralism* of the group members having different values and interests. Inside a multinational company people differ in their behaviour according to, for example, age, education, religion, ambition, nationality, language, expertise and position. Inside a EuroFed there is usually the pluralism of members differing according to, *inter alia*, national origin, size of turnover and profit, managerial style, market position, and organisational strategy. Every Commission DG has the pluralism of civil servants being different by, for example, national or regional background, style of decision-making, career aspirations, policy beliefs, and loyalty patterns. Such pluralism can fragment the larger organisation and transform parts of it into self-reliant lobby groups, which separately develop their own external networks.

Much of the same holds true at the semi-formal level of an established organisation. Here the *variety of role expectations* is normally most important. Staff and line people tend to have different expectations regarding each other's functioning: for example, the legal affairs staff with regard to those in public relations and the people in one product line with regard to those in another. A company like Philips, a DG like External Trade, an NGO like Greenpeace or a EuroFed like Unice is, at the semi-formal level, normally an amalgam of different sets of role expectations, based particularly on functional and territorial divisions. The amalgam can easily and centrifugally cause self-reliant behaviour from the constituent parts, including the establishment of new external networks.

Even at the formal level of an established organisation, internal cohesion can normally never be assumed. Already the formal division of *tasks and duties* makes the organisation internally divided. The Commission's DG Agriculture and DG Development have a real conflict of interests regarding meat exports to Sahel countries: one DG has to promote the (subsidised) exports on behalf of EU farmers and the other has to prevent them in order to protect the Sahel farmers. In an NGO, the steering committee, the bureau and the plenum have different formal positions, which can easily conflict. In most countries the national ministry of Transport has formal responsibility for both railway and road transport and is thus internally divided about the values of public versus private transport.

All these internal divisions, coming from informal pluralism, semi-formal role differences and formal task distributions are so *normal* that it is an abnormal or unnatural state of affairs for them to be absent. If the divisions are really weak, or absent, then, almost for certain, there is something wrong with the organisation. The explanation may be a crisis emanating from the outside, internal despotic rule, or simply a malfunctioning of members and units, neglecting their different values, roles and duties. The natural state of internal divisions can even be seen as a *richness*. This pluralism makes the organisation better adapted to the pluralism of the European environment. The variety of role expectations gives it more dialectical dynamics internally, and the different task allocations create for every formalised value of the organisation a strong stakeholder within it. Even their centrifugal forces can be seen as potentially healthy. They may increase the organisation's capacity for flexible and rapid responses to EU challenges. Its constituent parts can behave more self-reliantly, thus diminishing the costs of delayed action, and the external networks can be used as prospective antennae and protective shields.

The richness of internal divisions should neither be minimised nor maximised, but *optimised*. The economy of EU lobbying starts at home. Minimising the divisions may result in a blind obedience to orders and the organisation will then lose the rewards from the internal divisions and become, of course, most vulnerable at the top. Only in abnormal crisis-like situations, when all hands have to be on deck, may this be justified. Under normal circumstances such an enforcement of both coherence and co-ordination makes the organisation introvert, takes up a lot of scarce resources, like time and initiative, and puts a premium on obstruction. In the meantime, the external developments are taking place. There should be no attempt to maximise the richness of diversity either: a deeply divided organisation cannot act on the external playing field effectively. Competitors, having made their homework well, will try to exacerbate the internally dividing issues and to paralyse the organisation, and EU officials cannot take seriously an interest group with cacophonic or even contradictory voices, such as those that came from the Government of Malta regarding its membership request (in favour in 1993 and 1998, but against in 1996). Only 'sufficient' cohesion is needed, but this optimum is, inevitably, always a delicate balance between internal support and external effectiveness. It has to be constructed, over and over again, under the pressures of both internal divisions and external arena developments [Kobrin, 1982, V-VI-IX].

The big question, of course, is how sufficient cohesion can be realised. Here too, *preparatory homework* should drive the internal fieldwork. The internal arena can best be monitored in the same way as the external arena, outlined in the previous chapter and encapsulated in figure 4.2. For any EU dossier, the internal stakeholders are listed. They are usually the person doing the monitoring, colleagues in the office, the people in other staff and line offices, and the chief executive. Their issues and positions should be assessed and described realistically. One person can be responsible for this, for example the officer of public affairs management, the secretary or a board member. A better result comes from the simultaneous involvement of a few people or small groups. They separately assess the internal arena and discuss the observations critically, which may result in a more complete and reliable synthesis. In fact this is the duplica method now applied internally. Many multinational companies (MNCs) have regular procedures for questioning key people in the product and the different country units about their views on an EU dossier. The various responses inform the responsible manager about the internal arena. In government organisations, like ministries and agencies, people frequently express their differences by paper or in a meeting. This is not satisfactory, as positions on paper are hard to change and in a meeting the described facts and the personal strategies are easily confused. Trusted outsiders like consultants and even stakeholders can be asked to help make the description more complete and reliable.

Subsequently this homework has to result in the formation of a sufficiently cohesive position. This must balance the internal and the external arena, as they have been assessed. It forms the essence of strategy development, which we will continue to discuss below. The *building of cohesion* is usually seen as the final responsibility of the top managers. There is, of course, a lot of variation by type of organisation, to which we will return below. Companies can construct that cohesion more easily than voluntary groups and publicly controlled government organisations like the Commission. Even the culture of a country is a factor. If the cohesion is mainly constructed top-down, as is typically the German practice, then the cohesion is highly formal, requires a lot of signatures and time and tends to be poorly anchored [Nutt, 1999]. Dutch and Danish organisations, in contrast, have a reputation of a bottom-up approach, which includes staff and line units and even workers' councils. The more bottom-up, the better the cohesion can be anchored at the informal level, but the costs of time and effort in dealing with divisions are frequently the price to pay. French and British organisations usually rely on mid-level managers for cohesion, under approval from the top, which is frequently sufficient. Whatever the style, internal lobbying is always required, both window-out and -in. The relevant people inside have to be monitored and be kept sufficiently coherent and co-ordinated. They can be kept committed by providing them with information about the conclusions of the preparatory work, for example through the Intranet. MNCs sending out the aforementioned questionnaires frequently do this.

Sufficient cohesion is necessary, but of course not necessarily always achieved. An organisation can remain substantially and seriously divided on an EU dossier, even after a Teutonic top-down intervention. In such a case of *enduring dissent*, the organisation can best remain passive on the dossier, in order to avoid boomerangs. Heterogeneous EuroFeds like Unice have, for this reason, usually to abstain from taking positions on specific dossiers, because their members have conflicting specific interests. If a dissent develops into an almost permanent and paralysing cleavage, then the dramatic step of really dividing the organisation should be considered. Until 1998, the Philips company was internally deeply divided on the EU dossier regarding the imposition of copyright on compact discs. Its music-producing unit Polygram wanted this, but its unit producing CD-rewriters was strongly opposed. In 1998, Polygram was sold to the Canadian entertainment company Seagram and thus the internal cleavage was resolved. In a voluntary association such as a EuroFed, dissatisfied members usually anticipate such a dramatic decision. They simply start an ad-hoc coalition or a new EuroFed. In 1990, most European car manufacturers left the EuroFed CCMC because the French Peugeot group PSA continued to block a common position regarding the EU dossier on car imports from Japan. They formed the new ACEA in 1991 (with, ironically, PSA joining in 1994) [McLaughlin, 1994].

Useful knowledge
A second characteristic of the professional lobby group is the acquisition of knowledge that will be useful for getting the desired EU outcomes. The amateurish group is easily satisfied with its own impressions and perceptions of reality or it simply follows the personal wisdom of its leadership. Of course, the professional group is not an epistemic or academic faculty. It sees the acquisition of knowledge not as its primary objective, but only as an essential means for the realisation of its EU targets, such as a desired directive or exemption. These targets are also a means with which to realise the general and ultimate *raison d'être* of the lobby group, for example the making of profit or the maintenance of civil rights. The knowledge must, in short, be useful for the attainment of that higher goal [Lindblom and Cohen, 1979].

The most critical category of knowledge is *self-knowledge*. This requires a balanced insight into one's own desires and fears on one side and one's own capacities on the other. These desires and fears must have a better basis than the random collection of daydreams and nightmares. In a self-conscious lobby group they are equal to the general orientations and the specific targets mentioned before, as laid down in the strategy developed after critical discussions. This also has to be in balance with the capacity for action. The group has to know the state of its internal cohesion, as outlined above. Therefore it has to be familiar with the internal variety of informal values, semi-formal role expectations and formal tasks and duties, which all exist behind its official façade of unity. It must also be informed about the resources and skills at its disposal and, not least, about its perhaps poor image in the eyes of the other stakeholders. The whole matter of self-knowledge is so essential in EU lobbying that we will come back to it in the next section on strategy development.

The second category of required knowledge is *arena knowledge*, as discussed in the previous chapter. For any major phase in the life of the dossier at stake, it must include at least the primary stakeholders, including the EU officials, with their issues and their preferences. This implies that the EU officials lobbying for a desired outcome themselves have to be aware of the internal divisions inside a country's government and its civil society. The lobby group must also be familiar with the arena boundaries, because otherwise it can not exploit new stakeholders and issues outside. In addition, it has to assess, always, the precise nature of the arena, and in which areas the weather is usually volatile, with the winds changing from favourable to unfavourable and back again. In addition to all this 'software' knowledge, the organisation has to know the 'hardware' of the EU machinery, such as the important institutions and their components (chapter 2) and the manageable actors, factors and vectors, including the Triple P game (chapter 3).

Useful knowledge can be acquired from various *sources*. One is, of course, learning by doing. Failures may teach some success, but many lobby groups are slow learners and their experiences are often not remembered, reconsidered or taken as free lessons for the future. The more professional a group is, the more it organises its knowledge consciously. For this purpose most multinationals and EuroFeds have established a special unit of public affairs management, which is connected with other staff and line people and closely linked to the top managers. Among other tasks and duties, this unit performs the preparatory work regarding both the internal and the external arena. For example, it emails the questionnaire to relevant personnel inside, does the window-out monitoring and makes the quick scan of the arena. It can also make a benchmark of its own organisation regarding both the possession and the application of its knowledge, in comparison to those of competitors. In many cases it even proposes the best strategic balance between the reasoned desires and the capacity to achieve them.

In spite of all efforts to collect useful knowledge, even the most professional organisation has to act under *limited knowledge* [Kobrin, 1982, VII-VIII]. The required information about one's own organisation and the others is never complete or fully reliable. Uncertainty is the lot of every player, but of the amateur more so than of the professional. The latter applies the techniques of reasoned estimates and repetitive observations, described in the previous chapter, to improve its knowledge of the reality. Being more conscious about the relativity of its desires, it is also more capable of reconsidering its strategy, for both the general orientations and the specific targets. It always notices a new option or opportunity, for example a different dossier, a better moment for action or a friendlier stakeholder. It knows that its competitors and the EU officials have limited knowledge as well and that it is only the marginal difference of knowledge that is important, like the one point in a tie-break. In order to cover this crucial margin, the professional organisation, paradoxically, tends to overexpose its uncertainty. The amateur one, however, frequently camouflages its uncertainty by a show of self-confidence.

Optimal mix of resources and skills
Resources are the organisation's tools for survival. They are not fixed assets in permanent possession, but have to be acquired and constantly kept in good condition. A tool might be anything that contributes to the effective and efficient participation in EU politics. Even the strong desire to influence the process or the privilege to meet informally with a Commissioner might be seen as a resource. But more common is the limitation of the concept to only the *capacity for action* of an organisation, and not to include the categories of desires, compulsions and opportunities as well [Schlozman and Tierney, 1986, V]. Even then it remains a broad and dynamic concept. Sufficient cohesion, useful knowledge and good image, all taken here as indicators of professionalism, could be presented as important resources as well. In both the previously mentioned case studies and the limited research in the field [Kohler-Koch, 1998; Wessels, 1999; Koeppl, 2001], the most frequently mentioned resources are, however, expertise, networks, positions and financial means. In practice they are not separate from each other, but highly interchangeable. Expertise, for example, can be part of one's network, be the result of acquiring a position or be bought from a consultancy. A strategic position in the EU machinery may make networks or

finances redundant. Because of such interchange, it is impossible to conclude that one single resource is absolutely the most important.

The resource of *expertise* partially overlaps with the category of useful knowledge mentioned above. But self-knowledge and the political knowledge of how to manage an arena are usually not included. Expertise refers particularly to the technical aspects of a dossier or a single issue. In the EU system of compromise, every big fight, for example on equal health conditions at the workplace, tends to be rapidly split up into many small specific issues, such as regarding the noise or the radiation from a particular machine. The technical experts have the technical knowledge to settle these issues, and the public affairs expert can tell them how to do this successfully. Most lobby groups from the domestic level, especially the governments, have plenty of such technical experts ready at hand. Those from the Commission and the Parliament do not have them so numerous and have to insource them as members of an expert committee or an intergroup or simply as individuals invited to come along, thus offering them an excellent opportunity for lobbying.

In the pluralistic and fragmented EU area, *networks* are crucial for bringing together the different stakeholders. Most important is the informal network, because this is the precondition for the development of a stable semi-formal one, such as an ad-hoc coalition, which in its turn is the precondition for the formation of an authoritative formal organisation, such as a EuroFed. A formal platform without a stable semi-formal layer falls short of authority and can only survive artificially, for example thanks to a privileged legal position. Many a Council session is just such an artificial platform providing a privileged position for the national government. A semi-formal network without an underlying informality can easily lack stability and create its own misunderstandings, as frequently happens in Commission committees [Van Schendelen, 1998].

External *positions* are seen as crucial, because they link one's own group to the networks of stakeholders and, finally, to the EU machinery. The position may be that of an ordinary member of a EuroFed or an EU expert group, who sits around the table, monitors the others, voices maybe a few demands and uses the seat mainly as a means to improve a self-reliant plan of action. It may also be that of an informal leader, such as a big multinational in a fragmented EuroFed full of small to medium-sized enterprises (SMEs). A formally empowered position is not necessarily better than a merely informal one. It is not formal power but influence that matters, and the former, with its obligations of accountability, can even hamper the latter. In many a case, it is better to be the secretary running the apparatus invisibly than the formal chairman attracting all attention. Especially useful is the accumulation of positions. Some lobby groups have managed to position the same person as the secretary of an EuroFed, the expert on a committee, a member of an intergroup, and the representative of a working group. In contrast, the civil servants of the Commission hardly hold positions anywhere else.

Financial means are stressed as important resources, because of the costs of EU lobbying. Many variable cost items, for example those regarding expert-group work, are, however, reimbursed by the Commission. A lobby group can decide to invest more. The additional costs of a Brussels office (building, secretary, furnishings) can easily be as much as one hundred thousand euro a year [Greenwood, 1997, 103], which clearly discriminates against a lobby group with limited financial resources. The larger the budget of a trade association, the more contacts it appears to have with the Parliament, the Commission and the Council [Kohler-Koch, 1998]. Less well-off, usually small-sized ones can become richer by forming a collective group like a EuroFed. However, the concept of 'poverty' is not always easy to measure: Shell looks rich and Greenpeace appears poor, but both are rich if all the volunteers of the latter are capitalised. In any case, in 1998 Greenpeace was able to spend US$ 108 million on mainly political action [*Financial Times*, 20-09-00], which is more than the public affairs budget of most MNCs.

However important all resources may be, many professional EU lobby groups shift their political investments *from resources to skills*, which can be defined as meta-capacities for developing the capacity for action or simply as meta-resources. It is not the possession of expertise, networks, positions and budgets that is seen as crucial, but the development of the skills needed to acquire them at the right moment and in the right place and with the optimal mix. The skills refer to the activities of expertising (acquiring the expertise), networking, positioning and financing. The reasons behind this shift have everything to do with the efficiency of EU lobbying. Keeping all the resources in stock is an extremely costly affair. It is inefficient to collect, as a goal in itself, large and differentiated amounts of experts, networks, positions and budgets. Taking care of just one network is a time-consuming affair and demands continuous attention. It is more efficient to manage the supply of resources so that they are available at the right moment and place and in the desired mixture. The homework can reveal which mix of resources is needed for the fine-tuned fieldwork on a dossier.

A special skill regards the *research and development (R&D)* for useful new resources. In daily practice, many available resources hardly make a difference, because they are widespread or because they do not match the need in a specific case. The art is to develop new ones that really make a difference. In theory anything, even making a virtue out of necessity, can be used as a tool of effective EU lobbying. If it is also something new, then it may surprise the competitors and attract the EU officials. At the end of the 1990s, for example, new and efficient networks were formed by the use of electronic media; positions close to the accountancy firms working for the Commission were seized upon as advantageous tools; some losing stakeholders on the EU side, such as northern European steel manufacturers on the EU steel agreement, set up Washington liaison offices, thus taking position on two sides of the WTO table; companies in a politicised issue area like air transport or biotechnology discovered the method of setting up their own NGO (BONGO), in order to voice their opinion on consumer and environmental interests better; and the Commission developed more ingenious Triple-P practices, in particular on procedures of delegated legislation. Such new tools may be found by trial and error or by imitation, but by R&D the lobby group can be the first and take the lead. This and all other skills are ultimately a matter of political expertise. This meta-resource can be considered the single most important variable asset a lobby group may have.

A good image

The fourth requirement for a successful lobby group is a good image. Stakeholders and the officials feel attracted to the group when it behaves in an attractive manner. The idea of image has two dimensions, the first being its *general appeal*. The lobby group must have an image of both importance and agreeableness. By being seen as *important*, the group can avoid being overlooked and can have an anticipated influence on the others, who will take into account its existence and interests, even if it remains passive [Dahl, 1991]. There are, of course, different forms of importance. At one extreme, the lobby group is seen as having the power of, for example, a veto position (a minister in the Council) or a strong nuisance value (a blocking minority in a EuroFed). At the other extreme it is sympathy that makes the lobby group important, and thus attractive. It may be derived from its issue area, size, trade, social function or whatever highly valued context. In the 1990s, many NGOs promoting environmental issues ranked high on social sympathy. In between power and sympathy stand the variants of authority, prestige and respect, as enjoyed by, for example, the European Round Table of Industrialists (ERT) or the Economic and Financial Committee (EFC, previously the Monetary Committee). The image of *agreeableness* is the necessary addendum to importance. The lobby group must be seen as one with which it is a pleasure to make a deal, because it has a reputation of credibility for its words, loyalty to its promises and predictability for its subsequent actions. Without this, even the most powerful group may have a limited appeal, as it may be considered a monster not to be trusted. But agreeableness without importance is even worse, because it makes the lobby group a silly goose for the fox.

The professional lobby group always cares about its general image. It tries to make itself seen as important and agreeable. The more anticipated influence it has, the more it can save on the costs of lobbying. The more respect or sympathy it enjoys, the easier it can obtain a place around a decision-making table. The more it is seen as agreeable, the more comfortably it can come to a deal. A good general image, in short, is primarily a means to improve the efficiency of lobbying in the specific arenas. Image management really requires a lot of homework, as one has to influence the general affections of other stakeholders. Merely launching solemn statements, confessing social responsibility or sponsoring social needs is not sufficient, if necessary at all. If these activities have no impact on the EU stakeholders, then they are useless. If they contrast with the daily reality, they can even return as boomerangs. The preparatory work can even reveal some room for manipulation, for example the creation of the impression of being more important and more agreeable than others. But competitors doing their own homework well may unmask this impression management as being untrue.

The second dimension of a good image is the specific *supply side*. The amateur lobby group easily mistakes its own demand side, laid down in a so-called position paper advocating its preferences, as an attractive supply for its stakeholders. The professional group, in contrast, tries to meet the demand side of the primary stakeholders and to supply what makes them happy. By such an exchange it can make a deal. The supply of support is frequently demanded by stakeholders, most of whom feel weak on the competitive EU playing field and anyhow have to join a larger coalition. Commission officials have a strong appetite for detailed and reliable information regarding facts and trends in reality, and private interest groups, often having the information edge over governments, can supply this. Commission officials are also fond of the transparent aggregation of different interests. This saves them from doing the hard work of aggregation they themselves, while the transparency provides both views behind the scenes and signals to divide and rule if needed. In return they can supply scarce resources such as a desired draft proposal, a financial favour, a new procedure, another deadline or a better position inside. The high-ranking officials and the politicians have an insatiable appetite for good publicity through the mass media, in return for policy information and compliance. All this is usually true, but the best items for supply and exchange are always specifically attuned to the issues and the stakeholders at a particular moment in a current arena. They are different for the friendly, the unfriendly and the indeterminate situations. The clues come from the preparatory work.

Why Act, and for What?

The objective of a lobby group is to feel happy by winning an interest as a means to strengthen its ultimate objective, such as its licence to operate or its balance sheet. Circumstances and developments always challenge that sense of happiness. Perceived problems and expected threats may be called negative challenges, while perceived blessings and expected opportunities can be seen as positive ones. These are the two sides of the one coin of a challenge. In Ancient Greek times, this coin was called a 'problem', literally a rock thrown into the sea by playing gods, which endangered shipping on one side and provided shelter on the other. Today, 'problem' no longer means the coin, but only its endangering side. The dual objective of EU public affairs management is, however, still inspired by the Ancient Greek idea: to solve the negative challenges and to save the positive ones, as far as these by cause or consequence are related to socio-political processes. The inherent assumption is that it is possible to do this, but *what, precisely, is a problem and what is a blessing, and what is a threat and what is an opportunity?* The amateur will find the question superfluous, because he or she believes the answer is self-evident, at least as far as it applies to him/herself.

The professional knows that the answer is always a *value judgement* regarding a perceived or expected fact. It is the conclusion after the confrontation of a so-called fact (something that 'is or is not') with one's own so-called norm (something that 'ought to be or not'). Logically, the two are independent from each other and are only connected by the formula of the 'if... and if..., then...' approach: 'if this is the fact and if that is our norm, then we conclude that this is the challenge'. In the last resort, the fact has an absolute character: it does exist or does not, it is present or it is absent. The norm or value, however, has ultimately a relative character: it is one's own subjective viewpoint. Therefore, in the last resort every lobby group, including one's strongest enemy, is perfectly right about its chosen values. If, finally, the norm is positively loaded, one has a desire, and if negatively, a fear. *Figure 5.1* presents, at the top, the four situations that are logically possible. Two situa-

The challenges of public affairs management

I The nature of a challenge

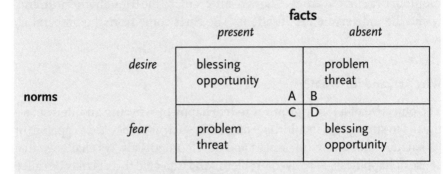

II The management of a challenge

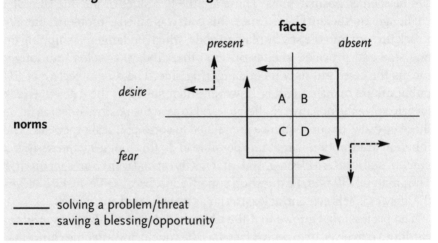

——— solving a problem/threat
------- saving a blessing/opportunity

Figure 5.1

tions can be described as representing a problem or a threat: in one the perceived or expected fact is not according to the desire (cell B), and in the other that fact is feared (cell C). The two other situations amount to a blessing or an opportunity: in one the perceived or expected fact is according to the desire (cell A) and in the other that fact gives no grounds for fear (cell D).

If one is a professional problem-solver, one can only be an optimist. One knows that, by logic again, the number of solutions is always twice the number of problems or threats. To create a *solution*, one might change either the fact or the norm. The lower part of figure 5.1 makes this clear. The first solution is that one tries to change the factual circumstances or developments. The way to do this is to turn cell B into A and/or cell C into D. This is a matter of carrying out, with plans of action, a lot of physical energy over several years with, of course, an uncertain outcome. The second solution is to change one's chosen norm and to opt for another one. Then one turns cell C into A and/or B into D. This is a matter of thought, which can be done fast and with the greatest effectiveness. The reassessment of a fact feared yesterday as something positive and that of an unfulfilled desire as something one should dislike merely requires a lot of mental energy. Marcus Aurelius, the Roman emperor, achieved such a change of attitude in his 'Meditations', after observing the breakdown of his empire around 180 AD. Paradoxically, most organisations (and people) are more doers than thinkers. To solve a problem or a threat, they prefer years of physical work above spending time on intellectual thinking. They consider it easier to change the facts than to change their norms. They are not professionals, as they miss half the number of solutions to a problem or a threat.

Changing either the facts or the norms has, of course, its *limits*. A fact is usually a variable, but not always a manipulable variable, at least not within the desired time period. The so-called problem of an unlevel EU playing field or the poor condition of Polish agriculture can hardly be solved in the short run. The variety of Europe, with all its regional cultures, is also an enduring fact of life. The change of norms has its limits as well. A company having its assets in a crisis sector, like textile manufacturing or shipbuilding in the past, cannot easily decide to move to another sector. Every lobby group has to respect dominant social norms as well, such as those regarding cartels, pollution and crime. If both the facts and the norms are not changeable, which is possible in theory but seldom happens in practice, then there is no solution to the problem, and if there is really no solution, then neither is there a real problem.

For the *saving* of a positive challenge (a blessing or an opportunity) the best practice of management is, of course, to preserve the *status quo* or to keep the situation moving in its favour. One has to preserve the facts of a situation, because they are seen as desired or free from fear, while at the same time checking, again and again, whether one still believes in the norm, whether it gives a desire or a fear. Most organisations (and people), however, hardly count their blessings and opportunities. As a consequence, they forget to preserve the benign facts and/or to validate their norms. They put their happiness at stake. Only the most professionals invest some of their energy in the saving of a blessing or an opportunity. They remember the fragility of every past happy circumstance. Paradoxically, most organisations do more to solve a negative challenge than to save a positive one, let alone to safeguard an old blessing. While trying to solve a problem, they may lose a blessing. While trying to prevent a threat, they may miss an opportunity.

So far, this reasoning is general and applicable to any field of human concern [Wartick and Mahon, 1994; Rochefort and Cobb, 1994]. It is, however, most relevant with regard to the management of EU public affairs. The EU playing field is always challenging. The facts are permanently changing, and most players have very different norms, reflecting their different cultural backgrounds and interests. This pluralism should invite one to reconsider one's own norms. The definition of the negative and the positive challenges or, in short, the *strategy development*, should be an almost daily concern of every lobby group [Hunger and Wheelen, 1998]. The amateur does this at random and incompletely. The professional has at least created some place and some time for doing it systematically and regularly. His or her strategy development takes place in the following three steps, plus two re-examinations of the agenda.

From the long list to the short list
The first step is the creation of an *awareness* about both oneself and the environment [Ackerman and Bauer, 1976]. Situations and trends, internally and externally, regarding both facts and norms are monitored and assessed. To put it simply: the cells of the upper part of figure 5.1 are filled with real cases, being the daydreams and the nightmares. A special PA official or unit may function as the engine, but many more people from both staff and line should be involved, to make the awareness more complete. The most difficult part of this work is the creation of self-knowledge and most of all the determination of what should be desired or feared. There is no absolute yardstick to determine the norms. They are in essence relative indeed. The best one can do is to keep them at least consistent with the other norms one holds for some time, otherwise one will end up throwing a boomerang. To regret this afterwards is a characteristic of the stupid. A notorious example has been provided by the Dutch Ministry of Agriculture on the 1993 Banana Dossier [Pedler, 1994]. In the first reading in the Council it supported the Commission proposal to protect the 'ACP bananas', thus supporting a (marginal) qualified majority. In the second reading, however, it supported the opposite case of a market liberalisation for the 'dollar bananas' (largely shipped through its harbour Rotterdam), and now it became part of the overruled minority. Finally it regretted its stupidity in not blocking the proposal during the first reading. The Ministry, being in two minds over what it

wanted to support, clearly lacked a consistent strategy. It is, of course, always difficult to develop a consistent strategy, and in many cases the strategy for tomorrow is only based on the evaluation of today's situations with the help of yesterday's norms. Awareness about both oneself and the environment is only a first step necessary in developing a better strategy. It results in the so-called *long list* of challenges, containing the blessings and the problems, the opportunities and the threats, the daydreams and the nightmares.

As a second step the *quick scan (figure 4.2)* is given to the challenges of the long list. For every selected case the main stakeholders and their issues and preferences are roughly identified. For a professional person or unit in EU public affairs management this can be largely a routine procedure, although every case is different. The next-best techniques of making the observations more reliable and complete, outlined in the previous chapter, can be used here. They cover both the reasoned estimate and the repetitive observation and they include, among other things, the use of the corporate memory and the involvement of various people from staff and line. The quick scan is, of course, not a goal in itself, but a mean to reduce the long list to a short list. Hardly any lobby group can simultaneously play on more than ten EU chessboards successfully. Only a very well-established NGO like Greenpeace, able to spend most of its affluent resources just on lobbying, can play on a few more, but even Greenpeace has to make a rational selection of priority dossiers, because the sum of desires and fears always outnumbers the resources. The development of the strategy for greater happiness is a matter of selectivity too.

The third step is the making of the *short list* or the *PA agenda*. An amateurish group finds this very difficult. Hardly being able to refuse a challenge, it overeats and, due to its corpulence, it can only move slowly. The professional lobby group is critical of the long list. It wants to pick the finest cherries, and does so by means of negative selection, discarding all challenges of poor quality until it is left with an agenda that can be realised successfully. Standard criteria of negative selection are the following *(figure 5.2)*.

i.   *Low relevance.* If the challenge scores low in terms of positive or negative impact, it is better for the lobby group to remain indifferent [Brown, 1979, 32]. This is clearly a matter of strategic thinking. For example, the 2000 draft directive on Liberalisation of Postal Services may affect every organisation sending ordinary post, but it is crucial for only a very few, such as the state-run post monopolies, the couriers and the mail-order firms.

Selecting priority dossiers for public affairs management

Monitor and scan current dossiers

If the dossier is assessed as:

1. hardly relevant by contents
2. damaging to internal organisation
3. having poor cost-benefit ratio
4. hardly urgent now
5. manageable by action elsewhere
6. free ride case (following winds)
7. without any chance (headwinds)
8. hardly making relevant difference

then (usually for majority of dossiers) remaining passive is rational

Figure 5.2

2. *Poor internal situation.* If the lobby group is internally seriously divided about a challenge, lacks sufficient knowledge, falls short of required resources and skills and/or expects a worsening image, it is better for it not to become active. Otherwise, it will become a loser in the best case and receive a boomerang in the worst case. An umbrella like ETUC is frequently internally divided on measures regarding the workplace and wisely does not to take specific stands.

3. *Adverse cost-benefit expectation.* This is more than a summary variable of the aforementioned two: all sorts of side effects can also be included. A great benefit from some action may be observed, but the costs of acquisition can make it unattractive. It is like the fine cherry at the very top of the tree, which is left to the birds. During the 2000 IGC for a new Treaty the governments of the small countries wanted to preserve their high proportion of Council voting points, but fearing the bill on other issues many conceded silently.

4. *Low urgency.* The lobby group can come to the conclusion that there is plenty of time for action. The challenge is in the future and immediate action is not necessary. The group consciously takes the risk that its competitors will act sooner, prearrange the arena and make it difficult to

intervene at a later moment. Green papers (suggesting a policy problem) and white papers (suggesting a policy solution) from the Commission are frequently seen as not urging action, although they may be early warnings of agenda setting.

5. *Good alternatives to EU PAM.* The mixed public-private multi-layers inside the EU may be taken as alternatives to EU public affairs management. Many an EU challenge can be solved or saved through either the national political system or the private sector. Farmers' groups frequently lobby their national government to reimburse the costs to them from EU measures on liberalisation, pollution or animal welfare. In a concentrated trade, like car manufacturing, the companies introduce many a standardisation themselves. In 1999, Philips decided to sell its Phonogram music division, because it felt endangered by the lack of good EU copyright regulation (and, as well, by its own CD-rewriter).

6. *Free ride available.* Often a free ride can be taken with another lobby group or coalition having the same preference but also a stronger interest in the outcome and better capacity for action. Small-sized companies, NGOs and governments frequently take a free ride with the bigger ones. The free ride is particularly rational if the arena is friendly: most probably the preference will prevail. The small air carriers like Virgin and Lauda hardly have to fight for air-transport liberalisation. They can take a free flight with British Airways, KLM and the US carriers, plus the consumer groups.

7. *Hardly any chance.* In this case the arena is assessed as extremely unfriendly, which is the opposite of the free ride case. There are mainly cold and fierce headwinds for the lobby group. If it were to become active, it could hardly proceed. Therefore it might just as well remain passive and save energy at least for getting compensation of its loss on another dossier. For example, the crofters in southern Europe have virtually no chance anymore of collecting from the EU rich agricultural subsidies they received in the past, and thus they can better lobby for something else compensating this loss.

8. *Hardly a relevant difference.* Even if the lobby group considers the challenge as relevant and feels it has a good chance of influencing the outcome, it may still believe that the created difference is at best hardly relevant. Comparing the situation before and after, it may feel it has been bitten by the dog instead of the cat (negative challenge) or pampered by the mistress rather than the wife (positive challenge). Then it is more efficient to stick to the cat and to the wife. Environmental lobby groups believing that the European Food Safety Authority (EFSA), composed of

the national authorities themselves, will hardly make a difference for food regulations, are better to remain passive regarding its establishment.

The EU agenda of public affairs management

The negative selection of the *priority challenges* can be easily made into a routine and even computerised. Every challenge on the long list can be given a score on the basis of each of the criteria. If one considers the criteria to be of unequal importance, then one can add one's weight to them at will. If, for example, a lobby group feels itself extremely rich, it can freely delete the cost-benefit criterion, as it can give this all the weight when it is feeling poor. If it wants to act anyway, for example for the purposes of publicity, then it can skip the free ride criterion. If it feels that the EU is endangering its mere existence, then it is better to give full weight only to the criterion of relevance. Under normal circumstances, however, not just one but many criteria have to be considered, and it may even be rational to give them all the same weight. This decision is, of course, one for the highest responsible management. Awarding scores to the challenges from the long list can be left to the rank-and-file people from staff and line. They usually have the expertise and information, but an EU public affairs office can give coaching on all this and will also collate the findings. The higher a challenge scores on the criteria, the less reason there is to become active on it. This negative selection of challenges should go on until preferably ten challenges at the most remain. These are the finest cherries, to be picked oneself. They are the rationally selected priorities, which form the short list or the PA agenda.

The removed challenges, the so-called *posteriorities*, have in fact been assessed as bearing higher total costs from political action than from adaptive passivity. Nevertheless, they need some follow-up care too. First of all, the challenges on the long list deserve a regular, for example quarterly, check on their low status. Perhaps the former assessment will need to be reviewed, due to a change of either facts or norms. Secondly, the causes of their low status may need to be dealt with at some stage: if, for example, the lobby group has to abstain from action due to its poor internal state (criterion 2), then it needs to address this. Thirdly, the consequences of a posteriority status may demand some action. For example, low urgency (criterion 4) should be used for at least some spadework and maybe for the safeguarding of a free ride (criterion 6). Finally, every posteriority can be used for the exploitation of some nuisance value. This is easier to do if one keeps one's own short list secret. Then, the other stakeholders, remaining uncertain about whether one becomes an active player or not, may provide some concession or compensation as a free gift, without costs.

Finally, after the three steps in the construction of the PA agenda, the professional lobby group makes *two re-examinations* of the agenda. First of all, it checks the selected PA agenda for its internal *coherence* and perhaps overlap. A lack of coherence or consistency may create a boomerang, as happened to many a national government from northern Europe in demanding both a reduction of EU regional subsidies (mainly financed by the North and spent in the South) and an increased allocation to its own regions. The search for coherence is an intellectual activity and should not be confused with the top-down decreeing of a coherent agenda on paper, as is the speciality of the French SGCI. Some selected challenges may have an overlap of issues and stakeholders as well. This creates room for a more integrated and thus more efficient approach. Secondly, the professional lobby group reviews its PA agenda as a set of *scenarios*. For every chessboard the leading question then is: what will happen if some fact or norm is changed? For sure, sooner or later one or both of them *will* change. A scenario helps to prepare oneself for that moment. This exercise is no different from the first step, when the challenge got its first definition. Its outcome can of course change the PA agenda. On second consideration a positive challenge may be seen as a negative one, or the reverse, or it may be that the challenge as yet does not pass the criteria of negative selection. All this is normal in the daily practice of thoughtful action under conditions of uncertainty and much better than acting thoughtlessly or overconfidently.

Matching the internal and the external arena
The amateurish group believes that its targets are clear: the problem or the threat has, simply, to be solved and the blessing or the opportunity, if identified at all, must be saved. Its action plan is directed at changing or preserving the factual side of the situation accordingly. It makes, however, a *threefold mistake*. Firstly, it neglects the normative dimension of any challenge. It is focused on doing, not on thinking, thus overlooking half the number of solutions. Secondly, it barely specifies the targets in advance and so it cannot determine precisely whether it has solved the problem or saved the blessing, in short whether it has ultimately been successful. At best, it reassesses the new facts according to the new norms of the day, but this is not a measure of (in)effectiveness but of (dis)satisfaction. Thirdly, its action plan is merely an introverted position paper, only containing its own perceptions and preferences, which it usually believes to be right. It hopes to overcome the nightmares and to preserve the daydreams. Its action plan is a dream or 'greatest happiness' scenario, only reflecting its demand side. It

is insufficient to achieve a deal and it may even tell the other EU stakeholders on which issues and items they can ask for a higher price.

The professional lobby group does it differently. At the *strategic* level, first of all, it brings all information about both the internal and the external arena together. This is, as it were, figure 4.2 again, but now including the home front in detail as well. The group has adopted the dossier as a priority and has determined its own issues and preferences. It has observed the facts and trends sufficiently, but it reconsiders its applied norms. Maybe some challenge will turn out not to be feared or desired, or perhaps even the whole dossier is not such a priority as previously thought. This reconsideration can save the group a lot of its energy. At this moment, in fact, the decision on whether *to go or not to go* is taken by the chief person responsible. If the group goes for the fight, it can of course repeat this critical strategic thinking at any time during the lobby process. Facts and trends may soon start to change, and if so they will require fresh thinking on norms, as Unilever discovered in 2000 when it decided to leave the GMO food arena. All this strategic thinking frequently results in a mixed decision on whether 'to go or not to go': regarding some aspects of the challenge the need for action is declared, but regarding some others it is not. Unilever, for example, did stop its GMO production and trade inside Europe, but not its research, and changed nothing outside Europe.

Secondly, the professional group defines in advance its *specific targets* or desired outcomes in the clearest way possible. If it wants to have a more benign EU regulation, it specifies for itself in advance how this should look and, if necessary, it does so in different variants. If it wants to receive or to keep a subsidy, it draws up for itself the amount required, the length of the period and the conditions. If it wants to get a friend parachuted into an important position, it defines for itself beforehand what sort of work to request which friend to do and in which position. Similar specifications are unambiguously and coherently made for any other desired outcome, such as the delaying of a decision, the reframing of an issue or the change of a procedure. This targets list is a position paper too, but it is different from the amateurish one. Firstly, it is clearly specified and thus suitable for measuring the level of success later on. Secondly, it is not simply introverted, but also attuned to the external arena. It is, in short, not the 'greatest happiness' scenario, but the greatest *possible* one.

Thirdly, the professional lobby group anticipates even more gloomy scenarios, as it is always more rational to prepare oneself for the thunder than for the sunshine. They are prompted by the question: 'What might happen if the arena turns from friendly to indeterminate to unfriendly?'. To prepare for the indeterminate situation, the professional group formulates a *next-best scenario*, preferably in several variants to provide flexibility. In such a scenario it includes some more concessions, which its preparatory work has revealed as probably acceptable to the crucial stakeholders. It is willing to accept a lower but still satisfying level of happiness. In addition, it develops for both the indeterminate and the unfriendly situation a *bottom-line scenario*. This equates with the targets one might maintain or win through the Court. Below this line, which is determined by the experts in legal affairs, it should never negotiate. For the unfriendly situation, in particular, the group finally works out a *loss-compensation scenario* as well, which covers possible linkages with other challenges or issues.

The *action plan* is the outcome of all this homework, now literally including the work at home. Its targets are internally sufficiently supported, unambiguously specified and realistically adapted to the arena situation. The plan contains the lists and schedules of activities, such as the actors to approach, the factors to use and the vectors to create. It connects, in short, all the homework to the fine-tuned fieldwork, to be outlined in the next chapter. All these preparations for the fight should, once again, not be taken as a sacrosanct goal. The lobby group blindly believing in its preparatory work is not a thoughtful professional but a naïve bureaucracy. The preparations are always only for some time to come and to the best of knowledge that is available, and as such tentative rather than definite. They usually regard a fight that has already started and is permanently changing, and thus requires a flexible response. The more proactive and the better researched, the more they help to achieve the desired outcomes.

With what Result?

The ultimate justification of a lobby action is that it creates a desired outcome. In daily EU practice the lobby group may be satisfied, of course, with less than the desired outcome. It may feel happy with a good compromise from the EU, enduring respect from the stakeholders and stable support from home. The desired outcome remains, however, the ultimate goal and is as such the reference point for the measurement of success. The professional group wants to see a *causal relationship* between its action and the EU outcome, the so-called dependent variable. Its action is not necessarily a case of doing something. As with the indeterminate arena, it may be a case of not doing anything and waiting-and-seeing. Whatever it decides, the group makes a conscious effort to influence or to make a difference as desired. In operational terms, the lobby group can be said to have influenced the EU, if it has more or less caused an EU outcome to be as it desired. However, that causality is always difficult to determine. Following David Hume [1748], one can even prove that, for at least two reasons, causality in social life is impossible to prove perfectly. The first reason has to do with time. Between the action and the outcome there is normally a lot of time, during which many more players try to influence the situation. The EU outcome is always a product of multiple competitive actors and factors, in short of multicausality. A single impact is impossible to isolate. Secondly, the lobby group can never know what would have been the outcome if it had remained absent. Maybe it would have achieved the desired outcome in any case, by sheer luck. The perfect control situation, necessary for the hard proof of causality, is not available in social life.

All this, strictly reasoned, may be considered true. The alternative, however, is not necessarily that one sees the social life as a collection of incidents beyond any explanation. In terms not of strict causality, but of *plausibility* one may determine some dependency of the EU outcome on the action of the lobby group. One can make use of at least the various next-best methods of assessing an influence or an impact [Van Schendelen, 1998, 13-17]. The best of these remains the *before and after* method: one compares firstly the action targets of the lobby group with the EU outcomes and tries to explain, as good and plausibly as possible, the latter by the former, and secondly those results with the action targets of the other stakeholders. Then one may see whether the lobby group has plausibly acted as a factor, or not. One can also recalculate its initial *chance* of creating a desired outcome; in doing so, as next-best methods, one assesses the resources, activities and networks at its disposal. The implicit theory is that if its resources are poor, its activities dull and its networks obsolete, then it has not been in the position to make a plausible difference, let alone one that it desired. Finally, there is the method of measuring the *reputation* for influence. One may ask the other stakeholders to give their frank opinion about the lobby group's performance in influencing outcomes. Not only an outsider can apply all these methods, but also every lobby group can do this to both itself and the others.

These next-best methods clearly have their shortcomings and that is why they are called next best. According to David Hume's fundamental view of social life, the before and after option is open to criticism, as the causality cannot be proven. The chance-based methods, suggesting causality as well, have the same weakness and, in addition, they replace the yardstick of the efforts to influence by (some of) the means of influence. Resources, activities and networks may contribute to influence, but they are not valid indicators of it: they tell us more about potential than about real influence. Besides, many more means should then be considered, such as a sufficient cohesion, technical expertise and a good image, to mention only a few from this chapter alone. The reputation method is not sufficiently reliable, because if one respondent can misperceive the real process of influence, then all the respondents can.

While all this may be considered true, every serious lobby group likes *to know* the impact of its actions. It desires this not as an intellectual goal in itself, but as a pragmatic means to improve its future behaviour. The amateurish group mainly learns by doing, if it learns at all. When it learns that one approach does not work well, then it simply tries another one, without much understanding of why the latter may be better than the former. The semi-professional group at least tries to learn some lessons in advance. It imitates those seen as the winners and wants to behave differently from those seen as the losers. In fact, it responds to reputations. The professional group does more. In addition to learning by doing and by studying the others, it is eager to know and to understand the variable impact of its lobby actions on the EU stakeholders. It wants to know whether, how and why its actions have contributed (or not) to the causes of the EU outcome. It invests in advance and afterwards in the gathering of knowledge, as it expects from this the greater return of achieving more desired outcomes in the future. It seeks a higher profit both from investments it has made and from the (already paid) costs of its previous mistakes.

In the professional approach the next-best methods are modified and integrated into a *systematic evaluation*. The starting point is the before and after comparison between the efforts to influence and the final outcome. Those efforts are the implementation of the action plan, containing the specific targets, the schedules, the scenarios and more, as outlined above. They are differentiated for the various phases of the decision-making process, so that even outcomes between times can be evaluated. After this comes the attempt to explain the similarities and the differences between the efforts and the outcomes. Of course, one should never take the similarities as the sole proof of success and the differences as that of failure, because the former may simply be due to good luck and the latter to bad luck, all unrelated to any action at all. But luck is occasional, not regular. If the similarities or the differences are regular rather than occasional, then they indicate the plausibility of some causal relationship between the efforts and the outcomes. The explanation can, of course, make use of all available general knowledge about regular factors of lobby actions, such as the capacity for action, the desires to participate, the compulsions to act politically and the invitations to join the arena, mentioned earlier. Such general knowledge can be used as a checklist of hypotheses to help explain the observed relationship in any specific case. Because the improvement of lobby success in the future is the purpose of such applied research into influence, the studious group has a special appetite for the specific factors under its control. These can be manipulated more than the others can, and so deserve an evaluation.

The specific factors certainly include the qualities of one's resources, activities and networks, as well as the many others outlined here. For the professional wanting to get an evaluation of its lobby performance they all have one common denominator: the *quality of the preparatory work* driving the action. This is tested with the wisdom of hindsight, as the student checks his test paper once again after the examination. The professional group is particularly interested in its unforced errors. These it can blame only on itself and not its competitors. For example, being misled by the smart Triple P game of a competitor is not necessarily an unforced error, but not to have allowed for this certainly is. The hindsight test is made, of course, for the various parts of the homework regarding both the internal and the external arena. If, for example, the group has been surprised by new facts and developments in the arena, it poses itself the critical question of why it has been surprised and how that can be avoided by better preparation in the future. It can make many critical comparisons, such as between one phase and another, one arena and the other, the recent past and the present, and itself and the main competitors. The critical review of the preparation provides more new self-knowledge and even inspiration for new R&D in EU public affairs management. The professional group stores the findings in its corporate memory, which is easily accessible to all its members, for example by intranet. All this sounds ambitious perhaps, and indeed, most lobby groups rarely evaluate their homework, if they have done any. As a result, they deny themselves the opportunity to strengthen the plausible relationship between their actions and the outcomes.

As the last next-best method the lobby group can measure the *reputation for influence* of both itself and the others on a recently completed dossier. Its own rank-and-file people are one source of respondents. Other potential sources are the EU officials subject to influences from everywhere, the befriended groups, the indifferent ones, and, if available, the peer groups of colleagues in EU public affairs management. It is rare to canvass the opponent lobby groups, although such a sports-like review of the match they have also been involved in may be extremely informative and may even result in a more friendly relationship. Every source has, of course, its strengths and weaknesses and may yield different results. The general weakness of rating reputation, however, is that it easily measures satisfaction at home or admiration in the external arena instead of the effectiveness of the lobby actions. Such measures may yet prove useful. The satisfaction indicates the level of happiness with the EU outcome and the backing for it at home, and the admiration can show the level of respect one gets on the playing field. The satisfying outcome, respect and backing remain the realistic prizes to win or to lose. Even if they are based on loose impressions, they are useful information. But if they are the products of only the management of impression, then they have nothing to do with evaluation.

Extra: the Multinational Model

No lobby group has its public affairs in a perfectly organised state at home, but some are more perfect than others. In the eyes of many players in the field [Koeppl, 2001; Kohler-Koch, 1998], the *multinational companies* (MNCs) in particular set the trend in managing their EU public affairs professionally, both externally and on the home front. They have to. Internally they have to cope with an exceptional variety of cultures, role expectations and formal duties. The differences between both the product units and the country units alone mean that internal dissent is, normally, their natural state of affairs. Externally, they are extremely challenged by the EU. Most EU decisions deal with the europeanisation of markets and sectors and thus particularly affect the multinationals. They are most dependent on EU decisions regarding, for example, the open market, standardisation, R&D subsidy and external trade. It was no accident that the EU policy programme 'Open Market 1992' was first planned at the Round Table of Industrialists in 1984 and first drafted in the PA Department of Philips in 1982 [Verwey, 1994]. The MNCs not only desire and have to lobby, but they also have the capacity to do so. They can usually fall back on sufficient financial means, technical experts, important networks and relevant positions. Most are also widely seen as having a good image and receive a lot of invitations, particularly from the Commission and the Parliament, to enter the corridors or rooms and to participate in expert groups or intergroups.

There is, in short, much to learn from the MNCs and their best practices of managing their home front [MacMillan, 1991; Pedler, 1995; Coen, 1998; Bennett, 1999; Sietses, 2000; Aerts and Verhaege, 2001]. Of course, they are far from all being the same. Some are more multinational than others or more organised by country units than by product units. All sorts of factors contribute to their variation, ranging from market position, economic sector and labour intensity to history, ownership, prestige and more. Nevertheless, most MNCs have a *basic structure* of their internal organisation in com-

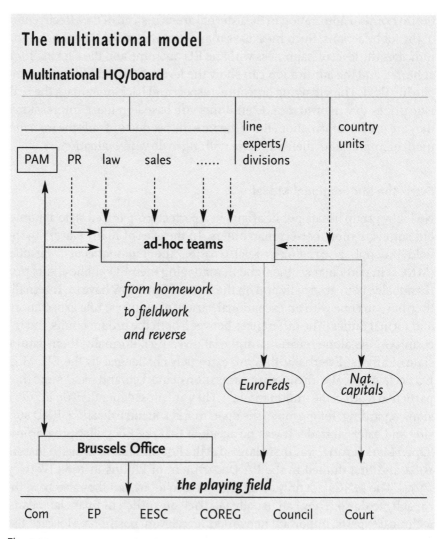

The multinational model

Multinational HQ/board

PAM PR law sales ...... | line experts/ divisions | country units

ad-hoc teams

from homework to fieldwork and reverse

EuroFeds

Nat. capitals

Brussels Office

the playing field

Com   EP   EESC   COREG   Council   Court

Figure 5.3

mon. *Figure 5.3* shows a stylised abstraction of it. The central unit is the *EU public affairs office*, located in the headquarters and under the direct responsibility of some member of the Central Board. It has three core jobs to do.

Its first task is to do all the *homework*, such as the monitoring of challenges, the making of the long list, the scanning of the arenas, the drafting of the action plans, the creation of scenarios, the retrieval of the corporate memory, and the evaluation of past 'games, sets and matches'. All this and more it does by taking into consideration both the external and the internal situation, both the past and the present, and both the perceived facts and the optional norms. At regular times, usually once every three or four months, it presents the results of its work to the responsible member of the Board. In view of the current strategy of the company, this person has to approve the proposed EU agenda of public affairs management for the next time period. This definition of the short list is seen as the key decision optimising the balance between internal support and external effectiveness. Most identified challenges are not placed on the short list. Country units and product units considering them still worthwhile are free to lobby on their own, unless this creates irritating turmoil inside the MNC. Every selected dossier is translated into specific targets, attuned to the external arena. In addition, the Board member uses the results of the preparatory work as input for strategy renewal. Old problems can, then, be reconsidered as blessings, or the reverse.

The second task of the public affairs office is the internal *implementation* of the short list. The standard approach is that for every priority dossier an *ad-hoc team* is formed, led by a kind of *chef de dossier*. The team consists of three categories of relevant people. Firstly, members from other staff units, such as from Public Relations (to keep in touch particularly on the issue of sound-in-public, to which we return in the next chapter), EU Law (for the formal sides of the dossier, including the bottom-line scenario), and Sales (because the management of public affairs also must ultimately contribute to the company's profits, a lesson learnt again by Shell during the Brent Spar affair). Secondly, experts from the relevant line management are included. They have the technical expertise on an EU issue of, for example, biotechnology, standardisation, transportation or engineering. In many cases they have a seat in an EU expert group or EuroFed as well; if not, the public affairs office helps to get them one. Thirdly, people from the various country units are part of the ad-hoc team. They may not only have different interests, which it is better to include rather than exclude, but also additional capacities and opportunities for lobbying. They can, for example, tap information from their own government, mobilise domestic support groups, and contribute to the company's multinational orchestra playing for the EU officials. The ad-hoc team usually meets more virtually than physically. The major tools of communication are the intranet, email, phone, fax and, sometimes, teleconferencing.

The third task of the public affairs office is to co-ordinate and to realise the external *fieldwork* with regard to the EU officials and the other stakeholders. For this it has two major tools. One is the aforementioned ad-hoc team, whose members operate as the multinational's orchestra, spearheading communication with the primary stakeholders. In many cases they already have a relationship with them, due to their line position, their national background and/or their membership of an association or an expert group. The second tool is the *Brussels office*, which almost every MNC has. The office is usually small-sized, consisting of one senior, one junior and a secretary. It has a location and a budget that permit hospitality. It serves primarily as the ears and the eyes of the company on the Brussels playing field. Going window-out, it monitors the competitors and officials and forwards the information to the central public affairs office. Secondly, it serves as the voice and the feet of the company in Brussels: going window-in, it fine-tunes here the efforts to lobby the process through, for example, coaching the line experts, talking with Commission officials, meeting competitors and engineering indirect links. It functions, in short, as a hub for the MNCs shuttle lobbying.

In many an MNC there exists the particular *issue of trust* between its Brussels office and the central public affairs office. The Brussels office needs a clear mandate, which gives room to manoeuvre, because otherwise it cannot fine-tune the actions, but the central one wants to keep control over what is done or left undone. British, Dutch and Nordic MNCs usually give their Brussels offices a free mandate for most window-out and -in activities, which are scrutinised regularly for the results. MNCs from the rest of Europe (and from the USA as well) usually see their Brussels office as merely their local desk having a strictly limited mandate, more for going window-out than window-in. Fearing that the local office may become an autonomous player, independent from the headquarters, they like to keep control over it at all times. The price they pay for this distrust in their own Brussels offices is frequently an unforced corporate passivity (or even absence) on the EU playing field. Waiting for new instructions from Frankfurt, Paris or Madrid, the local officer sees the play in progress and the instructions arriving too late. Some MNCs have moderated the issue of trust by compromising on distance: for example, the Brussels officer can, part of the week (usually Monday and Friday), be based at headquarters and even charged of co-directing the central public affairs office. Until recently such a bi-location or such a dual mandate demanded a lot of travelling. New communications technology, especially the intranet, can moderate this issue too.

The multinational model of EU public affairs management is, in a few catchwords, highly integrative through the inclusion of internal variety, professional by its focus on the homework, efficient in its plain and flexible structures and adapted to the challenging environment. Its organisation through a central public affairs office with flexible ad-hoc teams and a local support base, all under supervision of a Board member, is like that of a modern military intervention force. Not surprisingly, the MNCs have the reputation of being among the most successful lobby groups: scoring on issues, strengthening their position and enabling their people. Surprisingly, the MNCs stand almost alone in the way they organise themselves for the EU playing field. They are more admired in theory than followed in practice. It seems that most other EU lobby groups find the application of the multinational model difficult.

Other interest groups in comparison

SMEs and *local governments* usually have a weaker impetus for EU action, much fewer resources and skills, too parochial an image, and a more regional than European interest orientation. If they want to become influential at the EU level, they usually have to do this through the remote control of a national ministry and/or their association at either the national or the European level. Only a very few yet have a Brussels office, for example the Greater London Authority. Some have a special officer, but more on a travelling than a permanent basis and more for the monitoring (particularly of EU subsidies) than for window-in lobbying. This person acts mainly according to circumstances and is hardly embedded in an organisational structure with a public affairs office, ad-hoc teams and the like.

Regional governments usually have much more potential [Badiello, 1998]. Many are reasonably resourced, have their own Brussels office, feel compelled to lobby for subsidies and are invited to participate in semi-formal and formal EU meetings, ranging from expert groups to COR. Co-operating with other regions in Europe inside a EuroFed, a network or an ad-hoc group, they succeed in presenting an European face. But most are weakly organised at home. Their government background, with elected politicians and mass publicity on the home front, often makes it difficult to determine a short list of priorities with clear targets beforehand and critical evaluations afterwards. Their EU performance is frequently merely that of their small team in Brussels acting autonomously.

The *NGOs* vary in their effectiveness strongly. Most are just local or regional and have more or less the same problems with effective EU lobbying as the SMEs. But three categories of NGOs come close to the multinational model. First of all, the *protest NGOs* like Greenpeace and Amnesty [Jordan and Maloney, 1996; Jordan, 1997], which are usually excellently resourced and organised like an MNC, with ad-hoc teams and a Brussels office. Secondly, the *EuroFeds* [Greenwood, 1997; Greenwood and Aspinwall, 1998], which are usually based in Brussels and consider EU lobbying as part of their *raison d'etre*. They invest both in their European image and in the professional management of their EU affairs. Some, however, are largely national interest groups in a European disguise, for example the (British) Animal Welfare, the (German) SME-umbrella UEAPME and the (Italian) group of motorcyclists FIM. Almost all have a sort of PA office (often the secretariat) with ad-hoc teams (usually so-called working groups) and standard procedures for arriving at a short list or a common agenda. Many of their position papers are fairly well attuned to the EU arenas. Their two main weaknesses are often a lack of resources and internal dissent. Their larger members, who have their own alternative opportunities for lobbying, are frequently reluctant to provide finance and to compromise. The smaller members have less to contribute and to concede. All members can freely leave their EuroFed, as this is a voluntary association, and can form or join another one. Thirdly, there are the *hybrid NGOs*, like the GONGOs and the BONGOs. Frequently they are lobby platforms organised particularly by regional governments and MNCs, like CASTER by the regional governments lobbying for so-called steel interests and EACF by the national air carriers for what they call consumer interests. With the image of an NGO they feel that they are in a better position with regard to what others hopefully consider a general interest. This exemplifies their EU awareness and their ability to organise.

As a result particularly of the new Treaties in the 1990s with their broadening and deepening of EU policy areas, all *national ministries* feel that they are dependent on EU outcomes and want to influence them. They have to, because their autonomy to make binding decisions at home has become limited and pooled at EU level. At the Council level they all have their meetings and working groups, and the Commission invites them to take part in committees and agencies. Given such fine preconditions for EU lobbying, one might expect an MNC-like structuring of their EU affairs. Paradoxically, in most countries a ministry seldom has any kind of a public affairs office with ad-hoc teams for doing the preparation and planning the fieldwork. A Brussels office is a rarity; their people in the PR are primarily for liaison only with the Council. The long list with daydreams is seldom reduced to a short list with realistic targets and scenarios. Usually the policy experts, to compare with the line experts in the MNC, do the EU fieldwork almost alone and only in the committees of the Commission and the working groups of the Council. They are frequently poorly resourced and on most dossiers hardly co-ordinated. In their daily work they tend to deny the differences within their home ministry, to neglect the homework and to underestimate the fieldwork. The few exceptions to this general pattern are the small-sized Nordic ministries and those dossiers that are highly politicised at home.

That paradox has many specific causes, but also a few general ones such as the following. Except in the Nordic countries, most ministries, firstly, are large-sized *bureaucracies*. By their many formal tasks and duties alone they are already internally strongly divided. The top officials, being more political advisers than managers, have a span of control too limited for a sufficient building of cohesion. A ministry is usually run by self-reliant directorates and units, which only now and then take initiatives to establish MNC-like practices including a central desk, ad-hoc teams, a short list and even their own Brussels officer. Most ministries, secondly, have a *Council fixation* and see themselves as the powerful gatekeeper of EU decisions. They suffer from a cultural lag, since under Pillar I the bulk of EU decisions is made elsewhere and under Pillar II and III not many are taken. The small number of decisions they can influence falls in the last phase of the EU decision-making process. Here there is much less room for proactive lobbying than for last-minute crisis management. Their people in the national PR are also biased towards the Council and neglect particularly the semi-formal and informal layers of the Commission and the EP. Thirdly, the national ministries *stand alone* on the EU playing field. They do not have anything like a EuroFed for the proactive europeanisation of their interests, and the Council is no substitute for this. The main exceptions are the ministries of Defence, which now operate their NATO-linked Western European Armament Group (WEAG) and high-level committees, in north Brussels. The rest of the national ministries have an only national face or, more precisely, a national government one. They rarely form networks and coalitions with foreign nongovernmental stakeholders like MNCs and NGOs. The multinational model, in short, is still far beyond their reach.

The *national governments* differ the most from the multinational model. In theory, they meet most conditions for an excellent organisation. They have a strong interest in EU outcomes, many opportunities for influence, partly enshrined in Treaty texts, and plenty of manpower, financial means, expertise and other resources. They all have some domestic procedure and organisation for national co-ordination as well. However, with most governments the procedure is only started when the Council meeting approaches. Thus the earlier phases of Commission and EP involvement are neglected and so are decisions taken outside the Council by particularly the Commission (comitology). The procedure is usually an introverted effort on paper to create policy coherence and to justify the government's voting position in the Council to the national parliament [Van Schendelen, 1993;

Kassim and others, 2000 and 2001]. Therefore, even in the French SGCI case, the co-ordinating body bears no comparison to the public affairs office and the ad-hoc teams of the MNC. Neither is the PR the parallel of the Brussels office, as its members primarily act as liaison between their ministry and the Council [De Zwaan, 1995]. The governments seldom launch a proactive action based on careful preparation. Only when preparing for a new Treaty or for their Council chairmanship do they almost always establish at least a high-level ad-hoc team. However, the resulting position paper is usually the long list of daydreams and nightmares and not the short list of targets that would have more realistic application away from just the home front.

The popular idea that the national government must be united in its actions is for at least two reasons hardly realistic. Firstly, every government, here defined as all executive structures together, is internally *seriously divided*. The ministries and agencies are strong competitors with each other. They have their own formal tasks and duties, semi-formal sectoral loyalties and informal cultures, including party-political ones. Only on paper is the national government an organisation with its own parallel of a CEO and a Board, usually called the Prime Minister and the Cabinet. The more 'statist' governments of France and the UK are models for this [Schmidt, 1997 and 1999], but their co-ordination is little more than the recording of the outcomes of both self-reliant actions of the ministries and conflicts between them, made coherent on paper. Secondly, the national government, now defined as formally the highest layer of a country, is always confronted with a very *pluralistic home front*. The national parliament, civil society and the mass media are always divided about whatever new EU challenge there is. If they get wind of this, the private groups and the media usually receive it from their people in Brussels or their friends in the ministries at home. In some cases the private groups respond by launching a public campaign at home, and the journalists frequently give sensational coverage to it. MPs politicising the domestic issues involved often embarrass the government, forcing it to take side in public. A majority vote or, as in the Nordic countries, an instruction from parliament can settle the issue formally, but hardly in reality. Ministries and private groups having lost a domestic fight, usually feel more stimulated to lobby directly in Brussels.

Non-EU interest groups exhibit a wide variety of internal structures. At the upper end there is, for example, the US Mission in Brussels [Winand, 1998]. It operates like the multinational model and is connected to the staff and line experts of Washington. It invests much in preparation for the field-work. The American Chamber of Commerce comes close to it. At the lower end one may find foreign applicant governments, such as little Malta with its wavering preference for membership, and Poland where, at the end of the 1990s, four top politicians (the President, the Prime Minister, the Foreign Affairs minister and the European Affairs minister) vied with each other for control over EU affairs. Many of the non-EU countries' ministries are, however, much better organised. For example, the Hungarian Ministry of Transport is well organised for its interests in cross-border trucking. The country of Thailand, to support its exports, which are mainly dependent on the sale of tapioca to the EU, usually well prepares its fights with EU suppliers of animal food. Most foreign companies rely heavily on both their national governments and their associations. Only a few foreign MNCs, mainly from the USA and Japan, fit in with the multinational model. One of their main internal difficulties is to find a balance between the roles of headquarters and the Brussels office. Many have chosen to instruct the latter from the other side of the world, which is clearly a weakness.

Finally one can compare the EU institutions with the multinational model, and most interesting in this case is the *European Commission*. Many DGs come close to the multinational model. The Commissioner and the higher officials determine the short list. The *chef de dossier* functions as a sort of public affairs officer, who makes suggestions for this list, carries out the preparatory work and organises the fieldwork. Internally this person gets advice from different staff members, such as on EU law and on countries that need special treatment. A main window-out activity is the publication of green papers and white papers, which trigger the preferences of many stakeholders. They help to develop most of the realistic policy scenarios. Window-in activities take place particularly through the committees composed of representative experts from both private groups and governments. If they have a community of interests, they can be used practically as ad-hoc teams meeting as frequently as required to solve or to preserve the common interest. Then, the *chef* can promote this interest inside the Commission and the committee members can do this elsewhere, for example inside both the EP and their EuroFed, PR or national ministry.

From the Home Front to the EU Fieldwork

Organising one's home front is clearly a difficult job. It may take, indeed, over half one's energy available for the EU public affairs management. It requires a lot of homework. Nobody should blindly try to produce cohesion, knowledge, resources, skills, image, strategy, targets, scenarios and evaluations. All these internal ingredients for the cooking of success one should prepare carefully. This is purely a matter of *preparatory work*. The clearest example is the determination of the short list. This requires a reasoned selection from the long list of so-called challenges as identified by the examination of assessed facts and norms. Only after this can one really know what sort of ingredients one has to prepare, and what quantity and quality are required. The lobby group neglecting all this homework will almost certainly be punished by an extremely poor result from its EU actions.

The preparation for the home front is, of course, almost always *less than perfect*. In two situations this may be justified. Firstly, if the costs of perfection would exceed those of imperfection. Merely the factor of time pressure, for example caused by the deadlines of an EU process, may mean that the only real alternative to an imperfectly prepared action is no lobby action at all, which may be worse. The second situation is when one is better prepared than the best competitor, even if one's own preparation is less than good. For this, we used the metaphor of the tiebreak point previously. If the lobby group, however, observes that some of its competitors are organising their home front better, then it has to improve its own preparation for the match as well. This logic is indeed the hard reality of the EU playing field. More than ever, many interest groups want to create a desired outcome and invest in intelligent preparation for this at home.

The *multinational model* is, for sure, not the last word on optimising one's home front. It looks well designed: integrative, professional and efficient. It stands for co-ordinated self-reliance. For a growing number of lobby groups it functions as a standard or an example to follow. The establishment of a Brussels office has become particularly popular. This has raised, in consequence, many questions of internal organisation, ranging from the determination of the short list to the division of tasks and duties of public affairs management with regard to homework and fieldwork. The multinational model, looking so rational, is frequently applied only piece by piece, starting with a Brussels officer and, years later, creating important changes deep inside the organisation at home. The big question for research, of course, remains whether the model-like organisation of EU public affairs management does in fact create significantly more EU lobbying success. Both the theoretical logic of public affairs management and the MNCs reputation for influence among practitioners favour the multinational model, but this is less than empirical evidence. In any case, even if found necessary for success, the model can never be considered sufficient. It remains part of the preparation for the match and is not the match itself. The external fieldwork still has to come. This is a matter of fine-tuned lobbying and precise timing, the theme of the next chapter.

CHAPTER 6

MANAGING THE FIELDWORK

Lobbying: the Essential Link

After coming to the conclusion that its challenge should be solved or saved by lobbying on the EU playing field, the lobby group has to choose its ways and means of going window-out and -in. One option, of course, is to make use of the standard patterns of permitted or invited participation, such as the membership of a EuroFed, the request for consultation by the Commission, the Parliament hearing or, in some cases, the national co-ordination procedure at home. These orthodox ways have some advantages, such as their low costs of acquisition, the easy opportunities they provide to meet officials and their efficient window-out monitoring. Against these stand important disadvantages. The orthodox ways are open to many stakeholders, are therefore easily overcrowded and provide little opportunity to gain an edge over rivals. They are unfit for window-in activities. Being standardised, they are hard to engineer according to one's specific needs, for example, of timing and boundary control. Another option, more in addition to than replacing the former, is to develop unorthodox ways and means or forms of action. The popular key term for this is *lobbying*.

Originally, the term refers to the special practices of interest group representatives in the US Congress in the late 19th century [Milbrath, 1963; US/GAO, 1999]. Waiting in the lobbies of the Congress buildings, they urged the Congressmen passing by to vote 'yea' or 'nay' [Matthews and Stimson, 1975]. In the course of time, this 'lobbying' developed from merely corridor behaviour to a broader and more sophisticated set of activities, ranging from providing information to organising mass publicity and giving political or even financial support. The last-mentioned activity, which sometimes developed into bribery, has given lobbying a bad name among many ordinary people. The increasingly stricter regulation of lobbying in the USA since the mid-1920s, through both codes of conduct and registration, has barely improved this bad name. As a technical term it remains, however, useful. It refers to all sorts of *unorthodox actions of interest groups intended to bring desired outcomes from government.* So far we have used the term generally, as covering all window-out and window-in actions. From now on we will apply it specifically to the unorthodox variants. They are, once again, not necessarily cases of doing anything and also include cases of deliberate non-action or waiting and seeing. In either case, the lobby group is involved, visibly or not.

The definition deserves some elaboration. On the *receiving end* of lobbying are ultimately the governmental decision-makers. In the old US days these persons were primarily the elected politicians. In the Western political systems today, more and more the civil servants have become the ultimate targets of lobbying. They possess the bulk of delegated and discretionary powers. But in most systems, especially on the European continent, they are closely interwoven with representatives from organised civil society. For example, experts from the German company Siemens, the Portuguese Ministry of Social Affairs and the Italian Regione Lombardia circulate around the Commission semi-formally and informally. In fact, they may act as the real decision-makers, either being behind the text of an EU decision or making sure it is not made. The formal decision-makers, such as the Commissioner or the Council, may even remain ignorant of this. In consequence, not only the officials, but also the many other stakeholders around and even those inside one's home organisation are subject to EU lobbying. The adjectives of, respectively, 'political', 'social' and 'internal' lobby might be used to differentiate the three targets for lobbying, which are so closely connected in practice.

The lobby groups form the *sender side.* They can be citizens' groups, companies, trade associations and all other organisations forming part of civil society. Parts of any government can act as lobby groups too, either at their own initiative or having been persuaded by some affiliated private group. All national and most regional governments have their official representation in Brussels, but their people based here can also act as lobbyists. People from a domestic public agency or government desk can lobby on the EU playing field without having a formal representation or facility in Brussels. At the EU level, a Commission DG, a Parliament intergroup or a Council working group can behave as a lobby group, and their people individually as lobbyists as well. These EU officials are, in fact, both receivers and senders in the lobby process, a double role that gives them a most advantageous position. For the creation of a desired outcome, all these lobby groups may have, of course, their constitutional ways, regular procedures and other orthodox means as well. Citizens can join a political party or vote on election day; companies can formally appeal to a government or to the Court; in many countries, interest groups are formally consulted about government proposals; and Commissioners can always put forward a draft regulation. The use of these constitutional, regular and orthodox ways of influence are, however, not part of our specific definition of lobbying, even though they are frequently used in addition to it.

The action of influence must have an element of *unorthodoxy* falling outside the standard patterns of permitted or invited behaviour. The concept of (un)orthodoxy is, however, not easy to operationalise and to measure. Every bipolar concept has inevitably a lot of grey area, in our case resulting in degrees of (un)orthodoxy. Besides, an unorthodox practice today or in one arena, may be orthodox tomorrow or in another arena. Lobbying is also full of subtleties and therefore not easy to measure by indicators. For example, the Olivetti public affairs officer, who sends a personal letter to or calls the Parliament's rapporteur in order to influence his/her report, is clearly lobbying. So is the Commissioner, who offers the rapporteur a fine lunch in order 'to listen' or 'to make sure things are in order', but his formal letter in reply to a request from the rapporteur is not. Attending an organised hearing is not an activity of lobbying, but pressuring for its convocation or calling-off may be. The use of the break during a hearing in order to deal informally with other stakeholders is certainly a case of lobbying. The letter or lunch used for private affairs has, of course, nothing to do with lobbying, but every letter or lunch used for lobbying is best opened with some conversation about private affairs first, in order to create a pleasant and easy atmosphere for the business.

Some final comments on the definition are as follows. Firstly, lobbying should never be equated with influencing. It is only an unorthodox *effort* to create a desired outcome or influence, and there is, consequently, never any guarantee of success. Secondly, the definition suggests a one-way flow of actions, but this is only the basic pattern. In reality, there is almost always at least a two-way flow of communication and interaction. The EU officials having dual roles are the clear example of this *lobby shuttling*. Frequently, the pattern comes close to being a complex delta, full of side-streams, branches and channels [Deutsch, 1963]. Thirdly, the lobbying may be done as a full-time job, and there are many Brussels-based public affairs officers and consultants calling themselves professionals who do this. But most people practice the lobby only as a side-activity to their main job as, for example, a policy expert, line manager, civil servant or regional politician. Our notion of *professionalism* remains, once again, the mark of quality and not one of occupation. The full-time lobbyists can really be amateurs or cat burglars, whereas the part-timers can be the most professional.

EU lobbying we see as one of the fundamental parts of EU public affairs management, but also as *neither necessary nor sufficient* for getting the desired outcome. Every interest group can rationally abstain from lobbying in at least three situations. Firstly, if it wants to solve or to preserve its challenge by a non-EU action, for example at the domestic level or through the market. Secondly, if it has reason to believe that the decision-makers have already anticipated its potential influence and its desires regarding the outcome. Thirdly, if it considers as still sufficient the orthodox opportunities, such as offered by a EuroFed or the Commission. These three situations of rational non-lobbying are, of course, totally different from the situation in which the wait-and-see approach was considered the best. EU lobbying is also never sufficient to win the game. At the most it provides a better chance of winning than by the use of the orthodox opportunities alone. For this reason, lobbying the EU can be called essential for getting a desired outcome. But even without this ultimate effect, it remains useful as a triple tool: for window-out monitoring; for validating the three situations of reasoned abstention; and for strengthening one's position on the EU playing field.

The Surplus of Unorthodox Actions

On the EU playing field every interest group has really no shortage of potential actions for the creation of a desired outcome. It can choose from an infinite menu of possibilities of going window-out and window-in. Firstly, it can take the standard opportunities, mentioned above, for which it does not have to lobby in the specific sense. Secondly, it can fall back on the traditional techniques of influence, such as coercion, encapsulation, advocacy and argumentation, mentioned in the first chapter. Thirdly, it can make use of the many unorthodox techniques, which are discussed below. In fact, almost every variable is potentially instrumental. There are always manifold actors to approach factors to be used and vectors to construct. The options of 'exit, voice and loyalty' [Hirschman, 1970] or, in popular parlance, 'flee, fight, flirt', are only three out of many, and one always has the choice of using a technique leading in one or another direction, which poses a dilemma. *Figure 6.1* presents a selection of frequently occurring dilemmas of EU fieldwork. The two first-mentioned categories apply to the actors, being the EU officials and the other stakeholders, directly. The others refer to the factors and the vectors affecting them indirectly and they represent, as it were, dilemmas of meta-lobbying. The following exemplifies the dilemmas, which every lobby group can face.

The officials. The lobby group can support or oppose the position officials

Specific dilemmas of public affairs management

regarding	dilemma
officials	support or oppose their position / provide information or not / appease or disquiet
stakeholders	mobilise or demobilise / reward or punish / divide or unite
relations	formalise or informalise / stabilise or destabilise / use old or make new ones
procedures	simplify or complicate / accept or litigate / strict or loose interpretation
positions	recognise or challenge / take or leave / fill by merits or spoils
issues	politicise or depoliticise / broaden or narrow down / mix or separate
dossier life	relieve or hinder / preserve or transform / push or delay time
arena	enter or leave / one or another coalition / narrow or widen
decision	majorate or minorate / compromise or object / promote consensus or dissent
lobbying styles	supplying or demanding / low-key or high-key / direct or indirect / formal or informal

Figure 6.1

eventually adopt on an issue, thus making their life easy or difficult. It can favour or damage their private careers, for example by good or bad publicity. Officials from southern Europe, starting in Belgium and including Ireland, are used to practices of patronage and clientelism and thus to receiving subtle favours like lunches and loyalties in return for compliance. All officials have an appetite for reliable real-life information, which the lobby group can satisfy or not. It can also appease or disquiet the concerns of the officials. Making a drama out of, for example, global competition or the environment is an evergreen technique of disquieting them, frequently resulting in the rapid creation of an EU agenda. There are, of course, many more direct actions possible with regard to the officials, such as altering their level of prestige, competencies, budget, workload, organisation or recruitment. The officials themselves frequently play these lobby games against each other.

The stakeholders. One great dilemma is to mobilise more of them or not. More friends give more support, but they take a larger share of the game as well. Another dilemma is either to reward the friends and those who surrender or to punish the opponents and the defectors. It is also possible to engender either division or unity among groups of stakeholders. Sleeping stakeholders might be allowed to sleep or be woken up. Those wavering over an issue can be ignored, or convinced one way or another, or seduced in a different direction. The lobby group can deal with irritating players by either excusing them or accusing them in public, thus maybe bringing them either to obligation or to compromise. In 1998, Dutch Minister of Finance Zalm, defending his practices of fiscal aid to companies ('fiscal dumping'), forwarded to the Commission evidence collected through international accountancy firms, accusing most other governments of even worse practices. This stopped discussion on the issue for three years.

The relationships. The lobby group can make them either more formal or informal, with semi-formal options in between. If it is dependent on all three variants, then it has to cope with the dilemmas of their balance and timing. It can also make a relationship more or less stable. Conflict sometimes brings a better return than friendship [Coser, 1956], as the CCMC/ACEA case of the car manufacturers showed earlier. Another dilemma is over whether to stick mainly to old relationships or to develop new ones. For every lobby group this is a problem for cost-benefit analysis. Because of the continual turnover of EU officials and lobbyists it has anyhow much to invest in new relationships. After the 1999 reshuffle of the Prodi administration many Commission people had to build-up new networks for themselves.

The procedures. These are part of the Triple P game. One dilemma is over whether to simplify or to complicate them. Before the Commission's decision, in spring 2000, to allow Unilever to market its margarine Becel, the company pleaded for the procedure to be simplified. After that decision, it dropped its plea, considering that complexity was useful to keep new competitors out. Every lobby group can either accept or challenge a procedure as well and, in the latter case, even go to the Court. The tobacco industry did this in 1998, supported by Germany, when it questioned the basis in the Treaty for the Advertising Ban Directive. Another dilemma is over whether to lobby for a strict or a loose interpretation of a procedure. Both different language texts and various daily practices (precedents) allow room for interpretation.

The positions. As part of Triple P, a lobby group can either recognise or challenge established bodies and positions, such as committees, agencies and officials. The proliferation of committees in the field of waste management, to as many as 25, has partially been caused by outside lobby groups complaining about the composition of the existing committees. A lobby group can also either join or leave a body. The latter can be a sign of protest, but may also indicate its desire for more freedom of action. The recruitment of people for different positions is full of dilemmas: for example, whether to try for a national balance, to recruit sectorally or cross-sectorally, from inside or outside, and on merit or on the basis of patronage. The Commission decided in 2000, after many complaints about spoiled practices, to promote recruitment on merit.

The issues. One dilemma is over whether to politicise or to depoliticise them. A standard technique of the latter is to present an issue as 'technical', which many tend to equate with 'less relevant'. In order to depoliticise the issue, an expert group on railway safety frequently placed a mathematical formula on the first page of its report. Another dilemma is over whether to broaden a single issue or to narrow it down. In spring 2000, the lobby group of Europabio pressed for extending the proposed liability for GMO use to all sorts of industrial products, thus hoping to escape a specific regulation and to broaden its coalition. Another dilemma is over whether to combine the various issues in a package or to keep them separate. The Commission and the Council frequently combine issues in order to satisfy many stakeholders a little. The lobby group can also try to enlarge or to diminish the number of issues involved, thus manipulating the number of stakeholders, or choose to downgrade or upgrade an issue. The latter is a case of issue manipulation, of which *figure 6.2* lists many examples. One is the prohibition of child labour in the Third World, which sounds much more creditable than that of cheap textile imports from there, but it is the same issue. To this art of wording we will return below.

The life of a dossier. The lobby group can either help the passage of a dossier or make it difficult. The extreme example is the UK in the Council during the BSE affair (1996), when it simply blocked more than 50 dossiers (which became approved by rubberstamp afterwards). Another dilemma is over whether to preserve or to transform the dossier contents. Transformation, coming close to reframing the whole dossier, is an indirect technique of time management, which can solve or create a stalemate. A stalemate was overcome with the 1997 'Amsterdam' decision to reframe the matter of monetary stability as 'Stability and Growth'. A stalemate is frequently created by any successful lobby for subsidiarity, as happened in the 2001 EP session on fiscal harmonisation. There are many more direct techniques to push or to delay the decision-making process. The most direct is by moving a deadline forwards or backwards. Usually the former is more difficult than the latter, as it takes more energy to push than to delay.

The arena. The lobby group can choose either to enter or to leave a specific arena, with wait-and-see options in between. Inside the arena, it has the dilemma over whether to join one or another coalition. Frequently every coalition has its own mix of advantages and disadvantages, which make a marginal difference and offer a real choice. A strong dilemma, discussed before, is over whether to restrict or to expand the arena boundaries. Such a

EU examples of issue manipulation

the core issue	*the upgrade*
CAP (old)	food supply
CAP (new)	sustainability
cheap textile imports	child labour
tobacco smoking	liberty
taxfree shopping	employment
beer imports	public health
beer imports	environment
charging private transport	sustainable mobility
short truck-trailer coupling	social safety
handsfree car-phones	road safety
fur industry	animal welfare
laying hens	humane farming
subsidies to South Europe	social cohesion
ACP bananas	development aid
R&D subsidies	global competition
lower taxation (shoe repair etc.)	employment
competitive disadvantage (oil)	environment
ditto (Hungarian truckers)	social help
chocolate definition	development aid
subsidised food exports	humanitarian aid
procurements for CEE	stability
biotech R&D, trade, production	public safety
ditto (opposite)	development aid
oil stocks	security
SME support	employment
intervention in ECB	economic growth
non-intervention in ECB	monetary stability

Figure 6.2

change may result in a very different set of both issues and stakeholders. Alongside the combining of issues and dossiers the lobby group can also choose to make one arena overlap or be separated from another one. If the lobby group takes a long route or many routes to the EU (*figure 3.2*), then it encounters the arena dilemmas connected in series or in parallel. Every lane, junction and roundabout on its way to the final EU arena amounts to a prelude arena.

The decision. Regarding the EU decision itself, the lobby group has to decide either to majorate or to minorate its negotiation position. The first may give a better outcome in the short run, while the latter is an investment of goodwill in the long run or on another dossier. For so-called reasons of principle, the group can also choose not to participate in the negotiations at all and to abstain from them reluctantly. Such a position, intended to block the process by deepening the dissent, is of course risky. The EU officials and the other stakeholders can ignore it and continue with the even easier formation of consensus. The national governments in the Council, if it decides by unanimity, sometimes play the game of reluctance, but usually this is only reluctance until 'five to midnight' and part of a loss compensation game. In 2001, the Spanish government held up the Council decision regarding the timing of enlargement as a means of keeping its subsidies from the Cohesion Fund.

Lobbying styles. Standard dilemmas of lobby style are, among others, whether to supply or to demand, to be low-key or high-key, to act directly or indirectly, formally or informally, defensively or offensively, whether to be confrontational or appeasing, reactive or proactive. The question of style is widely considered as crucial. It is, in fact, the only one that is common to both the amateurish and the professional groups (*figure 3.3*). But their answers differ, as we shall see below at length. The theoretical dilemma over lobbying either legally or illegally is hardly one in practice. Every lobby group can easily meet the current prescriptions of registration and code of conduct and it has all the reason to fear the political isolation caused by scandals.

Coping with the Surplus

The most popular question posed by the dilemmas of EU fieldwork is 'What is *the best thing to do?*' Five types of answer are provided by EU practice. Firstly, there is the answer of the really amateurish groups: they just do something. Having an emotional feeling about an EU challenge, they want to go straight to an EU high official of their own tongue and to present their case in a prolix, loud and selfish way. If they see that route as too far or too costly, they make a stop in the national capital or association and try the same approach there. Driven by their emotion, they act almost Pavlovian, which is practically the same as *at random*. They go, as it were, to the ruler and voice their desire or fear. They are unfamiliar with the labyrinth constructed on a trampoline, as we characterised the EU playing field before. Fearing they will lose their way and to falloff, they keep their eyes fixed on the high officials and rush to them rapidly and loudly. They consider the many dilemmas to be a problem rather than a blessing.

A second answer comes from the manuals on EU lobbying [Gardner, 1991; Andersen, 1992; Randall, 1996]. They also keep it simple. They describe the EU pyramid of high officials, controlling units and dominant institutions, as if both the lower workfloor and the other stakeholders around are only subordinate and can be neglected. They are formalistic and belong to the first wave of the study of EU public affairs management, focused on the rulers. In addition, they give a number of *rules of thumb*, such as 'present with brevity and clarity', 'keep it low-key' and 'avoid overlobbying'. Although still vague, such lobby caveats may make sense, on some occasions. On others, however, a lengthy and woolly presentation, high visibility and an aggressive siege might be more effective, as we shall see below. The manuals, in short, hardly see the dilemmas and thus simplify the fieldwork.

Those on the receiving end of lobby actions in the EU give the third answer. According to the very small amount of field research, many Commission officials [Koeppl, 2001] and MEPs as well [Kohler-Koch, 1998; Katz and Wessels, 1999] want to be approached in low- key, friendly and informative ways at an early stage and not, as frequently happens, the opposite. Their *consumer demands* come close to the rules of thumb above. But what is good for the receiver is not necessarily good for the sender. The former wants to be in the driver's seat, the latter wants to achieve the desired outcome. Not surprisingly, according to many MEPs it is better to approach them than to try the Commission people. These findings are anyhow the result of limited research, based on formulaic written questions, not distinguishing between specific situations and neglecting most dilemmas mentioned above.

The fourth answer has been given by a very special group of senders, namely the commercial consultants. They have been interviewed in connection with the aforementioned MEPs' pilot study [Kohler-Koch, 1998]. Overall they have strong but barely varying opinions about the best ways of and moments for lobbying the Commission and the EP. *Almost everything* submitted to them in the questionnaire they apparently consider highly important. This has at least the suspicion of commercial self-interest. As really most important they rank the informal contacts with the Commission people during their preparation of a proposal and with the EP's rapporteur during the writing of the report. Other stakeholders and lobby styles have not been the subject of this small amount of research, let alone the many other dilemmas.

The final answer comes from the few theorists about EU lobbying. Their short answer to the question 'What is the best thing to do?' is: *it depends* on the situation of the arena. This is, of course, our position too. To make a lobby action more successful, with its yardsticks of effectiveness and efficiency, it must be fine-tuned to the specific situation. The professional lobby group, standing as a model for this answer, considers the surplus of dilemmas and variables of lobbying as a blessing rather than a problem. The higher their number, the more options it sees for solving or preserving a challenge. It can always find a friendly official, a supportive stakeholder, a pleasant issue, a promising dossier, a better moment, an open route and, in short, a chance to create a desired result. If there seem to be few such chances, it usually knows how to create them. Thanks to that surplus of dilemmas and variables, which is larger than that of the game of chess, it can usually escape a stalemate and overcome a setback. Its lobbying is not at random or based on rules of thumb, or focused on pleasing the receivers or the consultants. It is based on a choice that is as rational as possible.

The professional group has, of course, *no guarantee* of lobby success. It can neither predict precisely nor control perfectly the effects of its actions on its targets. For two reasons a precise prediction is always and everywhere impossible. Firstly, the relationship between an action and an effect is full of multicausality (same effect coming from different actions) and multifinality (same action producing different effects), in short with many weak correlations. Secondly, the many volatile variables are beyond the reach of a complete and a reliable calculation, as it with the simpler game of chess. Full control over the effects of lobbying is also impossible for, essentially, the same two reasons. The professional group therefore takes the complexity and the volatility of any EU arena as facts of life. It uses and even intensifies them, for example by creating new vectors and by crossing arena boundaries. The impossibility of a perfectly rational choice and thus a guaranteed success it does not consider a serious problem.

This best possible rational choice is, in fact, an *educated guess* or a calculation of the probable outcomes of a lobby action, given the specific situation. Thus it is anchored in the three main chapters of the preparatory homework. Firstly, that regarding the home front, whose results reveal what precisely the challenges are and what, given the internal arena, can be done about them. They are connected to the second chapter of the preparatory work regarding the external arena and resulting in the summary assessment of whether the arena is friendly, unfriendly or indeterminate for the challenges. The answers enable the setting of realistic targets, which are suitable for the conditions in the internal and the external arena. They also point to the best practices of EU public affairs management. Thirdly, there is the general homework regarding the crucial actors, factors, and vectors affecting the playing on the field. This covers not only general EU developments, such as the appearance of new agendas and new 'flesh and blood' practices, but also new practices of EU public affairs management, for example new methods of homework and newly developed lobby styles. Only in a book like this can the three chapters be separated. In daily practice they are closely connected and form one complex story.

Every lobby group is, of course, free to decide that choosing its actions at random, by rules of thumb, by serving the receivers or by following the consultants is no less rational than doing it by an educated guess. It then saves itself at least the costs of its own preparatory work. The chance of getting the desired return on such savings is, however, almost zero in practice. The lobby group acting at random makes itself dependent on sheer good luck, on the crumbs from the table. If it acts by rules of thumb, it can make all sorts of unforced errors. If it just serves the receivers or follows the consultants, it can make them much happier than itself. Our approach here remains *advisory* and not normative. There is no ultimate argument for why a lobby group should not be allowed to do all this instead of making a rational choice based on the best of its knowledge. But *if* the lobby group seriously wants to solve or to preserve a challenge, *then* it is better for it to base its actions on such a rational choice, and it can then save on the costs of inefficient or ineffective fieldwork. We shall now demonstrate this for the recurrent questions of the fieldwork, summarised earlier (chapter 3) as 'how to lobby, whom, where, with regard to what and when?'.

Lobbying Whom?

At any particular moment, on any dossier, the lobby group can go to hundreds of stakeholders, including the officials having a stake in the dossier. One thing is for sure: no group can approach them all, let alone all of them together at the same time. Every group has to be *selective*. The homework provides the best indications. Most helpful is the summary analysis of the arena (*figure 4.3*). If the wind is friendly, then the lobby group can confine itself to keeping the supporting stakeholders on board and, if possible, to arranging a free ride. If, on the other hand, the wind is unfriendly, then it is best to approach a few opponents in order to divide, if possible, the opposition and also some of the waverers in order to get them on board. The best opponents to approach are those who have been assessed as primary (important plus active) and as sharing the smallest number of preferences with the other opponents. The most attractive waverers are, by analogy, those having both a primary status and the highest number of mixed preferences. If, however, the winds are absent or are sidewinds, thus making the arena indeterminate, then it is rational to approach the most primary stakeholders among the many being either wavering or indifferent, or perhaps are just giving this impression. A little bit of argumentation and negotiation can bind them. The lobby group can read the names of these stakeholders from the vertical axis of its descriptive homework (*figure 4.2*).

It can also do this for *another dossier* on its short list. Usually it will find a number of stakeholders involved in more than one dossier, precisely as the lobby group is itself. Many lobby groups have a lot of contact with just one sector-related Commission DG and with only one or a few people inside. If such regular stakeholders take compliant positions on the different dossiers, then they deserve an intimate courtship. If they have mixed positions they can at least be approached with a compromise. If the lobby group considers them full opponents, then it is better for it to try to tackle them, thus liberating itself at a stroke from opponents on different dossiers. The lobby group can also work the other way around and identify those dossiers not on its short list, but of great interest to the primary stakeholders involved in the dossier with which it is concerned. Depending on their position on this dossier, it can easily support or tackle them on the other dossiers, thus creating redemption free of costs.

Two other pieces of preparatory work are also most useful. Firstly that regarding the *home front*. If well done, it provides the information on which people at home have the special expertise, status or relationship that is of interest to the stakeholders identified as crucial in the external arena. They can act as liaison and be incorporated in the external networking. Staff experts or line managers will frequently have already built up their own networks, which are now useful for the dossier at stake. In the multinational model of EU public affairs management these people are easily incorporated in the ad-hoc team. If there are no such persons at home, the lobby group still has some time, thanks to its anticipatory homework, to create and position them or to locate them among befriended stakeholders. Secondly, the *general* homework on developments related to the EU and to public affairs management can help to solve some dilemmas too. For example, the 1999 reorganisation of the Commission has set into motion a reshuffle of tasks and people inside it. Officials with new tasks usually suffer from a time lag with regard to information and contacts. The sooner the lobby group can serve them, the more it can get an edge over its competitors. In the EU, people and positions are more or less temporary and it is thus a matter of homework to keep the relevant EU directory updated. The same applies to developments in public affairs management. Two new practices are the identification of stakeholders by monitoring their websites and the networking with befriended stakeholders through email and intranet.

The examples make clear that the answer to the question 'lobbying whom?' depends on the specific situation. With knowledge of this, which is a matter for careful study, the lobby group can solve, at least partially, most dilemmas. Using figure 6.1 as a checklist, it can even profit from more dilemmas and activate more variables. For example, if it has identified a group of regularly befriended stakeholders it can launch a joint lobby with them for a special position on a procedure safeguarding the broader common interest, such as the position of an expert group under comitology. On the other hand, if it has found that, for a particular dossier, the few people from the Commission DG support it almost only, it can delay the process expediently by concentrating on lobbying them for a retardation of the formal deadline. The full solution of the many dilemmas can, however, only be reached after answering all the other questions relating to EU public affairs management, such as the next one.

Lobbying Where?

'Brussels' is only the *pars pro toto* name for the EU machinery, as it is the location of most institutions and offices. The relevant place of lobby action can, however, be anywhere. Of course it can be in the city of Brussels, in the EU buildings themselves, but also in the restaurants around them or in the offices of lobby groups. But it can also be in a hotel along the road to Paris, in the national capital holding the Council chair, in the building where a WTO panel meets or anywhere that stakeholders get together. Only the Commission officials do most of their lobbying in Brussels itself. They have it easy, because many EU stakeholders come to them spontaneously or by invitation, for example through their experts and lobbyists or by letter. All other lobby groups have to decide about the best location for lobbying. They cannot, of course, be everywhere at the same time and have to be selective once again. The matter of location may appear trivial, but without a meeting place it is hard to lobby and if it is not a satisfactory place it is difficult to become successful. Therefore the professional lobby group takes it seriously and selects rationally. The preparatory work on the former question 'whom?' can give the initial information on where to find the relevant locations as well. The stakeholders identified as crucial for some lobby action always have their settled locations and their more or less routine behaviour. The lobby group must get to know their behavioural map, but many stakeholders prefer to have low visibility and this inevitably makes the job more difficult. The professional group tries to collect this sort of information as part of the vertical axis of the arena description (*figure 4.2*) and to keep it up to date in its EU directory. A few consultancies specialise in selling this sort of information.

The choice of location can be optimised. For the *window-out monitoring* of stakeholders, Brussels is a relatively good place. The more wealthy lobby groups have their office or representation here. Many more travel to and from Brussels and can be monitored when entering the EU buildings, which are mostly also located here. But many stakeholders identified as crucial on a dossier are located elsewhere. The lobby group can, of course, send out or post some of its personnel to the same place, but this is a costly affair. Only multinational groups, like MNCs and Greenpeace can cheaply rely on their own local people elsewhere, but there are also other ways. Many national ministries can do so through their attachés at the embassies. Every group, wealthy or poor, can ask the befriended stakeholders living elsewhere to assist in monitoring other stakeholders located in the vicinity. Such an indirect use of locally based stakeholders is not only efficient in its cost savings, but is also often extremely effective, as these local people usually have a superior capacity to monitor: they speak the local language, have the contacts and represent a domestic interest. The identification of both the crucial and the befriended stakeholders elsewhere is clearly a matter of good preparation.

For its *window-in meetings* with a crucial stakeholder the professional group will try to dovetail the two behavioural maps. Brussels may seem to be an efficient location for the negotiations, but it frequently has the disadvantages of, for example, being full of social control, not having neutral terrain and not being at all relaxed. In any case, many crucial stakeholders live more outside than inside the city, in which case even Lisbon or Budapest may be a better place for the meeting. The lobby group can figure this out through studying the arena. By the same method it can arrange a multilateral meeting at least with the primary stakeholders on its side. Sooner or later the common interests have to be transformed into a strong and potentially winning (pushing or blocking) coalition, for which meetings are necessary. This is a matter of knowing and accommodating the usually complex agendas and schedules of the participants. Sometimes the lobby group enjoys the good fortune of already having regular contacts with most of the stakeholders it has befriended, for example through a EuroFed or an expert committee. Then it can use the day before the regular meeting to hold the special one. In the case of an expert committee, the Commission will even reimburse most variable costs of the meeting. Some members of expert committees lobby for more regular meetings mainly so that they can have the special meeting the day before.

An increasingly common question is whether a physical meeting can be replaced by a virtual one, such as by telephone, email, intranet and/or other information and computer technology (ICT) or, in short, *cyber-lobbying*. To some degree it can, but its potential, so far, is mainly limited to the window-out technique of monitoring and exchanging information. The internet provides a lot of information and the EU website is one of the best in Europe and most informative about agendas, positions and dossiers, from the draft to the final one. Most national newspapers have their own site and can be easily tapped for national background information. The major European and national interest groups have their own sites frequently revealing their short list, positions and activities. The intranet is increasingly used on the home front, particularly to inform personnel or members of the organisation. Some multinationals use it interactively as the virtual meeting place of their ad-hoc team. The use of email has become a standard practice, and teleconferencing is becoming more popular. A very special use of ICT, to which we will return below, is made particularly by NGOs for the sake of publicity, agenda-building and specific campaigning. But, in spite of all these new developments, the acquisition of really relevant information is still largely a matter of personal trust and contact. For window-in activities the virtual tools are even almost useless. Lobbying for deals and compromises requires a personalised approach for which a physical meeting is indispensable. The seemingly trivial question of location remains, in short, an important one.

Lobbying With Regard to What?

No lobby group can tackle all the issues of the dossiers on its short list at the same time. It has to be selective. For its specific *issue management* the professional group relies heavily on its homework. The main source of inspiration is the summary assessment of the arena, which gives the cues to the best practices, although they still have to be detailed. If, for example, the arena is essentially friendly, then the lobby group knows that it must keep the favourable issues high up and block opposing or hindering ones. From the cells of the arena description made earlier, it can deduce for which friendly issues it should produce supportive messages and for which unfriendly ones it should do the opposite. It can even personalise the mailing of messages, as it knows from the preparation which stakeholders are crucial either on its side or on the opposing side. If the arena is mainly unfriendly, then the lobby group can glean from its preparatory work on which issues and whom it can best lobby for compensation for loss. This homework can also reveal which unfriendly issues are the most suitable to be upgraded, resulting in another attractive Lorelei, such as identified in figure 6.2. As the main producers of such upgrades, many NGOs must have prepared well. They have hoisted such fine flags as 'public safety', 'sustainability' and 'humane farming', all hailed with satisfaction particularly by the MEPs. By such reframing a lobby group can mobilise more friendly stakeholders and, in fact, move the arena boundaries. From its preparatory work it can also discover on which issues it can better lobby to narrow the boundaries, in order to get rid of its opponents. If the arena, finally, is mainly indeterminate, then the lobby group can know from its homework for which issues (and even relating to whom) it has to intensify its monitoring, it should create an upgrade, or it needs to begin negotiating.

If the lobby group has carried out extensive preparation, it can even go beyond the issue boundary of an arena and use a totally different issue as the *Achilles' heel* of an opponent. In 2001, NGOs like (British) Oxfam raised in the EP the issue of the pricing of AIDS drugs, particularly for South Africa. The irritated pharmaceutical producers considered, *inter alia*, raising in Britain the developing issue of Oxfam's local business operations there as a BINGO, which to the irritation of other retailers are largely free from local taxes. Raising the issue should have been done, of course, indirectly through a stakeholder having a common interest in both the pharmaceutical producers and the British retailers. The preparatory work indicated that the British trade unions could have been mobilised. The pharmaceutical companies decided, however, to deal with the issue of AIDS drugs prices directly with the South African government, outside the EU. Making a virtue out of necessity, they promised cheap pricing in compensation both for approvals of new drugs and for further settlements inside the WTO, and they beautified their public image somewhat.

The lobby group can also practise *meta-lobbying* dealing with the factors and the vectors affecting an issue. The checklist of dilemmas can again be a source of inspiration. For example, the lobby group can decide to challenge the position of some opposing stakeholder, to move to another coalition or to lobby for a different procedure. Such behaviour may change the issues at stake. More specific is the meta-game of Triple P, intended to rearrange the playing field and thus to make the issues more friendly. The lobby group can get information for this meta-lobbying on issues from its homework regarding both the external arena and the general developments. For example, the conflict over the establishment of the European Food Safety Authority (EFSA) in 2000 was mainly about the layout of procedures and positions and hardly about the issues of food safety themselves. The latter usually only cause more tension and friction and can be better settled indirectly, by authorised procedures and positions. This is what DG Consumer Affairs proposed, at the suggestion and with support from some lobbying ministries, producers and retailers in the food sector. Having achieved a position on the EFSA procedures they can manage their food issues better in the future.

If the arena still remains unfriendly or indeterminate, the lobby group may have to return to its preparatory work on its home front. Maybe it has engaged itself in a *mission impossible*. Field experiences will be a useful input for a new internal study. They help in the checking of the reliability and the completeness of the previous one. The lobby group may come to the conclusion that it has to redefine the challenges, if necessary based on a reassessment of facts and norms. In an extreme case, it may conclude that its chances of winning something hardly exist or only at a disadvantageous cost-benefit ratio. Then it can better remove the dossier from the short list and put it on the long list, as Unilever did in 2000 with its GMO challenge. Thanks to its internal homework it can easily replace the new posteriority with a more promising dossier, the next one on its long list.

How to Style One's Lobbying?

The question of 'how to lobby' is the oldest one on the subject, going back to the days when lobbying was defined as only happening in political corridors. It is also the only question that is popular among both amateurish and professional lobby groups. No group lobbying for a desired outcome can escape it, because it is what finally shapes and styles its behaviour. Specific dilemmas are whether it should act supplying or demanding, formally or informally, and directly or indirectly. Very topical is the dilemma of whether it should act silently or noisily, in short how it should sound. Of course, it can behave at random, follow some rules of thumb, simply please the officials or do as consultants advise. All this would make a lot of preparation indeed superfluous. The following shows that those dilemmas can be better solved rationally, based on homework.

Supplying or demanding
Every lobby group has to develop both a supply and a demand side. Without the first it cannot make itself interesting to the other stakeholders and without the second it cannot get its interest included in the outcome. As far as some rule of thumb makes sense, the lobby group should be more conscious about its supply than its demand side. By an almost natural inclination it usually has the latter so much in the forefront of its mind that it must try hard not to forget its supply side. Besides, when entering an arena, it has to obtain and to maintain a position, which is better achieved through charming rather than demanding behaviour. For these two reasons the professional group invests consciously at least in its *image of charm*. It likes to be thought interesting, pleasant and friendly. It distributes such small symbols of agreeableness as a social small talk, a nice dinner or a golf party, and it hopes to be rewarded with a more informal relationship. Window-out it shows a strong interest in the problems of the others, thus trying to get information about their agendas in return, which is a useful input for the preparatory work. It also offers the other stakeholders, including the EU officials, help with the supply of expertise and support. What they say they need, if reliable, provides information about their strengths and weaknesses. EU officials for their part have on offer their capacity to push or block a desired outcome. All this charming and pleasant behaviour lays the ground for the crucial window-in practices, which must result in achieving the deals as desired.

The rational lobby group, in short, tries to satisfy its demand side by pushing forward its supply side. A good deal finally links up one's own demand and supply sides with those of the stakeholders crucial for obtaining a desired outcome. This behavioural style comes close to *political marketing* [O'Shaughnessy, 1990; Andrews, 1996; Harris and Lock, 1996; Dermody and Wring, 2001]. An EU arena is, indeed, usually a political market with open competition between multiple stakeholders and with rounds of wheeling and dealing among them, perhaps eventually resulting in a sufficient consensus. Most techniques of marketing can be used, ranging from branding and direct mailing to merchandising and export licensing. Their parallels in the EU arena are the build-up of a good reputation, the direct approach, the supply of desired values and the appointment of an intermediary. There is no point in arguing over who is right or wrong, as this is a zero-sum game. When for the closing of a deal some argumentation is called for, one says not what one wants to say, but what the other wants to hear. It is not intellectual, but salesman's talk.

The preparatory work provides the best possible *indicators* for the development of the supply side. The lobby group can, contrary to a popular rule of thumb, sometimes even demand more than supply. For example, in an overwhelmingly friendly arena it can take a free ride and get many of its demands fulfilled without having to supply much. By careful study of the situation, it can work out on which issues it can take a free ride and from whom. In a most unfriendly situation it might decide rationally, contrary to a rule of thumb again, to majorate aggressively its demand side in order to create a nuisance value, to get compensation for a loss or to delay the process. That aggression it has to fine-tune, of course, to the proper issues and stakeholders, which it can obtain from that homework. In a mainly indeterminate situation it has the least reason to push its demand side above its supply side, because it still has to build up its position here. The professional group chooses its specific style, however, with a wider view to both the near future and the other priorities of its short list, because it is always concerned about possible boomerangs. If it over-demands in the eyes of crucial stakeholders, it may get the bad image of a selfish player and be punished for it. But if it oversupplies, it might be seen as a softie and be taken advantage of as a result. It is all a matter of thoughtfully prepared lobbying.

Formal or informal
Many lobby groups have, again, an almost natural inclination to behave formally. Focusing on the desired end-result of the lobby process, they look for the signature of some high official or authority, such as the chairman of a EuroFed, a Commissioner or the Council. They aim to approach them formally, at an early stage, typically in the form of an official letter sent by the chairman of a lobby group to, for example, a Commissioner or the rapporteur. The EU process of secondary legislation, with its Commission proposal to the Parliament for Council approval, looks extremely formalised by its skeleton, encouraging many groups to behave accordingly. EuroFeds and national ministries frequently look no less formal. Many groups hold the *popular belief* that for a desired outcome formal approval is finally needed and even sufficient. Neither is true. If the desired outcome is for no decision to be taken at all, then no approval is needed either. If the desired approval has been granted, the required measure can still fail to be implemented or be blocked because of legal restrictions. One consolation, of course, is that the lobby group has not necessarily lost if the formal decision goes against its desire.

The best style of behaviour depends on the situation. In at least *four situations* the formal style of lobbying is not very appropriate. The first of these is when the lobby group wants no decision at all to be taken. This is a matter of delaying, which usually can best be achieved by informal and semi-formal practices. Secondly, if the lobby group has to go window-out, it should behave informally or semi-formally. It can more easily obtain crucial information through an informal chat or a pleasant meeting than by a formal letter. Thirdly, those who have to approve the desired decision, are seldom the same as the ones who create its contents. The workfloor is usually more crucial than the boardroom. The mid-level experts, clerks and other apparatchiks of a stakeholder can best be approached in non-formal ways. They are human beings, who also usually possess discretionary powers. Fourthly, if the lobby group wants to make a window-in deal with a supportive, an opposing or a wavering stakeholder, it should build it up informally. As said before, it is just like engaging a partner in life, which is best started informally, then leads up to some semi-formal formula of 'living apart together', and maybe results in a formal marriage. This does not work the other way around.

The latter also applies to the situation in which formal approval is really needed. This can best be *built up* step by step. The most effective lobbying starts informally. This usually provides the best monitoring and networking. Efficient tools are, for example, the nice restaurant, the pleasant outing and, for those who live around Brussels, the social networking in leisure time. If some informal consensus is being built, it can be put on semi-formal basis, for example that of an ad-hoc group, an expert committee or a working group. The common view must sufficiently reflect the interests of the stakeholders. During this process the prudent lobby group naturally keeps its own formal position paper, created at home, in its head or its luggage and never puts it on the table, because otherwise it cannot negotiate effectively and may lose face. In this respect the Commission officials have the disadvantage of being expected to be the first with a proposal. Hence they particularly like the more informal sessions. Finally, whenever necessary, the semi-formal group's position is put forward for formal approval, which is usually a matter of rubber-stamping.

From its earlier preparation, the lobby group can read which stakeholders should be approached informally and on which issues. To this it adds useful information about the personal *idiosyncrasies* of key people. One person may prefer a walk in the park or a leisurely drink, another a visit to a football match or a theatre. The regional office of Bayern from Germany even has on hand an aircraft to take people to a Bayern München football match. One person may like to talk about family or career, another about politics or philosophy. One takes familiarity as a sign of friendship, another takes it as impoliteness or even as contempt. One loves a phone call, another hates it as a violation of privacy. Many high officials only open the personalised and hand-written envelope and leave the pre-printed one to their secretary. Some people even dislike being approached informally at all and allow this behaviour only after a formal beginning. The professional lobbyist takes all these idiosyncrasies very seriously, as they are most helpful when trying to pass a physical or a mental threshold. There is a lot of exchange of such personal information between lobbyists. Some consultants have it for sale.

Direct or indirect

Another rule of thumb suggests that one can best approach a stakeholder directly, and the use of indirect ways is hardly mentioned. This neglect may cause an unforced error. By using an indirect method or so-called *U-turn*, the lobby group dissociates its message from itself and sends it through another medium. The indirect way has at least three advantages, which are neglected by amateurish groups relying on rules of thumb and the like. Firstly, the sender remains invisible or even anonymous and thus keeps its hands free. Secondly, the targeted stakeholders receive the message from a different source and thus may take it as more convincing or even as representing a more general interest. Thirdly, if opposition arises, this does not immediately strike back at the lobby group itself. The disadvantages are that the message may become distorted by the indirect transmission and, if it gathers support, can also be claimed by others. Whatever their (dis)advantages, there are many direct and indirect ways to lobby the other stakeholders. *Figure 6.3* presents a major selection, drawn from the case studies and the field research mentioned earlier.

The *direct ways* can range from informal to formal. Examples of the first are the face-to-face (*'lobby by body'*) contacts in the form of a personal visit or, for example, an invitation to the opera. Acting through a committee meeting, attending a hearing or launching a position paper are examples of more semi-formal ways. The sending of an official letter or a delegation to the highest official in charge, for example the chairman of a EuroFed or a Commissioner, is a case of a direct formal approach. All direct ways can be either low-key or high-key. In the latter case they rely on publicity. Examples are the publication of a brochure or an advertisement, the calling of a press conference or the organising of a public demonstration. The direct approaches can be either appeasing or confrontational: a hate site on the web

Examples of direct or indirect EU lobby styles

direct ways

personal visit, letter, phone, email
invitation for entertainment
committee membership
hearing participation
presentation of position
formal visit, contact, delegation
formal request, petition
folder or brochure
mass media participation
political advertisement
press conference
demonstration
hate-site, boycott, blockade, strike
litigation, Court procedure

indirect ways

(sub)national association
(sub)national government
(cross-)sectoral EuroFed
foreign (non-EU) network
ad-hoc group
affiliated interest groups
science and scientists
well-known personalities
mid-level civil servants
caretakers and friends inside
brokers and consultants
political parties
mass media mobilisation
undercover action

Figure 6.3

pillorying an opponent, a boycott and a legal procedure are examples of the latter.

The *indirect ways* also have many variants, ranging from informal to formal, low-key to high-key and appeasing to confrontational. Established routes are the U-turns via a domestic umbrella organisation and/or a EuroFed and/or a foreign (non-EU) platform like the WTO (*figure 3.2*). Ad-hoc groups and befriended lobby groups are also useful for making a message more general. Scientific studies, scholars and 'wise men' can be authoritative media, especially if they are under one's control but appear independent. The same holds true for popular personalities such as, for example, the Spice Girls, who demonstrated at the Parliament in 1998 against the draft Copyright Directive, to the great displeasure of music producers. People inside the system, like mid-level civil servants and friends, are excellent for plugging a message. Political parties are most useful for the politicisation of an issue, if this is needed. Many lobby groups use the mass media for disseminating information off the record and for promoting an EU issue and agenda. A lobby group can even act indirectly on its own behalf, for example by parachuting somebody into the Commission and by other undercover practices.

Most ingenious is the interconnection, in series or in parallel, of various U-turns. In this way one can arrange a *polyphonic orchestra*, sending the targeted audience the same message through various sound boxes, which is most convincing. In 1986, the members of EACEM, the association of sound engineering companies like Philips and Thomson, lobbied this way for HDTV [Verwey, 1994; Cawson, 1997]. Through their different units in the member countries they approached in parallel the various ministries, trade associations and other supportive stakeholders. The key people of those public and private organisations they subsequently linked in series to the relevant people in EuroFeds, the Commission, the EP and the Council, particularly at the workfloor levels here. In 1995, DG Environment, in co-operation with both national ministries and NGOs in its field, launched in a similar way a campaign in favour of so-called sustainability. Politicians can easily be used for such interconnection. They belong to party-political families extending from the local, regional and national level to the EP, the COR and the Council officially and, unofficially, often to the other EU institutions. There is a risk, however, that they will politicise the issue if they get involved, and that it will then be difficult to control. The interconnection of circuits therefore requires very professional fine-tuning, or else the end-result will be cacophony.

In daily EU practice many lobby groups appear to be biased towards the direct ways in all variants except the confrontational one. But the latter is becoming increasingly popular particularly among NGOs. Of the indirect ways, most prevalent are the use of a EuroFed and the national government. Perhaps many groups are not aware of the long menu of ways and underuse it. The professional lobby group wants to know this menu fully, of course, or else it cannot *fine-tune the lobby* to the current situation in the arena. The indicators for the best choice of method it also obtains from its homework. If it finds itself in a friendly arena, it can, for example, best bring both some informal visits to the friends it has identified in order to secure their support and engineer some U-turns for the wide distribution of supportive messages, thus keeping the wind blowing favourably. In a chilly arena it can best make use of, for example, scientific reports and the mass media for the reframing of the unpleasant issues, while it can find its compensation for loss during private talks behind closed doors. In an indeterminate arena it may be best to approach some crucial waverers by inviting them to a convivial meeting and providing them with so-called scientific evidence. Good preparatory study of the arena can also elicit information about the idiosyncratic preferences of stakeholders, their current networks being maybe useful as ready-made U-turns, and their needs for support at various stages along way. Such preparation can make the difference between lobby success and failure.

The Fine-Tuning of 'Sound'

A very special part of the big question of 'how to lobby?' regards the use of silence or noise, in short the *sound-button*. Many a lobby group is inclined to make a lot of noise on the EU playing field. It feels small and wants to attract attention. It sees something it desires or fears and then it wants to voice its pleasure or anger. If it is weakly supported domestically, it may want to show how great it is. Many lobbying styles are by their very nature noisy to a degree. Arrogant or pompous actions are soon widely known, and formal visits and letters are usually registered and easily noticed by the more than one thousand EU journalists: Brussels is a transparent village. Some direct and indirect ways are clearly used for making noise. A hate site on the web is intended to create publicity. It is impossible for some stakeholders to remain fully silent: national ministries and agencies are frequently called to their parliament or council, to account in public for their plans and actions, and NGOs like Greenpeace have to communicate with their thousands of members. They cannot easily control the information flow through a select committee or intranet.

Noise is, of course, a variable on a *continuum*. At one extreme there is just silence, meaning that the lobby groups operate behind closed doors and incognito for outsiders. At the other extreme there is the so-called outside lobbying, in which some stakeholders, frequently being NGOs based in the grass roots, compete with others through publicity campaigns, thus expanding the arena to the mass public. In between the two extremes there is the limited soundtrack for a selected audience, for example for the members of a EuroFed, a group of MEPs or some of the Commission officials. In spite of whatever inclination or inevitability, most EU lobby groups stick to the more silent approaches of, for example, behind-closed-doors meetings and closed networks or circuits. Issue-specific publicity campaigns, in the form of brochures, advertisements, press conferences or ICT-based actions for the mass public, mainly come from NGOs and USA-based interest groups operating in the EU, such as Philip Morris, the AmCham and the US Mission.

This low level of *outside lobbying* in the EU, in comparison to the USA, is striking. The explanation can hardly be a difference of competitive pluralism, at least not between lobby groups from civil society. But in the EU more than in the USA, these groups tend to be interlinked with all forms of government and already have their feet inside the mixed public-private systems, discussed in the first chapter and also existing at the EU level. So they may have less reason to lobby outside. The many young NGOs, however, are not yet nestled inside the governments and still have reason to lobby in this way. Two specific factors can explain the high volume of outside lobbying in the USA. Firstly, it is particularly focused on the members of Congress, who possess more legislative powers than the MEPs and have their vulnerable grassroots in the constituency. They have to be lobbied more intensively and can be lobbied via the populations of their constituencies, and thus through the mass media. Secondly, the litigation procedure that takes place in public is a conventional direct way of lobbying in the USA. These two specific factors are weak in the EU, where only the British have a pure constituency system, most mass media have low interest in EU affairs, and litigation through the Court is still an exceptional procedure.

The dramatic effect of noise, intended or not, is the mobilisation of more stakeholders. It widens the arena boundaries and absent stakeholders become stimulated to enter the arena, bringing their own interests and issues. They may even take the opportunity to build up a nuisance value so as to exchange it for another value. The new stakeholders delay the decision-making process, as they need time to find their position and to become party to the deal. Silence, in contrast to noise, has the opposite effects. It keeps the arena boundaries narrow and, if a compromise can be found, it usually speeds up the decision-making process. In EU public affairs management the variable of noise is not only relevant, but also risky. It is as easy to create noise, as it is difficult to create silence. Technically, noise is almost solely a one-directional variable of manipulation. Once the *ghost of noise* is out of the bottle, it is almost impossible to push it back. For this reason the prudent lobby groups fear it. In spring 2000, the Prodi Commission, although in favour of transparency, refused to publish its internal documents, on the grounds that this publishing would hamper the policy processes by attracting even more stakeholders and issues. In a noisy arena a lobby group cannot really control subsequent developments. The more unpredictable the arena becomes, the less the homework can be carried out sufficiently reliable and complete and the more the fieldwork has to be done haphazardly. The professional lobby group hates this situation.

This explains why, in the multinational model of EU public affairs management, the *sound button* is under the control of a member of the Central Board. The PR office may have a vested interest in continuously making a lot of pleasant sound, which yet remains sound, whereas the PA office may have strong reason to be firmly against any noise and to prefer silence. The dilemma over whether to turn the sound button in the one or the other direction is, then, a problem for the Central Board member. This person may dislike making sound if it damages the interests of the company at the political level, but on the other hand he/she may have reason to give priority to the interests of PR above PA, for example for the sake of market interests, and to accept the risk of a more unpredictable EU arena. Sometimes the damaging risk can be kept limited by some internal compromise, for example on the timing or on the contents of the sound, but even so the risk remains present.

The one-directional character of the sound variable also explains why many professional lobby groups believe that for the political arena silence is safer than sound. They fear the ghost from the bottle. Their management of sound is, in fact, *silence management*. They want to remain silent about their position in the arena and, especially, their real targets or lobby agenda and, most especially, about the specific interests or values lying behind them. Making the latter public would not only damage their effectiveness, but also be useless, because the other stakeholders, holding different interests and values, can, ultimately, not be converted. From their perspective they are fully right as well. Constructing a common interest out of various interests is the best result one can attain, and this form of engineering is better achieved under silence than noise. For communication with others there are plenty of ways available, such as meetings behind closed doors, closed networks and, if some noise is still considered helpful, indirect channels. If necessary, more ways can be created by applying special factors and vectors, such as by making a dossier more complex or technical, by bringing it under comitology, or by parachuting one's own people into the apparatus. The more a dossier is seen as 'low politics', the easier it is to negotiate silently and conveniently.

This preference to avoid the ghost of sound might be seen as a rational rule of thumb, but it has too many exceptions to be a real rule. The main ones regard the arena being or expected to become *unfriendly* at some stage of the dossier's life (*figure 4.1*). If a lobby group wants to push a proposal, but fears that this will not pass any of the six thresholds of the decision-making process, then it may feel like under sentence of death. It may have the same feeling about the reverse situation, when it fears that an undesired proposal cannot be blocked and will inexorably pass the next threshold. In such situations it can rationally cause noise. By doing this, it widens the arena boundaries, thus bringing in new stakeholders and issues and almost certainly delaying the process. But the release from hanging is never guaranteed. The crowds may love to see a loser put to death, as the *sans-culottes* applauded when Marie Antoinette was executed in 1792 on the Place de la Concorde. By making an identifiable noise, such as through lengthy jeremiads, the lobby group can even destroy its chance to get compensation for loss. If a lobby group feels itself close to a severe loss and wants to save itself by noise, then it is best for it, firstly, to reframe or upgrade its message and, secondly, to use only the most indirect or anonymous media, such as through befriended stakeholders and outside lobbying.

If the arena is or is becoming *friendly*, it is sometimes better for the lobby group to play noisily rather than silently. The friendly issues have to be kept buoyant, and orchestrating supportive sound indirectly and with preferably upgraded contents can do this excellently, for example by releasing new scientific evidence that the desired outcome will produce extremely positive effects for some high social value. This may even in the long run drive out growing counter-issues. In the meantime the friendly dossier can be protected by a public call to set a deadline for its introduction, as was done by the 1985 Round Table of Industrialists for the creation of the Open Market by 1990 (which became 1992). In the *indeterminate* arena the making of noise can also be rational. The many indifferent or wavering stakeholders here have to be put at their ease and won over. If they are dispersed over many countries and sectors, the lobby group may have no alternative to public sound, in which case it may start a public campaign for the reframing of the crucial issues. In accordance with its interest in a wait-and-see position, it can lobby in public particularly for more research and reconsideration.

In addition to these specific situations where sound is rational, there are at least four general ones. Firstly, to maintain or improve its *agreeableness* in the eyes of the competitors, every lobby group must have an active public relations or communication policy. This implies the use of sound in the public arena, but only general interests should be mentioned, never the specific issues. Secondly, some befriended stakeholders may want to get *good pub-*

licity. The EU officials are usually sensitive to lyric and high-grade publicity in the mass media. The lobby group should use this negotiating chip preferably only after having got the desired outcome and again only in general terms unrelated to its specific interests. In this manner the Eurogroup for Animal Welfare publicly thanked the MEPs for their vote on animal testing in April 2001. Thirdly, *new issues* are permanently arising and may need early reframing, in order to stop them being passed or blocked as early as the first or the second threshold. This can best be done in some of the most general and upgraded terms, such as sustainability, welfare or security. Finally, there is always some room for playing *theatre*. In order to distract or divert the attention of competitors, it may be rational to make a noise on something else than the real interest at stake. But the lobby group should remain credible and not be seen as a comedian.

The fine-tuning of the sound-button is, in short, fully dependent on professional *homework*. The lobby group making spontaneous noise is like the brainless bird making sound at seeing some bread in the garden and thus attracting 20 competitive birds plus the cat. The lobby group should neither have an equally brainless phobia about the ghost of noise, because then it will neglect the many rational exceptions. But given the one-directional nature of noise it is rational to adopt silence management as the best basis for the fieldwork. Thus the lobby group forces itself to identify the rational exceptions and not to make unforced errors. This is a matter of preparatory work and prudence. Without this, there can be no fine-tuning of sound or silence.

The Timing of the Fieldwork

'Lobbying when?' is the last of the leading questions relating to the fieldwork. The rule of thumb from the manuals urges the lobby group to be early in the process, because then it can prearrange the playing field and take the lead. An early player, however, is also visible at an early stage, expends from the start a lot of scarce energy, and can be bypassed by the competitors joining the match at a later moment. As in cycling, usually only the amateurs and the helpers rush ahead early. For the professionals the proper timing is always a difficult balance between being not too early and not too late. But when precisely is this? The *best timing* depends on the situation, which is dynamic due to the dossier life cycle (*figure 4.1*). So far this cycle has been presented in a stylised form with six phases and thresholds, developing from social problem formation to inspection.

In three respects, however, this stylised and analytical model falls short of reality. It is full of subtleties. Firstly, the difference between the various *phases* is frequently not clear-cut at all. One phase usually feeds forward and back to another phase. There is an EU saying that 'those who define the problem take half the decision'. Even the die of inspection is usually cast long before its own phase starts. Secondly, the *sequence* of phases is not fixed in reality. A dossier can start not in the first phase of social problem formation, but already halfway through the cycle, as a spin-off from, for example, another agenda, a package deal or a finding from an inspection. It can also bypass one or more of the following phases. An EU official may adopt a social problem as discretionary for direct policy implementation. An expert group may start to consider the constraints of inspection and end up with a new social problem. Thirdly, an *outcome* is never certain in reality. During every phase the officials involved can decide formally to terminate the dossier. Many a dossier even fades away without such a decision and dies as, for example, a non-problem or a non-output. This is usually the successful result of delaying and blocking actions by opposing stakeholders. Pushing a dossier through takes more energy than delaying or blocking it.

Subtleties are frequently also neglected when the model is applied. Firstly, *public attention* is assumed to be the highest during the formal decision-making phase and the lowest in the phases before and after. But this is usually only true for the formal phase of both primary and secondary legislation and then only for the few persistent issues, such as the B points. The bulk of Treaty texts, Council decisions and delegated decisions hardly get that attention during their formal phase. In contrast, public attention can be high for a green paper defining a problem, a white paper suggesting solutions, or an inspection report criticising a policy. Secondly, the *official bodies* are assumed to control a specific phase, as the EU skeleton also suggests [Schaeffer, 1996]. However, in every phase an official can play the role of a stakeholder and so can a non-official. EP intergroups and EuroFeds are major agenda-builders and experts from civil society in fact frequently make the decision. Companies behave as inspectors of competition policy and the Commission directs the delegated legislation almost from start to finish. Thirdly, the cycle is frequently regarded *as a whole* and seldom broken down into constituent parts, although, for example, an EP rapporteur can go through the full cycle individually, from redefining the social and the political problems to getting a formal decision from the plenum and to scrutinising the outcomes. The dossier life cycle, if interpreted and used realistically, thus has its potential at the micro level as well.

The best moment for lobbying is clearly not easy to determine. True, it depends on the arena situation, but for almost every dossier this is a dynamic affair, with stakeholders and issues changing during its life cycle, which is full of subtleties. In addition, in many policy fields the speed of the EU machinery for decision-making is faster than in the past [Jordan and others, 1999] and frequently faster than its counterpart in the national capital. According to the Commission [DN: IP/01/323, 2001] it takes on average about 20 months for a proposed act to be adopted by the EU and the same period again for it to be implemented by the national governments. It is, in short, impossible to define the best moment as a rule of thumb. Only two activities the lobby group should start at the earliest moment and continue afterwards. Firstly, the window-out *homework* regarding the external arena and the home front. This enables reasoned answers to the questions 'who acts why, for what, to whom, where, on what, how and with what result?', leaving open only the question of 'when'. The more alert and proactive the preparatory work, the more time there is for an anticipatory action. This can transform the factor of time from an independent to a dependent variable or, in other words, from the passive concept of time to the active one of timing. This *anticipatory action* should be the second early activity of a lobby group. This does not imply that it must always be early, but if it concludes from its preparatory work that an anticipatory action is necessary or helpful, then it should certainly do this at an early moment of whatever phase. For example, a company having to abandon a relevant EU challenge only because of its internal weaknesses must swiftly address them. A Commission official concluding that the playing field needs a rearrangement should quickly start a Triple P game. A national ministry observing that it falls short of a sufficient network must begin further networking soon. In short, every time-consuming activity considered important should be started early and be continued.

In contrast to these two early activities, the window-in activity of *negotiations* can usually best be done much later. In many a case the lobby group makes the best bargains not early on but much later. The timings for this *deadline lobbying* it finds through its preparatory work. In an unfriendly arena it can usually claim the best compensation for loss at only five-to-midnight. Crucial waverers can create the greatest impact if they are brought on board at a late stage. In a friendly arena the lobby group should not show its satisfaction early, for fear of revealing its interests. It is best for it to look reserved and in waiting for some time. In an indeterminate arena the wait-and-see strategies require that the lobby group remains slow to enter negotiations. Otherwise it will trade off some interests that it will need to be re-traded later, when the arena turns to friendly or unfriendly. If it learns from the homework that the best deal can be made at the latest moment, for example in the meeting of the Council ministers, then it should not act earlier. The early preparation and the anticipatory action will suffice here. This was the situation with the national air carriers in the 1992 Air Transport Slot Case [Van den Polder, 1994] and the French agricultural lobby in the 1998 Transgenic Maize Case [Bradley, 1998], mentioned earlier. But the lobby group can also be too late; precise timing is really an art.

While the preparatory work and the anticipatory actions can best be done at an early stage and the negotiations at a much later one, the *other fieldwork activities* of EU public affairs management cannot be allocated a single best time. In short: the former two should be done proactively and the other fieldwork activities should be reactive to the situation. For example resetting the strategy, updating the short list, extending the network or playing the Triple P game can all have many good or bad moments for action, but, dependent on the situation, some are better than others. For example, a EuroFed being in a friendly arena and wanting to speed up the process, should not necessarily arrange an early appointment with, for example, the EP rapporteur. Its absence or late arrival, so not alarming the opponents early on, could speed up the process the most. This is clearly a matter of detailed homework and no different from the delaying and the wait-and-see strategies in the unfriendly and the indeterminate arena respectively. The good moment for action here depends on the details. For example, the lobby group wanting to reframe an issue can hardly do so in the Commission's draft phase if the Commissioner has a personal commitment to the policy line. In this case, it is better to await or to anticipate the so-called decision-making phase of the EP or the Council, if this is going to happen. But usually it finds the Commission phase open and it is then better to try to reframe the issue at the interservice stage, when other DGs have their say, than at the expert meeting stage, as many experts tend to be cynical about reframing. But if the lobby group is the DG unit itself, then it can make good use of the early meeting of experts.

The dilemma of time and timing is, of course, not separate from the aforementioned *other dilemmas* of the fieldwork, for example those regarding lobbying styles. In the early phases of the life of a dossier and at the early stages of its involvement, the lobby group can usually best behave in a supplying, informal, indirect and low-key manner. This helps it to become accepted as an interesting stakeholder, to build-up relationships, to keep its hands free and to avoid early opposition. The early homework and the anticipatory actions should have those styles too. Then the lobby group will gather better information and greater opportunities at lower cost. But during the negotiations at the later stages it should become much more demanding in order to get the desired outcome and act formally if it wants a real decision, although the latter is not necessary if it only wants to block or to delay. The use of direct and noisy ways remains subject to the many considerations mentioned above. For all these public affairs activities not having an easily identified best time for action, the linkage to the other dilemmas should, in short, strictly depend on the specific situation and thus on the preparatory work. The amateur lobby group neglecting this takes the high risk of managing its EU public affairs in the wrong way at the wrong moment.

Extra: the Ideal Profile of the EU Public Affairs Expert

Improving the chance of getting a desired outcome from the EU is clearly a matter of fine-tuned and well-timed fieldwork and so a matter of special knowledge or expertise. This raises the question about the *ideal profile* of the expert in EU public affairs, working for a company, a NGO, a government, the Commission or whatever lobby group, or as a self-employed consultant. The work to be done can be distilled from figure 3.3. The person must be, in short, a threefold master: a *Socrates* in asking the same enduring questions for every case when it occurs, a *Max Weber* in developing the answers by preparatory work, and a *Niccoló Machiavelli* in applying the insights through fieldwork. The expert does all this dossier-related or specific homework and fieldwork both systematically and on time. Superficial work completed on time is as useless as perfect work that overruns time.

The specific skills needed for the preparatory homework range from pure to applied science. The three most *scientific skills* are the following ones. Firstly, the public affairs expert is research-minded, with strong descriptive and analytical capacities, and with a large appetite for valid and reliable observations or so-called facts. Secondly, the expert possesses a strong sense of relativism for values when assessing the facts, because no fact is good or bad by itself but only in confrontation with some independently selected value. Every value or position may be sensible, even those of the opponent. With such a phlegmatic approach, the expert can even turn a threat into an opportunity. All this is done, thirdly, with a critical or discriminating mind. The expert is conscious about, *inter alia*, the limits of his/her knowledge, the alternatives to every option, and the difference between shadow and substance.

There are three specific preparatory skills that come close to being *applied science*. Firstly, the expert remains familiar with the developing political science of the EU system, including the major actors, factors and vectors. He/she knows the relevant people, places and ways to enter the system. Thanks to this, the expert can compose menus for action on the playing field. Secondly, the public affairs expert, while keeping one eye on the EU, stays firmly within his/her own organisation, which is the source of every interest. This implies at least an overall knowledge of what happens at home: the internal dynamics, the main processes, and its position in society. Finally, the expert has a sense of pragmatic efficiency. There are always constraints of time, resources, knowledge, support and much more. Maximising the striving for perfection may bring an academic award, but also nullify one's position on the EU playing field. The expert wants to optimise or to search for the best possible way.

The specific skills for the fieldwork involve, first of all, the ability to make a two-pronged *connection with the preparatory work*. From one side, the public affairs expert is able to take field experiences as a source of inspiration for a different approach to the homework. Even a seemingly trivial piece of information may indicate an important change of issues or stakeholders, requiring additional arena analysis. From the other side, the expert is able to apply the homework to the playing field, of course after sufficient authorisation by some high official inside the organisation. For example, the building of a broader coalition, the upgrading of an issue, the supplying of support or the delaying of the decision-making process is driven by the preparatory homework. The applied expertise culminates in fine-tuning and precise timing.

The second specific skill required for the fieldwork falls in the area of *diplomatic psychology* [De Callières, 1716]. The direct fieldwork in particular is highly personalised behaviour. In the direct contacts with stakeholders, the public affairs expert looks communicative, reasonable and pleasant according to the various standards of the others. He/she masters the main languages, including body language and the informal codes. During the negotiations the expert is seen as reliable, offering and flexible. The person has a lot of patience and tenacity to cope with the long and difficult matches. A basic sense of humour and optimism is imparted, not only for its positive image but also for one's own mental survival. Due to the paradoxical necessity of remaining untroubled and yet looking human under all circumstances, the expert can try some theatre: smiling in stormy weather and grumbling when the sun comes out. As a diplomat he/she remains charming and respectful to the others who have different preferences, simply because the others are warriors with nuisance value, despite how irritating their preferences may be. The expert behaves like a sportsman, who is eager to score but in a courteous way, because there is always another match coming. All these qualities the expert performs in an unspectacular and quiet way, with a seeming concern only for the so-called general interest.

In addition to all these specific, dossier-related skills, the public affairs expert possesses two general attitudes. Firstly, the person has a *broad curiosity* regarding any development related to the EU playing field. The curiosity is not limited to the hard core of the EU decision-making mechanism with its variables such as procedures, personnel, issues and stakeholders. It extends to seemingly marginal developments such as the new political culture in Italy, the devolution of the French state, or the rapid industrialisation of Turkey. With some time lag all these developments may affect the EU playing field in the near future. The curiosity functions as the engine for the updating of one's understanding of the varieties and especially the irritating differences of Europe. It helps to get an anticipatory grip on the EU method of living together peacefully. Secondly, the expert has a *strong commitment* to his/her interest group and acts as a warrior on behalf of it. The public affairs expert wants to win or at least not to lose. This dedication gives him/her a licence to operate as a representative lobbyist. It also feeds back to the interest group, in the form of a flow of useful information and creative thinking. The expert is capable of defining a challenge, recommending how to save a blessing or solve a problem, and eventually helping to turn a threat into an opportunity.

If advertised, this ideal profile of the expert on EU public affairs management will certainly attract a number of applicants. Many of them hold the self-confident belief that they are naturally gifted and have the right talents for the job. They say they have the professional management of EU public affairs at their fingertips. But almost certainly only a very few applicants will come close to the profile. Expertise is always a scarcity, the reason being that expertise is a match of talents and skills to a specific role. The talents are, for example, those for assessing facts and values, for going through labyrinths constructed on trampolines, and for fine-tuning the fieldwork. To some degree they can be developed and brought out through training. But there are always people who hardly benefit from whatever training, thus making the difference between talent and training clear. Training without much talent can make a person a good player, but not a Kasparov. Talent without skills means a person has high potential, but is not yet a top player. Talent plus skills creates art.

Skills are easier to develop and to improve than talents. So far, most people working in the field of EU public affairs management have not received special training. They have developed their abilities through an *éducation non-permanente*. Only the happy few have received from their predecessor some teaching 'from father to son', including the inheritance of mistakes. Seniors rarely train juniors up to an advanced level. In most interest groups the learning takes place just by doing, with much trial and error. Most persons in EU public affairs management are self-made people. Coming from a different job, frequently in line management, they dropped without a parachute into the work of EU public affairs management. The lobbyists from government organisations in particular, including the EU institutions, have this career history and tend to confuse their old policy expertise with the new public affairs expertise. The lobbyists from MNCs and NGOs have usually had some limited training from a 'godfather'. Only some larger consultancy firms in EU public affairs management have created a few training facilities.

The public affairs official is, of course, not necessarily a person but can be a *small team* as well. This formula can be found among multinational organisations, like Shell or Greenpeace. This team is usually supported by other staff such as experts in European law, by line people for technical expertise, by colleagues from units in other countries and, if necessary, by specialised consultants. In a team all the work of public affairs management can be divided more according to the talents and skills of the members, but even this is more theory than practice. Most small teams are formed more by accident than by conscious intent. By the latter method, one can organise a team like a small orchestra and even gain an advantage from the limited research that has taken place on the best profile for a lobbyist. These findings suggest that officials who have been lobbied regard as the most influential lobbyists the full-timers, women and those from government [Nownes, 1999]. The full-timers are seen as more experienced and expert, the women as more patient and able to compromise, and government people as more concerned about the so-called general interest. These different virtues are easier to provide with a well-organised small team than by a single person.

There is, in short, much *room for improvement*. The easiest thing to organise and to improve is internal training. A senior should invest in some junior, even if the latter might overtake him/her or depart for a competitor. Regular short sessions with other staff and line personnel involved in EU affairs can at least create a common concern for the shortcomings on the home front and so a common agenda for improvements. The evaluation of any game played is, as outlined earlier, a great source of learning and training. Public affairs people invited from outside, even if they lack great expertise, may add value to internal training, because they stimulate learning by comparison. Recognised experts from outside can be asked to give a peer review. Another way of learning is by going out and meeting public affairs colleagues from other lobby groups informally, as happens in the Netherlands where four such circles exist. More formal is the enrolment at an institute or a school of EU public affairs management. There are a few vocational centres and short-term courses mainly at introductory level on offer, but frequently they have little to do with EU public affairs management in reality and, for example, only provide courses on EU policies and institutions.

There is no *university programme* in this field available in Europe. If it were to be established, it would need to be interdisciplinary. The major courses recommended are the following five: science and methodology, to understand value-relativism and research; political science, to understand the flesh and blood of the EU system; law, to know the EU skeleton; psychology, to comprehend the human dimension of public affairs; and economics, to grasp the issues of interests, scarcity and efficiency. Minor courses should be given on European cultural variety, European history, negotiations in complex situations, information retrieval techniques, communication studies, and special EU policy areas. Some European languages would have to be studied as options. Other electives, useful for the understanding of political engineering, would be chemistry (how to control an effect), construction (how to make a linkage stable) and mechanical engineering (how to make it work). Finally, the students would have to reproduce in practice and individually their exercises, case studies, case-related homework and essays and to participate for some time in a public affairs department of an EU-oriented lobby group. Such a university programme would, of course, not be a panacea. It would merely help to develop the talents people may have and to replace costly training by practical trial and error.

From the Potentials to the Limits of EU Public Affairs Management

At the end of the third chapter we explained our choice of starting the presentation of EU public affairs management with the homework on both the external arena and the home front and of ending with the fieldwork. This design is justified from an educational point of view. The homework should be the basis of the fieldwork. To avoid an egocentric approach towards the EU playing field, it is better to start with the external arena than with the home front. The alternative design, starting with the fieldwork, would only produce questions and no guiding answers. But, as emphasised before, the various activities of the preparatory work and the fieldwork, distinguished analytically, are closely interwoven in practice. All the questions and activities found in *figure 3.3* lie, in daily life, simultaneously on the table of every lobby group, whether it is conscious of this or not.

The paradox is that the more one keeps the various questions and activities separated analytically, the more one can safely interweave them for the production of a desired EU outcome. The greatest skill is in *interconnecting* all questions and activities systematically and acquiring new insights from them for both the fieldwork and the homework regarding both oneself and the arena. To do this perfectly is, of course, only a dream. Even in the easier game of chess such a multi-variable decision game can not be imagined perfectly, but one can strive for it. The more experience with homework and fieldwork one gets, the easier one makes the connections between the two and the more one grows in expertise. The reward will be a better choice of the next activity for the fieldwork and homework, which can bring the lobby group closer to the desired EU outcome. In every case of strong competition it is the margin that makes the difference.

By that interconnection of all questions and all activities one gets as much *homework-based fieldwork* as *fieldwork-based homework*. The preparatory work, then, is as much a source of inspiration for playing the game at home or in the arena, as playing the game is for the preparatory work. Through this process, one also creates a real *R&D* of EU public affairs management, resulting in even more options, tools, menus and dilemmas and, as well, in more manipulable factors and constructible vectors. The surplus of potential actions becomes even larger and is, theoretically, unlimited. For the professional this is not an embarrassing problem, but a pleasant opportunity providing a way through the EU labyrinth. What is unlimited in theory can, however, have its many limits in practice. That is the theme of the next chapter. To jump to a paradoxical conclusion: the professional, already taking greater advantage from the surplus of potential actions than the amateur does, suffers less than the amateur does from the limits in practice.

CHAPTER 7

THE LIMITS OF EU PUBLIC AFFAIRS MANAGEMENT

From Tantalus to SCARE

Our preceding chapters on the management of EU public affairs are full of buoyant spirits. The attractive flowers and trees of the EU playing field look like being within the reach of every lobby group. Of course, their harvesting is not easy and requires much homework and fieldwork, to be carried out carefully and energetically. But most lobby groups hold the optimistic belief that sooner or later a lot of flowers and fruit can be brought home as trophies and that they can prune, fructify or dig over the soil during their growth at will. Many even see room for planting better varieties. *Tantalus*, failing to pick the grapes in Hades, would have loved to go to Brussels. The EU decision-making machinery is certainly full of variables, which can be manipulated to get a desired outcome. But EU public affairs management is not without its limits. The mere pressures of time and efficiency make sure that not everything is a variable, let alone an easily manageable one. Not the sky is the limit, but the players, the playing field, the issues, the game, the audiences and all the other circumstances put together.

The various limits can be classed under different headings. One distinction is between the limits that are endogenously linked to a lobby group and those that exogenously come from wherever outside. Another distinction differentiates between structural limits, caused by patterned behaviour, and cultural ones, set by the individual and the collective minds. More concrete is the classification by communication categories or *SCARE*. The limits in this case come respectively the *Sender* being the lobby group, the *Channels* that transmit the messages, the *Arena* where all information is exchanged, the *Receivers* being the EU officials and other stakeholders, and the *Environment* conditioning the other four categories. In this approach all limits of EU public affairs management are viewed from the perspective of the lobby group sending a message. This message can have a substantial form and contents or be a so-called non-message, for example silence or an absence meant to convey a position.

We shall now examine this SCARE classification and for each category provide a number of typical limits. The identification of the limits mirrors that of the surplus of potential actions, shown in the preceding chapters, in two respects. Firstly, like the potential actions, the limits cannot be exhaustively listed. Their numbers are theoretically infinite. We confine ourselves here to the major limits existing in the daily life of EU public affairs management, as regularly stressed by practitioners in their interviews or observed by scholars in their case studies mentioned earlier. Secondly, for the management of these limits we shall discriminate again between the so-called amateurish and the professional lobby group. The catchword for the amateur is *nonchalance* and for the professional it is *prudence*. The professional is more scared than the amateur of making unforced errors and of thus becoming one of his own strong opponents. The prudent player remains conscious about the many possible limits, tries to escape or to extend them in advance, and respects the unmanageable limits.

The assessment of a limit is, of course, a matter for good preparatory work once again. In essence it is no different from that of a *challenge*, discussed in chapter 5. Every lobby group must, firstly, establish whether a limit exists in a particular circumstance or not. The same channel, arena and receiver may set limits for one stakeholder, but give a free passage to another. The limits are usually relative and not absolute. Secondly the group has to determine whether the limit, present or absent, is a problem or a blessing. If an existing limit is helpful for the group's targets, it is certainly a blessing, which might be preserved by efforts to keep it. If it is not helpful, then it is a problem, which might be solved either by alleviating the limit, or at least its consequences, or by reconsidering the extent of its harm. By analogy, the absence of a limit can be managed as either a blessing to preserve or a problem to solve. The professional lobby group does this sort of homework not only for its own organisation, but also for the most relevant other stakeholders. They all have their own variable collection of limits.

The Sender's Mental Limits

Public affairs management is a highly human activity. The person or team in charge of it has to search continually for the next best move. The possession and the use of brains, enriched by talents and skills, are crucial. Inevitably, however, all sorts of *human shortcomings* can play a disturbing role. For example, due to some personal drama one's private life can become an obsession and undermine one's performance of public affairs management. One's character may be so full of arrogance and vanity that one is, indeed, one's own formidable enemy on the playing field. Perhaps, one is mentally obsessed with one's interest, an opponent, an issue or something else that is part of the playing process. We shall now focus on these mental limits caused by human shortcomings and discuss three cases: emotions, dogmas and myths.

Emotions

The list of potential emotions is infinite. The lobby group can be brought into imbalance by, for example, the threat or the opportunity attached to a challenge. While carrying out his cost-cutting operation Centurion in 1992, the Philips CEO Jan Timmer emotionally blamed the Commission for what he called its postponing of the great HDTV opportunity. He only succeeded in attracting more opposition. The lobby group can also have the emotion of voracity, as a result of which it cannot reduce the long list to a manageable short list, because so much more looks threatening or promising. Another frequent emotion is that of political (in)efficacy, or holding the belief that it is one's fate to be a winner or a loser. Many emotions crop up during the game, for example resulting from the perceived unfair behaviour of another stakeholder. In such a case, many a lobby group feels disturbed and acts agonised. In the Biotechnology Dossier the opponents of GMO introduced the norm of 'zero risk' and publicly blamed the proponents for setting mankind at maximum risk. Part of the food industry behaved, indeed, as if emotionally imprisoned by this black-and-white debate. A lobby group can also have the emotional belief that some important stakeholders, such as Commission officials or MEPs, are autistic, biased, unreliable or in some way vicious. For their part, many EU officials display the emotion of distrust regarding what lobby groups really want. An emotional sender easily resorts to voicing its annoyance, thus throwing the tomahawk when remaining unaffected or offering the calumet could be more productive. A common emotion arises from the uncertainties regarding the arena: the inevitable lack of complete and reliable information may be upsetting, especially when both the stakes and the time pressures are high.

Emotions are a strong variable in the double sense that they can both strongly affect lobby behaviour and exhibit strong variation. Regarding the latter, there even exist specific *nation-wide* emotions, such as the British allergy towards EU federalism (the F-word), the French one towards takeovers by foreign companies and the Danish towards lobbying separately from the national government [Sidenius, 1999]. Some emotions are more bound to the *type of organisation*. SMEs frequently hold the emotional belief of inefficacy, while many a multinational regularly expects that it will be one of the winners. Issue-driven NGOs usually have their emotion anchored in their central policy value, such as 'green environment' or 'safe and healthy labour'. National ministries may attach emotional value to a specific EU dossier, especially if this has been given priority under pressure created through the political situation in the parliament, the leading interest groups and the mass media at home. Such a priority is seldom based on sound preparatory work and can soon create the problem of face-saving. The same can happen to a national government chairing the Council, if it is encouraged by its parliament to bring more and better order to the EU. In 1991 the Dutch government launched an overambitious campaign for European Political Union (EPU). In a few weeks it received its 'Black Monday' and became so bewildered that in 1997 it gave up on any ambition for its new chairmanship.

These and other emotions are part of human life. They are like earthquakes, which have to be taken as a part of nature. But the *professional* lobby groups know that, to some degree, these earthquakes can be foreseen and their most devastating effects controlled. The groups' awareness is the precondition of their prudence and is a matter of good preparation. It is not that the professional players have, necessarily, fewer emotions than the amateurs, who nonchalantly may neglect many causes of emotion as well, but that the professionals filter the emotive stimuli better and react in a more reserved way than the amateurs tend to do. They are disciplined about heeding their homework and remain concentrated on the targets. They take the emotions of other stakeholders as a useful indicator of their feelings of weakness (unless they are 'comedians'), and any unfairness from them they return as a free boomerang. In the multinational model the professionals are helped to remain cool by such measures as the critical ad-hoc team, the regular update of the short list and the construction of scenarios. Even so, they are still susceptible to emotional behaviour, but less so than the amateurs. This difference can be crucial for the desired outcome.

Dogmas
Dogmas are strong beliefs in being right and they tend to be immune to critical debate. Policy experts frequently believe that their policy proposal is the best one and during meetings with their colleagues from other member countries in an expert committee or a working group they can easily become involved in dogmatic clashes. Party politicians frequently claim the best ideology and preach to their audience that the only salvation is in fol-

lowing their message. Issue-driven NGOs tend to have great difficulty with any compromising on their core value. Many lobby groups are inclined to stick to a strategy once it is set, and, seeing a challenge, prefer to deal with the unpleasant facts rather than their fixed norms, thus rejecting half the number of solutions. A peculiar dogma is that of national co-ordination. Its source is usually the national parliament or even the constitution, requiring the national government to act as one body and to speak with one voice, thus denying all pluralism in the country. At EU level, one group's dogmas can easily irritate others, who perhaps also have the belief that they are perfectly right. Dogmas deny the concepts of pluralism and relativism of values [Galston, 1999]. They heat up the emotions and hinder the negotiations.

There seems to be some *national variation* in dogmas. Lobby groups from the Protestant areas of Europe, with the Germans at the top, frequently have the reputation of adhering to so-called expertise-based dogmas. After many conflicts and discussions on the home front, they have finally arrived at a policy position, which is rigidly advertised as also the best for Europe. National dogmas can also be based on a tradition or a value other than expertise. The French are frequently dogmatic on central planning, the Dutch on accommodative compromising, the British on rule of law and the Italians on flexible implementation. Some variation by *organisational type* seems to exist as well. Governments, usually lacking a public affairs unit within and using their policy experts as their agents, frequently take a dogmatic position, especially if their elected body instructs them. The same pattern can be found in private organisations, if policy experts set the tone. Many NGOs take their mission as their dogma. Companies tend to become dogmatic the more their core product or service is brought into discussion and especially when their licence to operate is at stake. For Philip Morris, smoking falls under the dogma of liberty.

Amateurish groups adopt dogmas more easily than *professionals* do, because the latter are more critical about their own strategic norms and values. In the multinational model, public affairs experts counterbalance the policy experts inside the organisation. They include the dogmas of other stakeholders in their plan of action. The professionals are more inclined than the amateurs to stay away from the public platforms, like press conferences and the mass media, which function as consuming markets for dogmas. They want to act publicly only in the special situations mentioned in the previous chapter, for example for the voicing of a politically acceptable dogma in order to attract support. They know that the real decision-making process consists of negotiations, which can best take place in inner rooms,

Ten popular EU myths

1. 'Brussels': a big bureaucracy
   The number of EU civil servants is extraordinary high.
2. Centralist union
   'Brussels' governs top-down.
3. Formal powers = real influence
   Those who have the formal powers are the ones who influence.
4. Corporatist union
   The employers, trade unions and officials together run the EU.
5. Elitist union
   Those running the EU form a closed group.
6. Dominant governments
   The national governments have the final say.
7. Democratic deficit
   The people and the parliament are politically marginal.
8. Paris-Berlin axis
   France and Germany together run the EU.
9. 'Not so relevant for us'
   The EU is much ado about nothing.
10. 'Towards one hotchpot union'
    All varieties are cooked to one average.

Figure 7.1

far away from such public platforms. Even a professional, however, is seldom free from all dogmas and may hold a sacrosanct value. The amateur is only less free, and this difference is important for the outcome.

Myths
A myth is a cherished preconceived image of reality. It is taken as true, but in fact it is merely fiction formed by, for example, tradition, prescripts, folklore, propaganda or tabloids. *Figure 7.1* exemplifies this through a number of popular myths about the EU, discussed in various places in this book. Most have a large following, even where they partially contradict each other. 'Brussels' is said to be a big bureaucracy, but in terms of budget or number of civil servants it is only a peanuts bureaucracy. The EU is seen as centralist, but a large part of its decision-making process is in reality firmly in the hands of public and private interest groups at its decentralised levels. The skeleton of formal powers is frequently mistaken for the flesh and blood of influence. The interest groups of organised management and labour, inter-

woven with the EU officials, make the EU look like a corporatist system, but in reality they rarely amount to a closed policy cartel in any way. The EU is seen as elitist, but usually it is an open decision-making system involving many competitive groups or, in short, a polyarchy, which is almost the opposite of an elitist system. National governments are seen as dominant, as prescribed by the Treaty of Rome, but in reality they are each only one player among many and, acting as part of the Council, they approve less than 20 percent of total EU law per year. With regard to the Parliament in particular, it is claimed that the EU has a democratic deficit, but in many respects, and in comparison to many national systems, it has more of a democratic surplus. The allegedly strong 'Paris-Berlin axis' is in reality a red-hot junction between two rivalling capitals. Small interest groups in particular frequently attach little relevance to the EU, but in fact they only feel small in a large relevant system. A hotchpotch Union has often been predicted, but this denies the existence of such clear trends as growing regionalism and cultural differentiation.

Every person or group believes some myths and is thus misled by their preconceived confusion of reality, but some are more under the influence of myths than others. There seems to be some *national* variation. Most myths are widely adhered to in the United Kingdom. The democratic deficit myth is popular in Scandinavia. The myth of formal powers is cherished in the formalistic countries of France and Spain. The myth of little relevance is, except regarding the stream of subsidies they receive, widely held in Greece and Italy, where any legislation is considered more recommending than binding. Some myths are typically for a particular type of *organisation*. Many a national government frequently maintains the myth of being a dominant government, except when it is defeated on an important dossier. Ministries of Home Affairs and Justice, having recently begun playing on the new field of Pillar III, tend to believe that their influence equals their formal powers. Newly arriving NGOs tend to believe that 'Brussels' is a huge bureaucracy, full of centralism and elitism; they have clearly much to learn. Among many SMEs the myth of little relevance is popular and used as an excuse for passivity.

Amateurish groups hold many myths. They follow the popular stereotypes, gossip and newspapers. In consequence, they limit considerably their own potential success with EU public affairs management. They go to Brussels, when they should really be at a lower, decentralised level, or they place their trust in the Council, although the Commission makes the real decision. They are, in short, misled by their preconceived images of EU reality. The *professionals* may have their myths as well, but usually in lower quantity and with less certainty. They act less from myth-bound reflex than through conscious reflection when faced with stimuli from the EU playing field. The discipline of preparatory work gives them the best possible protection against an enduring EU mythology. For example, their dossier-related inventory of the stakeholders is an open-minded exercise covering every observed stakeholder belonging to whatever layer, axis or platform. In the multinational model the professionals have such additional safeguards as the examination of the homework beforehand by somebody from the Board, the ad-hoc team working on it and its evaluation afterwards. One risk, however, is that they may generalise a single experience and thus construct a post-conceived image of reality with equally mythical contents. The dynamics and complexities of reality mean that nobody is fully free from myths. Some are only more free and less bound than others, but this difference may tip the balance towards winning or losing.

The Sender's Organisational Limits

Not only its mental situation, but also its state of internal organisation can set serious limits for a lobby group's EU public affairs management. Staff and line people may pass each other on the EU playing field, where the public relations (PR) staff can thwart the public affairs (PA) unit on the use of sound, and the legal staff can do the same on litigation. In a voluntary association such as a EuroFed some members can weaken the common position. In a multinational company the various country units may choose their own way to approach Brussels. Many a lobby group falls short of a good reputation or other important resources and its leadership can have a poor strategy or some other management deficit. In short, all organisational variables can limit the effectiveness and the efficiency of EU public affairs management. Here we shall focus on three typical cases: dissent, scarcity and lack of leadership.

Dissent

The lack of sufficient cohesion is one of the most common and most serious causes of a poor performance in public affairs management. Every lobby group has a certain amount of internal pluralism, indicated by different values, role expectations and duties. To some extent this may be considered a richness, because it promotes internal creativity and external adaptability. But this richness has its limits, and the internal dialectics may eventually hamper external performance. If a lobby group sends different messages to the same audience within a short time, then it may soon lose its credibility as a stakeholder, except in the very special case of a precisely directed and thus most cohesive 'comedy' performance. Every lobby group has a record of some serious dissent observed by other stakeholders, who can exploit it to their advantage. If the group has strong grass-roots layers, as usually exist in voluntary associations, then the appearance of dissent on a major issue is a normal part of its internal life and easily noticed externally. The same holds true for vertically segmented dissent, for example according to the divisions and the country units of an MNC, the ministries and the agencies of a national government, or the DGs and the task forces of the Commission. The calming of an internal cleavage costs a lot in terms of, for example, time, compromise and obedience. Sometimes the lobby group can even best abstain from playing on the EU field and consign the matter to its list of posteriorities.

Dissent may be a regular feature of every lobby group, but it is highly variable in its frequency, intensity, form, contents, methods of solution and other aspects. In practice, there are some patterns to the variations. Some seem to be *national*. In Denmark and the Netherlands many interest groups have grass-roots layers taking up a lot of internal debate and related costs. In France and Germany the internal dissent is often more embedded in procedures and formalities, and solved by a decree from the top to the rank and file who are trained in paying lip service. In Italy internal dissent tends to go along the lines of clientelistic factions, with the patrons in charge of seeking accommodation. More specific is the *organisational* variation. Government organisations are rather transparent in their dissent, because the mass media and politicians closely watch them. Their opposing stakeholders can easily identify and exploit the internal cleavages inside a ministry or directorate. Many NGOs are composed of voluntary members, who are confident about voicing their different positions on an issue. A confederation like UNICE or ETUC is more frequently paralysed by internal dissent than a more homogeneous federation like the CIAA (food industry) or the EMF (metalworkers) or a homogeneous ad-hoc group like Europabio (biotech firms). MNCs experience regular dissent among both their divisions and their country units. SMEs have it inside their regional and sectoral organisations, where they meet for the remote control of EU affairs.

The most striking variation is between the amateur and the *professional* lobby group. Through its preparatory work, the latter has an early-warning system regarding any internal dissent arising on an issue. It has some time to anticipate a clash, for example by using a procedure cutting across those of the opposing camps, by suggesting a compromise or by making an internal linkage with another dossier. If it fails to heal the cleavage, it can rationally decide to put the whole issue on its list of posteriorities and to remain passive, thus avoiding any further misinvestment. Thanks to its homework, it can also make some use of the observed dissent inside any other stakeholder. A relevant friend may thus be helped, a waverer won or an enemy split. Such a result, of course, has a good chance of success but is not guaranteed. The amateur group, however, does not even get the chance: because of its neglect of the homework it lacks the early warning system and can only muddle through.

Scarcity
Important resources such as expertise, networks, positions and financial means, are always scarcities, either by quantity or by quality. Even more so are the skills of acquiring expertise, networking, positioning and financing. Knowledge about the EU generally or about the arena specifically has limited reliability and completeness. A lobby group may have the finest image, including a good appearance and a nice supply side, but this is always less than sacrosanct. Time is almost always scarce. At the operational level of EU public affairs, qualified people are an utmost scarcity, and it takes a long time to get the talented well trained. Once they are qualified, they frequently switch to another position or another organisation, thus taking with them all their qualifications. In many cases a replacement has almost to start from scratch. Every asset, in short, is hard to obtain and can soon be lost. Scarcity is a fact of life.

There are hardly any indications of a *national* variation in scarcity, but the resource of networks and the skill of networking come close to having one. Interest groups from northern countries tend to be more rigid about networking than those from the southern areas and have, in consequence, a lower quantity and quality particularly of informal networks. The rest of the scarcities do not seem to be distributed differently according to the member countries. The variation in scarcity by *organisational* type looks more striking. The most notorious case of resource scarcity is the Commission, with its small staff and budget. Government organisations from the member countries frequently look important, agreeable and capable of supplying something of interest, but their specific resources and skills in EU public affairs management are often limited. Their expertise is mainly limited to the policy contents. Their networks and people operating inside the EU are frequently poorly supported. The established NGOs often have a strong nuisance value, a good level of agreeableness and, if they are not dogmatic, an interesting supply side. Many have facilities and skills for doing the preparatory work and for both networking and positioning. Some come close to the multinational model. Many MNCs regularly suffer from their own reorganisations, which disturb their EU public affairs management. During its Centurion operation in the early 1990s the Philips company experienced poor performance in Brussels. The newly forming NGOs and SMEs usually have the most limited resources and skills.

There exists a clear difference between the amateurs and the *professionals*. The latter manage their scarcities more prudently and in fact are more selective in, for example, adopting a dossier for the short list, developing a network, taking a particular route or negotiating over a target. Their selectivity comes from their homework. Through this they can save some of their scarce resources and skills or exploit them more successfully. Identifying their allies at an early moment, they can arrange cost-sharing of the monitoring, the networking and the other fieldwork. The amateurs, in contrast, behave more wastefully and are exhausted sooner. This difference can be dramatic for the desired outcome.

Lack of leadership

Management deficits can have many forms. No management is ever fully free from emotions, dogmas and myths. It can, for example, be emotional about a competitive stakeholder, dogmatic about its strategy once set and mythical about its position on the EU playing field. It is also never free from dissent and scarcity within the organisation. All this is normal, but the special duty of management is to control and to relieve all these mental and organisational limits. Here it meets its own limits: its decision on strategy is frequently not based on a regular and open-minded assessment of preferred norms and observed facts, but on an indolent compromise between, for example, the old and the desired strategy, one or another emotion, or two rival board members. Frequently it starts its consensus management not by stimulating the rich internal dialectics, but instead with leaping to a formally imposed consensus. Even if it starts in the right way, it may fail to transform the dialectics into a better synthesis. Many managers have a poor span of control, thus leaving to drift the various units of line and staff, including those in public affairs management. All this may result in poor control over the homework and fieldwork of EU public affairs indicated by, for example, a poorly reasoned short list, a wasteful fight with PR over sound, and an imbalance between targets and financial means.

All the management deficits have their variations. They may even be *nation-specific*. In countries where some emotions, dogmas and myths are particularly persistent, as suggested above, the interest group managers usually have great difficulty in overcoming them. Lobby groups in Germany,

France and Spain, frequently being rather hierarchical, tend to fall short in the dialectic management of consensus. In the Netherlands, managers are, for the opposite reason, often indolently compromising on setting strategy. In the Protestant countries managers frequently underestimate the importance of informal networking, including the undignified wining and dining. More specific are the *organisational* variations. The management of government organisations, such as national ministries and the Commission, frequently fails to develop a realistic next-best scenario and to keep its staff and line cohesive. There is enormous variation among the smaller-sized regional and local governments, but some, like the German Länder and the Spanish region of Cataluña, have a reputation of strong leadership over their EU public affairs. EuroFeds and other NGOs are frequently characterised by a weak position of the management. The chairman or the board is usually selected, replaced and pressurised by the grass roots. Many MNCs are so large and vertically segmented that their management has only limited control over operations. In many cases it has a well-resourced EU public affairs unit at its disposal, but under-uses its potential. The management of SMEs has to meet, in addition to its internal limits, the external ones of their regional and sectoral associations, necessary for remote control.

Amateurishly organised lobby groups have clearly more management deficits than *professional* ones. They are more affected by their mental limits and by their internal dissent and scarcities. Their managers are more doers than thinkers and more led by reflex than by reflection. They are, in short, highly dependent on good luck and frequently suffer bad luck. The management of professional groups, in contrast, oversees its EU public affairs more or less as sketched in the multinational model. It has its mental and organisational limits better under control. It has an early warning system obtained through its homework, and can use this to anticipate and take measures to alleviate some limits. Its management deficits are, in short, usually less numerous, but it still encounters limits to its ability to manage EU public affairs successfully. However, these are less the result of its own deficits and more because of external circumstances mentioned below.

The Limits of Channel Management

A channel is a transmission system for sending messages. There are many different types of channels. *Figure 7.2* presents a selection of the analytical variety. Through the various possible combinations the number of channels can be infinite. A channel can be one-way, for either the sending or the receiving of a message, or be two- (or more) way, for interactive communi-

Variety of channels for public affairs management

one way or two/more ways

single or multiple (network)

connected or dead end

parallel or in series

direct or indirect

open or closed

general or specific

natural or artificial

permanent or revolving

established or newly developed

Figure 7.2

cation. There may be just one channel or a multiple channel system, forming a network. A channel can be connected either to a receiver, or to another channel or have a dead end. If there are more channels, they can be parallel or be connected in series. Channels may go directly or indirectly to some place, which can be compared with the direct and indirect ways of lobbying a stakeholder, as discussed in the last chapter. A channel can be open or closed. In the former case, it is free, like the road, and in the latter case it requires a fee to be paid, a ticket to be obtained or a password to be given, as for the toll-road, a party or an intranet. The channel can also be general for any member of the public or specific for only a particular group. Some channels are natural like a river, while others are artificially constructed or engineered like a canal or a pipeline. A channel can be either permanent and not dependent on being used or temporary and existing only as long as it is used, like a moving vehicle. Some channels are old, established and tested, while others are newly developed and experimental.

Channel thinking is highly inspired by the three metaphors of water, sound and electricity. Through cybernetics and systems analysis it has made its imprint on political science [Deutsch, 1963; Easton, 1965]. In the applied science of political management, with EU public affairs management as a special chapter, the key question for every sender is *how to get a message, in the desired form and with the desired contents, delivered only to the desired place and at the right time.* Much can go wrong with this objective. During the channel process, the form can be affected and the contents changed. The message may be delivered to the wrong place and at the wrong time. These four problems of form, content, place and time can occur in combination, resulting in 24 different problem cases. The message can even be lost, disappear and not be delivered at all. If the transmission itself is good, it may have been delivered not exclusively but be widespread, resulting in politicising rumours going around.

All these problems are not due either to the sender or to the receiver, but they are *channel-related*. Many causes are possible. It may be that the chosen channel is not correctly connected to the desired place or has a dead end. Or it may have a limited capacity, so delaying the delivery. Or perhaps the channel has a filter, affecting the form or the contents of the message. Or maybe it produces its own noise and echo, thus making a message widespread. All these and more channel characteristics are, of course, variables. To some degree they can even be manipulated or managed by both the sending lobby group and any other stakeholder. The former wants to get the message delivered as desired, while the latter may like to distort, change, delay, misplace, obstruct or politicise the transmission. Both have many options, but any option has its limits as well. Now we shall discuss three typical cases of channel limits: power, quality and configuration.

Power

Some channels are more powerful than others are, just as there are turbulent rivers and calm waters. National ministries and EuroFeds, if used as channels of information and influence, tend to be powerful with regard to, for example, the Commission officials. The ministries have some nuisance value at the Council level, for example by linking different dossiers in a complex way. The EuroFeds are considered authoritative, because they aggregate the interests of sectoral groups from different countries, thus saving the Commission officials a lot of hard work. But the same national ministries may be a dried up channel with regard to MEPs or to stakeholders from different countries, while the EuroFeds have little authority over each other. For communication with the members of an expert committee or a working group, scientific reports are usually more powerful vehicles than the mass media, but for communication with the mass public their status is almost the reverse. For the publicising of a political claim a prestigious press conference in central Brussels is a lively channel, but for the pursuit of inside negotiations it can reverse the current.

The power of a channel, in short, depends much on the relationship between the sending and the receiving side. It is strongest if there is a balance of interests between the two sides. Whether a message can indeed be delivered to the right place, at the right time and with the planned form and contents subsequently depends on the channel system. The two sides have to be connected, of course. That can happen in the many different ways shown in *figure 7.2*. Some ways are certainly more powerful than others, but they are less so by necessity than by specific circumstances related particularly to the arena and the life of the dossier. If there are many opposing stakeholders, it may be better to use, for example, channels in parallel rather than in series, thus decreasing the chance of the transmission failing. Even better, in a case of such opposition, may be to combine parallel and indirect channels, thus concealing oneself as the source of the sound. The opponents may try to reverse the current, for example by the issuance of a countermessage through the same channel, thus causing severe confusion, or they try to change the EU decision-making procedure so that the sender's desired place and time become irrelevant.

It is clearly possible to manipulate the power of a channel, but this possibility is limited, as to a large degree the power belongs to the channel and not to its users. For example, a general channel like the mass media is extremely difficult to keep under control. Even a specific and closed channel like an intranet is not easy to keep specific and closed in practice. The management of *the power limits*, as far as possible, requires good preparatory work. This helps to identify which channels are the most powerful and how their power can remain under some control and perhaps be made immune to opposing actions. But for obvious reasons, outlined in the previous chapters, even this homework has its limits. Nevertheless, any difference of prudence can make a lot of difference to the desired outcome. The amateur group neglecting its homework uses the power of a channel like a novice sailor. In order to transmit its message to 'Brussels' it goes, for example, directly to the mass media or to the national government, with all the risks of becoming overpowered. As a trained sailor, the *professional* group prudently tries to avoid such an outcome. It fears falling at the mercy of the waves and usually prefers a channel with power and safety in balance. However, the professional has no guarantee, but only a better chance of not being sunk.

Quality

Some channels keep a message intact during transmission, but others do it much less. In the pure case both the form and the contents remain unchanged and the message is delivered complete and pure only at the planned time and in the planned place. In many a case the transmission, however, has a poor quality. Several *variants of mistransmission* can be distinguished. One is that the channel adds signals, which affect the form and/or the contents of the message. The mass media produce a lot of channel noise. A message can be misformed or changed when it goes via national government, due to bureaucratic conflicts or so-called national co-ordination. A second variant is that parts of the form and/or the contents are lost during the transmission. A channel usually contains some filters, locks and lock-keepers. For example, in a Parliament session, the rules of order, the timetable and the clerks can be selective in the recording of a message. A third variant regards the delivery on time and at the right place. The message may end up at a different address by going down a side-channel. Many a company or an NGO trying to send some idea to the Commission through its EuroFed sees it falling off the table, never reaching the Commission, and being consumed by someone else. In a fourth variant the transmission itself is kept intact, but not exclusive. The channel may have a memory system, which can be tapped by others. A formal letter to or from the Commission may arrive perfectly at its destination, but due to its registration it might be noticed, identified and read by other stakeholders and journalists.

Channels have a large amount of *quality variation*. The informal face-to-face contact in, for example, a fine restaurant is the channel with normally the highest potential for quality. The time and place are fixed, the form is determined and the contents are directly transmitted from mouth to ears. But the meeting can be leaked or be noticed by others, such as the secretary, the chauffeur, or an opponent or a journalist passing by chance. Even some traces of the meeting, such as an invoice or a scribble, can be left behind. All other channels contain even more risks of mistransmission. In contrast to the informal meeting, a press conference is almost like shouting out the message. Journalists attending the conference can interpret the message how they want. The off-the-record tip to a journalist is just stored in his/her memory and may be ferreted out by others. Every channel has its limits, giving a chance of faulty rather than intact transmission.

No lobby group on the EU playing field can do without channels, however. Everyone is dependent on others and has to communicate. To some degree an interest group can manage *the quality limits* and make them slightly wider or narrower. The sender can take some measures to check the quality of the transmission during the process and afterwards. But it is most difficult to take safeguarding measures in advance. It is much easier for an opponent to engender a mistransmission than for the sender to prevent it, as it is easier to spread rather than stop rumours. Amateur groups suffer more from the channel limits than the *professionals*. The latter have better knowledge of the usual quality of a channel than the former. For many situations they know that they should prudently choose a less risky channel, take some measures of quality control and widen a few limits. If they play the role of the opponent, they know how to narrow the limits of a channel used by the enemy sending a message. But they are aware that even such an act of channel management must be considered prudently, because it may boomerang back.

Configuration

A channel is usually not just a connection between two or more places, but a configuration of many transmission elements created by nature or mankind. The main ones are capacities, flows, regulators, collectors and sites, as in the following examples. The Commission's free *capacity* (after taking into account its current workload) to channel new political demands is very limited due to the small size of its apparatus. The volume or the contents of new messages easily overload it. Traffic jams at the Commission and/or overflows to other channels are some of the usual consequences. The Parliament is renowned for its multiple and parallel *flows* to and from institutions, countries and interest groups. Some flows it accelerates, for example through an intergroup like the one on animal welfare. Others it delays, as happened to the GMO dossier in the late 1990s. Some it converts into a circular flow, like the one on workers' codetermination. The multiple and parallel flows can easily collide inside the Parliament, which then may adopt contradictory resolutions that shock some MEPs and the watching public. Every channel has its *regulators* propelling, slowing or redirecting flows. Some are inherent to the flow, such as the developing issue that has its own momentum propelling it forwards, the traffic jam that slows down the flow, and the circular course that redirects. Others are constructed, such as the secretariat of a EuroFed, the whitebooks of the Commission, or the decision deadlines. Channel *collectors* are, for example, the *chef de dossier* of the Commission, the rapporteur of the Parliament, and the public affairs official of a lobby group. More abstract collectors are the memory storage, the bureaucratic pipeline, and the policy dossier itself. The *sites* of a channel refer to the areas around it, such as the expert groups around the Commission. They connect with other channels, provide room for overflows and feedback-loops, and receive all sorts of more or less fertile residues.

All such elements, together forming the channel configuration, may be considered *limitations or facilities*. On the one hand, they put limits on a perfect transmission: much can go wrong, due to the channel system. A local government, a Commission unit, or a multinational NGO, wanting to send a message to an EU stakeholder, may end up in a traffic jam, a circular flow, a dried-up channel, a pipeline and/or an overflow. On the other hand, all these elements are three-fold facilities as well. Firstly, they enable the watching of the channel process, because every element is a potential indicator. Monitoring them is most useful homework for the improvement of one's fieldwork. Secondly, all the limitations also exist for the opposing stakeholders. One has seldom any reason to fear that a message sent by them will go through whatever channel smoothly and perfectly. Again, by monitoring the configuration one can observe their bad or good luck and respond accordingly. Thirdly, as partially manipulable variables, the elements provide some room for configuration management and engineering. An example is the aforementioned Triple P game, which intends to make a configuration by the early instalment of lock-keeping persons, positions and procedures.

The configuration elements place limits on every sender, but the *professional* lobby groups can also take advantage of the facilities. They monitor a configuration carefully, watch the streaming closely, and intervene at will consciously. By such prudence they can, to some extent, widen the limits for themselves and narrow them for their opponents. Even a small widening or narrowing, for example regarding a deadline or a ranking, can strongly improve the outcome. But the professionals can never fully get rid of all these channel-related limits and their consequences either, many of which fall outside their control.

The Limits of Arena Management

The four main components of every arena, discussed earlier, are the issues, the stakeholders, the life of the dossier and the boundaries. Each of these components sets its limits, every time a new conflict arises, for every lobby group. As contested facts, values or instruments, the issues are claimed by many stakeholders. The involved lobby groups have to be alert and frequently active in order to become part of a winning coalition. If they do not really lose, they consider it a good win. The life of a dossier is always unpredictable, and consequently it falls largely outside the control of a single group. The boundaries of an arena are normally diffuse, permitting the entry and exit of issues and stakeholders. Each lobby group, being always only one of many, has every reason to feel itself overwhelmed more by the limits than by the opportunities of an EU arena. From the many arena limits, and continuing the discussion of them from the first chapters, we select the following three: pluralism, complexity and dynamics.

Pluralism
Europe is full of irritating differences of opinion regarding perceived facts, preferred values and cherished instruments. According to many a lobby group, the source of both the differences and the irritations lies, of course, outside itself. Harmony seems reigning inside the group and disharmony as coming from outside. But almost every issue is also embedded in strong public and private organisations. Cultural differences are usually differences between interest groups and frequently even within them. They can be found among EU institutions, (sub)national governments, NGOs and business organisations. The resulting competitions come close to a *civil war*, no matter how civilised. Each lobby group can have only a marginal grip on its development and outcomes. It may try, of course, to push or to block the passage of an issue or a dossier. But many other stakeholders will try as well, with the result that the dossier's life frequently ends up like a truck with many drivers behind the wheel, steering in different directions. It is also an open truck, easily permitting passengers to jump on or off. Its trailer-load of stakeholders and issues is seldom fixed. In such a pluralistic setting many stakeholders are eager to develop their own networks, coalitions and cartels, in order to get some grip on the arena and its outcomes. But even the most corporatist arena allows the insiders only limited control. There are always some challengers inside and many more outside.

The pluralistic character of the EU poses significant limits for every lobby group [Hoffman, 1963]. An arena is seldom inviting: only the stakes may attract, as the grapes did Tantalus. The lobby group nonchalantly entering an arena runs all the risks of becoming isolated or even victimised, so it must behave prudently. Any issue can be a threat or an opportunity, every stakeholder can be a friend or an enemy, every dossier can come to a good or a bad end, and any boundary can become wider or narrower. The professional player, behaving prudently, tries to figure out all these possibilities. From his/her preparatory work can be obtained the indicators for drawing conclusions. It may also reveal which other stakeholders are acting prudently and therefore have to be taken seriously. The professional group can discover finally that, *thanks* to the pluralistic nature of the EU, there are always some beneficial issues and some friendly stakeholders, both inside and outside the EU institutions. It only has to discover them by its homework, and later it can more or less manage them in its the fieldwork. In this way, it can even contribute to an increase or a decrease in the arena's pluralism, for example by launching a new issue or by compromising on an old one. But it can never dictate the desired outcome, and neither can any competing stakeholder. This is the essence of pluralism. The professional understands this better than the amateur, and through its prudence it has a better chance of getting a desired outcome.

Complexity

Every arena is like a labyrinth and even a seemingly small issue is full of complexity. The contested facts, values and instruments are related to different interest positions, each being right in its own way. Even such a black-and-white dossier, as the Tobacco Advertisement one, is complex like an Ancient Greek drama, with all parties defending noble but irreconcilable values: the one liberty and pleasure, and the other safety and health. Most stakeholders have complex structures as well. For example, the Commission is full of both horizontal and vertical segmentation, not to mention its assistant bureaucracy of thousands of expert committees. There is almost always an important difference between the skeleton and the flesh and blood of an organisation. This is also true for the relationships between interest groups. They range from a rather formalised EuroFed to a highly informal ad-hoc network. Frequently they cut across both institutional and territorial borders. This makes it difficult to identify their membership and has resulted in such a vague and modish concept as *governance* [Kohler-Koch and Eising, 1999; De Schutter and others, 2001; COM Governance, 2001]. The dossier's life is no less complex. It can have an early death and always has its mini-loops inside institutional phases. There is no fixed relationship between an institutional phase and a decision-making phase, as every EU official and other stakeholder can take part in every phase. Comitology looks even 'a dark glass' [Bradley, 1992], and the combining of dossiers is a very complex practice. Last, but not least, the arena boundaries are seldom fixed, rigid and concrete and usually variable, diffuse and abstract, in short, complex. They almost always cut across those of other arenas, thus facilitating even more combining of issues and dossiers.

The nonchalant interest group can easily lose its way in the arena looking like a labyrinth. Becoming upset by the normal complexities, it may lose its way even more and it will usually ask for a reduction in the complexity. The professional player, however, sees both the limits and the opportunities caused by complexity. Assuming that every labyrinth has a structured pattern, however irregular this may be, it tries to understand it. *Thanks* to the complexity it at least enjoys the extra room created for playing by those who lost their way. It discovers that there is always more than one front door, back door, hopper window, passage, connection, by-pass, exit or escape. The expert can even try to increase the complexity for others and especially for the opponents, for example by helping to engineer a fake entry or another dead end. The professional group remains, however, conscious about the limits of all those advantages from complexity and prudent about the use of their opportunities. It may lose its way as well or fall into its own trap. Complexity sets its limits on all, but on some more than on others. This margin is usually important.

Dynamics

An arena is always to some extent dynamic like a trampoline. The issues can rapidly change, due to newly chosen values, perceived facts or preferred instruments. A main factor governing this is the Commission itself. It repeatedly launches new decisional values, research reports and policy proposals. Stimulated by a new Treaty, by one of the other institutions or by a stream of lobby groups it even brings out new issue and policy areas, as it did around the millennium with those on public health and taxation. Or it reframes old ones, such as changing from production-oriented to sustainable agriculture. The lobby groups have changing agendas, in the best case because of their reassessment of the challenges and the short list. Their organisations change as well: they reorganise themselves, are fused or split, and have a turnover of personnel, thus changing their capacities and their performance; the 1999 Commission started a major reform of itself; NGOs may beget a GONGO or a BINGO. All stakeholders can break off an engagement with others and enter another one. The life of a dossier is full of dynamics. The many lobby groups try to push or to block its development and do this in different directions. Through their negotiations they can bring a dossier to life or put it to death and even, by an agreement on reframing, to reincarnation. Many a dossier spills over into different policy areas. The arena boundaries are not less mobile. Old issues can fade away and new ones arise, as happened with the Biotech dossier in the late 1990s when its issue changed from product improvement to human safety. Old stakeholders can leave and new ones enter the arena, as happened in the same case.

In every arena the lobby group has reason to feel that it is on a trampoline. It can easily fall down and/or off. Expertise is, of course, also rewarding here. *Thanks* to the dynamics, the professional group, recognising some patterns of change, can survive longer and sometimes even make a leap forwards. It has comparative advantage over the amateurs, who usually ask for a more static arena. Therefore, the professional might try to make the arena even more dynamic, for example by pressurising for deadlines or provoking new stakeholders to enter the arena. The professional group creating scenarios can prepare itself for change and thus anticipate events. Even in bad times it knows that a better moment will always come. By its timing and its time management it hopes to create a great difference in order to promote the desired outcome. Notwithstanding all these potential rewards, even the most professional group is limited by the arena dynamics. It has to respect the natural forces of any boisterous and wild arena, but through prudence it will cope better with it than the amateurs.

The Limits at the Receivers' Side

It is not only the stakeholders, including the EU officials, who are the receivers, but also outside groups not yet involved and the mass media. The outsiders, not being on the 'mailing list' of the sender, may have received the message by accident, by an echo or by tapping the channel. As a result, they may become stakeholders as well. All these receivers can limit the effectiveness of a message. It may have been sent, channelled and gone through the arena perfectly, but yet not have been absorbed by the targeted receiver as desired. One possible cause is that the reception has been simply absent or weak, for example owing to too much concentration on internal affairs, a confusion or an indifference on the part of the targeted receiver. A second possibility is that the message has been received well, but has been interpreted wrongly, in which case it might be regarded as more urgent than it is, linked to the wrong dossier or otherwise given a different meaning. Even if it is received and interpreted correctly it can still fail by the third filter of reactive behaviour. The receiver can, for example, overreact, not react at all or do the opposite to what is desired. All this can happen not only with a message with form and content, but also with a so-called non-message, for example a non-verbal action or the silence of a sender. To put all this succinctly in terms of communication theory: the message may not have been registered (by a *syntactic* filter), understood (by a *semantic* one) or taken into account (by a *pragmatic* one) correctly [Cherry, 1966]. From the many receiver-related limits we select the following three for elaboration: inattention (syntactical), satiation (semantic), and neutralisation (pragmatic).

Inattention
While a sender can have its mental and organisational limits, so can a receiver. The emotions, dogmas and myths it holds can lead to a most selective perception filtering the message. Some signals may be neglected and

others over-registered. A receiver suffering from internal dissent, scarcity or lack of leadership can be equally inaccurate in its reception of a message. The *syntactical* case of neglect or inattention may thus have many causes. For example, an EP rapporteur with a bias towards a particular outcome is easily blind to the counter-message provided by the sender. A national ministry, believing it is perfectly right on its policy position, will for a long time remain deaf to any warning report from the playing field. A national parliament, believing the myth that it is always the Council that decides, shall neglect the so-called 'pre-phases' of real decision-making. A small-sized lobby group can be inattentive due to its limited resources and its belief in the myth that the EU is not that relevant. Many lobby groups have the experience that both their strong opponents and close allies hardly take in their messages, as the former may not be at all receptive and the latter may feel glutted. The inattention is frequently caused by poor internal organisation, in which case the receiver may be introvertedly focused on the internal dissent or the pending reorganisation. Or perhaps its public affairs function is scattered over various units, not linked to the management, or simply unmanned due to vacancies or staff holidays.

Every stakeholder can have such a syntactical filter of inattention at its *input side*. Amateurishly organised receivers tend to be more inattentive than professional ones. Their antennae are poorly attuned to the stakeholders that are potentially relevant for them. Often they do not have personnel responsible for monitoring, or they are hardly aware of their own mental and organisational limits, which make them deaf or blind to a message. By their poor organisation of the intake they limit the effectiveness of the sending lobby group. If the latter is also an amateurish group, then it may become irritated and inclined either to send a stronger message or to renounce the targeted stakeholder altogether. Through their preparatory work the professionals, in contrast, try to anticipate the attention limits of a targeted receiver. When they observe that a receiver is inattentive, they also consider the advantages that may be gained from this. They can even send fake messages, in order to test the attention of a stakeholder. If they regret the receiver's inattention, they try to repeat the message prudently, for example indirectly and quietly. But even the best professional cannot prevent or remove all causes and cases of inattention among all targeted receivers. Nobody can be seen or heard by those who remain blind and deaf.

Satiation

One variant of the *semantic* filtering of an incoming message is that the receiver may soon have had enough of it. Most information has a rapidly decreasing marginal utility or, to put it differently, an explosive marginal irritation value. Receiving a message twice, in the same form and with the same contents, is in the best case taken as an indicator of disorganisation on the part of the sender and in the worst case as an insult to the receiver. MEPs frequently complain about lobbyists repeating themselves, as the latter do about the former. Most receivers feel bored with those lobby groups that believe that only they are perfectly right on an issue and so send their argumentation again and again. The reiteration of identifiably the same findings of research is often counterproductive through its provocation of counter-research. Receiving the same arguments pro or against a proposal again and again is usually felt to be boring and bothersome. The nice Lorelei labels used for the upgrading of a core issue (*figure 6.2*) tend to become obsolete after about seven years on average. So-called over-lobbying easily activates the filter of satiation at the receiver's side. In such cases the receiver may soon lose any interest in the message at all and even become irritated. Satiation, in short, always lies in wait.

The semantic filter of satiation can always become active during the *throughput* of a message. The amateurishly organised receivers are most vulnerable to this. They are inclined too easily to believe that they have already received a message, as they tend not to read it closely but only cursorily, missing the details. Feeling satiated they can also easily feel fed up and irritated, which may weaken their attention capacity even more. The professionals, however, take the reiteration of a message they receive as information in itself and try to figure out whether it is the result of, for example, the nervousness or the disorganisation of the sender or maybe something else like the echo from a channel. Then they can even benefit from their findings and, for example, soothe the sender or exploit its poor internal organisation. The amateurish senders, when believing that the targeted receiver is indifferent through satiation, may react in an even more irritating fashion, such as by repeating the same contents in a stronger form or through more channels without disguising the source. The professional senders, in contrast, will already have been more prudent, preferring to send a really important message through a 'polyphonic orchestra' (as mentioned in chapter 6), with the help of the befriended stakeholders that were identified through the homework. They like to construct new platforms, such as a BONGO, a federation or an ad-hoc coalition. Much of their R&D is directed at finding fresh forms for the same contents. Any reiteration, then, comes to the receiver as if from a different source. The professional senders also gain free advantage from the irritation to the receivers caused by their amateurish competitors. They do not whine or whimper. To exacerbate the receiver's satiation with those amateur messages, they can even stress the parrot-like sound of their opponents. But even they cannot fully prevent or overcome the risk that they themselves may fall victim to the satiation of a targeted receiver. All receivers have their moments of satiation and indigestion.

Neutralisation

No sender is the only one with a message sent to a targeted receiver. On every dossier the latter receives different messages from mutually opposing senders. The receiver has, in theory, many *pragmatic* options for response, ranging from doing nothing to meeting the request or doing the opposite of what is suggested. In practice, the receiver has less freedom of choice, for example due to its own interests, current commitments or power positions. But this freedom can be restored by the *paradox* of cross-pressures: the higher the number of contradictory messages there is, the lower the impact of each tends to be and the larger the menu of options. The many lobby efforts to influence one particular stakeholder should, in mathematical terms, not be added together or multiplied, but divided by each other, because they create room for manoeuvre. The limit of neutralisation, which is found everywhere, is a corollary of the paradox of cross-pressures. The Commission *chefs de dossier* and the EP's rapporteurs, in particular, being approached by many competitive stakeholders, usually enjoy the paradox. Many other stakeholders also receive messages from a large amount of competitors inviting them to take their side. If one offers support to a targeted receiver, another stakeholder may overbid. If one presents some evidence, another may show it to be false and refute it. If a message gets public attention, then it may become neutralised in a mass debate. So-called research is vulnerable to neutralisation because it may take only three months to deliver a piece of counter-research.

To some degree, every stakeholder receiving messages has such a pragmatic filter of neutralisation at its *output side*. The professional receivers will feel happy with it: thanks to the cross-pressures they have more room for a reasoned choice. Under the flag of 'democratic consultation' many EU officials are even eager to stimulate more stakeholders to send different messages. This not only saves them a lot of monitoring costs, but also gives them more freedom of choice. Neutralisation is a limit for the sender, but a freedom for the receiver. The amateurish receivers, however, may feel unhappy with all the cross-messages. They have to choose and, because of the poor state of their preparatory work, they find that difficult. At the senders' side too, the amateurish groups regret the neutralisation limit, except when they get their opponent neutralised by accident. They dream of being the only sender. If their report is refuted within three months, they become upset and maybe aggressive, thus making new mistakes. The professional senders, however, consider the neutralisation limit as a normal characteristic of a pluralistic system. As part of their arena analysis they explore the probable cross-pressures on a targeted receiver in advance. Thanks to this homework, they can better *immunise* their own messages against the cross-messages and produce their own cross-messages against those of the opponents in plenty of time. To achieve a better bargaining position, they may simulate or stimulate new messages crossing with other ones. On the GMO dossier the counter-messages from lobby groups like Europabio finally gave the Commission the legitimate option of not closely following the Greenpeace coalition's line. But no sending lobby group can always or fully control the neutralisation limit, as this belongs to the receiver.

The Limiting Environment

An EU public affairs communication system is seldom a closed one containing only the senders, channels, arena and targeted receivers involved in the dossier at stake. There are usually *openings and gaps* both to and from the outside. A sender can fail to keep its message in a closed circuit, for example because a journalist uncovers the evidence of a conflict, or because, feeling weak, it looks for outside support. Channels can produce all sorts of echo and noise, attracting attention from outsiders. Stakeholders and issues inside the arena can disappear. Receivers can be accountable to an open forum, as happens to Commissioners in the Parliament and Council members in their national parliament. In addition, there is the case of reverse openness, from the outside to the inside. Outside interest groups hearing about a dossier may want to interfere, in order to influence the process, to cash in on their nuisance value or to receive some other return. Lobby groups that are not well established, such as SME alliances, citizens' groups and lobby groups from applicant member-states or non-EU countries, frequently do this at a late stage. Journalists from mass media or sectoral media love to enter an arena and nose around, to please their readers. All these outsiders bring in their own norms, expectations, values and interests, which can become relevant inside the arena. They may push or block, for example, new agendas, changing decision-making practices, or specific mixed-economy patterns. In fact, they indicate the widening of europeanisation. We now present the following three examples of the limits-setting environment: reputation, prescripts, and outside groups.

Reputation

The reputation of a person or a group is never a stable property, but a temporary assessment of its conduct by others according to their norms and morals. A widely respected good reputation gives a licence to operate on the playing field, while a bad one makes it difficult to get a message across. An MNC like Philip Morris, widely seen as the major producer of 'scandalising tobacco', is frequently evaded by other stakeholders and especially by EU officials. Companies with cartel-like market practices easily lose face in Brussels as well. A good reputation, in short, is part of the social responsibilities of any interest group. Both the contents and the forms of its lobby behaviour contribute to it. A social reputation can be acquired not only by *achievement* but also by *attribution*. Government administrations tend to have a better social reputation than NGOs and the latter better than companies [Eurobarometer, autumn 2000, 98], and this is reflected in the relative levels of trust in each as protectors of the so-called general interest. However, this reputation is only an image because there is no good criterion with which to measure, for example, policy-making on healthy food as of a more general interest than the lobbying on it, or the latter more than the retailing of healthy food. In order to earn a better reputation by a cheap attribution, companies set up a BONGO and NGOs a GINGO. A good social reputation is, however, not sufficient for getting a message across. A government or NGO that does not respect, for example, procedures, deadlines or demand sides is easily vilified. Any behaviour inside the EU system can be observed by groups in society and result in a bad reputation. The lobby group pushing its interest in a too sneaky or dirty way can be scandalised by social groups and be blacked in Brussels, as happened even to the Santer Commission trying to cover up Commissioner Edith Cresson's misbehaviour in 1998.

Amateurish lobby groups tend to be nonchalant about reputation limits. If they have a good reputation, they see it as a fixed value, but if it is bad, they hope that nobody cares. Wanting to pick a pretty flower along a ridge, they take high risks with their reputation and frequently topple into the gorge of fallen names. This fate occurred to Greenpeace after it had provided false information on the Brent Spar oil platform in the mid-1990s. *Professional* groups know that their competitors, other stakeholders and journalists can watch them. They are prudent and allow the flower on the ridge to grow. They respect the various norms and morals, maybe not by conviction but at least through fear of being scandalised if they offend [French, 1983, I]. This *Praxismoral*, as it is called in Germany, is encompassed by their preparatory work. They take into account that lobbying styles allowed in one country, sector, or arena may be abhorred in another. They try to manage their own reputation, for example by upgrading their contested interest, by outsourcing risky behaviour to a network, or by creating an image of openness. Shell did the latter in its 1999 *Listening and Responding* campaign aimed at creating a better dialogue with its stakeholders. Prudent groups also try to build up an upper standard or a premier league of players with selected membership. For example, the US Mission in Brussels has built up a great reputation and high prestige [Winand, 1998]. But however prudent its anticipation or management may be, no lobby group can fully control reputation limits, as they are ultimately set by others.

Prescripts

In 1991 the Dutch MEP Alman Metten (a socialist) privately published *The Ghost of Brussels*, in which he reported that he had received within about three months almost 150 written requests from lobby groups, 90 percent from industry alone. He concluded that EU lobbying is neither transparent nor balanced and proposed both a register of lobbyists and a strict code of conduct. His action produced much mass-media attention and resulted in the first EP hearing on lobbying in January 1992 [Doc En/CM/118767]. On 13 May 1997, the EP established rules for lobby groups accredited by the Parliament (*figure 7.3, upper part*) to complement a registration and accreditation procedure. Meanwhile, the Commission and the Council, but not the Court, formulated their own codes of conduct for both the outsiders and their personnel and issued registration forms. The new Prodi Commission, after all the public scandals of 1998 and the following investigations by the Committee of 'Wise Men', considered the sharpening of its regulations a top priority. All these codes and forms can be seen as *semi-formal* prescripts set by the EU institutions in response to social demands. To some extent they regulate and make transparent both the sending and the receiving of lobby messages, in whatever form, by their personnel. More *formal* prescripts, other than as laid down in the public and civil law applying to all EU citizens, do not exist. Various associations of lobbyists, such as the Public Affairs Practitioners PAP (*figure 7.3, at the bottom*), have made informal codes of conduct. Apparently, they see codes as a tool with which to create a better image.

Amateurish lobby groups may take the view that everything not forbidden or prescribed is permitted or left open. They may come to the conclusion that the specific prescripts are mildly and loosely formulated, thus leaving much freedom of lobby behaviour. Acting nonchalantly, they may at the very least become scandalised and at the most lose their license to move around the arena. *Professional* groups interpret the prescripts strictly, moni-

Codes of conduct

European Parliament

In the context of their relations with Parliament, the persons whose names appear in the register provided for in Rule 9(2) shall;

a   comply with the provisions of Rule 9 and this Annex;
b   state the interest or interests they represent in contacts with Members of Parliament, their staff or officials of Parliament;
c   refrain from any action designed to obtain information dishonestly;
d   not claim any formal relationship with Parliament in any dealings with third parties;
e   not circulate for a profit to third parties copies of documents obtained from Parliament;
f   comply strictly with the provisions of Annex I, Article 2, second paragraph*;
g   satisfy themselves that any assistance provided in accordance with the provisions of Annex I, Article 2* is declared in the appropriate register;
h   comply, when recruiting former officials of the institutions, with the provisions of the Staff Regulations;
i   observe any rules laid down by Parliament on the rights and responsibilities of former Members;
j   in order to avoid possible conflicts of interest, obtain the prior consent of the Member or Members concerned as regards any contractual relationship with or employment of a Member's assistant, and subsequently satisfy themselves that this is declared in the register provided for in Rule 9(2).

Any breach of this Code of Conduct may lead to the withdrawal of the pass issued to the persons concerned and, if appropriate, their firms.

*Rules on the declaration of Members' financial interests

PUBLIC AFFAIRS PRACTIONERS

This code of conduct applies to public affairs practitioners dealing with EU institutions. As public affairs practitioners providing essential democratic representation to the EU institutions, the signatories to this code (see below) are all committed to abide by it, acting in an honest, responsible and courteous manner at all times.

In their dealings with the EU institutions public affairs practitioners shall:

a   identify themselves by name and by company;
b   declare the interest represented;
c   neither intentionally misrepresent their status nor the nature of their inquiries to officials of the EU institutions nor create any false impression in relation thereto;
d   neither directly nor indirectly misrepresent links with EU institutions;
e   honour confidential information given to them;
f   not disseminate false or misleading information knowingly or recklessly and shall exercise proper care to avoid doing so inadvertently;
g   not sell for profit to third parties copies of documents obtained from EU institutions;
h   not obtain information from EU institutions by dishonest means;
i   avoid any professional conflicts of interest;
j   neither directly nor indirectly offer nor give any financial inducement to any EU official, nor Member of the European Parliament, nor their staff;
k   neither propose nor undertake any action which would constitute an improper influence on them;
l   only employ EU personnel subject to the rules and confidentiality requirements of the EU institutions.

Any signatory will voluntarily resign should they transgress the code.
For more information, contact: GPC Government Policy Consultants

Figure 7.3

tor their application closely and respect them prudently. They consider them as both a blessing in disguise and a comparative advantage. By observing the prescripts correctly, they gain a seemingly legal status and they can keep the amateurish groups at a distance. Of course, they may try to influence the prescripts, which are always open to reformulation. In the early 1990s they offered their own informal codes to the officials of the institutions, in order to influence the drafting of the semi-formal prescripts. This sort of lobbying is no different from influencing whatever new regulation, although it is more closely monitored by the attentive mass public than the average regulation is. The prescripts have become a new category of limits. They exist for all lobby groups but the professionals apply them internally better than the amateurs. This margin of prudence may make a crucial difference for the desired outcome.

Outside groups

There are always newly arising interest groups, which sooner or later may enter the playing field. In 1980 hardly any MNC, regional government, city government or national NGO had its own facility in central Brussels. At best, they had indirect representation through the established national umbrellas that had their own EuroFeds. Interest groups from outside the EU area were almost completely absent, with neither direct nor indirect representation, and many mass-media organisations had only a temporary reporter in Brussels, to cover Belgium, NATO and the EU all together. A *few decades later* most established interest groups from governments and civil society have both a network of indirect linkages and a direct presence on the playing field, either temporarily or permanently. Hundreds of non-EU interest groups have established their facilities in Brussels as well, and many mass-media organisations have set up permanent desks for the EU alone. New outside groups can be expected in the *future*. Interest groups from SMEs, local governments, national agencies and social categories such as immigrants and the aged are in the early years of the new millennium still frequently absent, but this is likely to change. Any new enlargement of the EU brings in new interest groups and social categories dealing with different aspects of, for example, religion, literacy, trade, income and tradition. Sooner or later their values and interests will come to play a stronger role inside the system and change existing cultural balances. The newcomers will set lobby limits for the insiders. At the very least they want to be taken into account.

Amateurish groups inside the system tend to see these groups as intruders. Fearing that they may lose what another group receives, they are inclined to see lobbying for a desired outcome as a zero-sum game. Because they are already inside, they hope to protect their interests through acquiring Triple P privileges. With their own people in strong positions on favourable procedures they want to establish new elitist policy cartels in an otherwise pluralist environment, thus mobilising the groups in opposition to them. In early 2000, the discussion about enlargement towards Central Europe provided many examples of this zero-sum thinking. Spanish interest groups were worried about losing their valuable EU subsidies to the applicant states, and, many small member-state governments feared having to give in on voting points, EP seats and other old privileges. *Professional* groups inside the system are more prudent. They see the EU decision-making processes as variable-sum games, and even regard their old subsidies and privileges as bargaining chips for another desired outcome. They view new interest groups of, for example, immigrant shopkeepers, retired people or applicant states, merely as new stakeholders. They incorporate them in their preparatory work and in their lobby business in the normal way. In the mid-1990s, the Dutch lobby groups on road transport, from both the ministry and the private sector, offered their EU support to Hungarian truckers, their major competitors outside. The professional groups also try to make use of the particular issues promoted by the new groups. A special EU policy for immigrant shopkeepers can be of great value for many producers and public agencies. The issues of growth and welfare in Central Europe are useful for lobbying in favour or against EU policy changes and thus for blocking or pushing current policies. The professional groups that most want to establish links with outsiders entering the arena tend to be those that feel they are in an unfriendly arena and therefore want to widen its boundaries. Knowing from their homework which of the coming outsiders can provide new opportunities or set new limits on their EU public affairs management, the professionals are more proactive than the amateurs in harvesting the former and turning the latter into a virtue.

Extra: the Limited National Governments

A national government can be seen as a prominent example of a public interest group. Through its usual rhetoric it gives the image of having almost unlimited capacity to influence EU outcomes. It claims to be the national body and voice. Yet, in comparison to many private interest groups, it frequently has important *comparative disadvantages* regarding the EU playing field. The comparison between public and private lobbying cannot, of course, be seen as black and white, as the two categories lie on a continuum that also includes the many variants of NGOs, described earlier. Any comparison should also have as much *ceteris paribus* as possible. So national governments can best be compared with the MNCs, as summarised in the multinational model. Both categories are large-sized and have a conglomerate structure, fragmentation by divisions, a multi-layer operation, high complexity of internal decision-making and much internal pluralism. The three most striking comparative disadvantages of governments are: transparency, pressures from elected politicians, and an obsession with the so-called general interest.

National governments score high on *transparency*. Their many formalised procedures frequently have a public character. If a ministry wants to have a national law, it has to make public its proposal. In the Nordic countries, citizens and journalists can urge government officials to make public even internal documents. By written or unwritten constitution the exercise of power is divided among several institutions. In the EU area, government is almost a synonym for *limited government* [Friedrich, 1974]. Much information has to be presented to the national parliament, either according to the constitution or at the MPs' request. Because of divisions inside and among the ministries many facts and values relating to past, current or planned decisions and policies leak out unofficially into society, and in federal countries like Germany the competition between regional governments creates even more openness. Journalists have a relatively easy job of getting news from inside their national government. Because of all this openness, national governments are awkwardly placed not only as senders but also as receivers of lobby messages: information provided can easily become publicity.

Multinational companies and even NGOs like Greenpeace have an easier position. Internal proposals for strategic management do not have to be made public and can usually be kept inside the organisation. There is seldom any legal entitlement for outsiders to demand inside information. Shareholders and other stakeholders normally receive only summary information through yearly reports and official statements. Some information may leak out or be obtained by journalists unofficially, but its volume is usually much less than that from the national government. The *tragedy* of government transparency is that it gives the national government, in comparison to private stakeholders, a disadvantage on the EU playing field. Competitors are aware of its intentions, and can easily anticipate and exploit its internal divisions. Government behaviour is usually noisy and thus predictable; many lobby groups distrust it because of its propensity for leaks, and they consequently prefer to bypass it.

The *pressures from elected politicians* are a second comparative disadvantage. Especially in the Nordic countries the national MPs can instruct their government regarding its behaviour in the Council. They can impose any national dogma on their government, ranging from a policy preference to a financial *juste retour* ('I want my money back') or a high-ranking EU position. Due to their natural party-political competitions, they commonly politicise issues regarding the EU openly, thus potentially adding emotional content to the government's behaviour. They like to hang on to the myth of an EU composed of member-state governments based on parliamentary sovereignty. Frequently they deny the pluralist nature of the EU at large and take an uncompromising position. All this is more the case in the northern than in southern countries. In the latter, the government frequently behaves more in a more authoritarian way and the parliament is less critical of EU integration [Raunio and Wiberg, 2000]. But the northern example is beginning to reach the South. More than ever before the MPs of the French *Assemblée Nationale* or the Spanish *Congreso* put forward their EU demands to their governments, requiring information about Council sessions, and politicising home issues in order to bring about EU action. In all countries, in short, MPs are to some extent and increasingly exerting pressure on their governments regarding EU affairs [Norton, 1995; Bergman, 1997; Katz, 1999-A].

Multinational companies do not have a representative body discussing in public and instructing or questioning the Board on its EU public affairs management. Their shareholders tend to regard the management of EU affairs as an executive task. Their workers' council meets in closed session and is usually primarily interested in its own labour issues. Managers are free to meet their stakeholders behind closed doors. The *tragedy* of parliamentary democracy is that it can bind the national government rigidly before, during and after its activities on the EU playing field. Because of conditions at home the government can be seriously limited in its room to manoeuvre at the EU level. Any new election can change these limits yet again, thus even making the government's position inside the EU unstable. Parliamentary procedures and practices take much time and energy from the government as well. Parliamentary democracy is, in short, a strain on both the effectiveness and the efficiency of the national government as an EU interest group.

The obsession with the so-called *general interest* is a third comparative disadvantage. A national government is expected to consider all sorts of interests at home; it cannot simply choose in favour of only the well-established groups, discriminating against, for example, the SMEs, the aged or the unemployed people. It may decide not to choose the latter, but then it may have to account publicly for that decision at home and increasingly at the EU level. The national government is also expected to bear a special responsibility for so-called collective goods, which are consumer goods delivered free or at a subsidised price through the government. In most countries infrastructure, public health and public transport are examples of these, and they are increasingly subject to the EU open-market regime. The national government cannot, of course, be everybody's friend. It has to make choices for its so-called general or national interest. In practice, this is a decision-making procedure, involving only some or all ministers, the national parliament perhaps, and, in a relatively corporatist situation, even the major private interest groups. The outcome is always that many interests at home are not included. The by-passed interest groups then frequently take their own by-pass route directly and self-reliantly to Brussels.

The multinational company can, much more easily, cope with different interests inside it. Even its most dominant interest is always specific and flexible. The Board can simply close or sell a division or a unit holding back the rest of the company, as Philips did with its Polygram division in 1998. A government cannot close its department for aged people or sell it to the private sector so easily. The *tragedy* of the general interest orientation is that the national government always has to consider many different specific interests, even those with hardly any public voice. When making a choice, it always has to follow a complex procedure or has to make a complex compromise. It cannot easily define a short list and, for every dossier on this list, clear targets. It usually has too many priorities, adopted under domestic pressure. The problem for the national government, in short, is that its home front is the whole of the country, which is always extremely pluralistic. Its attempt to define the general interest is, in fact, a mission impossible.

The three disadvantages or tragedies do not imply, however, that the national governments are tragic heroes like those that existed in Ancient Greek mythology. In comparison to at least many decentralised governments, NGOs and SMEs at home, the national government has some comparative advantages at the EU level as well, particularly in its manpower, budget and formal powers, in short its resources. In comparison to all interest groups, including the MNCs, it even has at least three *comparative advantages*. Firstly, more than other groups or organisations, it can formally use the traditional influence techniques of coercion by law and by encapsulation. At home it has much power of delegated legislation and a large budget, both of which can be used for making others more compliant. In the EU it can formally contribute to both primary legislation (Treaty formation) and secondary legislation (Council decision-making). Secondly, the national government does not have to live with a rigid yearly profit-and-loss account, as the MNC and many other interest groups have to do. If it desires, it can allocate to a targeted EU dossier almost unlimited resources for any length of time. Thirdly, inside the EU and partially laid down in Treaty texts, it has the most recognised image of any public authority, which is a lobby facility in itself. However, regional governments and sectoral groups in particular challenge this image at home, indicating that its strength is only comparative and not absolute.

In spite of these advantages, the three tragedies frequently induce national governments to behave highly amateurishly on the EU playing field. Its transparency, pressures from the national parliament and obsession with the general interest often make it noisy, inflexible, and over-demanding. These shortcomings cannot be repaired in a simple way. No national government is free to end its current transparency, to become remote from MPs, or to deny pluralistic interests. Of course, it can *compromise* a little bit on the values of transparency, parliamentary government and general interest. It can try to keep some of its messages confidential, unwritten or behind diplomatic barriers. By delegation, decentralisation and privatisation it can shift dossiers away from parliament to, respectively, the administrative apparatus, the lower level authorities and civil society. Free from national parliamentary involvement and through domestic lobbying it can then keep some control and influence over the dossiers passed to others. An alternative is to overload the parliament with documents, thus making it practically impotent and having to follow the government line. It can reduce the general interest to an open procedure of negotiations between domestic interest groups, thus to a kind of open tender. The government then has only to protect that procedure and it can accept any final compromise as its EU position in the Council. In the future it might decide to split its Council voting points, as if they are seats, into some in favour and some against a Commission proposal, according to the domestic balance. All national governments already practise these three main compromises to some extent.

Even without compromising on the three values the national government can make *virtues out of necessities*. Through its transparency it publicly shows that it has a friend inside for almost every outside interest group, thus easily attracting allies free of cost. In an unfriendly EU arena it usually needs secrecy and silence less than publicity and noise, which are therefore not necessarily a hindrance. In most countries, the government has control over the majority of MPs, and it can often easily turn them into partners, signing the instructions it has drafted. It can use the so-called general interest for elegantly disguising any option that may be disputed with regard to a specific interest. In fact, all national governments manage to some degree their comparative disadvantages in these ways. If they cannot dispose of them, they have to use them. Even the Danish government, often eager to proclaim its own virtues, provides fine examples. After the negative referendum result on the Treaty of Maastricht in 1992, it used domestic noise to get a protocol to it. It usually drafts its instructions from the national parliament itself, and then uses them as pressure on the Council. Its ban of foreign beer imports, to protect its domestic beer producer Tuborg, it presented as a general interest of health and the environment.

To some degree the national governments might further reduce their comparative disadvantages through the *professionalisation* of their lobby organisation. This is primarily a matter of further preparatory work. Basic transparency may be an inevitable fact of government life, but a display of division and turmoil is not. By monitoring and analysing its home front better and in advance, the national government can create and exhibit more internal cohesion. MPs are part of parliamentary democracy by definition, but this is not the case with their politicising and dogmatic behaviour. Leadership from the executive can bring at least the majority of MPs to a more compromising position. This too is a matter of homework on the party-political stakeholders and issues inside the parliament. It is no different from bringing the members of a voluntary trade association to a majority position. The so-called general interest, finally, may be a dominant belief of society, but it does not necessarily require a long list of general demands. By selective homework they can be reduced to a short list of priorities.

The big problem for the national governments is that, while they want to be successful on the EU playing field, they rarely manage to realise the basic *preconditions* for success inside its apparatus. There is seldom, for example, a kind of EU public affairs office or systematic approach for the carrying out of both anticipatory homework and attuned fieldwork far before and beyond the Council meeting the following month. Their offices of national coordination are more for silencing the home front and particularly the national parliament than for preparing the EU playing field. The ministries themselves also seldom have such an EU public affairs office or approach. They tend to rely on their policy experts alone, as if line people can replace specialised staff. Their talented and skilled people in the management of EU public affairs are usually scarce, self-taught, insufficiently resourced and without a promising career perspective. A short list with clear targets is seldom made, let alone a substantial analysis of selected arenas. Preparatory work, again, is an exception rather than a rule inside the national government at large. Fieldwork alone, without preparatory work, can only lead to amateurish behaviour. Circumstances such as transparency, pressurising MPs and a belief in the existence of general interest thus make the final performance frequently even worse. Most national governments have been assessing their difficulties in achieving the preconditions for lobby success since the mid-1990s.

Yet, even if the national governments develop smarter compromises at home, make more virtues out of necessity and better realise the preconditions for successful EU actions, they will never be able to overcome all the limits of EU public affairs management. No player can. The limits, summarised under the label of SCARE, remain just as applicable to any national government. It will, for example, always be troubled by its own myths and internal dissent, remain dependent on channels that distort and which are beyond its control, be surprised by the dynamics and the complexity of EU political life, encounter inattentive or incommunicative receivers, and run up against reputations and outside groups. But all such limits are variables and, as such, partially manageable. There is no real reason why the national government must be so much like Tantalus.

The Limits of EU Public Affairs Management: a Problem or a Blessing?

All the limits discussed above may seem self-evident. Yet, they are largely neglected in the literature and by the buoyant zealots of public affairs management. They are, however, discussed informally by the professionals working in the EU practice. As a reminder, these professionals are not necessarily those with a full-time or commercial status of public affairs manager, but only those who prudently prepare for the fieldwork, whatever their job position. These professionals regard the *understanding* of the limits as most useful knowledge for various reasons. They want to respect the limits falling outside their control. They want to be aware of the ones applying to their rivals in order to use them. They especially hope to enjoy the advantages created by rivals' nonchalance. They want to influence the direction of those limits that are slightly manageable. They may even be able to arrange the environment for some of the limits and play about with them. Already aware that all the many possibilities of EU public affairs management have their limits, they understand conversely that all these limits can also provide possibilities. Then they can make fewer unforced errors, enjoy virtues out of necessities, and manipulate the room for manoeuvre.

The various limits of EU public affairs management clearly have not an absolute but a relative status. The same limit can exist for one lobby group, but be absent for another. The presence or the absence of the same limit one group may consider a problem and another a blessing. This assessment should depend, of course, on the specific arena situation. Because of this, the professional group tries to identify its comparative advantages and disadvantages as well. The former it wants to save as blessings and the latter to solve as problems. It may even try to devise and to create more disadvantageous limits for rivals. So far we have considered all such possibilities and limits of EU lobbying, including their so-called problems and blessings, primarily from the perspective of a lobby group. In the next and final chapter we shall review EU lobbying from the broader outside perspective of *democracy*. We shall examine whether all the EU lobbying by public and private interest groups, and especially its professional variant, is good or bad for EU democracy.

CHAPTER 8

LOBBYING AND EU DEMOCRACY

Democracy as a Criterion

Lobbying on the EU playing field is frequently and publicly *criticised* for its so-called damaging effects on the democratic functioning of the EU. What lobbyists do behind their desks, when organising their homework, is not a matter of public concern. During the previously mentioned 1992 EP hearings on lobbying, the critical side of the debating forum had three major accusations. Firstly, that the already most dominant interest groups in society, such as, allegedly, the industrial multinationals, lobby the most. The inference here was that they create an imbalance of decision-making, to the disadvantage of the weaker interest groups such as workers, consumers and small enterprises. Secondly, that much lobbying takes place behind closed doors. By inference, this creates a lack of transparency, which frustrates competitors, the mass media and other officials. Thirdly, that much lobbying involves a lot of abuses and immoral practices, such as document robbery, blackmail and bribery. The inference here was that this should be forbidden.

Whether these accusations and inferences were valid or not, they brought the public debate on lobbying under the framework of democracy. The critics of lobbying believed that the allegedly dominant opaque and immoral lobbying was putting EU democracy in danger. This framework is, of course, only a public *choice* out of many alternatives [Graziano, 1998]. The phenomenon of lobbying could have been (and, in the future, can be) debated within different frameworks as well. Three examples are given here. One alternative framework of evaluation is provided by the criterion of integration [Greenwood, 1997, X; Sinnott, 1994]: do the various stakeholders, lobbying for their issues and coming from different countries, sectors, regions and other constituencies, contribute to a more stable EU decision-making system or not? A second alternative framework might be that of efficient EU decision-making: does lobbying make it easier for EU officials to come to a decision or not? A third framework addresses the welfare of citizens:

279

does lobbying contribute positively or negatively to socio-economic welfare or nothing at all?

Given the current dominance of the democracy framework, we shall focus here on the *impacts* of EU lobbying on EU democracy. In academic language, democracy is the dependent variable and lobbying the independent one. An effect of lobbying may be positive, negative or indifferent for the state of EU democracy. The positive and negative ones are the most relevant for the debate and form our focus here. In order to assess these effects, we shall have to define what is meant in Europe by the word 'democracy'. But before we can begin to do this, we shall have to put aside four different, but closely related and equally interesting questions.

Firstly, we shall by-pass the preliminary and substantial question regarding the *applicability* of nationally born notions of democracy to the EU system [Christiansen, 1994; Weiler, 1995]. We shall simply pursue the current public debate, in which they are applied. Secondly, we shall not enter into a discussion about the question of what *the best concept* of democracy is. As we shall see below there is no criterion to help determine this. In consequence, we shall, thirdly, not raise the question of whether the EU is *democratic at all* [Andersen and Eliassen, 1996]. To this question as many answers are possible as different notions exist. For example, the claim of a 'democratic deficit' [Dehousse, 1995] is as serious as that of a 'democratic surplus' [Meunier-Aitsahalia and Ross, 1993]. Finally, we leave the *inverse* relationship between democracy (as the independent variable) and interest group behaviour (as the dependent one). An open society, active citizenship and limited government are, indeed, excellent democratic preconditions for the flowering of lobby groups [Popper, 1945]. Our single question remains: do lobby groups have specific impacts on EU democracy?

Notions of Democracy

In Europe (and elsewhere) not just one, but *many notions* of democracy are popular. Many are disputed at home and even more at the aggregate level of the EU [Pollack, 2000-B], where their variety, developed over the years, becomes clear [Schmidt, 1997; Pinder, 1999]. For example, in countries with a presidential-like system, like France or Britain, there is frequently more emphasis on the notions of accountability and rule of law and less on those of pluralistic competition and consensual decision-making than in countries with a parliamentary system, like Italy or Sweden. In countries with strong political parties, like Spain or Greece, the notions of parliamentary governance and discursiveness tend to be popular, while those of corporatism and responsiveness are frequently more popular in countries with well-developed interest groups, like Austria or the Netherlands. Established social groups, like the educated and the wealthy, compared with weakly organised groups such as small shopkeepers and workers, tend to attach more importance to the notions of direct channels and limited government and less to those of competitive elections and common identity.

More fundamental than this sociological explanation of the variety of notions of democracy is the main conclusion from the science of knowledge that, ultimately, every value has not an absolute, but a *relative* status [Brecht, 1959]. A scientifically sound criterion to determine the single best notion of democracy is simply beyond reach [Lord, 1998, 15]. This idea of relative values opens the door to manifold competitive and newly arising notions of democracy. They all may make sense. 'Democracy', in fact, is an open container full of different notions, negatively held together by their common contrast to the (equally broad) notions of tyranny, despotism and the like [Pennock, 1979; Dahl, 1989; Held, 1996]. The notions differ largely on what they stand for positively. They are variously presented as core ideas, preconditions, elements, indicators, factors or outcomes of democracy. Some notions are value-related, such as 'freedom', 'tolerance' and 'legitimacy'. Others are process-related, such as 'elections', 'majority rule' and 'responsiveness'.

Sometimes, however, the notions of democracy differ only in appearance. Different words can be used to mean the same fundamental idea. For example, 'liberty', 'freedom' and 'autonomy' are frequently used as synonyms for the personal capacity to act as one wants [Pennock, 1979, II; Dahl, 1989, VII]. But the reverse happens as well: the same word is used for different ideas, sometimes even by the same author. For example, democracy is, on the one occasion, seen as containing such elements as legitimate authority and identity and, on another, as one element of the wider notion of legitimate authority [Lord, 1998; Beetham and Lord, 1998]. An established taxonomy of notions of democracy is clearly absent.

For our purpose it is not necessary, if possible at all, to decide upon the best definition of the concept of democracy with regard to the EU. For the construction of our dependent variable it is sufficient to assemble the most popular notions of democracy as they feature in the public debate about the EU. They are listed in *figure 8.1*, subdivided into four categories, respectively related to the input side of the EU, the throughput of decision-making, the output side, and the feedback-loop in civil society [Easton, 1965]. We shall briefly explain them.

Input notions

The general idea of the input concept of democracy is that the decision-making system must be *open* to all sorts of people and groups wanting to get a desired outcome. The openness is not discriminating or selective, but gives an equal and fair chance to every desire regarding the outcome of a decision. A desire may involve anything: one or another decision or no decision at all regarding binding laws, policies, allocations, implementations, recruitment, sanctions and any other outcome. Openness, equality and permeability are not necessarily real for every moment for every desire. Some thresholds and time lags may exist, but after some time every type of demand, information or support, intended for the officials and coming from whomever, should find its way into the system. The pluralism of civil societies, with all its competitions, should have, in short, a continuation inside the system.

This permeation is facilitated by at least three specific *vehicles*. Firstly, there are the regular competitive elections, based on equality and fairness, for at least the purpose of distributing the formal positions of power. Secondly, there exist several direct channels for the transportation of desires. They may range from a national referendum to a private visit and from an orderly petition to a street protest. Finally, there are the indirect channels,

Popular notions of democracy

Input notions
- openness, permeability
- pluralistic competition
- competitive elections
- direct channels
- representative channels

Output notions
- legitimacy
- limited government
- rule of law
- accountability
- responsiveness

Throughput notions
- representation
- majority-vote decisions
- consensual decisions
- polyarchy, opposition
- legitimate authority
- discursiveness
- transparency

Feedback notions
- citizenship
- tolerance
- identity
- freedoms and rights
- linkages to input

Figure 8.1

by which the various desires of civil societies can be represented. They may be political parties, interest groups, mass media, bureaucracies and any other platform with an intermediary capacity.

All these general and specific input notions have some degree of *popularity* in European countries. Of course, people and groups differ in their preference for one or another input notion and for one or another formula for each, as the following examples may show. The greater openness of the French government to the employers' organisations than to the trade unions is a national issue there. In all countries, the electoral system is regularly the subject of debate, particularly regarding the balance between proportionality and districts. Direct channels are relatively popular in countries like Denmark and Finland, in regions like Flanders and Bavaria, and in concentrated interest groups like the consumer electronics sector and the environment movement. Examples of strongly supported indirect channels are the political parties in Italy and Belgium, the mass media in Britain, the bureaucracies in the Netherlands, the churches in Austria and the trade unions in Germany. These various preferences frequently clash, of course, at the EU level.

Although the input notions are still in a process of europeanisation, they all have been put into practice to some extent at the *EU level*. Here there exists substantial openness to old and new desires. National, regional and sectoral issues tend to permeate easily into the system and are a major factor of both the expansion and the reform of policy fields, like those of the environment and agriculture. Some established groups may take a lead, but the current overtaking by SMEs, NGOs and regions indicates a remarkable degree of equality for those entering the system after some time [Bouwen, 2001]. The pluralistic competition inside the member countries clearly has a perhaps imperfect, but still real continuation at the EU level. There are elections, although they are only direct for the seats of the Parliament and held on a national basis. There are plenty of direct channels available. They range from the Danish or Irish referendums to the corridor lobbying and street protests in Brussels. All major indirect channels exist and are used by political parties, interest groups, civil servants and journalists from the member countries. In some cases these input arrangements may be considered to be still weak and in development. For example, the political parties are rarely organised on a transnational basis and journalists function more as sports reporters at the output side, commenting upon scandals and scores, than as providers of information at the input side. But these arrangements nevertheless reflect the existence of input forms of EU democracy [Harlow, 1999].

Throughput notions

The general idea here is that governance must be *representative* of what the people desire. This idea of representation is another container-like one, which was developed particularly in the 1960s. A group of officials may be said to be representative if it mirrors the demographic distribution of the people (for example by age, sex and ethnicity), their opinions and/or their interests [Birch, 1964 and 1971]. This may apply to an elected body, but also to a nominated one such as a committee, a corporatist platform or a bureaucracy (Krislov, 1974]. The representatives are assumed to act both on behalf and in behalf of the larger population, instead of whom they govern. In their so-called 'acting for the people' [Pitkin, 1967 and 1969], they may behave as either a delegate or a trustee [Pennock and Chapman, 1968], although the latter does not necessarily precludes the former [Conniff, 1977]. Regarding the elected politicians, there exist the two formalistic notions that their position is made representative by the ballot box automatically and their institution by the constitution as well. Some notions of representation even jump ahead to the output side and the feedback-loop of the governance system and emphasise the responsive allocation of desired outcomes [Eulau and Prewitt, 1973] and the promotion of civil society [Pateman, 1970].

Two other groups of throughput notions of democracy may be seen as more specific. The first is focused on the *methods* of governance. One variant is the notion of majority rule, usually with an amendment for a qualified majority in case there is an inequality of either size or passion [Dahl, 1956; Dahl, 1989]. Another variant replaces this amendment by the notion of consensual or even consociational governance, by which different preferences are continually accommodated by new compromises [Lijphart, 1977; Taylor, 1996]. More in-between is the variant emphasising the notion of polyarchy and, inside a body, of opposition, preventing the rise of a dominant majority [Dahl, 1971]. The second group stresses specific *values*. Somehow the representative officials are expected to exert legitimate authority [Friedrich, 1963], to discourse comprehensively [Fishkin, 1991; Elster, 1998] and/or to behave transparently [Deckmyn and Thomson, 1998; Bunyan, 1999], to mention only the most popular values.

All these throughput notions of democracy have differing levels of *popularity* in European countries [Schmidt, 1997], as the following few examples show. In Britain, there is a threefold strong belief in elected representation based on party-political delegation, in majority decision-making, and in the value of transparency. Most popular in the Germanic countries are functional representation by experts acting on behalf of their segment of society, consensual decision-making and the value of discursiveness. In France the preference for functional representation is more limited to administrative experts representing the so-called legitimate authority of the elected president and parliament, while the value of transparency is more stressed after rather than during the decision-making. In Italy there is basic support for electoral representation on a party-political trustee basis, for consensual governance and for polyarchy and opposition. In the European area a single dominant set of throughput notions of democracy is clearly absent. The various notions compete with one another.

To some degree they all have been put into practice at the *EU level* [Hayward, 1995]. All institutions have a demographic composition representative of at least the nationalities. At the administrative level this is an informal arrangement (the *fourchette*), but at the political one it is formalised through seats, voting points and positions. The political parties have their formal representative platform in the Parliament, the interest groups in the EESC, the regions in the COR and the member states in the Council. They deliver into the system a wide variety of opinions. In the form of expert groups, comitology and agencies there is a lot of functional representation. This is closely linked to the Commission, which acts as a bureaucracy representing the sectoral and regional constituencies in particular. Electoral representation is directly rooted in the Parliament and indirectly in both the COR (almost fully recruited from subnational councils) and the Council (governments based on elected national parliaments). In addition there are the special linkages between the EP and the national parliaments [Norton, 1995; Katz and Wessels, 1999].

The specific notions of throughput democracy also have some EU design. All main *methods* of governance have been put into practice. Majority-vote decision-making is present in the College of the Commission, the Parliament (under co-decision even with an absolute majority rule) and the Council (qualified and normal majority). But in all institutions the informal routine is consensually directed at reaching a broad compromise. Polyarchy and opposition are vested in both formal power distributions and informal cleavages. Examples of the latter are policy conflicts, xenophobia, and disagreements even about the application of notions of democracy, as shown in *figure 8.2* [Neunreither, 1998]. The *values* of legitimate authority, discursiveness and transparency are hardly at issue as such, but substantially in their application. Examples are the contested authority of the Commission, the discursiveness of the Parliament and the transparency of the Council. These issues are subject both to new proposals and to public debate, which indicates that the values underpinning them are regarded as serious notions of democratic governance.

Categories of Political Opposition in the EU

---

1. **Systemic opposition to the EU**
1.1 National sovereignty; no transfer of powers
1.2 Limitation of scope of possible competencies (free trade, etc.)
1.3 Ideological reservations (socialist vs. capitalist integration)
1.4 Cultural identity
1.5 Xenophobia
1.6 Global solutions (regional co-operation outdated)
1.7 Internal balance of power (e.g. Germany too influential)
1.8 EU undemocratic (insufficient citizen rights, etc.)

---

2. **Politics-orientated opposition**
2.1 Reform of the institutional system (re-weighting of votes)
2.2 Re-examination of financial framework (balance between contributors)
2.3 Application of basic principles (subsidiarity, transparency)

---

3. **Policy-orientated opposition**
3.1 Reform or further evolution of internal EU policy areas (CAP, research, environment, etc.)
3.2 Reform or application of external policies (CESP, WTO negotiations)
3.3 Topical issues within EU policies (e.g. price of bananas)

---

from: Kh. Neunreither: Governance without Opposition, in Government and Opposition, vol. 33/4, october 1998, p. 429. Reprinted with kind permission from the publisher.

Figure 8.2

Output notions

The general idea of output notions is that a result of governance should be *legitimate*, which means that it should be widely considered as acceptable. There are various potential sources of legitimacy [Easton, 1965, XIX; Schaar, 1981, I]. The ideological and policy-related objectives of governance can be seen as sympathetic if they meet such popular social needs as health, employment, education and housing. The throughput process can be a source of legitimacy as well if it is taken as fair and just. Then even a disappointing outcome is accepted as 'all part of the game' and a compromise reached among opposing groups after transparent discourses as 'the best possible result'. The outcome of a careful aggregation of many different interests is often considered as coming close to the so-called general interest. A special source of legitimacy is the personal authority or the charisma of the responsible officials. Margaret Thatcher, Felipe González and Helmut Kohl (the former 'heads of state' of Britain, Spain and Germany respectively) had their moments when they could speak *ex cathedra* and get what they wanted to do or not to do accepted. Also special is the legitimacy provided by prestigious vehicles such as, in many countries, tradition and science. If an outcome links up nicely with a famous past or is based on scientific evidence, it may be more easily accepted.

More specific output notions of democracy are the following and two come close to being *methods*. One is limited government, which from the point of view of public affairs management by government might be seen as a vice (chapter seven), but from that of democracy it is widely considered a virtue. The notion has at least three dimensions: checks and balances among the institutions of governance, decentralisation to subnational and functional authorities, and government restraint regarding the private spheres and sectors. The last two dimensions are also covered by the notion of subsidiarity. The other notion of method regards rule of law: outputs of governance should ultimately be based on formally binding decisions, produced through prescribed procedures, approved by a formally representative platform and open to judicial appeal. Specific output *values* exist as well. One is that the officials producing outputs should be accountable for what they do or not do [Lord, 1998, III]. The minimum requirement is that the nominated officials are accountable to the elected ones, and the latter to the electors. Another popular value is that the outputs should be responsive to the desires imported into the system at an earlier stage [Eulau and Prewitt, 1973]. This responsiveness may be general, in the sense that the government performs what it has promised to the people (during the elections or in the parliament), but also be particularised for special regions, sectors or groups [Eckstein, 1971].

All these output notions of democracy have variable levels of *popularity* in European countries. The outputs of governance there are widely considered legitimate and implicitly taken as acceptable, as is indicated by the relatively high levels of civil obedience and low levels of civil protest in most countries [Van Deth, 1997]. When strong protests exist, they are mainly limited to the special issues of regional separatism (such as in the Basque region, Corsica or Northern Ireland) or sectoral decline (farming, trucking or mining, for example). All countries have some forms of limited government in one or more of its three dimensions (checks and balance, decentralisation, private liberty). Most notable is Germany, which scores high on all three. France is apparently at the opposite end of the spectrum, but behind the formal show of central state dominance lie the increasing realities of, *inter alia*, conflicts between the *Matignon* and the *Elysée*, administrative decentralisation, and sectoral privatisation. The notion of the rule of law is most popular in Britain. In the Continental countries it also includes soft law (semi-formal agreements), being the outcome of consensual decision-making, or so-called rule of consent. In all countries the value of accountability is in some way contained in formal arrangements with representative councils and the electors and in more informal codes of practice with the mass media. Every government is widely evaluated, both by public opinion and through the ballot box, for its perceived responsiveness. In countries like Italy, Belgium and Greece, clientelism involving selected groups is part of this.

The different notions and practices of output democracy belong to a process of europeanisation and vie with each other at the *EU level*. To some degree, they all exist in some form. Legitimacy is rooted in popular policy values ranging from open market to healthy food, in decision-making procedures that are generally accepted as basically fair, and in special vehicles such as charismatic leadership (like that of Walter Hallstein or Jacques Delors), tradition (from the old *Idea of Europe* to the practices of representation), and science (as in the role of expert groups) [Schmitt and Thomassen, 1999]. People in the southern countries attach even more legitimacy to EU institutions than to their national ones [Norris, 1999]. The notion of limited government occurs in the developing practices of institutional checks and balances and, with regard to both the domestic levels and the private spheres, in the concept of subsidiarity. The main form of EU control is still through the law. Discretionary decisions regarding subsidies and procurements must also have a legal basis. The binding laws are formally devised according to procedures based on Treaties, approved by representative platforms and, unlike many national constitutional arrangements, open to appeal at the Court. The maintenance of law, vulnerable through its dependency on national co-operation, is yet remarkably effective, but more for civil societies than for the national governments. Evidence of accountability is found in three developing formal practices: EU officials are becoming gradually more accountable to the Parliament, Council ministers to their parliament at home, and both, indirectly, to the various ballot boxes. In addition, there is accountability to the challenging interest groups and the mass media. Responsiveness to earlier demands can be seen both in general policies and in specific support for selected regions and sectors.

Feedback notions

The general idea in this case is *citizenship*. The people are not just subjects of governance, but citizens having the individual capacity to internalise the values of governance selectively (civic spirit) and to behave accordingly (civic behaviour). As the governance system should be open and permeable at its input side to citizens' demands, so the citizens should be open to demands from governance. Their internalisation may be selective. If citizens reject values of governance, they ultimately have to account for this in front of a court. The same idea applies to groups and organisations of citizens, the so-called corporate citizens, including NGOs and companies. With their civic spirit they take into consideration both the desired and the perceived functioning of governance. Through their civic behaviour they express their own views, which may range from full support to intense protest. A democracy cannot exist without its civil society [Seligman, 1992; Fine and Rai, 1997; Ehrenberg, 1999; Fullinwider, 1999].

There are more specific feedback notions, two of which concern *values*. Firstly, given the pluralistic character of society, the citizens need to be tolerant of each other [King, 1976]. Irritating differences can then be solved in a peaceful way. Standard procedures and regulations are available in order to promote social tolerance and to keep pluralism alive. Secondly, to avoid any breakdown of society, citizens should have some stable sense of group identity [Lord, 1998, IV]. This may be related to a social indicator (such as sex, income, age or ethnicity), a belief system (a religion or ideology), a region ('the Flemish'), a sector (like agriculture, banking or education) and/or a nation ('La France'). The more overlap there is between the identities, the more social cohesion there is. Two other specific notions involve *methods*. Firstly, the citizens should possess substantial freedoms and rights to act as a citizen [Friedrich, 1963]. This notion implies, negatively, that the citizens are entitled to have some private sphere free from the governance system and, positively, that they are entitled to participate in ('free for') the system if they wish. For example, the formation of public opinion or collective action is fully a matter of free choice. Finally, the cultures and structures of civil society should be linked to the input side of the governance system. The feedback channels are part of civil society itself and consist particularly of political parties, interest groups and the mass media [Luttbeg, 1968]. Without these the system of governance can never reflect the general notions of openness, representation and legitimacy and be called democratic.

All these feedback notions of democracy have some degree of *popularity* in the European countries, but in each only a few individual or corporate citizens display a high level of civic spirit and behaviour and most only moderate or low levels [Van Deth and Scarbrough, 1998]. The fact that, in public opinion, the few are presented as a model for the many, indicates the prescriptive support for the notion of citizenship. Tolerance is a high-ranking social value as well, measured by the public disapproval of any discrimination against, for example, immigrants, women or the aged. New or deviant values and activities are accepted as part of the pluralism of society, as long as they do not break the current laws. All sorts of group identities exist in the European countries. Those based on belief systems and nationality, however, seem to be weakening in most countries (except Scandinavia), while regionalism is an increasingly significant notion of group identity in countries like Spain, Germany and Belgium [Marks, 1996-B]. Basic freedoms and rights have been institutionalised everywhere [Zincone, 1999]. Freedoms from governance are being requested more than before, as indicated by the issues of privacy and privatisation, which have spread from the North to the South of Europe. Feedback linkages to the governance are supported everywhere, but in the northern countries there is evidence of a shift from political parties to interest groups and the mass media [Richardson, 1995; Klingemann and Fuchs, 1995].

As part of the europeanisation of the overarching notion of democracy, the various feedback notions and practices compete at the *EU level*. Individual citizenship is seemingly the weakest-realised notion here [Niedermayer and Sinnott, 1998; Harlow, 1999]. But corporate citizenship, in the form of attentive and participatory civil organisations, to some degree representing the people as individuals as well, is highly developed, as extensively illustrated in this book. There is a medium level of individual tolerance for people from other EU countries, as indicated by sympathy scores, which tend to be the highest for one's own countrymen (except in Italy and Belgium) and higher for people in the North than for those in the South [Eurobarometer 46, 1996, B 46/7]. Corporate tolerance is indicated by the preparedness of these organisations to settle their disputes and irritations through peaceful compromise. If they possess (semi-)formal positions inside the EU system, they usually continue to show their tolerance with highly consensual decision-making. Most people feel they have some EU identity, particularly on utilitarian grounds [Gabel, 1998; Van Kersbergen, 2000], but this feeling is generally not as strong as their district, regional and country identity [Eurobarometer 51, 1999, 8; Scheuer, 1999]. Among corporate citizens sectoral identity is the strongest. At the end of the 1990s the notion of freedoms and rights is rapidly growing and acquiring some formal status through a Charter or Constitution. The main linkage system between civil society and the EU is through the organised or corporate groups. The mass media and the political parties, however, still have a mainly national focus. They connect back to the EU via the indirect channels of domestic officials.

The Impacts of EU Public Affairs Management on EU Democracy

All the various notions of democracy clearly play some role at the EU level, but they are all *disputed* as well. Some people praise, for example, the direct channels on the input side as superior to the representative ones, but others take the opposite view. Others again differentiate further and prefer the direct channels to be open only to individuals, and the representative ones only to political parties. Their preferences thus conflict with those of others, who put their trust in, for example, interest groups as agents of democracy. Many believe that the two types of channels are at least partially and potentially contradictory as they channel into the system different demands from different sources. Others, however, see this difference not as contradictory but as complementary. This sort of critical debate exists regarding all other notions as well. The preference for either majority-vote or consensual decision-making is just one other example. No notion has absolute or unconditional support. According to many, even the topical notions of, for example, transparency, the rule of law and tolerance should have their limitations in practice.

As said earlier, it is not our objective to assess here the state of EU democracy. Given the disputed nature of the many notions, such an objective would be impossible to achieve and remain controversial. For our case, it is sufficient to observe that all notions have achieved some form of realisation at the EU level. The state of EU democracy is clearly an amalgam of these notions, each having its own support basis somewhere in the European area. As an example of europeanisation, these practices of EU democracy can be seen as compromises between the often irritatingly different notions of democracy in the EU countries, regions and sectors. The contested character of the notions at these lower levels is continued at the EU level, but there becomes more intense due to their greater heterogeneity. Our objective here is only to explore the *dependency* of EU democracy, reflecting the many different notions, on the behaviour of lobby groups. Do the practices of EU democracy have to be explained by that behaviour? Do these lobby groups have a positive or negative (or no) impact on them?

Input impacts
The EU is clearly a relatively open and competitive system. Three indicators, *inter alia*, are the constant influx of new issues resulting in new agen-

das, the regular permeation of new regime and policy values, and the massive involvement of so-called representative experts. The strong competition between issues, values and experts reflects the pluralism of the supplying countries. The lobby groups play a significant role in keeping the system *open and competitive*. The positive proof of this is their role in the decision-making process, as documented by the many case studies. The negative proof is provided by an imaginary control situation in which lobby groups are absent. If this were the case, the EU would be a system only of COM officials, MEPs, members of EESC and COR, Council ministers and Court personnel, with only two types of linkages with the member countries. One of these is the direct election to the EP and the other the indirect linkages between the Council, EESC and COR on one side and the national capital and society in the home country on the other. This virtual system would certainly be much more closed to many issues, values and people from private and even public interest groups and be altogether much less open and competitive than it is in reality now.

Regarding the so-called vehicles of input democracy the lobby groups have different impacts. There is hardly any evidence that they play a role in the direct *elections* to the EP, but, from their viewpoint on the EU, some try to influence party manifestos, lists of candidates and public debates at the domestic level. Britain is the great example here. *Direct channels* are, however, mainly created by lobby groups, many of which regularly send a representative to Brussels for window-out and window-in activities. Some have their own Brussels office and/or a consultant on the spot and/or some of their rank and file as experts on the EU work floors. Most *representative channels* are also constructed by interest groups. The outstanding example is, of course, provided by the numerous umbrella organisations representing companies, trade unions, professional groups, environmentalists, consumers, decentralised governments and others [Landmarks]. The Commission and the Parliament in particular bring together the channelled issues, values and people, thus functioning as a kind of representative bureaucracy and parliament. The political parties are only directly linked to the EP elections and indirectly to the Council and the COR. The mass media are almost absent on the EU input side.

The lobby groups may be most helpful, but are not sufficient for the EU input democracy. In terms of *equality of entry*, some types of lobby groups tend to have stronger positions than others [Bouwen, 2001]. The more established groups, like national ministries and multinational groups, usually have a permanent ticket to enter their policy sector, but they seldom they have a passe-partout, entitling them to enter any room. In the field of DG

Development Aid, for example, neither the German company Siemens nor the French Ministry of Social Affairs are established players. Like many others, they have to knock on the door, or go in via the back door. Professional groups find the system particularly open and permeable, because they carry out a lot of preparatory work before their lobbying. They are simply smarter than the amateurs and can arrive early in the right place. The electoral vehicle is potentially most open to NGO-like lobby groups, which give the impression of standing for a so-called general interest. The direct channels are mainly used by the better-resourced groups, which can afford the costs, like multinational organisations and national ministries. The representative channels are the least discriminating, as they are open to every group meeting the minimum conditions of organisation. But there always remain some insufficiently organised outside groups, such as retired people and immigrant entrepreneurs, which we shall discuss in the section on feedback impacts.

The lobby groups can have at least two *negative impacts* on EU input democracy. The first comes from the lobby groups as individuals. Many lobby groups try to make the system of access and entrance to the EU less open, not for themselves but for their competitors. This is the paradox of openness leading to closure. These groups try to form a coalition on the access routes, in order to get priority at the entrance. Once inside, they aim to erect thresholds, keeping their rivals both at a distance and behind them, and also to transform their coalition into a policy cartel, which may include EU officials [Gobin and Smets, 1998]. The second negative impact comes from the lobby groups in combination. Because so many groups want to come in and to permeate, they can easily overload the system through either the volume or the contents of their demands. This is the paradox of openness creating its own blockage. Some issues, values and groups are then held up, stockpiled, refused or otherwise not provided entrance. Each of these negative impacts may result in an imbalance of lobby groups on the input side.

The inequality of entry and the negative impacts are, however, at least partially addressed by three system-linked *correction mechanisms*. Firstly, many doors are opened from the inside. Because of their appetite for new or controversial information, support and demands, the EU officials themselves frequently invite in even the incipient, the amateurish and/or the penniless interest groups that have a European orientation. Many incumbent groups, wanting to turn the tide inside the arena, also widen the arena boundaries and open the doors. Entry thresholds are, in short, frequently only temporary. Secondly, the number of lobby groups scrambling for position outside makes the system more open and competitive than it already is.

Many more groups feel they have the desire, the capacity, the compulsion and/or the invitation to enter and to participate. They often get some form of permanent ticket, professionalise themselves, find cheap ways to be present or join a representative channel. Thirdly, the overload problem is tackled by the early arrangement of inputs, such as through new expert committees and consultation procedures. This has happened in the field of waste management, where numerous competitive lobby groups have acquired a semi-formal place in one or more of the around 25 expert committees.

The scores and successes of EU input democracy are, in short, importantly, and to a degree even increasingly, caused by lobbying interest groups. This dependency is neither necessary nor sufficient, but it does exist in daily practice. Those scores tell, of course, only part of the story of EU democracy. However different, for example, the positions of interest groups may be on the input side, they should never be equated with differences of final impact. The former gives *only the chance* of exerting influence in a democratic way. The latter depends as well on the positions lobby groups adopt both during the throughput and on the output side of the decision-making process, which may be very different from their initial positions. Except for the few outsiders, all lobby groups have at least a good chance to enter the system sooner or later.

Throughput impacts
In many respects the EU decision-making system is fairly representative for the member countries but this is *not necessarily* the direct result of lobby group activities. Commission civil servants and MEPs can act, of course, as their own agents of representation, for example by circulating, soliciting opinions or anticipating interests. Part of the representative character of the system has also been created by more formal practices, such as those regarding the recruitment of people and the distribution of positions. But even with these two factors of EU representation the presence of lobby groups is frequently one of the operative causes. With these groups nearby the officials act rationally by anticipating their demands even more and by establishing practices of recruitment and distribution that recognise lobby groups' wishes. In addition, there is the daily new impact from lobby groups coming into the system. By making available their experts, these groups make the work floors of the EU demographically more representative of the various sectors, regions and countries. By providing information, even if selective, they stimulate the representative and discursive character of the opinions on policy held by the officials [Neyer, 2000]. By indicating

their support, they promote a decision-making process more representative of the various interests.

This supply of experts, information and interests is also *insufficient* to bring about a more representative decision-making process. The supply can be unbalanced if it represents only one category of interests. The officials can be self-obsessed or nonchalant for whatever reason. Almost always the supply leaves some room for choice and manoeuvre. The officials even enjoy the paradox that, the stronger the competition among lobby groups, the more they are likely to find themselves in the position of a trustee with a free mandate to devise a compromise acceptable to the larger arena. Many officials have indeed a vested interest in strong lobby competition, which provides on one side more free experts, information and support and on the other side more freedom to decide. But this freedom is only that of a cook who has to make dinner with ingredients provided by the diners themselves. The output side, where legitimacy is expected, casts its shadow here. But the more varied the ingredients provided, the more the kitchen is representative of what nature offers, and the lobby groups are at least very helpful in this regard.

The *methods* of democratic decision-making are also dependent on the presence of lobby groups. This dependency is, once again, selective. Lobby groups prefer the majority-vote method only if this is most likely to give them the result they desire. Aware that the official bodies formally control this method, they usually prefer consensus to a majority vote. Normally, they see the consensus position achieved adopted by those official bodies. They prefer the large chance of winning a part of the game by consensus to the small chance of taking the full game by majority vote. For the same reason, they are quick to register their opposition to what they dislike. With a nuisance position they may get better negotiating terms and a larger slice of the game. If the arena is highly competitive and turning to stalemate, they usually defer to the supreme role of the officials who cook up a representative compromise. Whether the lobby groups like it or not, the more they compete, the more they contribute to the polyarchic method of decision-making.

The lobby groups enhance the democratic *values* involved in the throughput process as well. The individual group does not, of course, primarily demand legitimate authority, discursiveness and transparency in the processing of the dossier at stake. In essence, it values most highly winning or at least not losing the desired outcome. But, knowing that such an outcome is frequently indeterminate for a long time, it has a next-best preference for these three values. It considers them safeguards against conspiring practices by rivals. Anyhow, those who fear to lose a match usually demand that a legitimate authority makes the decision in a discursive and transparent way. They then still have more opportunity for intervention. The special issues of the authority of the Commission relying on expert committees, the discursiveness of the Parliament sympathising with popular views, and the transparency of the Council preferring closed doors, have, indeed, been politicised by lobby groups feeling themselves frequently at loss. Many come from Britain. Their clear support for the three values is at least partially based on their self-interest, which is usually the most solid basis for support.

The lobby groups can, however, have *negative* impacts on the democracy of the decision-making process as well. Given their primary drive to win or at least not to lose a game, many individual groups may regard democracy not as a goal in itself, but as a means and/or a code to use flexibly. The professional groups know that the forms, methods and values of democratic decision-making may determine the specific outcome. Therefore, they try to include these variables in their *Triple P* meta-game. The amateurish groups, in contrast, tend to neglect this. The professional group feeling that it is on the winning side may strongly dislike any proposal to make the decision-making process more representative than, from its point of view, it already and sufficiently is. It may even eschew the three throughput methods. By the majority-vote method it runs the risk of being identified as a privileged minority, by the consensual one of having to make wider concessions, and by the polyarchic one of attracting new challengers. It may also have little interest in furthering the values of authoritative, discursive and transparent decision-making. The professional group in a marginal position or in a losing mood is usually no different in its instrumental approach to democracy, but only in its final preferences. It is inclined, then, to pledge for more representative, consensual and polyarchic decision-making and for a more strict application of the three values. It may remain silent only on the majority-vote method, because that might reveal that it represents only a very small minority itself.

Such reductions of the scores of democracy are subject to some system-bound *correction mechanisms* as well. Firstly, no arena has fully closed boundaries. There are always watching groups still considering whether to join, and these are at least a source of social control. Intruding into an arena, they can make it more representative by both their quantity and their variety. If professional, they can challenge the current forms, methods and values of decision-making and counterbalance the Triple P efforts of their opponents. The mass media, in addition, have a special appetite for reporting on so-called undemocratic practices. Secondly, the EU officials frequently have a vested interest in making the process more democratic, because this will bring them, ultimately, into the driver's seat. For a different reason, lobby groups inside an arena that are in a losing mood can have the same preference for more democracy, as it is an instrument that can hinder the near-winners. Thirdly, the output side may already have cast its shadow. The final decision or outcome needs legitimacy and, particularly, both accountability and responsiveness. There are more quality tests of democracy to come.

Output impacts

The outputs of EU decision-making are widely considered as coming closer to the various notions of output democracy. They are particularly seen as substantially legitimate or acceptable, reflecting limited government and rule of law, and being both accountable and responsive. In all member countries an absolute or relative majority of people supports their EU membership, being the summary indicator of its acceptance [Eurobarometer, autumn 2000, 33]. These scores of democracy on the output side are *not necessarily* the products of lobbying interest groups, of course. Many national politicians, MEPs, Commission officials and Court judges have contributed at least to the formation of both the formal prescripts and the basic practices of this democracy. Those of limited government and the rule of law in particular are firmly rooted in Treaties, which have been drafted by national governments and approved by national electorates (parliaments or electors in a referendum). The officials have validated most forms of both accountability and responsiveness as well, but these may have been promoted by lobby groups as engineers of democracy, at either the domestic or the European level. Behind every new Treaty or official memorandum there is really a great deal of lobbying by many interest groups [Edwards and Pijpers, 1997; McDonagh, 1998]. Many groups finally achieve some results from earlier permeation and participation on the output side of the decision-making process.

The achievement of *legitimacy* is, indeed, frequently at least partially managed by lobby groups. If policy values attract much sympathy and thus acceptance, they have usually earlier been promoted by lobby groups. Examples are the popular values of an open market, healthy food and social cohesion. So-called fair practices, which may make acceptable even an undesired outcome as being 'all part of the game', are frequently constructed by lobby groups themselves. Examples are the open consultations and expert meetings, reflecting the EU work floors. Many groups add a measure of their own charisma, as is done by the European Round Table, adopt a tradition like functional representation, and carry out their operations with a show of science and expertise. Output legitimacy is, in short, at least partially the product of lobby groups, ranging from national ministries to local governments and from trade associations to NGOs.

This is no different for the identified *methods and values* of output democracy. Lobby groups have imposed many limits on the government of the EU, resulting in a more complex system of governance. Special citizens' groups have pressed for the EP to be a checking and balancing power. The committee system, run by interest groups, is such a power. Regional and sectoral groups have been a strong factor of decentralised participation in EU affairs. Industrial groups have clearly stimulated the trend from so-called positive to negative integration, exemplified by the creation of a more open market and a more autonomous civil society. Together with their governments, the lobby groups from the majority of countries with a legalistic tradition (the South of Europe, plus Britain and Germany) have contributed much to the EU practice of bringing the compromises on decisions under the rule of law. Through their regular appeals to the Court they continue to strengthen this practice. British citizen's groups in particular have successfully pressed for more accountability. Both the general and the specific responsiveness of the products of EU policy can only be explained if lobby groups are taken as a factor.

The existence of lobby groups is, of course, *not a sufficient* condition for the creation of EU output democracy. The officials who approve and sign the decisions may remain deaf or blind to their actions. They may give priority to the values of their office or themselves, as happens in every system. As players too, they can patronise selected lobby groups by applying discriminating procedures. They may even undermine the practices of limited government by making deals and coalitions across institutional, territorial and sectoral boundaries. Officials outside the Court can weaken the supremacy of law through their capacity to interpret the regulations as discretionary or to fall back on 'soft law'. They can use the procedures of accountability for highlighting only their own performances, in short for giving themselves good publicity. They may sometimes keep responsiveness limited to their own preferences or to selected client groups. All this can happen at any level and it happens to varying degrees in the EU as well.

The lobby groups can even have *negative impacts* on the scores of output democracy. The rationale for such an approach is, again, their prime aim of coming the closest possible to the desired outcome for a dossier. The professional groups are best able to identify opportunities for managing or manipulating the practices leading to legitimacy, but as prudent players they make an inconspicuous and thus modest use of them. They may also take advantage of the practices of limited government, the rule of law, accountability and responsiveness. They know how they can fare under these prestigious flags. At the moment of final decision-making, the established groups can use a position of influence to get preferential treatment. Their establishment may even be only regionally or sectorally based. For example, a region like Saxony is then patronised by someone from there based at the Commission and an NGO like Greenpeace by an EP rapporteur with a green soul. The better-resourced groups, frequently having an office in Brussels, can exert daily pressure on the officials to get their interests legitimised, legalised and responded to more or less as they demand. The output side can, in short, reflect great inequality among lobby groups, especially between the professionals and the amateurs.

Three system-linked *correction mechanisms*, however, prevent all these potentially negative impacts from easily becoming reality. Firstly, inside the official decision-making system many legal and social controls on the officials remain operative, even if a few are not. The rapporteur with a green soul has to get his report adopted by the shadow rapporteurs, the parties and the plenary. Commission officials are subject to control through the existence of competitive offices, higher officials and the other institutions. The 1999 demise of the Santer Commission was a dramatic example of such control, being highly effective after a short time lag. Secondly, even more controls emanate from the lobby groups themselves and are caused by their quantity and their variety. They spend a lot of energy on closely watching each other. The comparative advantages of the most professional, established and resourced groups become smaller since many more groups sufficiently attain these characteristics. Groups perceiving that they are on the losing side and cannot join the winning side may launch a critical campaign, blaming the officials for a lack of legitimacy or accountability. The mass media need only a wisp of smoke in order to report a big fire, which may burn the officials. Thirdly, the feedback mechanism can cast its shadow. If an output is widely considered as falling short of democracy, it may evoke serious feedback reactions. The lobby group aware of the risk of scandals disciplines its behaviour beforehand.

Feedback impacts

The EU outcomes clearly have some democratic impacts on the member societies. Citizenship is stimulated to some degree, as both individual and corporate citizens receive information, however incomplete and unreliable it may be, about outcomes ranging from draft directives and institutional changes to final decisions and scandals. What happens inside the EU system can flow to the outside at any moment. There will always be some citizens, who react to received information. This is where *citizenship* comes in as the feedback loop of democracy. If the citizens react, they do this at least through their civic spirit. They may develop new beliefs, values or judgements regarding the EU or confirm old ones. In some cases they even react by civic behaviour. This may be in their neighbourhood, society at large, the market or the domestic political system, thus potentially feeding back through indirect channels. Or they may react by more direct civic behaviour, for example by lobbying in Brussels, with the objective of bringing their civic spirit to the attention of EU officials. This behavioural reaction applies more to corporate than to individual citizens.

The EU outcomes can even affect specific *values and methods* of feedback democracy. Examples are the following. The extension of the internal market has reinforced the value of tolerance for people, products and ownership from foreign countries. Intolerance meets more retaliation than in the past. The common decision-making by 'Brussels', where one's own national government has become at most only one player among many, has given expression to new forms of the value of identity. Regional identity in particular has become much more important. Freedoms and rights, as methods or even as preconditions of feedback democracy, have been strengthened by such EU outcomes as sectoral liberalisation, limited government and free movement. Linkage systems have been stimulated particularly by Commission invitations to interest groups to provide information and to sit on expert groups. The political parties and the mass media are, however, still more a dead-end route at home, only informing their public, rather than being a fixed part of the feedback loop.

Lobby groups have contributed to all these feedback impacts. Of course, they are *not necessary* for their creation. In theory EU officials and politicians alone could have produced these impacts. Formally, they are frequently at least co-producers of them, as they approve or block many outcomes. But what they do (or do not), is in practice usually the result of negotiations with and among many public and private lobby groups. They are entitled to sign if they wish a proposal provoked by these groups. Citizens' reactions to the legislation on, for example, GMOs, chocolate or asylum are, implicitly, reactions to results of those negotiations with lobby groups. This is equally the case for the EU impacts on the values and the methods of feedback democracy, as the aforementioned examples make clear. The extension of the open market, reinforcing the value of tolerance, is claimed to be the result of lobby behaviour from MNCs. Regional groups have acted as a strong factor behind the widening of the EU decision-making mechanism, giving focus to more regional identities. Subnational and private lobby groups have strongly pushed the EU policies of decentralisation and privatisation, as forms of limited government creating more freedoms and rights. The formal invitation of the Commission to interest groups to function as a feedback linkage is in practice often one inspired by such groups acting as a waffle iron squeezing the EU officials.

The lobby groups are, however, *insufficient* for the promotion of democracy in the EU. Citizenship can be stimulated by the EU, but at the same time hampered by other determinants such as, for example, welfare, education, free time and social interest [Milbrath and Goel, 1977]. Their unequal distribution may explain why there is so much variation of EU citizenship between corporate and individual citizens and even within each category. Thanks to the EU the values of tolerance and identity have acquired new meanings and forms, but their status in society is also dependent on more than the EU with its lobby groups alone. For example the respect for pluralism, being a core value of European integration, is also determined by the social situation at street level and frequently becomes the focus of tension here. The formation of new identities, such as the regional ones, is in many cases primarily caused by local factors such as language or religion and only catalysed via the EU. Lobbying for the proclamation of freedoms and rights through the Official Journal is not sufficient, as it must take into account wider social demands and adequate infrastructures as well. EU stakeholders pushing for more and better feedback linkages can fail in their efforts, as the weak linkage positions of the political parties and the mass media demonstrate.

The groups lobbying under the EU flag can even have *negative* impacts on the state of democracy in the various societies. If the people come to believe that the EU is only a sort of republican court with lobbying groups and factions patronising them, they may lose some civic spirit and behaviour and become more indifferent and passive. Individuals and outside groups, such as retired people and immigrant shopkeepers, may even get the feeling that they are not clients at all. The values of tolerance and identity, enhanced by many sectoral and regional groups, may develop in the opposite direction of rising social conflicts and cultural confusion. For a job vacancy, a house purchase or even a parking place the people may dislike competition from equally entitled foreigners. The loss of national identity can result in damage to democratic practices at home, such as a decline of parliamentary control and voting turnout. The EU may challenge some domestic freedoms and rights, such as the Dutch coffee shops selling soft drugs, the Austrian Cabinet formation in 2000, the Spanish sports involving animals, the British working hours and the French appetite for 'unhealthy' cheese. The decline of political parties in all the member states [Mair, 1990], widely seen as a negative development, is probably partially due to the success of interest groups at the EU level [Richardson, 1995].

These potential or real negative impacts remain limited, so far, by the workings of at least five *correction mechanisms*. Firstly, the EU officials, getting feedback on negative lobby impacts, frequently interfere and take some measures to deal with them. Commission officials, for example, like to get outside groups on board; MEPs include weak special interests within their intergroups; Council ministers, under pressure from public opinion, fight for maintaining such domestic assets as coffee shops and cheese. Many EU lobby groups, secondly, search for new support groups and potential clients. In the field of DG R&D policies, for example, big companies have made many alliances with SMEs. At the domestic level, thirdly, protest groups may arise. In most countries the main example here is of the national parliament feeling marginalised on EU affairs [Norton, 1995]. In such cases, the parliament feeds back its feelings of concern either indirectly through its government or, as in the case of Denmark, even directly in Brussels. Fourthly, formerly outside groups learn to organise themselves better for EU action. The previously weak groups of consumers and workers are respected EU lobby groups now. Groups of patients or retired people are growing in significance, and immigrants' groups may follow. Finally, there is social control by society. If a lobby group is widely seen as misbehaving according to some notion of democracy, it can acquire a poor reputation and an isolated position among its citizens, customers or members at home and subsequently at the EU level. The fear of this boomerang is a self-correcting mechanism.

Improving EU Democracy by EU Lobbying

The relationship between lobby groups as the independent variable and EU democracy as the dependent one is for two reasons more complex than as it has been described above. Firstly, there is the *multifinality* of lobby groups. They create more impacts than solely on democracy, as is shown by the following few examples. By their group formations they contribute to the integration across borders of private and public interests and organisations. Their direct settlements of irritating differences, such as in the field of labour relations, whether achieved under the Social Dialogue or not, improve the social stability of the EU. Their creation of standards contributes to EU economic growth and welfare. By making available information and manpower to the Commission, they promote the effectiveness and the efficiency of the EU decision-making machinery. In addition, they have their specific impacts on the formation of EU special policies, such as on the environment, agriculture or R&D. All such impacts on values other than democracy can subsequently, as intermediate variables, contribute positively or negatively to EU democracy. The lobby groups are, of course, usually driven not by the intention to create such impacts, but by their selfish ambition to win or not to lose a desired outcome. Selfishness has thus many side products, including highly appreciated ones [Mandeville, 1705].

Secondly, there is the *multicausality* of EU democracy. Many more independent variables than lobby groups alone have their impacts on it. Among them are the following three. The EU officials themselves are a first one, as we mentioned before: independent from lobby groups, they can contribute to EU democracy. Positive examples of such contributions are the formal proposals, based on notions of formal democracy, from the Commission to regulate public accountability, from the Parliament to receive more formal powers, and from the Council to apply a Charter of Rights. A second cause is the mass media. Their contributions to EU democracy are negligible or negative rather than positive. Most of them are poor observers of EU developments both in and on behalf of their public. They hardly report about anything more than the official statements, the scandals and the results of games surrounding decision-making, as if they are covering Eurosports. On the basis of such information, citizens can hardly come to a reasoned judgement useful for their citizenship. Ideally for EU democracy, most journalists of the mass media should be trained and resourced much better than is the case at present. The potential of cyber-democracy may become a third cause of EU democracy in the near future [Hague and Loader, 1999; Kamarck and Nye, 1999; Wilhelm, 2000]. The basic assumption is that the citizens and the EU officials can be brought closer together through various ways of direct communication, to the benefit of EU democracy.

Under consideration here, however, is not how EU democracy can or should be explained or strengthened. Given all the contested notions of democracy at the EU level, the dependent variable is still developing and not yet sufficiently stable. We remain focused on the lobby groups as one important factor of EU democracy. This is not to deny the importance of the many other factors, such as the officials, the mass media and the electronic means. They have their impacts on EU democracy too, either directly or, as far as they condition the role of lobby groups, indirectly. Our core observation is simply that the lobby groups have some impacts on the state of democracy in the EU. Inevitably they contribute to an europeanisation of notions of democracy. In many cases they determine the practices of democracy, at least partially. Some impacts fit nicely with current notions of democracy and can thus be considered positive. Others are potentially or really at odds with them. These negative impacts are, however, subject to system-bound correction mechanisms. Our leading question now is *how EU democracy can benefit more from lobby groups*, even if such a benefit is only an unintended side product of the lobbying. This big question can be simplified as follows. Can the positive impacts be strengthened and increased? Can the negative ones be reduced or blocked? Can the correction mechanisms be promoted and reinforced?

Strengthening the positive impacts
Referring to figure 8.1, we conclude that lobby groups have positive impacts on all elements of democracy, as covered by the various notions, with two exceptions. One is the input method of competitive elections and the other the throughput method of majority-vote decision-making. Most lobby groups keep their hands off these. Willy-nilly they contribute to the realisation of the other notions positively, some more than others. Of course, only the *active* groups contribute positively. The passive ones are irrelevant on the positive side. In the sections above, the established and the professional groups came out as the most important among the active groups. The first category, usually not falling short of resources, has not only the capacity and the drive, but frequently also an invitation from the officials to participate in the decision-making process. The *established* groups produce the high-quantity of beneficial lobby impacts on democracy. The second category of professional groups overlaps only partially with the established ones. Most of the latter may behave amateurishly, while some newcomers may act most professionally. The *professionals* produce the best-quality impacts on democracy. Thanks to their preparatory work they prudently respect the many limits of behaviour. For example, they try to supply useful information and support to the officials, to promote a legitimate consensus, and to behave as a corporate citizen. In their public relations campaigns they sometimes like to put those positive side effects on EU democracy on their credit side, thus impressing the public.

The positive impacts can, in consequence, be strengthened by a triple approach: by the *activation*, *establishment* and *professionalisation* of many more interest groups in their capacity as EU lobby groups. The more and the better lobbying is practised, the more it produces beneficial impacts on democracy. A few amateurish or professional lobby groups may be a danger to democracy, but a surplus of professional groups is a blessing to it. All together, they can keep the system open and competitive, make the process more representative and discursive, bring the officials into the driver's seat of polyarchy, and create a more developed citizenship and feedback linkage, to mention only some effects. Time is already on the side of the triple approach [Meny and others, 1996, I]. Increasing numbers of interest groups are becoming more active on EU affairs, are building up a more established position as lobby groups and are professionalising themselves. They do so under pressure from both the perceived relevance of the EU and the stronger competition from the numerous other stakeholders. They are also encouraged to do so by the Commission officials and the EP members, in particular, who have a vested interest in the active and professional lobbying by established groups.

Reducing the negative impacts
The main negative impacts of lobbying on EU democracy, mentioned above, can be briefly *summarised* as follows. The lobby groups, which enter and permeate the system successfully, may set up thresholds for others, form closed coalitions and overload the system on the input side. During the decision-making process the insiders may act as a closed shop, making a strong claim of representation and consensus, paying lip service to polyarchy and legitimate authority, and minimising external discursiveness and transparency. On the output side they may counter the democratic practices of legitimacy, limited government, rule of law, accountability and responsiveness, or they may manipulate them so that they can benefit from their protective flags. At home they may dispirit individual citizens and outside groups, disregard the values of civil tolerance and common identity, and discredit the freedoms and the linkages of competitors.

Such negative impacts may come not only from the active groups. Paradoxically, the *passive* interest groups contribute to them as well, precisely because they are passive and leave to the active ones their room for action, thus weakening the competition. In an essentially open system like the EU, a threshold or a closed shop, erected by the active few, can only endure if the many remain passive. Among the active groups, the many *semi-established* ones in particular create the bulk of negative impacts. Falling short of, for example, a strong organisation, an established presence and a permanent ticket to move around, they are more concerned about their impacts on stakeholders than on democracy. In contrast, the non-established groups, playing only occasionally, have hardly any impact on either, while the best-established groups have most to lose in becoming the talk of the town. The most serious negative impacts, however, come from the *semi-professionals*. They master some techniques of political engineering, such as smart homework, Triple P and issue manipulation, but are indiscreet in the application of these skills. They try to pick the flowers on the ridge by, for example, erecting a threshold for competitors, obstructing transparency or limiting the freedoms of others. In contrast, the real amateurs lack the skills to damage democracy seriously, while the full professionals respect the limits of EU Public Affairs Management prudently and especially the risk of a boomerang from scandals caused by allegedly undemocratic behaviour.

The negative impacts can best be reduced by the same aforementioned triple approach. Firstly, the more the many domestic interest groups are *activated* to play a role as EU lobby groups, the smaller the stratum of passive groups providing room for the active few. The best form of activation usually comes from the rank and file of these interest groups and ultimately from individual citizens. Even the mass media and the political parties, now constituting little more than a dead end at home, might contribute to that activation perfectly well. They should make the people more aware and concerned about their interests in the EU. Secondly, the better *established* the lobby groups become, the more they will have to lose by creating negative impacts on democracy. Their greatest risk is of becoming scandalised and isolated and thus losing their ticket to operate. In fact, they are stimulated to *professionalise* themselves, and this is the third key to the reduction of the negative impacts. The more the lobby groups become fully professional, with both technical skills and a sense of prudence, the less they cause serious damage to democracy. Time, again, is already on the side of the triple approach. Public interest groups are increasingly activated by the citizens and private ones by their members or workers. The rank and file push their interest group towards being better established on the playing field. At the receiver's side of EU lobbying, the officials and the other stakeholders, fearing any fall-out from scandals, demand more prudent behaviour.

Reinforcing the correction mechanisms
Of course, there will always remain some negative impacts from lobbying on EU democracy. Nobody can prevent a lobby group, wilfully or otherwise, installing an undemocratic practice or distorting an existing democratic one tomorrow. Only a tyrannical system, unconcerned about democracy at all, can forbid lobby groups officially, but it is, paradoxically, always run by one lobby group itself, for example by the military, the clergy or the party. In a democracy, lobby groups are an essential part of the system [Popper, 1945]. Their positive impacts on democracy can be taken for granted and

Self-regulating EU lobby-democracy

Input side
- scrambling groups outside
- openings from the inside
- provision of positions

Throughput
- officials' self-interest
- watching groups
- output anticipation

Output side
- internal controls
- external controls
- feedback anticipation

Feedback
- official interferences
- looking for support
- protest groups
- new groups
- reputation

Figure 8.3

enjoyed as free benefits. Their negative impacts can be reduced not only by the threefold approach mentioned before, but also by a reinforcement of the system-bound correction mechanisms. These mechanisms are summarised in *figure 8.3.*

We came to the conclusion above that the system-related correction mechanisms are most dependent on both the *quantity* and the *quality* of the active lobby groups. The higher the number of active groups, the more of them will enter the EU arenas, increase the competition, bring the officials into the driver's seat and search for new support from the outside, thus stimulating new entrants. The higher the number of established groups, the more there will be to create all the aforementioned effects continually, to care about their established positions and to recognise the value of professionalisation. The better the quality of lobby groups, the more they behave adequately, proactively and prudently, driven as they are by the double desire to win a current game and to keep their licence for a further game. Of course, any increase in active, established and professional lobby groups may attract more lazy, wandering and amateurish groups as well, but as followers they are hardly a danger to democracy as long as they behave as followers and not as leaders. Many newcomers take, indeed, the active, established and professional lobby groups as an example to follow.

Any effort to strengthen the correction mechanisms should, therefore, be focused on increasing both the quantity and the quality of the active lobby groups. The first is a matter of *stimulating the participation* of all sorts of interest groups at the EU level. There is, however, hardly any need for a kind of official EU stimulation policy for this. Many interest groups already have strong desires to participate, resulting from perceived threats and opportunities. Many also feel sufficiently compelled by their competitors in the market or the policy sector. The invitations from inside the EU are usually at most a temporary problem, as many officials and groups inside want to get new groups on board. Most obstacles to participation relate to insufficient capacity on the home front, as manifested by internal dissent, a lack of knowledge, a poor mix of resources and skills, and/or a bad image. To improve them is primarily a job for the interest groups themselves, maybe with some coaching from outside. The second focus on *quality improvement* is strongly dependent on the quantity of lobby groups. The higher the number of the active and the established groups, the stronger the competition and the social control among them. Competition stimulates their preparatory work and social control their prudence. These two factors hardly need a specific EU policy approach either. If there is a wider intake of lobby groups, the increase in both competition and social control will follow almost automatically.

To keep the system open and competitive only some kind of a watchdog is needed. The analogy is provided by DG Competition, which rarely develops specific competition rules for different trades, but relies on general rules to keep all commercial markets open and competitive. A similar approach is appropriate for the political market of EU decisions. *Open entry* and *fair competition* are the two preconditions for the strengthening of the in-built correction mechanisms, which subsequently promote EU democracy. To a great extent, the currently competing lobby groups already fulfil these two preconditions. A single or a few groups may try to close off the entrance, but the effort usually fails due to both the pressures from outside and the invitations from inside. A single or a few groups may also try to play tricks, but a boomerang endangering their licence to operate usually will hit them. A watchdog will be helpful to strengthen the two preconditions, and the best possible is *public opinion* supported by critical mass media. If some closed shop or unfair practice is observed and made public, then there will always be an EU official or another stakeholder eager to open a door, to provide a position or to interfere in the process, and they do this already, even without a well-developed EU mass media. Although the notions of openness and fairness are not clear-cut and still differ by arena, sector or country, they are also in a process of europeanisation. More and more lobby groups, therefore, take a safety margin: wanting their behaviour to be free from the risk of being misunderstood and thus scandalised, they are prudent.

The idea of a basically self-regulating lobby democracy is not new. It is the core idea of James Madison's *Paper 10* of *The Federalist* papers [1788]. A lobby group, called a faction, is seen as a normal phenomenon of free human life. If such a selfish group is seen as devilish, then there are two possible solutions. One is to remove the causes. This can only be done either by tyrannical rule or by an equalisation of interests, which are respectively undesirable and impossible. The other solution is to reduce the negative effects of lobby groups. This can best be done by keeping the system as open as possible and by attracting into the system the maximum number of groups having the highest variety. They all will compete with each other. One or a few devils can best be exorcised by the mobilisation of as many devils as possible. Then they will not become saints, of course, but only human beings socially controlled by other human beings. This ingenious vector rather than factor approach is the solution Madison recommends. In addition he pleads for a limited government, with many formal checks and balances, in order to prevent the state itself becoming a devil.

Extra: Improving EU Democracy by the Study of EU PAM

Our proposition here is that the study of public affairs management at the EU level can greatly contribute to EU democracy, as measured by the various notions of democracy. The better *developed* this study is and the more *widespread* its knowledge and insights are, the smaller the chance of closed shops and unfair practices. Those two conditions are inseparable. A solely well-developed science can be used for better or worse. Those who master it exclusively have the choice of both and can use their knowledge for either peaceful or aggressive purposes. But if the science becomes widely spread among many, it loses its potential to overpower others. If this happens, the others counterbalance everyone who has mastered it, and all together they promote respect for each other and abstention from aggression. The widely diffused knowledge, however, must have a sufficiently sound scientific basis as well. If people take their beliefs or myths as knowledge or neglect chain reactions, they may cause a lot of damage as well, maybe not by criminal intention but by stupid mistakes, which is, according to the French politician Charles De Talleyrand-Périgord (1754-1838), even worse. In short, both the development and the diffusion of sound knowledge regarding *how to push the buttons of 'Brussels'* may enhance EU democracy.

In chapter 2 we characterised the current state of knowledge about EU decision-making as widely considered unsatisfactory. Many grand theories and big concepts, mainly derived from international law and international relations, have been launched and applied to the EU. They have, however, hardly any explanatory power, let alone predictive value. The critical new trend has three components. The first one is *empirical* research, which shifts the intellectual interest away from the skeleton to the flesh and blood of EU decision-making. What are the so-called facts, arrived at by transparent methods and not refuted by evidence? What are their explanatory causes or factors and what their probable consequences? And which vectors might produce similar consequences? The second component is *inductive* reasoning. Which interpretation of the described facts and their mutual relationships makes sense? Is there a driving force behind it, for example the influence of lobby groups? How can this new conjecture be further tested? The final component is *mid-level* theorising. If some interpretation is repeatedly considered reliable and valid, how then can it be systemised into some coherent theory? The old pretension to cover the whole and to tell a grand story is clearly replaced by the modest ambition to make mid-level statements. These must be reliable and valid at least for the crucial variables of some part of the system, for example a policy sector, a type of arena, or an influence approach.

Mainly younger, often American, scholars have given rise to the critical new trend, but they were not alone. The many lobbyists, in particular, needing to know *how the EU is really working*, criticised the old body of pretentious knowledge silently, by preferring to rely on their own trials and errors and, in some advanced cases, on their own R&D for EU public affairs management. They identified, for example, the work floors of the EU, the mid-level Commission official and the delegated legislation. They developed their own methods of homework, Triple P practices, fine-tuned styles of lobbying and more. Much of their knowledge gathered in practice is still not accepted by many academics, but there are always some scholars and some practitioners who like to walk over the bridge between *academia* and *societas*. They have organised their joint meetings, activities and outlets, mentioned in the extra section at the end of chapter 1. The scholars want to gather more valid and reliable knowledge and the practitioners more relevant and useful insights. Together they have a common interest in improving the knowledge basis of EU public affairs management and in supporting the critical new trend.

If kept exclusive, the better knowledge and insights might be used against EU democracy as well, of course. But they already tend to be rapidly disseminated among many people, particularly by four *channels of diffusion*. Firstly, the growing results from research on EU public affairs management get wide circulation through many more new books and the specialised *Journal of Public Affairs*. Secondly, many consultants working for various lobby groups gather comparative experiences and disseminate this knowledge among their clients. Many of them also participate in the aforementioned networks with academics, in order to stimulate or to tap their brains. Thirdly, on a more or less commercial basis, private organisations and postgraduate schools are increasingly offering open courses on EU public affairs management in Brussels and elsewhere, as advertised in the *European Voice*. The lecturers usually come from the same mixed networks of experienced practitioners and researching academics. Finally, there are the few university programmes with at least a research-based major or minor course on the EU decision-making machinery and/or the behaviour of interest groups. The students here get a basic taster and perhaps an appetite for more. But a specific programme on EU public affairs management still does not exist. Taking in overview, the knowledge and insights are not exclusively held by just a few: they are spread around and available to anyone who wants to master them.

In terms of contents, these channels disseminate in particular three *types of knowledge*. Firstly, they provide the results of research. As in a restaurant, the consumers are less interested in the cooking than in the meals. They want to know the facts of, for example, the EU work floors and the networking of various officials. Secondly, useful tools are taught. The people are most interested in checklists regarding, for example, the making of a short list of dossiers, fine-tuned lobbying or the internal organisation of EU public affairs management. They show much less interest in the methodology behind the construction of a checklist. Thirdly, the contents are mostly highly prescriptive in terms of do's and don'ts. The checklists have a breakdown of what it is better to do or not to do. The frequently silent criteria are effectiveness and efficiency: people want to know how to score better and more easily. The prescriptions are usually placed in a longer-term perspective, with attention given to chain reactions and thus also with an emphasis on prudence. The contents, in short, are most focused on useful and relevant knowledge. As such they are more attuned to the demand side of the practitioners than the supply side of the researchers. This wider diffusion of more research-based knowledge and insights anyhow indicates a popularisation and democratisation of EU public affairs management.

There remains, however, room for further improvement, and two priorities can be suggested. First of all, the *diffusion* needs more ramified channels and balanced contents. The current channels are mainly used by private organisations with an EU-wide position, such as MNCs, EuroFeds and NGOs like Greenpeace. They need ramification towards both the interest groups of governments and, to serve the smaller-sized groups, the regional and the local levels. Many interest groups, especially in the southern countries, still lag behind in the awareness and the practice of EU public affairs management, not to mention its body of knowledge. Electronic means (e-learning) and visiting scholars (a travelling faculty) should be used more for its diffusion. Their contents deserve a better balance between the demand side of the practitioners and the supply side of the researchers. The better understanding of the methodology behind those results, checklists and prescriptions may not only turn some consumers into producers of knowledge, but also educate them all to a more critical level.

Secondly, the channels of diffusion should be fed with a higher quality and quantity of knowledge or, in short, with better and more *research agendas* [Andersen and Eliassen, 1995]. Three agendas, all related to EU democracy, are given here. One concerns the limits of EU public affairs management, the current knowledge of which comes more from practitioners than from systematic research. In particular the limits set by the arena, the receivers and the environment are relevant for the state of EU democracy. The negative effects from the possible practices of closed shops and unfair competition are just one example. If the published results of research refute such practices, they are useful for their unmasking of a popular belief. If not, they will certainly alert the mass media, acting as the watchdogs of EU democracy and, subsequently, strengthen the correction mechanisms. Once published, tricks simply become less effective. The second agenda regards the question of why selected categories of interest groups, such as immigrant shopkeepers and national ministries, frequently fall short of activism, establishment and professionalism. These three features of lobbying have the strongest discriminatory impact on EU democracy. The results of research can help the currently passive, wandering and/or nonchalant interest groups to strengthen their lobby capacities, to engineer an efficient establishment and to improve their professionalism. The third agenda is focused on the europeanisation of the various notions of democracy. Such an agenda of classical political science might help all EU stakeholders to adapt their behaviour better to the rising common norms of EU democracy.

These two priorities are justified here for their contributions to the broad value of EU democracy, but they can be based on other values as well. As said before, EU lobbying can also be seen as an important factor of, for example, European integration, efficient EU decision-making and/or socio-economic welfare. These highly valued outcomes can also benefit from the science of EU public affairs management. It is, of course, not necessary to have any other justification for whatever study than simply 'wanting to know' or 'art for art's sake'. Nevertheless, here we advocate those two priorities of research as being of benefit to EU democracy, through which EU lobbying has recently been politicised.

Reflection for the Action

The EU is a most ambitious experiment of living together peacefully in Europe, partially or fully replacing the old practices of accommodation by patience, leniency, war, imitation and ad-hoc negotiations. The machinery of common EU decision-making has acquired the reputation of highest *relevance*, thanks to the priority of EU law over domestic law in particular. All sorts of interest groups coming from the pluralistic member societies try to intervene in the workings of the machinery, which provides much openness and permeability. Frequently, they get a more or less desired outcome, being the decision as pushed for or the prevention of a feared decision. The EU officials and politicians inside the machinery largely welcome the arrival of new issues and stakeholders, which give more relevant contents to the machinery. Like the lobby groups, they also make use of the vectors of europeanisation, so integrating the domestic and the European level, and also the public and the private sectors more than before. The EU has, in short, become a major place for political action.

Traditional techniques of influence are less effective and efficient here. Coercion cannot really work in a system characterised not by centralised but by fragmented power. Encapsulating others by the creation of personal and budgetary dependencies also has a very limited effectiveness in such a system, as it is easily counter-balanced by competitors. Advocacy, ranging from the social variant of propaganda to the legal one of litigation, clearly also has its limits in a system full of different values and rules. Much of the same holds true for the technique of argumentation. Like in the ancient Greek drama, all the opposing stakeholders on an issue are capable of proving how right they are in their position. All these traditional techniques reflect an attitude of superiority or even arrogance of one over the other. This may have worked in the more stratified domestic societies of the past, but is much less effective at the EU level. Not one single country is dominant here, let alone one public or private lobby group.

The new influence technique of *public affairs management* and especially its professional application is better adapted to the realities of the EU than the traditional techniques. It is essentially based on respect for the many (frequently irritating) different values and stakeholders in any arena. However, the respect is not for the value or the stakeholder as such, but for its power of resistance. It can best be compared with the respect fighting soldiers have for each other, when they want to survive a complex and uncertain battle. That respect is, first of all, demonstrated by their careful preparation for the battle and by their prudent behaviour during it. The EU lobby groups, taking their public affairs seriously, want to likewise survive and when going window-out, they prepare themselves well and act prudently. They search for the best ways within the labyrinth and the best moments on the trampoline of EU decision-making. But different from real soldiers and the time-period of Machiavelli, they cannot hope to kill-off their opponents forever. They have to lobby for peace, by negotiating a deal and finding a compromise, in short by going window-in with crucial stakeholders and by settling issues. This is a second indicator of respect.

This approach of any EU arena, euphemistically called 'playing field', requires a lot of *reflection* for the action. There are so many challenges, options, menus and dilemmas that the game of chess may look easy. At its home front, the lobby group has to consider the real nature of the challenges and the presence of such preconditions as a sufficient cohesion and a good appeal. The mere downsizing of the long list of EU daydreams and nightmares to a short list of realisable targets requires intense reflection. For every specific arena, one has to observe and consider the issues at stake, the stakeholders involved, the time dimension and the arena boundaries, and also to reflect on their best management. The fieldwork is full of dilemmas, such as with regard to the styles of behaviour, the use of voice and the timing of an activity. The number of potential actors to approach, factors to use and vectors to create are always too high to manage them all. The lobby process is full of limits also requiring attention. The lobby group must be aware of all this and make decisions at the same time.

Reflection for the action improves the *chance of success*, but is in itself neither necessary nor sufficient for it. A lobby group can also act haphazardly or by reflex. It may even achieve a desired outcome in this way incidentally, with some good luck. However, the chance of this happening is slight and in a number of cases practically absent. If one wants to win, or at least not lose, regularly either a game or one's respect from others and/or one's backing at home, one is advised to act through reflection. The more thorough the reflection, the better the chance of success, although there are never any guarantees. Reflection is always more or less imperfect, due to, for example, incomplete information, lack of time or unreliable sources. Even with thorough reflection, the lobby group may be a victim of bad luck caused by an unforeseeable event, like the fall of the Commission Santer in 1998-99 or the sudden rise of the hot issue of 'terrorism' in September 2001, to mention two high-profile cases.

The reflection is not the goal, but a most useful means to increase the chance of a more successful EU lobby *action* in a specific arena. This does not imply that specific activities always have to follow. After reflection, every lobby group may come to the conclusion that it can better remain passive, for instance because it considers the cost-benefit ratio of any further action to be unattractive. It is then at least mentally active through its awareness of the lobby situation. If it decides to play an active role it has to prepare itself thoroughly, which ranges from effectively organising the home front to carefully analysing the arena. The purpose is to find and to establish optimal positions in regard to issues, stakeholders, moments and boundaries considered relevant. During the preparatory work, the balance of activities will gradually shift from window-out to window-in behaviour. Finally, the lobby group has to negotiate on issues with stakeholders in order to become part of the winning coalition. All these activities have been previously summarised under the catchwords of 'preparatory homework' and 'fine-tuned fieldwork'.

If the lobby group wants to find the approaches that will *score the highest* on efficiency (cost-benefit ratio) and effectiveness (desired outcome), it must make a substantial investment in collecting reliable information on itself and the EU arena, and also reflect on this. That investment is an ongoing activity. It must start before the action and continue during the action, and even afterwards. Only then can the lobby group gather the information needed for making sound decisions regarding its participation in the arena, its responses during the interactive lobbying and its primary lessons to be taken for the next game. The so-called 'best practices' are never permanently fixed, but are dependent on new insights and are thus constantly in development. Many lessons can also be taken from others, like other groups lobbying on the same dossier, people working on the receiver's side or in the transmission channels, watching journalists and colleagues, and academics researching lobby group behaviour. In public affairs management, the professionals are insatiable in their demand for enhanced knowledge and learning.

They are also *prudent* for two reasons. Firstly, every arena contains certain risks. A lobby group may become part of the winning coalition, but part of the losing one as well. During the lobbying in the arena, it may lose old friends, find itself in a hostile setting, be caught in manipulation of the issue, be treated as a scapegoat, become divided at the home front or be subjected to any other experience suitable for a nightmare. It may ultimately have to live with a most undesired outcome from the EU for many years, for example, a law establishing huge costs of adaptation or giving the competitor a substantial advantage. Therefore, like the soldier wanting to survive in a risky field, the professional lobby group wants to behave prudently by preparing itself consciously and by acting cautiously. Secondly, it wants to keep its license to operate in any other arena considered relevant, at the same time or in the future. By acting prudently in every arena, the lobby group may sometimes lose its interest at stake, but keep its respect from others and its backing at home. If, however, it becomes subject of controversy or scandal due to its nonchalant behaviour, it may be out of any other arena at the same time or in the near future, thus almost certainly losing even more interests.

One primary conclusion from all this is that *the most professional* lobby groups make the largest contributions to EU democracy. They respect others and behave prudently. Willy-nilly, they help to strengthen the system-bound correction mechanisms. The semi-professional or more nonchalant groups not only make more mistakes to their own disadvantage, but also care less about things such as reaching a compromise, the criticism from public opinion, or the presence of outsiders' groups. However, they are more or less established and active on the EU playing field, thus being in the position of learning by practice and making at least a small contribution to participatory democracy. The many interest groups that remain passive for whatever reason, but nevertheless complain about the EU outcomes and procedures have the worst influence on EU democracy. They should participate and assume their role as a lobby group, preferably in a professional manner. They can then become part of a winning coalition regularly and, willy-nilly, contribute to EU democracy.

The second primary conclusion is that the flowering of *the study* of public affairs management, being highly dependent on open and competitive democracy, also makes a significant contribution. It fosters the opportunity for many more groups of people to lobby the EU in an active, established and professional manner, and it diminishes the possibility that only a few groups will win the games, the sets and the matches. In short, EU democracy is dependent on many groups and ultimately on many people knowing how to participate in the machinery of decision-making, including how to lobby professionally. Thanks to nature, they all possess a substantial mental capacity, which is the most important tool for acquiring that knowledge. Of course, they are also free to allow that capacity to remain inadequately used or not used at all. Such people and groups may feel that they have many reasons to complain about undesired EU outcomes and so-called undemocratic practices. They could better complain about their own ignorance and nonchalance. The prevention of more complaints of this type has been the educational objective of this book.

REFERENCES

Roman numbers behind reference in text refer to chapters; Arabic numbers to pages.

Ackerman, R. and Bauer, R. (1976), *Corporate Social Responsiveness*, Reston: Reston

Aerts, S. and Verhaege, S. (2001), *Improving the Government Relations Function*, Oxford: ECPA (occasional paper)

Alkhafaji, A. (1989), *A Stakeholder Approach to Corporate Governance*, Westport: Quorum

Andenas, M. and Türk, A., editors, (2000), *Delegated Legislation and the Role of Committees in the EC*, London: Kluwer

Andersen, C. (1992), *Influencing the EC*, London: Kogan Page

Andersen, S. and Eliassen, K. (1993), 'Norway: National Corporatism Challenged', in: Van Schendelen (1993), pp. 265-301

Andersen, S. and Eliassen, K. (1995), 'EU Lobbying: The New Research Agenda', in: *European Journal of Political Research*, volume 27, 4, pp. 427-441

Andersen, S. and Eliassen, K., editors, (1996), *The EU: How democratic is it?*, London: Sage

Andrews, L. (1996) 'The relationship of political marketing to political lobbying', in: *European Journal of Marketing*, volume 30, 10, pp. 68-91

Andriessen F. and others (1999), *Advancing the Union*, London: ICRI

Arp, H. (1995), *Multiple Actors and Arenas: EC Regulation in a Polycentric System*, Firenze: EUI (Ph D.)

Azzi, G. (2000), 'The Slow March of European Legislation: The Implementation of Directives', in: Neunreither and Wiener (2000), pp. 52-67

Badiello, L. (1998), 'Regional Offices in Brussels', in: Claeys and others (1998), pp. 328-344

Bainbridge, T. (1995), *Penguin Companion to the EU*, London: Penguin

Bauer, R. and De Sola Pool, I. (1960), *American Businessmen and International Trade*, Glencoe: Free Press

Bauer, R. and others (1963), *American Business and Public Policy*, New York: Atheston

Beetham, D. and Lord, C. (1998), *Legitimacy and the EU*, London: Longman

Bellier, I. (1997), 'The Commission as an Actor: an anthropologist's view', in: Wallace and Young (1997-A), pp. 91-115

Bennett, R. (1999), 'Business Routes of Influence in Brussels', in: *Political Studies*, volume 47, pp. 240-257

Bergman, T. (1999), 'National Parliaments and EU Affairs Committees', in: *Journal of European Public Policy*, volume 4, 3, pp. 373-387

Berrington, H. (1998), *Britain in the Nineties*, London: Frank Cass

Bertrand, G. and others (1999), *Scenarios Europe 2010*, Brussels: European Commission (working paper Forward Studies Unit)

Bindi, M. (1998), 'The Committee of the Regions', in: Van Schendelen (1998), pp. 225-249

Birch, A. (1964), *Representative and Responsible Government*, London: Unwin

Birch, A. (1971), *Representation*, London: Pall Mall

Bisson, T., editor, (1973), *Medieval Representative Institutions*, Hinsdale: Dryden

Blondel, J. and others (1970), 'Legislative behaviour: some steps towards a cross-national measurement', in *Government and Opposition*, volume 5, 1, pp. 67-85

Bouwen, P. (2001), *Corporate Lobbying in the EU: Towards a Theory of Access*, Firenze: EUI (working paper SPS 01/5)

Bradley, K. (1992), 'Comitology and the Law: Through a Glass, Darkly', in: *Common Market Law Review*, volume 29, 4, pp. 693-721

Bradley, K. (1998), 'The GMO Committee on Transgenic Maise', in: Van Schendelen (1998), pp. 207-222

Brecht, A. (1959), *Political Theory*, Princeton: Princeton U.P.

Brown, J. (1979), *The Business of Issues*, New York: Conference Board

Buchholz, R. (1990), *Essentials of Public Policy for Management*, Englewood Cliffs: Prentice Hall, 2nd edition

Buchholz, R. and others (1985), *Management Response to Public Issues*, Englewood Cliffs: Prentice Hall

Bunyan, T. (1999), *Secrecy and Openness in the EU*, London: Kogan Page

Calori, R. and Lawrence, P., editors, (1991) *The Business of Europe*, London: Sage

Caporaso, J. (1974), *Structure and Function of European Integration*, Pacific Palisades: Goodyear

Carr, F. and Massey, A., editors, (1999), *Public Policy in the New Europe*, Cheltenham: Elgar

Carrol, A. (1989), *Business and Society: Ethics and Stakeholders Management*, Cincinnati: South Western

Cawson, A. (1995), 'Public Policies and Private Interests: the role of business interests in determining Europe's future television system', in Greenwood (1995), pp. 49-61

Cawson, A. (1997), 'Big Firms as Political Actors', in: Wallace and Young (1997-A), pp. 185-205

Cherry, C. (1966), *On Human Communication*, Cambridge, Mass.: MIT Press

Christiansen, T. (1994), *European Integration Between Political Science and International Relation Theory: The End of Sovereignty*, Firenze: EUI (working paper RSC 94/4)

Christiansen, T. and Kirchner, E., editors, (2000), *Committee Governance in the EU*, Manchester: Manchester U.P.

Christiansen, T. and others, editors, (1999), 'The Social Construction of Europe', in: *Journal of European Public Policy*, volume 6, 3, pp. 527-719 (special issue)

Cini, M. (1996), *The European Commission*, Manchester: Manchester U.P.

Claeys, P. and others, editors, (1998), *Lobbying, Pluralism and European Integration*, Brussels: EIP

Coen, D. (1998), *The Large Firm as a Political Actor in the EU*, London: Routledge

COM (European Commission)
  – *Europe in Figures*, periodical
  – *Eurobarometer: Public Opinion in the EU*, Brussels, bi-annual
  – *General Report*, Brussels: annual
  – (1999), *Designing Tomorrow's Commission*, Brussels
  – (2000), *Reforming the Commission*, (two parts), Brussels
  – (2001), *European Governance*, Brussels (white paper)
  – (2001), *Improving and Simplifying the Regulatory Environment*, Brussels (interim report to the Stockholm European Council)

Conniff, J. (1977), 'Burke, Bristol and the Concept of Representation', in: *Western Political Quarterly*, volume 30, 3, pp. 329-341

Coplin, W. and O'Leary, M. (1976), *Everyman's Prince*, North Scituate: Duxbury (2nd ed.)

Coplin, W. and O'Leary, M. (1983), *Political Analysis through the Prince System*, New York: PSA

Corbett, R. (1998), *The European Parliament's Role in Closer EU Integration*, London: Macmillan

Corbett, R., Jacobs, F. and Shackleton, M., (2000), *The European Parliament*, London: Harper

Corbey, D. (1995), 'Dialectical Functionalism: Stagnation as a Booster of European Integration', in: *International Organization*', volume 49, 2 pp. 253-284

Coser, L. (1956), *The Functions of Social Conflict*, London: Routledge

Curtin, D. (1997), *Postnational Democracy: The EU in Search of a Political Philosophy*, Utrecht: Utrecht University

Daemen, H. and Van Schendelen, M. (1998), 'The Advisory Committee on Safety, Hygiene and Health Protection at Work', in: Van Schendelen (1998), pp. 129-147

Dahl, R. (1956), *A Preface to Democratic Theory*, Chicago: Chicago U.P.

Dahl, R. (1971), *Polyarchy*, New Haven: Yale U.P.

Dahl, R. (1989), *Democracy and its Critics*, New Haven: Yale U. P.

Dahl, R. (1991), *Modern Political Analysis*, Englewood Cliffs: Prentice Hall (5th ed.)

De Callières, M. (1716), *On the Manner of Negotiating with Princes*, (edition University Press of America, Washington, 1963)

De Schutter, O. and others (2001), *Governance in the EU*, European Commission, Brussels

De Zwaan, J. (1995), *The Permanent Representatives Committee*, Amsterdam: Elsevier

Dean, J. and Schwindt, R. (1981) *Business, Government and Society: Reading Lists and Course Outlines*, Durham: Eno River Press

Deckmyn, V. and Thomson, I., editors, (1998), *Openness and Transparency in the EU*, Maastricht: EIPA

Dehousse, R. (1995), 'Constitutional Reform in the EC', in: Hayward (1995), pp. 118-136

Dehousse, R. (1998), *The European Court of Justice*, London: Macmillan

Dermody, J. and Wring, D., editors (2001), 'Political Marketing', in *Journal of Public Affairs*, volume 1, 3, pp. 198-280 (special issue)

Deschouwer, C. (2000), *The European Multi-level Party-System*, Firenze: EUI (working paper RSC 00/47)

Deutsch, K. W. (1963), *The Nerves of Government*, New York: Free Press

Dinan, D., editor, (2000), *Encyclopedia of the European Union*, London: Macmillan

Dogan, R. (2000), 'A Cross-sectoral View of Comitology: Incidence, Issues and Implications', in: Christiansen and Kirchner (2000), pp. 45-61

Donnelly, M. and Ritchie, E. (1994), 'The College of Commissioners and their Cabinets', in: Edwards and Spence (1994), pp. 31-61

Douglas, M. (1985), *Risk Acceptability According to the Social Sciences*, New York: Russel Sage

Downs, A. (1957), *An Economic Theory of Democracy*, New York; Harper and Row

Easton, D. (1965), *A Systems Analysis of Political Life*, New York: Wiley

EC Committee (1994), *Issue Management Summary*, Brussels: American Chamber

Eckstein, H. (1971), *The Evaluation of Political Performance*, London: Sage

Edwards, G. and Pijpers, A., editors, (1997), *The Politics of European Treaty Reform*, London: Pinter

Edwards, G. and Spence, D., editors, (1994), *The European Commission*, Harlow: Longman

Edye, D. and Lintner, V. (1996), *Contemporary Europe*, London: Prentice Hall

Egeberg, M. (1999), 'Transcending Intergovernmentalism? Identity and Role Perceptions of National Officials in the EU decision-making', in: *Journal of European Public Policy*, volume 6, 3, pp. 456-474

Ehrenberg, J. (1999), *Civil Society*, New York: New York U.P.

Eipa (1991), *Subsidiarity: the Challenge of Change*, Maastricht: Eipa

Elgie, R and Griggs, S. (2000), *French Politics*, London: Routledge

Elgström, O. and Smith, M., editors, 'Negotation and Policy-making in the EU', in: *Journal of European Public Policy*, volume 7, 5, pp. 673-834 (special issue)

Elster, J. (1998), *Deliberative Democracy*, Cambridge: Cambridge U.P.

Emerson, M. and others (1988), *The Economics of 1992*, Oxford: Oxford U.P.

EP (European Parliament)

– (1999) *Activity Report 1993-1999*, Brussels

Eulau, H. and Prewitt, K. (1973), *Labyrinths of Democracy*, Indianapolis: Bobbs-Merrill

Everson, M. and others (1999), *The Role of Specialised Agencies in Decentralising EU Governance*, Brussels: European Commission,

Falkner, G. (1998), *EU Social Policy in the 1990's*, London: Routledge

Fine, R. and Rai, S., editors, (1997), *Civil Society: Democratic Perspectives*, London: Frank Cass

Fischhoff, B. and others (1981), *Acceptable Risk*, Cambridge: Cambridge U.P.

Fishkin J. (1991), *Democracy and Deliberation*, New Haven: Yale U.P.

Fligstein, N. and McNichol, J. (1998), 'The Institutional Terrain of the EU', in: Sandholtz and Stone Sweet (1998), pp. 59-91

Flora, P. (1988), *Growth to Limits: Unity and Diversity*, New York: Walter De Gruyter

Franklin, M. and Scarrow, S. (1999), ' Making Europeans? The socializing role of the EP', in: Katz and Wessels (1999), pp. 45-60

Frederick, W. and others (1996), *Businessmen and Society*, New York: McGraw (6th edition)

Freeman, R. (1984), *Strategic Management: A Stakeholder Approach*, Boston: Pitman

Freeman, R. (1999), 'Divergent Stakeholder Theory', in: *Academy of Management Review*, volume 24, 2, pp. 233-236

French, P. (1983), *Ethics in Government*, Englewood Cliffs: Prentice Hall

Frieden, J. and Rogowski, R. (1996), 'The Impact of the International Economy on National Policies', in: Keohane and Milner (1996), pp. 25-47

Friedrich, C. (1963), *Man and his Government*, New York: McGraw-Hill

Friedrich, C. (1974), *Limited Government*, Englewood Cliffs: Prentice Hall

Fullinwider, R. (1999), *Civil Society*, Lanham: Roman and Littlefield

Gabel, M. (1998), *Interests and Integration*, Ann Arbor: Michigan U.P.

Gaffney, J., editor, (1996), *Political Parties and the EU*, London: Routledge

Galston, W. (1999), 'Value Pluralism and Liberal Political Theory', in: *American Political Science Review*, volume 93, 4, pp. 769-778

Gardner, J. (1991), *Effective Lobbying in the EC*, Boston: Kluwer

Garman, J. and Hilditch, L. (1998), 'Behind the scenes: an examination of the importance of the informal processes at work in conciliation', in: *Journal of European Public Policy*, volume 5, 2, pp. 271-284

General Report: see COM

George, S. and Bache, I. (2001), *Politics in the EU*, Oxford: Oxford U.P.

Gigerenzer, G. and others (1989), *The Empire of Change*, Cambridge: Cambridge U.P.

Gobin, C. and Smets, I. (1998), 'Reflecting on European Lobbying', in: Claeys and others (1998), pp. 24-33

Goetz, K. and Hix, S., editors, (2000), *Europeanised Politics?*, London: Frank Cass

Gorges, M. (1996), *Euro-corporatism?*, Lanham: University Press of America

Gottweis, H. (1999), 'Regulating genetic engineering in the EU', in: Kohler-Koch and Eising (1999), pp. 61-82

Grant, W. (1989), *Pressure Groups, Politics and Democracy in Britain*, London: Philip Allan

Graziano, L. (1998), 'Lobbying and the Public Interest', in: Claeys and others (1998), pp. 36-50

Green Cowles, M. (1997), 'Organizing Industrial Coalition', in: Wallace and Young (1997-A), pp. 116-140

Greenwood, J. (1997), *Representing Interests in the EU*, London: Macmillan

Greenwood, J. (1998), 'Corporatism, Pluralism and the Capacities of Euro-groups', in: Claeys and others (1998), pp. 83-109

Greenwood, J. and others, editors, (1992), *Organised Interests and the EC*, London: Sage

Greenwood, J., editor, (1995), *European Casebook on Business Alliances*, Englewood Cliffs: Prentice Hall

Greenwood, J. and Aspinwall, M., editors, (1998), *Collective Action in the EU*, London: Routledge

Greenwood, J. and others (1999), 'The Capacities of Euro Groups in the Integration Process', in: *Political Studies*, volume 47, 1, pp. 127-138

Guyomarch, A. and others (1998), *France in the EU*, London: Macmillan

Haas, E. (1958), *The Uniting of Europe*, Stanford: Stanford U.P.

Hague, B. and Loader, B., editors, (1999), *Digital Democracy*, London: Routledge

Hall, P. (1993), 'Policy Paradigms, Social Learning, and the State', in: *Comparative Politics*, volume 25, 4, pp. 275-296

Hanf, K. and Soetendorp, B. editors, (1998), *Adapting to European Integration*, London: Longman

Harding, C. (1992), 'Who Goes to Court in Europe?', in: *European Law Review*, volume 17, 1, pp. 105-125

Harlow, C. (1999), *Citizen Access to Political Power in the EU*, Firenze: EUI (working paper, RSC 99/2)

Harris, P. and Lock, A. (1996), 'Machiavellian Marketing: the Development of Corporate Lobbying in the UK', in: *Journal of Marketing Management*, volume 12, pp. 313-328

Harris, P. and others, editors (2000), *Machiavelli, Marketing and Management*, London: Routledge

Haverland, M. (1999), *National Adaptation to European Integration*, Firenze: EUI (working paper RSC 99/17)

Hayes-Renshaw, T. and Wallace, H. (1997), *The Council of Ministers*, London: Macmillan

Hayward, J., editor, (1995), *The Crisis of Representation in Europe*, London: Frank Cass

Heath, R. (1997), *Strategic Issues Management*, London: Sage

Heath, R. and Nelson, R. (1986), *Issues Management*, London: Sage

Held, D. (1996), *Models of Democracy*, Oxford: Polity Press

Helms, L. (2000), *Institutions and Institutional Change in the Federal Republic of Germany*, London: Macmillan

Henning, R. (1993), 'Sweden: From Adaptions to Lobbying', in: Van Schendelen (1993), pp. 249-264

Hirschman, A. (1970), *Exit, Voice and Loyalty*, Cambridge, Mass: Harvard U.P.

Hix, S. (1999), *The Political System of the EU*, London: Macmillan

Hix, S. (2000), *How MEPs Vote*, (mimeo), London: LSE

Hix, S. and Lord, C. (1997), *Political Parties in the EU*, London: Macmillan

Hoffman, S. (1963), 'Discord in Community', in: Wilcox and Haviland (1963), pp. 3-31

Hofstede, G. (1984), *Cultures Consequences*, London: Sage

Hofstede, G. (1994), *Cultures and Organisations*, London: Halper Collins

Hojnack, M. and Kimball, D. (1998), 'Organized Interests and the Decision of Whom to Lobby in Congress', in: *American Political Science Review*, volume 92, 4, pp. 775-790

Hosli, M. (1999-A), 'The Netherlands and Coalition Formation in the EU Council', in: *Acta Politica*, volume 34, 1, pp. 67-91

Hosli, M. (1999-B), 'Challenges to the EU Council', in: *International Political Science Review*, volume 20, 4, pp. 371-392

Howell, K. (2000), *Discovering the Limits of European Integration: applying grounded theory*, Huntington: Nova

Hudock, A. (1999), *NGOs and Civil Society*, Oxford: Polity Press

Hume, D. (1748), *An Enquiry Concerning Human Understanding*, London: Cadell

Hunger, J. and Wheelen, T. (1998), *Strategic Management*, Reading, Mass: Addison Wesley (6th edition)

Hurwitz, L., editor, (1980), *Contemporary Perspectives on European Integration*, London: Aldwyck

Huxham, C., editor, (1996), *Creating Collaborative Advantage*, London: Sage

Jacobs, F. and Corbett, R. (1990), *The European Parliament*, Harlow: Longman

Joerges, C. and others (1999), *The Law's Problems with the Involvement of Non-Governmental Actors in Europe's Legislative Processes*, Firenze: EUI (working paper Law 99/9)

Joerges, C. and Vos, E., editors, (1999), *EU Committees: Social Regulation, Law and Politics*, Oxford: Hart

Jones, B. and Keating, M., editors, (1995), *The EU and the Regions*, Oxford: Clarendon

Jordan, A. (1997), *The Protest Business*, Manchester: Manchester U.P.

Jordan, A. and Maloney, W. (1996), 'How Bumblebees Fly: Accounting for Public Interest Participation', in: *Political Studies*, volume 44, 4, pp. 668-685

Jordan, A. and others (1999), 'Innovative and Responsive? A longitudinal analysis of the speed of EU environmental policymaking 1967-1997', in: *Journal of European Public Policy*, volume 6, 3, pp. 376-398

Jørgensen, K. (1997), 'Studying European Integration in the 1990's', in: *Journal of European Public Policy*, volume 4, 3, pp. 486-492

Kamarck, E. and Nye, J. (1999), *Democracy.Com*, Hollis: Hollis

Kassim, H. and others, editors, (2000), *The National Co-ordination of EU Policy* (volume I), Oxford: Oxford U.P.

Kassim, H. and others, editors, (2001), *The National Co-ordination of EU Policy* (volume II), Oxford: Oxford U.P.

Katz, R. (1999-A), 'Representation, the Locus of Democratic Legitimation and the Role of the National Parliaments in the EU', in: Katz and Wessels (1999), pp. 21-43

Katz, R. (1999-B), 'Role Orientations in Parliaments', in: Katz and Wessels (1999), pp. 61-85

Katz, R. and Wessels, B., editors, (1999), *The EP, the National Parliaments and European Integration*, Oxford: Oxford U.P.

Kavanagh, D. (2000), *British Politics*, Oxford: Oxford U.P.

Keohane, R. and Hoffmann, S. (1990), 'Community politics and institutional change', in: Wallace (1990-A), pp. 276-300

Keohane, R. and Hoffmann, S., editors, (1991), *The New European Community: Decision-making and Institutional Change*, Boulder: Westview Press

Keohane, R. and Milner, H., editors, (1996), *Internationalization and Domestic Politics*, Cambridge: Cambridge U.P.

Keohane, R. and Nye, J. (1997), *Power and Interdependence*, Boston: Little Brown

Key, V. (1964), *Politics, Parties and Pressure Groups*, New York: Crowell

King, P. (1976), *Toleration*, London: Allan and Unwin

Kingdon, J. (1984), *Agendas, Alternatives and Public Policies*, Boston: Little Brown

Kirchner, E. (1992), *Decision-making in the EC*, Manchester: Manchester U.P.

Klingemann, H. and Fuchs, D., editors, (1995), *Citizens and the State*, Oxford, Oxford U.P.

Knill, C. and Lehmkuhl, D. (1997), *The Globalisation of European Interest Representation: the Case of the Consumer Electronics Industry*, Firenze: EUI (working paper SPS 97/9)

Knoke, D. (1990), *Political Networks*, Cambridge: Cambridge U.P.

Knoke, D., editor, (1996), *Comparing Policy Networks*, Cambridge: Cambridge U.P.

Kobrin, S. (1982), *Managing Political Risk Assessment*, Berkeley: California

Koeppl, P. (2001), 'The acceptance, relevance and dominance of lobbying the EU Commission', in: *Journal of Public Affairs*, volume 1, 1, pp. 69-80

Kohler-Koch, B. (1997), 'Organised Interests in European Integration', in: Wallace and Young (1997-A), pp. 42-68

Kohler-Koch, B. (1998), 'Organised Interests in the EU and the EP', in: Claeys and others (1998), pp. 126-158

Kohler-Koch, B. and Eising, R., editors, (1999), *The Transformation of Governance in the EU*, London: Routledge

Krasner, S. (1999), *Sovereignty: Organized Hypocrisy*, Princeton: Princeton U.P.

Kreher, A. (1996), *The New European Agencies*, Firenze: EUI (working paper RSC 96/49)

Kreher, A., editor, (1998), *The EC Agencies between Community Institutions and Constituents*, Firenze: EUI

Krislov, S. (1974), *Representative Bureaucracy*, Englewood Cliffs: Prentice Hall

Kurian, G., editor, (1998), *World Encyclopedia of Parliaments and Legislatures*, Washington DC: Congressional Quarterly Press

Landmarks (annual), *The European Public Affairs Directory*, Brussels: Landmarks

Laurencell, S. (1979), *Lobbying and Interest Groups: a Selected Annotated Bibliography*, Washington DC: Congressional Research Service

Legendre, A. (1993), 'The State's Power under Pressure', in: Van Schendelen (1993), pp. 51-66

Leonard, M. (1999), *Networks Europe*, London: Foreign Policy Center

Leonardi, R., editor, (1993), *The Regions and the EC*, London: Frank Cass

Lewis, J. (2000), 'The methods of community in EU decision-making and administrative rivalry', in: *Journal of European Public Policy*, volume 7, 2, pp. 261-289

Lijphart, A. (1997), *Democracy in Plural Societies*, New Haven: Yale U.P.

Lindberg, L. (1963), *The Political Dynamics of European Economic Integration*, Stanford CA: Stanford U.P.

Lindberg, L. (1970), 'Political Integration as a Multidimensional Phenomenon', in: *International Organization*, volume 24, 4, pp. 649-731

Lindblom, C. and Cohen, D. (1979), *Usable knowledge*, New Haven: Yale U.P.

Loewenstein, K. (1973), *The Governance of Rome*, The Hague: Nijhoff

Lord, C. (1998), *Democracy in the EU*, Sheffield: Sheffield Academic Press

Loughlin, J., editor, (2001), *Subnational Democracy in the EU*, Oxford, Oxford U.P.

Luttbeg, N., editor, (1968), *Public Opinion and Public Policy*, Homewood: Dorsey

Machiavelli, N. (1513), *The Prince*, edited by A. Gilbert (1964), New York: Hendricks House

Macmillan, K. (1991), *The Management of European Public Affairs*, Oxford: EC-PA (occasional paper)

Mair, P., editor, (1990), *The West European Party System*, Oxford: Oxford U.P.

Majone, G., editor, (1996-A), *Regulating Europe*, London: Routledge

Majone, G. (1996-B), 'The European Commission as regulator', in: Majone (1996-A), pp. 61-79

Majone, G. (1996-C), 'Regulatory legitimacy', in: Majone (1996-A), pp. 284-301

Maloney, W. and Jordan, G. (1997), 'The Rise of Protest Business in Britain', in: Van Deth (1997), pp. 107-124

Mandeville, B. (1705), *The Fable of the Bees: Private Vices, Public Benefits*, London: Garman (1934)

Marks, G. and others, editors, (1996-A), *Governance in the EU*, London: Sage

Marks, G. and others (1996-B), 'Competencies, Cracks and Conflicts: regional mobilization in the EU', in: Marks and others (1996-A), pp. 40-63

Massey, A. (1999), 'Public Policy in the New Europe', in: Carr and Massey (1999), pp. 27-43

Matthews, D. and Stimson, J. (1975), *Yeas and Nays: normal decision-making in the US House of Representatives*, New York: Wiley

Maurer, A. (1999), *(Co-)governing after Maastricht: the EP's institutional performance 1994-1999*, Brussels: European Parliament

Mayes, D. editor, (1992), *The European Challenge: industry's response to 1992*, London: Harvester Wheatsheaf

Mazey, S. and Richardson, J. (1996), 'EU policy-making: a garbage can or an anticipatory and consensual policy style?' in: Meny and others (1996), pp. 41-58

Mazey, S. and Richardson, J., editors, (1993), *Lobbying in the EC*, Oxford: Oxford U.P.

McCormick, J. (1999), *Understanding the EU*, London: Macmillan

McDonagh, B. (1998), *The Paradox of Europe: an account of the negotiation of the Treaty of Amsterdam*, Dublin: Europe House

McLaughlin, A. (1994), 'ACEA and the EU-Japan Car Dispute', in: Pedler and Van Schendelen (1994), pp. 149-166

Meny, Y. and others, editors, (1996), *Adjusting to Europe*, London: Routledge

Meunier-Aitsahalia, S. and Ross, G. (1993), 'Democratic Deficit or Democratic Surplus', in: *French Politics and Society*, volume 11, 4, pp. 57-69

Milbrath, L. (1963), *The Washington Lobbyists*, Chicago: Rand MacNally

Milbrath, L. and Goel, M. (1977), *Political Participation*, Chicago: Rand Mac-Nally

Mitchell, R. and others (1997), 'Toward a theory of stakeholder identification and salience', in: *Academy of Management Review*, volume 22, 4, pp. 853-896

Molle, W. and others (1993), *Bargained Administration in Europe*, (mimeo), Rotterdam: Erasmus University

Moravcsik, A. (2000), 'Integration Theory', in: Dinan (2000), pp. 278-291

Morgenthau, H. and K. Thompson (1985), *Politics among Nations*, New York: Knopf, 6th edition

Neunreither, K. (1998), 'Governance Without Opposition', in: *Government and Opposition*, volume 33, 4, pp. 419-441

Neunreither, K. and Wiener, A., editors, (2000), *European Integration after Amsterdam*, Oxford: Oxford U.P.

Neyer, J. (2000), 'Justifying Comitology: The Promise of Deliberation', in: Neunreither and Wiener (2000), pp. 112-128

Niedermayer, O. and Sinnott, R. (1998), *Public Opinion and International Governance*, Oxford: Oxford U.P.

Niskanen, W. (1971), *Bureaucracy and Representative Government*, Chicago: Aldine Atherton

Norris, P. (1999), 'The Political Regime', in: Schmitt and Thomassen (1999), pp. 74-89

Norton, Ph., editor, (1995), 'National Parliaments and the EU', in: *Journal of Legislative Studies*, volume 1, 3 (special issue)

Nownes, A.J. (1999), 'Solicited Advice and Lobbyist Power: evidence from three American States', in: *Legislative Studies Quarterly*, 24, pp. 113-123

Nugent, N. (1999), *Government and Politics of the EU*, London: Macmillan (fourth edition)

Nugent, N. (2001), *The European Commission*, London: Palgrave

Nugent, N. and O'Donnell, R., editors, (1994), *The European Business Environment*, London: Macmillan

Nutt, P. (1999), 'Surprising but true: Half the decisions in organisations fail', in: *Academy of Management Executive*, volume 13, 4, pp. 75-90

O'Shaughnessy, N. (1990), *The Phenomenon of Political Marketing*, London: Macmillan

Page, E. (1997), *People who run Europe*, Oxford: Clarendon

PARG (1981), *Public Affairs Offices and Their Functions*, Boston: Public Affairs Research Group Boston University

Pateman, C. (1970), *Participation and Democratic Theory*, Cambridge: Cambridge U.P.

Patterson, L. (2000), 'Biotechnology Policy', in: Wallace and Wallace (2000), pp. 317-344

Pedler, R. (1994), 'The Fruit Companies and the Banana Trade Regime', in: Pedler and Van Schendelen (1994), pp. 67-92

Pedler, R. (1995), *The Management of Public Affairs*, Oxford: ECPA (occasional paper)

Pedler, R. and Schaeffer, G., editors, (1996), *Shaping European Law and Policy: the Role of Committees and Comitology in the Political Process*, Maastricht: EIPA

Pedler, R. and Van Schendelen, M., editors, (1994), *Lobbying the EU*, Aldershot: Dartmouth

Pennock, J. (1979), *Democratic Political Theory*, Princeton: Princeton U.P.

Pennock, J. and Chapman, J., editors, (1968), *Representation*, New York: Atherton

Peterson, J. (2001), 'The Choice for EU Theorists', in: *European Journal of Political Research*, volume 39, 3, pp. 289-318

Pierre, J. and Peters, B. (2000), *Governance, Politics and the State*, London: Macmillan

Pijnenburg, A. (1998), 'EU lobbying by ad-hoc coalition', in *Journal of European Public Policy*, volume 5, 2, pp. 303-321

Pinder, J., editor, (1999), *Foundations of Democracy in the EU*, London: Macmillan

Pitkin, H. (1967), *The Concept of Representation*, Berkeley: California U.P.

Pitkin, H., editor, (1969), *Representation*, New York: Atherton

Pollack, M. (1997), 'Representing diffuse interests in EC policy-making', in *Journal of European Public Policy*, volume 4, 4, pp. 572-590

Pollack, M. (1998), 'The Engines of Integration?', in: Sandholtz and Stone Sweet (1998), pp. 217-249

Pollack, M. (2000-A), *International Relations Theory and European Integration*, Firenze: EUI (working paper RSC 00/55)

Pollack, M., editor, (2000-B), 'Democracy and Constitutionalism in the EU', in *ECSA Review*, volume 13, 2, pp. 2-7 (http://ecsa.org)

Popper, K. (1945), *The Open Society and its Enemies*, London: Routledge and Kegan Paul

Previdi, E. (1997), 'Making and Enforcing Regulatory Policy in the Single Market', in: Wallace and Young (1997-A), pp. 69-90

Randall, H. (1996), *A Business Guide to lobbying in the EU*, London: Cartermill

Raunio, T. (1997), *The European Perspective: transnational partygroups in the 1989-1994 EP*, Aldershot: Ashgate

Raunio, T. and Wiberg, M. (2000), 'Does Support lead to Ignorance?', in *Acta Politica*, volume 35, 2, pp. 146-168

Richardson, J. (1995), 'The Market for Political Activism', in: *West European Politics*, volume 18,1, pp. 116-139

Richardson, J., editor, (1996-A), *European Union: power and policy-making*, London: Routledge

Richardson, J. (1996-B), 'Policy-making in the EU: Interests, Ideas and Garbage Cans of Primeval Soup', in: Richardson (1996-A), pp. 3-23

Richardson, J. (1996-C), 'Eroding EU policies: implementation gaps, cheating and resteering', in: Richardson (1996-A), pp. 278-294

Ringland, G. (1998), *Scenario Planning*, New York: Wiley

Roberts, G. (2000), *German Politics Today*, Manchester: Manchester U.P.

Rochefort, D. and Cobb, R., editors (1994), *The Politics of Problem Definition*, Kansas: Kansas U.P.

Rometsch, D. and Wessels, W., editors, (1996), *The EU and member states*, Manchester: Manchester U.P.

Rosamund, B. (2000), *Theories of European Integration*, London: Macmillan

Rose, R. (1984), *Understanding Big Government*, London: Sage

Rosenthal, G. (1975), *The Men Behind the Decisions*, Lexington: Lexington Books

Safran, W. (1997), *The French Polity*, New York: Longman

Sandholtz, W. and Stone Sweet, A., editors, (1998), *European Integration and Supranational Governance*, Oxford: Oxford U.P.

Savage, G. and others (1991), 'Strategies for assessing and managing organizational stakeholders', in: *Academy of Management Executive*, volume 5, 2, pp. 61-75

Schaar, J. (1981), *Legitimacy in the Modern State*, London: Transaction

Schackleton, M. (2000), 'The Politics of Codecision', in: *Journal of Common Market Studies*, volume 38, 2, pp. 325-342

Schaeffer, G. (1996), 'Committees in the EC Process', in: Pedler and Schaeffer (1996), pp. 3-24

Schaeffer, G. and others (2000), 'The Experience of Member State Officials in EU Committees', in: *Eipascope*, 2000, 3, pp 29-35

Scharpf, F. (1994), *Community and Autonomy: Multilevel Policy-making in the EU*, Firenze: EUI (working paper RSC 94/1)

Scheuer, A. (1999), 'A Political Community?', in: Schmitt and Thomassen (1999), pp. 25-46

Schlozman, K. and Tierney, J. (1986), *Organised Interests and American Democracy*, New York: Harper and Row

Schmidt, V. (1996), *From State to Market: the transformation of French business and government*, Cambridge: Cambridge U.P.

Schmidt, V. (1997), 'European Integration and Democracy: the differences among member states', in: *Journal of European Public Policy*, volume 4, 1, pp. 128-145

Schmidt, V. (1999), 'National Patterns of Governance under Siege', in: Kohler-Koch and Eising (1999), pp. 155-172

Schmitt, H. and Thomassen, J., editors, (1999), *Political Representation and Legitimacy in the EU*, Oxford: Oxford U.P.

Schmitter, Ph. (1996-A), 'Some alternative futures for the European polity', in: Meny (1996), pp. 25-40

Schmitter, Ph. (1996-B), 'Imagining the Future of the Euro-Polity with the Help of New Concepts', in: Marks and others (1996-A), pp. 121-150

Schmitter, Ph. and Streeck, W. (1999), *The Organization of Business Interests*, Köln: Max Planck Institute (mimeo)

Scott, A. and Hunt, M. (1965), *Congress and Lobbies*, Chapel Hill: North Carolina U.P.

Seligman, A. (1992), *The Idea of Civil Society*, Princeton: Princeton U.P.

Sharpe, L. (1993), *The Rise of Meso Government in Europe*, London: Sage

Shaw, J. (1995), *EU Legal Studies in Crises?*, Firenze: EUI (working paper RSC 95/23)

Sidenius, N. (1999), 'Business, governance structures and the EU: the case of Denmark', in: Kohler-Koch and Eising (1999), pp. 173-188

Siedentop, L. (1999), *Democracy in Europe*, London: Allen Lane

Sietses, H. (2000), *The Fragmented Interest Representation of Big Dutch Business in the EU*, Rotterdam: Erasmus University (mimeo Faculty of Management)

Simon, H. (1960), *The New Science of Management Decision*, New York: Harper

Sinnott, R. (1994), *Integration Theory, Subsidiarity and the Internationalization of Issues*, Firenze: EUI (working paper RSC 94/13)

Spinelli, A. (1965), *The Eurocrats*, Baltimore: Hopkins U.P.

Stone Sweet, A. and Caporaso, J. (1998), 'From Free Trade to Supranational Polity: the European Court and Integration', in: Sandholz an Stone Sweet (1998), pp. 92-133

Stone Sweet, A. and Sandholtz, W. (1997), 'European integration and supranational governance', in: *Journal of European Public Policy*, volume 4, 3, pp. 297-317

Stone Sweet, A. and Sandholtz, W. (1998), 'Integration, Supranational Governance and the Institutionalization of the European Polity', in: Sandholtz and Stone Sweet (1998), pp. 1-26

Taylor, P. (1996), *The European Union in the 1990's*, Oxford: Oxford U.P.

Telò, M., editor, (2001), *European Union and New Regionalism*, Aldershot: Ashgate

Thompson (1967), *Organizations in Action*, New York: McGraw Hill

Töller, A. and Hofmann, H. (2000), 'Democracy and the Reform of Comitology', in: Andenas and Türk (2000), pp. 25-50

Tombari, H. (1984), *Business and Society*, New York: Dryden

Treu, T., editor, (1992), *Participation in Public Policy-making*, Berlin: De Gruyter

Urban, S. and Vendemini, S. (1992), *European Strategic Alliances*, Oxford: Blackwell

US/Congress (1977), *Senators: Offices, Ethics and Pressures*, Washington: GPO

US/GAO (1999), *Federal Lobbying: Differences in Lobbying Definitions and their Impact*, Washington: General Accounting Office

Van den Polder, R. (1994), 'Lobbying for the European Airline Industry', in: Pedler and Van Schendelen (1994), pp. 103-119

Van der Heijden, K. (1996), *Scenarios*, New York: Wiley

Van der Voort, W. (1997), *In search of a role: the ESC in EU Decision-making*, Utrecht: University of Utrecht

Van der Voort, W. (1998), 'The Economic and Social Committee', in: Van Schendelen (1998), pp. 250-273

Van Deth, J. and Scarbrough, E., editors, (1995), *The Impact of Values*, Oxford: Oxford U.P.

Van Deth, J., editor, (1997), *Private Groups and Public Life*, London: Routledge

Van Kersbergen, K. (2000), 'Political allegiance and European integration', in: *European Journal of Political Research*, volume 37, 1, pp. 1-17

Van Kippersluis, R. (1998), 'The Waste Management Committee', in: Van Schendelen (1998), pp. 47-67

Van Rens, P. (1994), 'Dutch Trade Union Federation and the EU Works Council', in: Pedler and Van Schendelen (1994), pp. 283-300

Van Schendelen, M. (1984), 'The European Parliament: political influence in more than legal powers', in: *Journal of European Integration*, volume 8, 1, pp. 59-76

Van Schendelen, M. (1990), 'Business and Government Relations in Europe', in: *European Affairs*, volume 4, 2, pp. 81-87

Van Schendelen, M. (1996), 'The Council decides: does the Council decide?', in: *Journal of Common Market Studies*, volume 34, 4, pp. 531-548 and volume 35, 1, p. 171

Van Schendelen, M. and Jackson, R., editors, (1987), *The Politicisation of Business in Western Europe*, London: Croom Helm/ Routledge

Van Schendelen, M., editor, (1993), *National Public and Private EC Lobbying*, Aldershot: Dartmouth

Van Schendelen, M., editor (1998), *EU Committees as Influential Policymakers*, Aldershot: Ashgate

Van Thiel, S. (2000), *Quangocratization: Trends, Causes and Consequences*, Utrecht: ICS

Verwey, W. (1994), 'HDTV and Philips', in: Pedler and Van Schendelen (1994), pp. 23-40

Vos, E. (1990), *Institutional Frameworks of Community Health and Safety Regulation: Committees, Agencies and Private Bodies*, Oxford: Hart

Waddell, H. (1952), *The Wandering Scholars*, London: Constable

Wallace, H. (1997), 'Introduction', in: Wallace and Young (1997-A), pp. 1-16

Wallace, H. and Wallace, W., editors, (1996), *Policymaking in the EU*, Oxford: Oxford U.P. (3rd edition)

Wallace, H. and Wallace, W., editors, (2000), *Policymaking in the EU*, Oxford: Oxford U.P. (4th edition)

Wallace, H. and Young, A., editors, (1997-A), *Participation and Policy-making in the European Union*, Oxford: Clarendon

Wallace, H. and Young, A. (1997-B), 'The Kaleidoscope of European Policymaking', in: Wallace and Young (1997-A), pp. 235-250

Wallace, W., editor, (1990-A), *The Dynamics of European Integration*, London: Pinter

Wallace, W. (1990-B), 'Introduction: the dynamics of European integration', in: Wallace (1990-A), pp. 1-24

Warleigh, A. (2000), 'Citizenship practice, NGOs and policy coalitions in the EU', in: *Journal of European Public Policy*, volume 7, 2, pp. 229-243

Wartick, S. and Mahon, J. (1994), 'Toward a Substantive Definition of the Corporate Issue Construct', in *Business and Society*, volume 33, 3, pp. 293-311

Wasserman, P. and others, editors, (1988), *Encyclopedia of Public Affairs Information Sources*, Detroit: Gale

Weiler, J. (1995), *European Democracy and its Critique*, Firenze: EUI (working paper RSC 95/11)

Werts, J. (1992), *The European Council*, Amsterdam: North-Holland

Wessels, B. (1999), 'European Parliament and Interest Groups', in Katz and Wessels (1999), pp. 105-128

Wessels, W. (1997), 'The growth and differentiation of multi-level networks', in: Wallace and Young (1997-A), pp. 17-41

Westlake, M. (1994-A), *Modern Guide to the European Parliament*, London: Pinter

Westlake, M. (1994-B), *The Commission and the Parliament*, London: Butterworth

Westlake, M. (1995), *The Council of the EU*, London: Cartermill

Wheelen, T. and Hunger, J. (1998), *Strategic Management and Business Policy*, Reading: Addison Wesley (6th edition)

Wilcox, F. and Haviland, H., editors, (1963), *The Atlantic Community*, New York: Praeger

Wilhelm, A. (2000), *Democracy in the Digital Age*, London: Routledge

Willis, D. and Grant, W. (1987), 'The UK: Still a Company State?', in: Van Schendelen and Jackson (1987), pp. 158-183

Winand, P. (1998), 'The US Mission to the EU in Brussels', in: Claeys and others (1998), pp. 373-405

Wincott, D. (1996), 'The Court of Justice and the European policy process', in: Richardson (1996-A), pp. 170-184

Wind, M. (1996), *Europe Towards a Post-Hobbesian Order? A Constructivist Theory of European Integration*, Firenze: EUI (working paper RSC 96/31)

Wright, V. (1996), 'The national co-ordination of European policy-making: negotiating the quagmire', in Richardson (1996-A), pp. 148-169

Wurzel, R. (1999), 'The Role of the EP: interview with Ken Collins MEP', in: *Journal of Legislative Studies*, volume 5, 2, pp. 1-23

Young, O (1968), *Systems of Political Science*, Englewood Cliffs: Prentice Hall

Zincone, G. (1999), *Citizenship: between State en Society*, Firenze: EUI (working paper RSC 99/31)

INDEX